Literacy

Literacy Lessons
Teaching and Learning with Middle School Students

Margaret J. Finders
Washington University, St. Louis

Susan Hynds
Syracuse University

Upper Saddle River, New Jersey
Columbus, Ohio

Library of Congress Cataloging in Publication Data
Finders, Margaret J.
    Literacy lessons : teaching and learning with middle school students/by Margaret J. Finders, Susan Hynds.
      p. cm.
    Includes bibliographical references and index.
    ISBN 0-13-030384-4 (pbk.)
    1. Language arts (Middle school) I. Hynds, Susan. II. Title.

LB1631.F56 2003
428'.0071'2—dc21

2002032138

Vice President and Publisher: Jeffery W. Johnston
Editor: Linda Ashe Montgomery
Development Editor: Hope Madden
Editorial Assistant: Laura Weaver
Production Editor: Linda Hillis Bayma
Production Coordination: Carlisle Publishers Services
Design Coordinator: Diane C. Lorenzo
Cover Designer: Bryan Huber
Cover Image: Corbis Stock Market
Production Manager: Laura Messerly
Director of Marketing: Ann Castel Davis
Marketing Manager: Darcy Betts Prybella
Marketing Coordinator: Tyra Cooper

This book was set in New Baskerville by Carlisle Communications, Ltd. It was printed and bound by R.R. Donnelley & Sons Company. The cover was printed by Phoenix Color Corp.

IRA/NCTE Standards on pp. 196 and 233 from *Standards for English Language Arts*, by the International Reading Association and the Council of Teachers of English. Copyright 1996 by the International Reading Association and the National Council of Teachers of English. Reprinted with permission.

Photo Credits: pp. 120, 123, 126, 195, and 222, Susan Hynds; pp. 259 and 260, Harry Webb.

Pearson Education Ltd.
Pearson Education Australia Pty. Limited
Pearson Education Singapore Pte. Ltd.
Pearson Education North Asia Ltd.
Pearson Education Canada, Ltd.
Pearson Educación de Mexico, S.A. de C.V.
Pearson Education—Japan
Pearson Education Malaysia Pte. Ltd.
Pearson Education, *Upper Saddle River, New Jersey*

Copyright © 2003 by Pearson Education, Inc., Upper Saddle River, New Jersey 07458. All rights reserved. Printed in the United States of America. This publication is protected by Copyright and permission should be obtained from the publisher prior to any prohibited reproduction, storage in a retrieval system, or transmission in any form or by any means, electronic, mechanical, photocopying, recording, or likewise. For information regarding permission(s), write to: Rights and Permissions Department.

10 9 8 7 6 5 4 3 2 1
ISBN 0-13-030384-4

*To Anna, Sally, Elizabeth, and to all the
middle school students and their teachers who
have taught us so much*

Preface

Jeez, can I write this over? This is just junk. I thought it was just for you. If we're gonna share it, I want to do it over. I thought this was just for you. This is just junk.

Ryan, 7th grader

Ryan, a seventh-grade student, can teach us much about the significance of the peer dynamic in a middle school literacy classroom. When he thought his writing was just for his teacher, quality was not particularly important, but when his teacher suggested that he share with his peers, well, that was something different.

In this book, you will meet middle school students like Ryan. You'll meet their teachers and their student teachers, and you'll have an opportunity to grapple with the complexities that shape literacy lessons in a middle school classroom. Changing school settings, shifting social networks, and fluctuating expectations based on gender roles place middle school students at a pivotal juncture in their lives.

The major difference between being an English *major* and being an English *teacher* is having an intimate knowledge of students and schools. In this text we will focus on that intimate knowledge, specifically in the middle school. We will examine research- and theory-based approaches to practice. We will ask you to consider questions such as, What is the teacher's role? What is the student's role? How do current theories translate into practice? What tacit assumptions inform our professional practices? How do we build and implement curriculum? In this text we hope to provide you with the necessary tools to seek answers and grow as professionals.

Literacy Lessons will provide tools for inquiry. Our goal is to invite you into the ongoing professional conversations that unite and divide scholars in the field. To do this, we emphasize methods of inquiry rather than mastery of content material. For example, we ask you to look through different lenses to examine what might be lost and gained by a particular teaching approach. Similarly, we ask you to examine a set of national or local standards and consider how these standards might play out differently in diverse classroom settings.

We intend in *Literacy Lessons* to provide support for you through guided teaching experience, tools for reflection, and an understanding of teaching as a situated process. As you read this book, you'll notice the following features:

- **Guiding Questions.** Each chapter opens with a list of questions that address the focus of the chapter. Here you will be asked to speculate on key issues, examine

your own assumptions, connect your experiences to theoretical issues, and articulate your emerging understandings of the chapter content.
- **A Case for Consideration.** Each chapter opens with a short vignette of a middle school classroom. In these opening cases, we present a range of issues and preservice and in-service teachers offer answers and questions about the particulars of their classroom experiences. Immediately following each case is a series of prompts for you to address through discussion, writing, or situated role play. We ask you to unpack the embedded issues and speculate on possible teaching strategies to support your students' literacy learning.
- **Standards in Practice.** This feature invites you to consider various aspects of your teaching philosophy and practice in light of such standards as the INTASC English Language Arts Standards, National Board Certification Standards, National Middle School Association recommendations, NCTE/IRA Standards, and your own state standards. You will be asked to consider both the obstacles and opportunities that particular standards pose for you and your middle school students.
- **Your Fieldwork Journal.** Your Fieldwork Journal is designed to support the development of reflective practice by providing tools for inquiry and opportunities for guided reflection. We will ask you to use a variety of informal inquiry techniques to examine the complexities of planning and teaching. You might be asked to make observations, conduct interviews, or analyze artifacts as a way of enriching your understanding of teaching and learning in the middle school classroom.
- **Language Lenses.** Chapter 6 introduces the four language lenses: (1) reading and viewing, (2) writing, (3) talking and listening, and (4) language study. In subsequent chapters, you will see how various forms of literacy might look through these lenses. Thus, you are encouraged to think constantly and concretely about how you might integrate the language arts in every aspect of your teaching.
- **Literacy Lessons.** Literacy Lessons showcase teachers working with concrete literacy strategies and teaching techniques such as literature circles, peer response groups, cultural critique, and grammar mini-lessons. These Literacy Lessons offer multiple models and techniques for approaching literacy teaching and learning. Examining practice through Literacy Lessons means taking a critical stance and developing deeper understandings of social, political, and ethical teaching at the middle school level.
- **Resources.** Each chapter concludes with a section of print and electronic resources designed to promote further inquiry and continued professional development.

Still today, texts that address middle school students rarely acknowledge diversity in a richly contextualized manner. In sharing the stories of colleagues who teach in middle schools across the nation and showcasing complex issues at the center of middle school teaching, we hope *Literacy Lessons* will offer even the most experienced teachers among us the resources to improve our literacy programs. Our aim is to tap your intellectual curiosity and rouse you to continue your professional conversations beyond this text. In the voices of teachers and students that follow, we hope you will recognize your own struggles and successes as teachers and lifetime learners in the middle school classroom.

Acknowledgments

The idea of developing a book for middle school language arts teachers could not have come to fruition without the incredible support and insights of many people. Friends, colleagues, and family members have been supportive, inspiring, and sustaining. We appreciate the conversations and connections with parents, teachers, and students. For reasons of privacy, there are many whose names do not appear here.

In particular we would like to thank the preservice teachers whose writing appears on these pages. A special note of thanks to Rhiannon Bell, Jason Berrier, Jennifer A. Campbell, Jim DeAngelo, Noah Garfinkel, Rebecca Harkavy, Audra Keiser, Shonda Isaacs, Jerry McLaughlin, Tanya M. McRorie, Keith Newvine, Trina Nocerino, Cari Sue Palma, Ellen Paradise, Jennifer Peters, Cheryl Sawaztke, and James Smith.

We would also like to thank several teachers who have taught us a great deal over the years about working with early adolescents; some taught across the hall, some opened up their classrooms as research sites, and others shared their stories over cups of coffee. We are particularly grateful to those whose words appear in this book: Ellen Barton, Herm Card, Benjamin Clardy, Amy Craig, Elizabeth Dixon, Mary McCrone, Sue Peters, Dona Ward, Harry Webb, Joe Wilson, Gary Zmolek, and doctoral student Noshin Jihan.

This text has benefited from an extensive review by many talented colleagues: Peggy Albers, Georgia State University; Dennise Bartelo, Plymouth State College of the University System of New Hampshire; Marjorie Hancock, Kansas State University; Sandra Hurley, University of Texas at El Paso; Kenneth Kaufman, Loyola University, Chicago; Patricia P. Kelly, Virginia Tech; and Cynthia Leung, North Dakota State University.

It is collaboration that has brought this book to life. Our collaboration began with a phone call to a professional colleague and ended in remarkable friendship. We thank each other for the guidance, insights, hard work, and not-so-gentle prodding that we gave to each other. Across the kitchen table and the country, we wrote and talked and wrote together.

Most important, we appreciate the middle school students who have helped us think deeply about what it means to teach and learn in middle schools. Our special thanks to Jenny Aiken, Cesar Gomez, Casey Grady, Youngin Hahn, Mallory Hohm, Jaclyn Kinney, Jason Mechlin, Shannon Nolan, Stephanie Vaughan, and their classmates in middle schools across the country.

Contents

chapter 1 Middle Schoolers and Middle School   2

Guiding Questions   2
A Case for Consideration: Teen Mothers in Different Times   2
A Bundle of Raging Hormones: The Invention of Adolescence   3
Monitoring Your Teaching: Your Fieldwork Journal   5
Beyond Biology   7
From "Mini" High School to Middle School   8
   Interdisciplinary Teams   13
   Advisory Programs   13
   Varied Instruction   13
   Exploratory Programs   14
   Transition Programs   14
Standards in Practice   17
References   18
Resources   19

chapter 2 English Language Arts from Mid-Century to the Millennium   22

Guiding Questions   22
A Case for Consideration: The World Across the Hall   22
Exploring Your Teaching History   25
From Texts to Political Contexts: Literacy Learning Then and
   Now   26
Our Shifting Views of Literacy and Its Teaching   27
   Literacy as Text: Product-Centered Approaches   30
   Process-Centered Approaches   32
   Social/Contextual Approaches to Literacy Teaching   37
Standards in Practice   42
References   43
Resources   45

chapter 3 Planning and Adapting Instruction for Middle School Learners 48

Guiding Questions 48
A Case for Consideration: The Techno Trio 48
Beyond Print: How We Think About Literacy Learning 50
Planning for All Students 52
Starting to Plan 58
    Goals 58
    Support for Learners 60
    Assessing Materials and Resources 61
Planning for Multiple Intelligences 62
Jumping In: Collaborative Planning 64
Organizing Lesson Plans 66
    Weekly Calendar 66
    Daily Lesson Plans 68
    Formal Instructional (or Unit) Plans 70
Interdisciplinary Planning 71
Long-Range Planning With Middle School Students in Mind 72
    Sketch Out Your Overall Goals 72
    Identify Relevance and Usefulness 73
    Choose an Organizing Framework 73
    Design a Culminating Activity 74
    Investigate Materials and Resources 74
    Include Evaluation 74
    Describe Techniques, Strategies, and Procedures 75
Formalizing Long-Range Plans 76
Grading Rubric for the Unit Plan 82
Planning for Change 83
Standards in Practice 84
References 86
Resources 87

chapter 4 Including Middle School Learners With Disabilities 88

Guiding Questions 88
A Case for Consideration: Mr. Carlisle's First Days 88
Individualized Educational Program 90

Contents   xiii

     Modifications   95
         Activity Modifications   95
         Instructional Modifications   96
         Materials Modifications   96
         Environmental Modifications   96
     Supports   97
         Consultative Support   97
         Collaborative Teaching   98
         Individual Support   98
         Peer Support   98
     Interaction With Peers   99
     Considerations for Supporting Each Learner in the Middle School Classroom   101
     Evaluation of Student Performance   104
     Standards in Practice   107
     References   107
     Resources   108

chapter 5   Integrating Assessment   110

     Guiding Questions   110
     A Case for Consideration: Managing the Mess   110
     Assessments! Assessments! Assessments!   112
     Integrating Assessment   113
     Considerations for Assessment in the Middle School Classroom   114
     Performance Assessment of Authentic Learning Tasks   115
     Beyond Paper-and-Pencil Tests: Tools for Alternative Assessment   118
         Learning Logs as a Form of Assessment   118
         Graphic Representation as an Assessment Tool   119
         Assessment Conferences   120
         Assessing Small-Group Work   121
         Assessment of Performances and Demonstrations   122
         Assessing Student Participation in Large Groups   122
         Assessment of Inquiries and Investigations   123
         Portfolio Assessment   128
     Grading: The Final Act   128
         Creating a Grading Rubric   128

Beyond Traditional Tests and Quizzes   130
Collaborative Rubrics: Assessment as a Teaching Tool   134
The Dilemma of High-Stakes Testing   136
Standards in Practice   142
References   143
Resources   144

chapter 6 Language Lenses: Integrating the Language Arts in the Middle Grades   146

Guiding Questions   146
A Case for Consideration: A Constant Voyeur   146
Integrating the Language Arts: Teaching for Diversity   149
Challenging Some Myths About Language   150
  Myth: Speech Is an Inferior Form of Language   150
  Myth: Learning to Read Must Precede Learning to Write   151
  Myth: Fluency in One Language Interferes With Fluency in Another   151
Language Lenses   152
"Making a Fire in Our Hands": One Final Thought   164
Standards in Practice   165
References   165
Resources   166

chapter 7 Reading and Viewing in the Middle Grades   168

Guiding Questions   168
A Case for Consideration: Making Room for Poetry   168
Reading and Viewing in New Times   170
Reading and Viewing for Multiple Purposes   170
Reading and Viewing With Middle School Students   172
Considerations for Reading and Viewing With Middle School Students   173
Differences Between Literary and Nonliterary Reading   174
Inviting Students' Responses to Literature: Stances Versus Hierarchies   175
Strategies for Comprehension and Understanding   176
Strategies for Critical Reading and Viewing   178
Inviting All Readers   179

Contents   xv

    Text Selection in the Middle School Classroom   181
        Locating Texts   181
        Censorship and Text Selection   181
        Organizing Instruction   182
    Creating a Classroom Climate for Reading and Viewing   183
        Organizing for Whole Class Instruction   183
        Organizing for Student-Selected Reading   187
        Organizing for Small-Group Reading Experiences   187
        Organizing for Workshop Teaching   188
    Assessment Issues in the Reading and Viewing Classroom   191
        Responding   191
        Evaluation   193
        Grading   194
    Standards in Practice   195
    References   196
    Resources   198

chapter 8   A Focus on Writing   202

    Guiding Questions   202
    A Case for Consideration: To Assign or Not to Assign   202
    Writing With Middle School Students   203
    Balancing Acts: Writing Instruction in the Middle School   210
        Comfort and Challenge   211
        Collaboration and Privacy   211
        Choice and Control   214
        Physical Activity and Solitude   217
        Correctness and Creativity   218
        Personal and Public Writing   218
    Creating a Classroom for Writers   219
        The Writers' Workshop as a Structure for Learning   221
    Assessments of Written Literacies   224
    Monitoring Progress: Formative Assessments   225
        Anecdotal Records   225
        Writing Logs   226
        Conferences   226
        Writers' Journals   226
        Peer Group Records and Checkpoints   227

Writing Rubrics 227
Writing Portfolios 228
Reflective Windows 229
Using Technology Effectively With Middle School Writers 230
Standards in Practice 233
References 234
Resources 235

chapter 9 Talking and Listening in the Middle Grades 238

Guiding Questions 238
A Case for Consideration: Beyond the "Official Meaning" 238
The Many Faces of Talking and Listening 239
Purposes and Forms of Oral Language 240
Talking and Listening With Middle School Students 243
Leveling the Field: Race, Class, Gender, Culture, and Oral Language 244
Talking and Listening to Explore 245
   Character Role Plays 246
   "To Tell the Truth" 247
Talking and Listening to Learn About Talking and Listening 249
   Interpersonal Communication: Exploring the Language of Self and Others 249
Talking and Listening to Connect and Transform 252
   Breaking the I-R-E Pattern: Inviting Students' Genuine Responses in Class Discussion 252
   Question Cue Cards 257
   KWL Activity 257
Talking and Listening to Showcase and Perform 261
   Speeches, Demonstration, and Presentations 261
   Beyond Round-Robin Reading: Oral Interpretations, Choral Reading, and Readers' Theater 263
Evaluating Oral Language and Listening 266
Standards in Practice 270
References 271
Resources 272

chapter 10 A Focus on Language Study 276

Guiding Questions 276
A Case for Consideration: "I Never Thought About Words Before" 276

What Counts as Language Study 278
Discourse Communities and Communicative Competence 280
Helping Students Understand Their Discourse Communities 282
Standardization and "Powerful" Language 284
   Guiding Practice With Varieties of English 285
Playing With Language 288
Language Study Across the Curriculum 289
Language Diversity and Grammar Instruction 289
   Teaching Grammar and Usage in the Middle School 290
   Second Language Learners 290
Monitoring Language Development 291
   Skills to Remember 292
   Goals and Growth Records 295
   Portfolios 296
   Error Analysis 296
Standards in Practice 298
References 299
Resources 299

chapter 11   Entering the Profession: Lessons for Literacy and Life   302

Guiding Questions 302
A Case for Consideration: Teaching in Troubled Times 302
Professional Support: Where Do You Go From Here? 304
   Professional Memberships 305
   Help Down the Hall 306
Securing a Job 308
   Gaining Experiences 309
   Preparing a Professional Portfolio 311
Standards in Practice 315
References 315
Resources 316

Index 319

Literacy Lessons

chapter 1

Middle Schoolers and Middle School

GUIDING QUESTIONS
1. How have our views of early adolescents shifted across time?
2. What are the differences between middle school and junior high school?
3. What are the key components of an effective middle school?

A CASE FOR CONSIDERATION

Teen Mothers in Different Times

A tintype photograph captures a young bride in white eyelet, poised beside her husband, who stands awkwardly in a borrowed suit. Supported by parents, family, and friends, 14-year-old Joy Dunlap married 28-year-old William Walter Meadows. It was considered a beautiful and proper wedding, but Joy's friends whispered that it was "about time" for her to marry. She was, after all, 14, a grown woman still living in her mother's house, still cooking for her father. When Joy was 15, her family celebrated the birth of her son, Walter, who was welcomed into the world by all.

Eighty years later, things are very different for 15-year-old Angel. As a teen mother, Angel describes herself through the eyes of adults in the following manner: "The biggest thing is slut 'cause I had a baby. No teacher called it to my face. But they looked upon me like that. They looked at me like I was nothin' at all 'cause I had a baby when I was 13." Angel was expelled from her middle school and ordered by the courts to attend an alternative school because of her frequent truancies and her "early" pregnancy. Angel, pregnant for the second time, explained, "Yeah, they thought, 'You're no good. You'll never amount to anything.' The sheriff, the teachers, and they kept saying it, 'You're no good.' That's what they think, but I take care of myself. I take care of my son. I take care of him when he's sick. I make sure he's got what he needs. I'm a good mom to Tyler."

Although both Joy and Angel had babies as teenagers, teachers and other community members viewed their lives quite differently. In fact, Joy was never considered a "teenager." That word didn't enter our language until about 1938, and Joy turned 14 in 1912. Neither Joy nor Angel completed the eighth grade, but Joy's world was different from Angel's, who turned 14 in 1996. Although Joy Meadows was 15 when she had her first child, she was never considered a "teen mother." She was, in fact, not considered exceptionally young. Angel, on the other hand, was placed in an alternative school for her sexual misconduct, her middle school teachers' worrying about her "running around with a man nearly twice her age."

FOR DISCUSSION

- Joy wasn't expected to go to school beyond the elementary grades. Angel was court ordered to attend an alternative middle school. What might account for such different perspectives?
- Assumptions about appropriate schooling for early adolescents have shifted dramatically over the past 100 years. What assumptions do you hold for teaching early adolescents today?

A BUNDLE OF RAGING HORMONES: THE INVENTION OF ADOLESCENCE

Many of us worry that teaching early adolescents will be a negative experience. Some worry that by teaching language arts in a middle school, we will be forced to abandon our subject matter and focus solely on classroom control. For instance, one of our colleagues reported, "Most of my students have only heard horror stories about this age group." Another said, "I'd never wanted to teach middle school. They are nothing but a bundle of raging hormones." Even those who express interest in middle school teaching worry:

> *I look forward to their enthusiasm. I want to teach middle schoolers because they're still little kids. They still like to have fun with learning. You don't have to worry so much about apathy, but you DO have to worry about classroom control.*

Preservice teachers may tend to focus on classroom management plans rather than young adult books, integrated curriculum, multiple intelligences, or other important aspects of middle school pedagogy. After working in a middle school with real, live middle school students, these same preservice teachers speak enthusiastically about their amazing students, the ways in which they can think deeply about their work and the world around them. One reported, "You know, I wouldn't want to work anywhere else. Middle school offers the best of both worlds: students young enough to have real fun with learning and old enough to do some real critical thinking." Another

> What expectations do you hold for working with early adolescents? Do your expectations about early adolescents match the common concern for control?

said, "I'm embarrassed about how I underestimated my students at first. When we planned our trip to the zoo, my students weren't just little kids going to see some animals. They weren't just getting out of school for the day. They were scientists and authors who got on that bus ready to do some serious study."

Expectations for teaching in a middle school may be based in part on the stories that you have heard or images of early adolescents as presented in the popular media. Images of school cafeterias or after-school detention rooms, although often quite humorous on the big screen, may shape how we come to view what it means to be an early adolescent. Talk shows fill the airwaves with images of "out-of-control" early adolescents and distraught parents. Popular media images of classrooms often portray the teacher in even worse light. Such images tend to invade our cultural assumptions and shape what we view as "normal" behaviors. It is difficult to examine our own stories and underlying assumptions because what is considered ordinary is just that—so ordinary that it is invisible. These assumptions guide what we expect of our students, our colleagues, and ourselves.

Our assumptions about early adolescence will also guide our curricular decisions and shape our daily interactions with our students. Literacy Lesson 1–1 illustrates how assumptions about early adolescence left invisible and unexamined shaped one teacher's interactions with early adolescents. As you read the following Literacy Lesson, look for the ordinary. What do Mr. Stone's words and actions suggest that one should consider normal? What is considered inappropriate and out of the ordinary?

Literacy Lesson 1-1

Mr. Stone Graduates From Elementary School[1]

Mr. Stone was a popular sixth-grade teacher in a self-contained elementary classroom. Students often requested to be in his classroom. "He made learning fun," they said. He did lots of hands-on activities and took great pride in the fact that he knew each of his students well. The students enjoyed the nicknames he gave them, and an overwhelming majority noted that he was their all-time favorite teacher.

After teaching sixth grade for many years, Mr. Stone elected to accept a position as a seventh-grade language arts teacher. At the beginning of his first year as a seventh-grade teacher, he worried, "I won't be able to be so close to them. I won't know them as well. They won't need me in the same way. I won't know their parents or brothers and sisters like I do now. It will definitely be different. I'll just be more distant. That's all there is to it." Teaching in junior high also had its positive side for Mr. Stone. He looked forward to interacting with students "more academically" as he put it.

"I like my new students, but it's very, very different," he says. "My students are 'hormone hostages' and Sarah's group serve as the fashion police. Girls tend to run in packs," he laughed. "There's a herd of them coming down the hall now."

---

[1] From *Just Girls: Hidden Literacies and Life in Junior High* (pp. 28–29) by M. Finders, 1997, New York: Teachers College Press. Copyright 1997 by Teachers College Press. Reprinted with permission.

Mr. Stone's changes were apparent to his former sixth-grade students. One commented, "He like changed to a totally new person." Another said, "He's meaner." One girl who had been especially fond of Mr. Stone explained, "He acts like he doesn't even know me." Another commented, "He's not as nice as he used to be. He never laughs. He doesn't tell jokes. He doesn't call me Sunny [the nickname he gave her] anymore." Students reported that Mr. Stone told fewer stories about his family and himself and seemed more distant. "He just sticks to the books now," one student reported.

For a variety of reasons, Mr. Stone dramatically altered his classroom practices to fit into the new environment. Likewise, the head of his English department viewed the role of a middle school teacher as much different from that of an elementary teacher. In a discussion on hiring another new language arts faculty member, she expressed reservations for a candidate who, like Mr. Stone, had been an elementary school teacher:

She may not be happy because she'll expect too much contact with the kids. Kids this age don't want teachers to know that much about them. Not even their parents. They want to be on their own. Elementary teachers get too close. She'd better not hug any of them.

Think about how Mr. Stone's views of early adolescence governed how he should teach. The students he was working with were actually only about 4 months older than they had been at the end of their sixth-grade year, but Mr. Stone's view of this change seemed to demand dramatic changes. It seemed obvious to him that he would need to "be more distant."

Like Mr. Stone, your assumptions of early adolescents will guide your curricular decisions and shape your daily interactions with students. We judge the value and worth of others based on our assumptions of what counts as "normal" behaviors. Such assumptions have grave consequences for those whose experiences do not match our own. As a teacher you will want to reflect on your actions and the underlying assumptions.

MONITORING YOUR TEACHING: YOUR FIELDWORK JOURNAL

Throughout this book, we ask you to tease out the assumptions you hold about your students. We ask you to think about assumptions that circulate about early adolescence and how those assumptions might translate into teaching beliefs and practices. The ways teachers envision their early adolescent learners have everything to do with how they will teach these learners.

Effective teachers of any age group learn to examine the assumptions that guide their practice, to monitor their own teaching, and to modify instructional approaches to support all learners in their classrooms. Each chapter will include one or more features titled "Your Fieldwork Journal." The intent of the fieldwork journal is to give you a variety of methods of inquiry in order for you to gather and examine information about yourself, your students, and your teaching practices.

Your fieldwork journal supports the development of an inquiry-oriented approach to teaching. You'll gain tools to be a teacher researcher, which simply means that you'll learn to make close observations of students and teachers at work and to think critically about your observations and the assumptions that undergird them. The fieldwork journal includes focused writing experiences (short journal entries designed to support reflective thinking) and classroom inquiry activities (research strategies such as interviewing, recording observations, and analyzing artifacts). Begin now with Your Fieldwork Journal 1–1.

Your Fieldwork Journal 1-1

Becoming a Middle School English Teacher: Expectations and Assumptions

To begin, you will need to set up your fieldwork journal. All you will need is a three-ring binder, dividers, and paper. You may want to maintain an electronic component as well. As you begin, you will want to label each entry so you can revisit your views and document change over time. Your label should include a title that will help you focus your views and reflect on them later and a date for each entry. For example, your first entry might read as follows:

1–1 Expectations and Assumptions, Date:

1. List your expectations for this text. What do you anticipate you will learn and do? What do you imagine are (should be) the central goals set for this text?
2. Briefly describe your views in working with early adolescents (ages 10–15). What do you expect, anticipate, look forward to, and/or worry about in working with middle schoolers?

Your own experience as an early adolescent may influence how you answered questions 1 and 2.

3. Jot down five attributes that these people might have used to describe you as an early adolescent: (A) parent, (B) best friend, (C) teacher.
4. Think back to your experience as a sixth-, seventh-, or eighth-grade student. Describe a scene from your school experience as an early adolescent. At first, write quickly and try to capture as much detail as you can. Let your pen fly and attempt to get lost in the experience. As you're writing, try to capture the images and feelings of the experience.

Many of us have humorous, painful, or embarrassing stories to tell about our adolescent experiences. We may remember some disagreements with our parents, our naive bravado in entering competitive sports, or our changing bodies that we feared might forsake us in public. The changes during adolescence are great. Psychological and biological changes are never more rapid. Gender roles become more rigidly enforced. Shifts in social expectations for the early adolescent are equally dramatic. It is no wonder that parents and teachers often voice fear for the impending arrival of adolescence; yet the concept of adolescence did not exist before the last two decades of the 19th century (Klein, 1990). Klein succinctly describes the creation of adolescence based on social and economic factors:

> Basically, industrialization occurring during the later 1800s created the need for a stage of adolescence; the Depression created the legitimized opportunity for adolescence to become differentiated from childhood and adulthood; and the mass media influence/blitz of the 1950s crystallized this stage by giving it a reality all its own. (p. 456)

Adolescence as a life stage solidified due in large part to economic conditions, specifically the Depression. Palladino (1996) explains that up until the 1930s most people in this age group worked for a living on farms, in factories, and at home. She writes, "They were not considered teenagers yet or even adolescents for that matter" (p. 5). She argues that it was this mass coming together in a school setting that solidified adolescence as a distinct age group. In other words, it was the school setting where a majority of teenagers spent the majority of their day together that gave birth to adolescence. The economic conditions of the time created the need, and the life stage was thus created. The emergence of adolescence as a life stage had as much to do with the economic conditions as it did with "raging hormones," the theory popularized by G. Stanley Hall.

BEYOND BIOLOGY

In this country, G. Stanley Hall became known as the father of adolescence with the publication of his 1904 two-volume set *Adolescence*. Hall conceptualized the period of adolescence as biologically determined, with little consideration for social or cultural influences (Santrock, 1993). According to Hall, hormonal factors account for the marked fluctuations in adolescent behaviors (Brooks-Gunn & Reiter, 1990). Although we make the case that adolescence as a life stage is based on social and economic conditions, clearly we do not deny the tremendous biological events that occur at this developmental stage. But we want to focus your attention on how those biological changes are perceived and experienced at any historical moment. Social and cultural conditions dictate how one should act and how others might react to them. Clearly you can see how Joy's marriage to a man twice her age was considered appropriate so she might be better cared for, while Angel's relationship was considered promiscuous. We are not suggesting that one should view either Angel's or Joy's actions as good or bad, right or wrong. Rather we use their stories to demonstrate that coming of age is shaped by the social and historical events of the time. The times governed how Joy and Angel should dress, talk, act, and be judged. Joy covered her body completely, while Angel's dress revealed her developing body. Even judgment about body shapes and sizes is shaped by the historic period. Brumberg (1997), for example, chronicles the changing images and expectations of American girls' bodies as shaped by the events of different historical periods, noting that attention was at one time focused on the size of hands.

Most often, understanding of the historic, economic, social, and cultural complexities that shape the lives of adolescents disappear, and we tend to hold tightly to a singular, biological view of the "normal" adolescent, which includes the following assumptions: (a) adolescents sever ties with adults; (b) peer groups become increasingly influential social networks; (c) resistance is a sign of normalcy for the adolescent; and (d) romance and sexual drive govern interests and relations (Finders, 1997). Yet this view may be based for the most part on middle class assumptions. Class, race, gender, and individual life circumstances influence how one comes of age in this country. In cross-cultural anthropological studies, for example, Schlegel and Barry (1991) note that in middle class homes where child labor is not needed, adolescents of both sexes are likely to spend a good deal of time with same-age peers. But girls in working-class homes or in families of Hispanic or of recent Middle Eastern or Asian extraction may be expected to spend their after-school time at home, whereas boys may be with peers or at work outside the home.

We understand early adolescents as individuals with complex histories, but often the complexities of their lives are forgotten when we begin to think about teaching in the middle school. If we hold narrow, negative views of early adolescents, we can hardly envision an engaging literacy curriculum. "Out of control" as the identifying trait of this life stage serves to solidify adolescence as a period of incompetence. A holding facility was needed; junior high schools were created. It is no wonder that junior highs are so often characterized as "wastelands."

With the arrival of adolescence came the creation of the first junior high schools in 1909. Everhart (1983) describes two factors that explain the evolution of schooling to include junior high schools: (a) the perceived need for student retention and (b) the growing recognition of adolescence as a separate stage in the life cycle. Child labor laws and compulsory schooling laws in the early 1900s solidified the demand for a new school structure, the junior high school.

FROM "MINI" HIGH SCHOOL TO MIDDLE SCHOOL

To meet the needs of early adolescents, the first junior high schools appeared in 1909 in Columbus, Ohio, and in Berkeley, California, in 1910 (Everhart, 1983). As schools for early adolescents began to appear across the nation with different grades and different philosophical orientations, the need for a clear definition became evident. The junior high school emerged specifically to support the academic preparation for high school.

Until the 1960s schools for early adolescents were constructed as junior or "mini" high schools, with a focus on subject matter knowledge and little consideration for the social, physical, or psychological needs of the early adolescent. Most students left their self-contained elementary classroom and entered a comprehensive junior high school where they met with individual content teachers for discrete blocks of time. Class periods were linked by 3- to 5-minute passing times with little attention to connections across content boundaries or the need for physical activity.

Typically, the structure and schedule of the junior high school, as opposed to the middle school, divided each day into seven or eight discrete segments in which

TABLE 1-1 School Orientations

Junior High School Orientation	Middle School Orientation
• Focus on subject matter. • Staff schools with teachers who are expert in subject matter. • Establish individual student schedules. • Expect students to take responsibility for their own learning. • Employ a curricular model based on independent subject matter and competition.	• Focus on adolescent learner. • Staff schools with teachers who are expert at teaching early adolescents. • Establish small communities of learners. • Connect learning to local community. • Include families in the education of the early adolescent. • Employ a curricular model based on interdisciplinary teams and collaboration.

students received daily instruction in math, science, social studies, and language arts. Often an alternating schedule provided for instruction in music, art, and physical education. Some junior high schools offered an exploratory strand of instruction on such subjects as foreign language, home economics, and industrial arts. Also, at the junior high, extracurricular activities became available: plays, band, orchestra, vocal music, volleyball, tennis, football, basketball, wrestling, and track. Early on, home economics and industrial arts were segregated by gender. Similarly, extracurricular opportunities were segregated and more readily available for boys. But the 1972 federal law Title IX prohibited sex discrimination in education, which resulted in junior high schools offering athletics and other extracurricular activities to girls equal to those that were available to boys.

Middle schools, as an alternative to junior high school, emerged in the 1960s, offering a more transitional form of schooling between elementary and high school. As noted earlier, junior highs were envisioned as preparatory programs for high schools. The middle school orientation brought a shift in focus from the subject matter to the early adolescent learner. This change in focus necessitated a change in the grades included in the school. Typically junior high schools include grades 7–9, while middle schools include grades 6–8 or 5–8 (see Table 1–1).

Two landmark reports called our attention to the needs of early adolescents in school settings: the California State Department of Education's *Caught in the Middle: Educational Reform for Young Adolescents in California Public Schools* (1987) and Carnegie Council on Adolescent Development's *Turning Points: Preparing Youth for the Twenty-First Century* (1989).

The California report represents the work of the Superintendents' Middle Grade Task Force and identifies students in this age group as at risk in the following ways:

- **Intellectually.** Early adolescents face decisions that have the potential to affect major academic values with lifelong consequences.
- **Physically.** At no other point in human development is an individual likely to encounter so much diversity in relation to oneself and others.
- **Socially.** Adult values are largely shaped conceptually during adolescence.

> As you read through the recommendations for effective middle school education, think back to your own junior high or middle school experience. You may find that regardless of when you went to school and regardless of whether your school was called a middle school or a junior high, there are remnants of both orientations. Probably no one school is purely one or the other.

- **In the development of moral and ethical choices and behaviors.** Early adolescents want to explore the moral and ethical issues that are confronted in the curriculum, in the media, and in the daily interactions they experience in their families and peer groups.

When you consider the tremendous social, intellectual, and physical changes facing early adolescents, you can see that the large, comprehensive junior high school was not serving them well.

The Carnegie Council on Adolescent Development, established in 1986, focused the nation's attention on the challenges of the adolescent years. Although published in 1989, the council's recommendations remain consistent with views of effective programs for middle school learners. The report offers the following recommendations:

1. Create small communities for learning.
2. Teach a core academic program.
3. Ensure success for all students.
4. Empower teachers and administrators to make decisions about the experiences of middle grade students.
5. Staff schools with teachers who are expert at teaching young adolescents.
6. Improve academic performance by fostering health and fitness.
7. Reengage families in the education of young adolescents.
8. Connect schools with communities.

The middle school movement attempted to align the structure and curriculum of the school to better serve early adolescents. Most important were the changing views of what the curriculum should include. The National Middle School Association (NMSA), founded in 1973 to promote effective changes in middle level education, established a set of guiding principles that have come to define exemplary middle level education. The responsive middle school, according to the NMSA, is characterized by: a shared vision, educators committed to young adolescents, a positive school climate, an adult advocate for every student, family and community partnerships, and high expectations for all. It should be noted that the concluding report of the Carnegie Council (1995) suggested that, 10 years later, middle schools were doing much better in the social aspects of schooling for early adolescents, but the recommendation for academic rigor and high expectations for all had been all but ignored.

It's difficult and complex to balance the needs to develop both social and academic competencies. Clearly, there are no simple ways to design and implement literacy lessons that will be responsive to the needs of all middle schoolers. In the following Literacy Lesson, student teachers in language arts and science worked together to implement exemplary middle school practices as they were coming to understand them. As you read about their planning, look for specific places where they infused components of effective middle school practices and ways that their planning might be strengthened. In Literacy Lesson 1–2, you'll see a project overview and rationale for an integrated language arts/science unit written by a teaching team that included two science student teachers and two language arts student teachers in Indiana.

Middle Schoolers and Middle School

Literacy Lesson 1-2

Planning a Smashing Unit

This is a unit plan to die for! Incorporating topics that students have learned in their science and English classes, eighth graders will work together to construct an "educational" haunted trail. The trail will consist of traditional elements of haunted house types of displays, but it will include a number of stations that will, in their own eerie way, demonstrate and celebrate learning in science and language arts.

The trail will be made up of a number of different stations that students will work together to conceive and build. They will be asked to create items that integrate the things that they have been studying in class. For example, students will read original and found poems and stories. Also, students will be introduced to the art of oral history, and they may share stories that they have written or collected from the community. A guest speaker will introduce students to Dia de los Muertos (Day of the Dead), so students may share the memorials to their friends and loved ones that they have written and read. Students will make observations of the cemetery ecosystem. They will identify different flora and fauna. Students may share their contour maps and research projects on life in the cemeteries. They may decide to set up a rock sample station and ask guests to identify rocks and minerals.

The haunted trail is designed as an opportunity for our students to "show off" what they have been learning. They will invite parents and friends to adventure on this trail of "horrors," allowing students to share and enjoy the conclusion to the unit that we call "The Graveyard Smash."

A Graveyard Smash Rationale

By now, upon mentioning to others that our integrated studies unit topic is cemeteries, we have become accustomed to the double takes and raised eyebrows. Typical remarks include, "What'ya goin to teach the kids to do, dig their own graves?" Well, er, no. Snide comments aside, cemeteries constitute one of those rare topics that easily bridge the sciences and the humanities. More important, we are convinced that students will be engaged. How can we be so sure? As a subject, cemeteries are not typically addressed in the classroom; confronted with this novel area of study, students will not feel as though they are revisiting materials that they have previously encountered year in and year out. Equally important, cemeteries are a vital aspect of most any community. Also, as students progress through adolescence, they become increasingly curious about issues pertaining to death and mortality. The relevance and potential for engagement, we believe, will encourage students to exhibit a positive attitude toward learning. Inasmuch as we believe in our topic's worthiness, excitement has characterized the planning stages of our unit design, consequently we have generated an abundance of ideas. Incidentally, we are consciously providing more activities than we would need for 10 days. (Fifteen days, in all likelihood, would be more ideal.) At any rate, the choice of cemeteries has proven to be a fertile topic, and we imagine it would be an enlightening experience for students and teachers alike.

In our efforts to make this unit design as educational and stimulating as possible, we plan for the eighth-grade class to take a field trip to one of the large public cemeteries in the local community. As safety is a strong consideration here, teachers and parents will act as chaperones for this half-day outing. We expect either a community historian or groundskeeper will be present to give an introduction to some aspects of the graveyard we intend to visit. Language arts and science teachers will have visited the graveyard beforehand and be ready to explore topics of interest. (We have in mind, for example, finding and recording particularly compelling or witty epitaphs and finding and recording aspects of the graveyard's faunae and florae.)

We are confident that our integrated unit design incorporates many Indiana English/Language Arts Proficiencies and Essential Skills. Some of our curricular goals include, but are not limited to, the following: Students will view themselves as readers, using school and public libraries/media centers to collect stories, reading a variety of materials (including the Internet), constructing meaning through collaboration with others, and critically examining what they read. As far as writing is concerned, students will view themselves as writers. They will generate ideas for writing from research and from collaboration with others and use process strategies to create and revise their writing. Particularly with our inclusion of guest speakers from the community, students will become more proficient listeners in a pleasant environment of learning. Students will also be expected to examine critically what they hear and not just become passive participants during these presentations. Proficiencies specific to the culminating activity include the following: selecting reading materials and sharing what they read, speaking to learn, collaborating with other speakers, and adapting their speech to different audiences.

The science curriculum for this unit plan incorporates a wide variety of the Indiana Proficiencies. Lessons topics involving the life sciences include ecosystems of the cemetery, human life expectancies, and even animals (blood-sucking animals). These lessons would integrate proficiencies that address interdependence of life, human identity, and physical health. Other integrated science studies would include lessons of the undetectable motions of the ground called *creep,* mineral and rock identification of tombstones, and the creation of a scale map of the cemetery with age contour lines. This project helps kids learn about research methods as well as the direct study of contour and scale. The cemetery has proved to be a wonderful way to integrate the various aspects of science while at the same time involving the community.

Perhaps you can hear the enthusiasm that Noah, Jennifer, Brian, and Justin felt in designing their first interdisciplinary middle school project. Their overview and rationale demonstrate attention to important aspects of exemplary middle school practice. They tapped local community resources, invited parents, crossed disciplinary boundaries, and created a project that was collaborative rather than competitive. Even their culminating activity was envisioned as a celebration of learning rather than a graded competition. The National Middle School Association lists five key components for exemplary middle school programs: interdisciplinary teams, advisory programs, varied instruction, transitional programs, and exploratory programs.

This project was a smashing success even though Jennifer and Noah, like most middle school teachers, were operating under many constraints. The first obstacle they encountered was that their school didn't organize students into teaching teams, so scheduling was a problem. They weren't able to implement the project as they had at first imagined because the science classes don't meet at the same time as the English classes, and these classes include most but not all of the same students. They did find solutions to these difficulties, and they felt their haunted trail was a success.

> As you read the following hallmarks of the exemplary middle school, think about how the graveyard project maps onto the five key components. How did Noah, Jennifer, and the others attend to these five components? In what ways might the project be strengthened even more?

Interdisciplinary Teams

Teachers from different disciplines work together as a team, sometime referred to as a *family*. Teams of teachers are assigned to the same group of students, which creates a small community of learners within a larger school. Teams ranging from two to five members in two, three, or four subject areas provide support for early adolescents by building a greater sense of belonging. Usually the teaching team shares a common planning time, which allows for collaborative teaching across disciplinary boundaries. This structure, with its built-in opportunities for flexible scheduling, allows for variety to plan and implement a curriculum that supports both social and academic competencies. Teams may plan a field trip, for example. They may sponsor such family activities as an "Evening with the Stars," a student-organized dinner and stargazing event. With close contact among teachers and students, teachers are better able to tap students' interests, maintain close connections with parents, and respond to the unique needs of students on the team.

Advisory Programs

Advisory programs foster strong adult-adolescent relationships and a sense of belonging to the school community. A regularly scheduled time is built into the school day for students to meet with their advisor, who may be a teacher, an administrator, or other staff member. To be well known by a significant adult in the school setting enhances an early adolescent's chances for success. Advisory groups are small by design to allow students opportunities to share concerns, explore careers, plan academic programs, discuss local and global issues, or address any personal, school, or community issues that may arise. Advisors get to know individual students, their interests, and their families. This time may be used to allow students opportunities to participate in planning school events and even in establishing school policies. In advisory meetings, students gain opportunities to serve as leaders and experts, which builds positive self-esteem and enhances engagement in the learning community.

Varied Instruction

The content of the curriculum starts with students' interests, often built around their own real-world questions. "Real" and "relevant" are the keys to success for a middle school curriculum. Opportunities for physical movement and hands-on (maybe even bodies-on) learning activities are vital in a middle school. The three *C*s for learning in a middle school are collaboration, cooperation, and community. Exemplary middle school programs deemphasize competition and support collaborative learning groups. Often, learning projects are integrated through community-based activities. Culminating activities are often designed as opportunities for students to celebrate their learning and to make a contribution to the community. Flexible scheduling may allow for instruction across age groups. Understanding the need for tapping multiple intelligences, middle school teachers try to structure learning opportunities that actively engage students and accommodate individual differences.

Exploratory Programs

Enrichment for all learners gives early adolescents opportunities to explore a broad range of academic, vocational, and recreational topics. Exploratory strands may be made available for 1-day exploration fairs, 1- or 2-week mini-courses, or full-semester courses. Courses in such areas as career choices, health, foreign languages, or intramural sports give middle school students a chance to explore new challenges beyond the curriculum. Tapping their curiosity may lead to more comprehensive investigations later. For instance, an exploration into student government or local community affairs may pique a student's interest and lead to memberships in school and community organizations. Through exploratory strands, middle schoolers also get to share their expertise, often serving as teachers or leaders. The exploratory strand allows both middle school teachers and students to participate as teachers and learners; changing roles can be deeply satisfying to all.

Transition Programs

To ease the transition into middle school, teachers, counselors, and school administrators set up opportunities for incoming students to meet them and visit the building before actually making the move to the middle school. Often, a visitation day is set in the spring so incoming students can see the school and meet their new teachers before summer vacation begins. During the first weeks at their new middle school, students attend orientation sessions that allow for additional opportunities to meet with school personnel, learn about school activities, have their questions answered, and calm their fears. Advisory groups can serve an active part of the transition program. Attentiveness to creating a smooth transition can mean the difference between success and failure throughout the middle school years—and beyond.

Now that you know something about middle school philosophy and practices, we invite you to investigate how those around you view and experience schooling for early adolescents. For Your Fieldwork Journal 1–2 entry, we'll ask you to compare views of adolescence and schooling with those about whom you have just read.

Your Fieldwork Journal 1-2

Middle School Experiences: Schooling for Early Adolescents

Set up two interviews with friends or relatives who are not middle level educators. The purpose of your interviews is twofold: (a) to collect views of schooling for early adolescents and (b) to document middle school experiences. Take time to design open-ended questions. Think about ways to elicit stories from your interviewees. Ask your interviewees to describe their impressions of what one might expect teaching middle school. Also ask them to share their histories as early adolescent learners. Ask them what they remember about making the transition from elementary school to high school.

Now record their answers in your field notebook. At first, attempt to record their views without making judgments. Use a "double-entry" journal format (see accompanying table) to record specifics of the conversations on one side of your notes, and then, on the other side, reflect on the meaning of these behaviors or conversations.

Double-Entry Journal	
Observations	**Reflections**
Write down what is observed. In making your observations, you may consider the following questions: • What is said? • What is seen (facial expressions, gestures)? • What gets "center stage"?	Jot down inferences about your observations. In making your inferences, you may speculate on some of the following questions: • What is not seen? • What is hidden? • What do these activities suggest that one is supposed to value? • What is considered appropriate/ordinary? • What is taken for granted? • What is considered inappropriate/out of the ordinary?

Now write a brief reflection. Do more than simply describe the conversations. In your reflections, can you identify patterns in the observed behavior that suggest certain attitudes? For example, in reflecting on the language used, do you note any biological, animal, or other metaphors? What do your interviewees take as "normal," "ordinary," and "unusual"? What do your interviewees take as surprising? What do these things suggest about what should be considered "normal"? Consider the years that they were in school, and look through the interviews for evidence of experiences that match/mismatch junior high or middle school orientations.

Speculate on how the views presented might be constructed by various political, historical, and ideological forces. In other words, guess why they believe what they believe, why their school experiences were what they were. What was happening in the world at the time? What was happening in a particular region?

Many schools were not philosophically or financially able to undertake such dramatic changes from junior high school to middle school. Some schools changed in name only. Some changed from grades 7–9 buildings to grades 6–8 buildings but did not implement the philosophy or practices that accompany the shifts from junior high school to middle school. Oftentimes school administrators and teachers did not have any knowledge of middle schools, and changes were implemented solely to accommodate building needs. Moving all ninth graders to the high school might alleviate overcrowding in a city's junior highs, for example. Even today, many middle schools remain "mini" high schools.

Although the five components are considered to be vital elements of the exemplary middle school, many factors are at work to make middle schools unable to enact all of them. Financial constraints, for example, may make scheduling classes difficult for interdisciplinary groups. Likewise, team planning time is often dropped.

Shifting orientations can be challenging at the teaching level as well. Often teachers have had little or no experience in working across disciplines. Jennifer, Noah, and the other student teachers in Margaret Finders's university program faced great challenges to work with those outside their discipline. One reflected, "Working together has definitely NOT been easy. Time to plan is doubled." Another observed that "those science teachers, ugh, they don't think like we do." Science student teachers voiced similar concerns about "those English teachers." Working as a member of an interdisciplinary team, Sarah began her reflection on the experience like this, "I hate group projects. You never have time to do them well." She concluded this reflection on a brighter note:

> *In working through this project, I really learned how teachers with diverse specialties can enhance overall learning. Because of her biology background, Stephanie was able to introduce aspects of frontier life that I would never have considered, like land and climate issues. Because of her English background, Shonda was able to develop the ideas of genre and bring in literature of the period and writing to have real-life implications for students.*

For this group and others the opportunities were greater than the obstacles.

In addition to the many economic and structural reasons why middle schools have not been able to enact all of the recommendations to become the kinds of places where early adolescents thrive, perhaps one of the key reasons is the lack of trained professionals to teach early adolescents. For more than 60 years literature has been calling for middle school teacher preparation; regardless, the majority of middle school teachers have no specialized preparation and have been prepared to teach other age groups in other kinds of schools (McEwin, Dickinson, Erb & Scales, 1995, p. 3).

What does all of this mean for you as an English language arts teacher of young adolescents? What are the specialized knowledge, skills, and dispositions needed to be a highly successful English language arts teacher? Unfortunately we can't give you a single bulleted list. We don't believe there is a singular, tried-and-true, one-size-fits-all view of effective literacy instruction for middle school teaching. We believe that instruction must be contextualized. Certainly we believe that specific practices lend themselves to effective literacy teaching and learning in the middle grades or we wouldn't be writing this book. Throughout the remainder of this book, we emphasize methods of inquiry rather than mastery of disciplinary material. We ask you to look through different lenses to examine what might be lost and gained by a particular pedagogical approach. Similarly, we ask you to look at sets of national standards and recommendations and inquire how these standards might play out differently in diverse classroom settings.

In the next chapter, you'll see how views of English language arts, like views of early adolescence, are situated historically. We invite you to consider how English language arts teaching and learning has shifted across time.

We turn your attention now to two sets of recommendations and examine how conceptions of early adolescents might influence our roles as middle school literacy teachers. In the Standards in Practice section, we ask you to examine sets of state and national standards. We do not ask you to embrace them uncritically; rather we want you to become critically aware of them, to examine them in order to understand diverse perspectives and the ways in which your classroom might be supported or constrained by external agencies.

Standards in Practice

The National Middle School Association Research Summary #5 "Young Adolescents' Developmental Needs," lists the specialized needs of early adolescents ages 10–15. According to this report, early adolescent learners:

1. need physical activities.
2. need positive social interactions with adults and peers.
3. need opportunities for creative expression.
4. need to feel a sense of competence and achievement in their work.
5. need meaningful participation in families and school communities.
6. need opportunities for self-definition.

You can find the complete report on the NMSA Web site at *http://www.nmsa.org*. Now think about how these recommendations might translate into English language arts curricula. Create your own list of recommendations for middle school literacy teachers. What do you think are the five most important things a middle school language arts teacher should do/think/be? (Keep each item short and to the point.)

Top Five List of "Shoulds" for Middle School Teachers
1. A middle school language arts teacher should . . .
2. A middle school language arts teacher should . . .
3. A middle school language arts teacher should . . .
4. A middle school language arts teacher should . . .
5. A middle school language arts teacher should . . .

A set of recommendations for teaching English language arts to early adolescents already exists. You may have heard of some teachers achieving National Board Certification. The National Board for Professional Teaching Standards (NBPTS) offers advanced voluntary certification for experienced, highly competent teachers. This organization has created sets of standards for what accomplished teachers should know and be able to do. You can download their standards for board certification in Early Adolescence/English Language Arts (EA/ELA) from the following address: *http://www.nbpts.org/*. Now create a list of recommendations according to the NBPTS.

Top Five List of "Shoulds" for NBPTS Middle School Teachers
1. A middle school language arts teacher should . . .
2. A middle school language arts teacher should . . .
3. A middle school language arts teacher should . . .
4. A middle school language arts teacher should . . .
5. A middle school language arts teacher should . . .

Finally, write a brief reflection on this exercise
Based on the NBPTS list of competencies for exemplary English language arts teachers of early adolescents, what seem to be the underlying assumptions about early adolescents? In what ways do the EA/ELA standards match/mismatch the NMSA recommendations? Last, how do they match/mismatch your views for exemplary practice?

REFERENCES

Brooks-Gunn, J., & Reiter, E. O. (1990). *At the threshold: The developing adolescent.* Cambridge, MA: Harvard University Press.

Brumberg, J. J. (1997). *The body project: An intimate history of American girls.* New York: Random House.

Carnegie Task Force on Education for Young Adolescents. (1989). *Turning points: Preparing youth for the twenty-first century.* Washington, DC: Carnegie Council on Adolescent Development.

Carnegie Task Force on Education for Young Adolescents. (1995). *Great transitions: Preparing adolescents for a new century.* Washington, DC: Carnegie Council on Adolescent Development.

Everhart, R. (1983). *Reading, writing and resistance: Adolescence and labor in a junior high school.* Boston: Routledge & Kegan Paul.

Finders, M. (1997). *Just girls: Hidden literacies and life in junior high.* New York: Teachers College Press.

Klein, H. (1990). Adolescence, youth and young adulthood: Rethinking current conceptualizations of life stage. *Youth and Society, 21,* 446–471.

McEwin, C., Dickinson, T., Erb, T., & Scales, P. (1995). *A vision of excellence: Organizing principles for middle grade teacher preparation.* Westerville, OH: Center for Early Adolescence and National Middle School Association.

National Middle School Association. (2002). Research Summary #5 "Young adolescents' developmental needs." Available at http://www.nmsa.org/research/ressum5.htm.

National Middle School Association. (1995). *This we believe: Developmentally responsive middle level schools.* Columbus, OH: Author.

Palladino, G. (1996). *Teenagers: An American history.* New York: Basic Books.

Santrock, J. W. (1993). *Adolescence.* Dubuque, IA: Wm. C. Brown.

Schlegel, A., & Barry, H. III. (1991). *Adolescence: An anthropological inquiry.* New York: Free Press.

Superintendents' Middle Grade Task Force. (1987). *Caught in the middle: Educational reform for young adolescents in California Public Schools.* Sacramento: California State Department of Education.

RESOURCES

Print

Allen, H. A., Splittgerber, F., & Manning, M. L. (1993). *Teaching and learning in the middle level school.* Upper Saddle River, NJ: Merrill/Prentice Hall.

Beane, J. A. (1993). *A middle school curriculum: From rhetoric to reality.* Columbus, OH: National Middle School Association (NMSA).

Coleman, J. S. (1961). *The adolescent society.* New York: Free Press.

Dickinson, T. (1993). *Readings in middle school curriculum: A continuing conversation.* Columbus, OH: NMSA.

Eccles, J., Lord, S., & Midgley, C. (1991). What are we doing to early adolescents? The impact of educational contexts on early adolescents. *American Journal of Education, 99,* 521–542.

Eccles, J., Wigfield, A., Midgley, C., Reuman, D., Iver, D. M., & Feldlaufer, H. (1993). Negative effects of traditional middle schools on student's motivations. *The Elementary School Journal, 93,* 553–574.

Feldman, S., & Elliott, G. (1990). *At the threshold: The developing adolescent.* Cambridge, MA: Harvard University Press.

Hynds, S. (1997). *On the brink: Negotiating literature and life with adolescents.* New York: Teachers College Press.

Kellough, R. D., & Kellough, N. G. (1999). *Middle school teaching: A guide to methods and resources.* Upper Saddle River, NJ: Merrill/Prentice Hall.

Manning, M. L., & Bucher, K. T. (2001). *Teaching in the middle school.* Upper Saddle River, NJ: Merrill/Prentice Hall.

McEwin, C., Dickinson, T., Erb, T., & Scales, P. (1995). *A vision of excellence: Organizing principles for middle grade teacher preparation.* Westerville, OH: Center for Early Adolescence and National Middle School Association.

Moore, D., Bean, T., Birdyshaw, D., & Rycik, J. (1999). *Adolescent literacy: A position statement for the Commission on Adolescent Literacy of the International Reading Association.* Newark, DE: The International Reading Association.

Muth, K. D., & Alvermann, D. (1999). *Teaching and learning in the middle grades.* Needham Heights, MA: Allyn and Bacon.

Takanishi, R. (1993). Changing views of adolescence in contemporary society. In R. Takanishi (Ed.), *Adolescence in the 1990s* (pp. 1–7). New York: Teachers College Press.

Walley, C. W., & Gerrick, W. G. (1999). *Affirming middle grades education.* Needham Heights, MA: Allyn and Bacon.

Watson, C. R. (1997). *Middle school case studies: Challenges, perceptions, and practices.* Upper Saddle River, NJ: Merrill/Prentice Hall.

Wiles, J., & Bondi, J. (1993). *The essential middle school.* Upper Saddle River, NJ: Merrill/Prentice Hall.

Wilhelm, J. (1996). *Standards in practice, 6–8.* Urbana, IL: National Council of Teachers of English Press.

Electronic

Adolescence Directory On Line. ADOL is a directory of Web documents that focus on the social, emotional, and developmental needs of adolescents. ADOL exists as a way to help educators, parents, health practitioners, researchers, and adolescents access Web resources.

http://education.indiana.edu/cas/adol/welcome.html

Center for Adolescent Studies. The Center states that its mission is to advance the understanding of the psychological, biological, and social features of normal adolescence. It serves as a resource of research on transition into adolescence.

http://education.indiana.edu/cas/index.html

Middle Web Resources. This Web site explores the challenges of middle school reform and provides resources for educators and parents.

http://middleweb.com/index1.html

National Board for Professional Teaching Standards. The NBPTS is an independent organization governed by a 63-member board of directors. Its mission is to establish high and rigorous standards for what accomplished teachers should know and be able to do to develop and operate a national, voluntary system to assess and certify teachers who meet these high standards.

http://www.nbpts.org/

National Council of Teachers of English. The NCTE middle-level strand offers research and resources for middle-level English language arts teachers.

http://www.ncte.org/middle/

National Middle School Association. The NMSA is an organization of professionals, parents, and others interested in the educational and developmental needs of young adolescents. NMSA is the only national educational association exclusively devoted to improving the educational experiences of young adolescents.

http://www.nmsa.org/

chapter 2

English Language Arts From Mid-Century to the Millennium

GUIDING QUESTIONS

1. How have our assumptions about literacy teaching in the middle grades changed over the past 50 years?
2. How have these changing assumptions influenced the teaching materials and techniques of junior high and middle school teachers?
3. How have your experiences as a student influenced your current assumptions about literacy and its teaching?

A CASE FOR CONSIDERATION

The World Across the Hall

In Mr. Owens's seventh-grade English classroom, students sit in rows of desks waiting for the class period to begin. Some are chatting with neighbors and friends; others are tearing paper out of notebooks or stuffing personal items temporarily inside their wooden desks. Steam escapes from a row of radiators beneath the large classroom windows. On a table along the back wall is a yellow cardboard box with colored dividers, which seems to hold teaching materials of some kind. A stack of worn grammar books sits in the corner, flanked by a filmstrip projector and a pile of dittoed multiple choice quizzes. An American flag and the teacher's heavy wooden desk dominate the front of the room. Some due dates and a few spelling words are written on the dusty blackboard.

After a few moments, Mr. Owens steps to the front of the room and tells students to take out their grammar books. Students each turn to different pages in large workbooks with slick green covers. They are supposed to work at their own pace, completing as many pages in one class period as they can. Some of them start right away, while others shuffle to the back of the room to sharpen pencils or dig in purses and pants pockets for pens. Suddenly the activity stops as the principal, Mr. Jones, enters the doorway. There are some nervous looks as Mr. Jones begins:

> Good afternoon, students. I have an announcement to make. As you know, last week was the end of the first marking period. Some of you worked very hard this term, and we're very proud of you. You did much better than your classmates and your efforts have paid off. Will the following people please gather up your things and move to the "A" classroom across the hall?

As Mr. Jones calls out the names, the mix of apprehension and relief in the room is almost palpable. Some students shift uneasily in their desks; others gather their books and belongings for the move across the hall. As soon as the three students leave the room, Mr. Jones's face turns somber.

> Now, just as there are those who worked up to their full potential, there are others who, unfortunately, failed to live up to our expectations. Will the following people please take your belongings and move to the "C" classroom next door?

The students watch in stunned silence as their classmates file out the door.

FOR DISCUSSION
- What do you make of this scenario?
- What do Mr. Owens and Mr. Jones seem to assume about the purpose of school?
- When do you think this incident took place?

This event happened routinely in the junior high school Susan Hynds attended from 1959 to 1961. Though his name has been changed, "Mr. Jones" was Susan's principal. Every marking period, without fail, Mr. Jones marched into her classroom with **THE LIST,** as Susan and her classmates waited in nervous anticipation. As you read this story, you probably suspected that it didn't happen in a modern-day classroom. In what ways does this picture compare or contrast with the memories of your own middle or high school? How do you think students would respond to a scenario like this today?

Now compare Susan's account with that of someone who attended an urban middle school from 1988 to 1990. Noshin is a doctoral student in literacy education, who was a middle school student nearly three decades after the time Susan described in the opening case study. In many ways, her experience provides a stunning contrast to Susan's.

> *In seventh grade we read* A Day No Pigs Would Die. *I will never forget that book. I remember feeling disgust (like I really wanted to throw up). The author must have*

used vivid language for me to remember and feel so much. I don't remember so much about my teacher teaching, except that she asked a lot of questions and we had to take a test on it. But I do remember that she seemed to enjoy the story, too.

I remember other things, too. That I had to do a paper. I wrote about the homeless, and that was really my first research paper. That I studied so much about Shakers that I never wanted to know another thing about them, though I was *fascinated at the time. That my friend Holly did a research paper on building plans for a local mall that was so thorough that all seventh graders were made to listen to her presentation (it* was *interesting). That we had to read a story written by a local author about an overweight girl who develops better eating habits and slowly gains self-awareness and self-esteem, and the author came to our class and visited and talked with us. I felt I could relate to that book, I think because I was overly anxious and self-critical during that time. It helped me to see that things can get better and you can do something about your own life.*

What I remember about eighth-grade English, more than anything, is the ambience. I couldn't tell you what we wrote or did, but I do remember that most of the time it was a nice change from most other rooms. We had a stage in our room and lots of books and different areas in which we could do things. It's funny, but I don't have any recollection of the teacher talking or doing things; I can kind of picture her in the background somewhere. I do remember having discussions with other students and also that I used to hang out in different parts of the room. I also have a vague memory of being in a certain part of the room that was very colorful. I also remember there was an area with stuff to read, and there was a Redbook *magazine that I used to enjoy reading. I would sometimes read* Redbook *after that time in my life. I think we also had computers in the room, but I don't remember using them.*

At this point, you are probably marveling at what a difference a decade—or, more accurately, three decades—can make in the life of a middle school student. The "ambience" that Noshin talks about, the room with its stage platform and comfortable reading spaces, the fact that she could read *Redbook* magazine during English class, the opportunities for social interaction and for researching current topics like homelessness—all these factors stand in striking contrast to Susan's memories of multiple choice quizzes, spelling lists, and fierce academic competition.

There's an old adage that we never remember what our teachers taught us; we only remember how they treated us. If you think back to your own memories as an early adolescent, chances are, you'll remember bits and pieces of things that distressed or impressed you about English class. Like Noshin, you may not remember exactly what your teachers said or did, but you will surely remember how you felt. If you trace these feelings back far enough, you may make some important discoveries about the assumptions from which your teachers might have been operating. The purpose of this chapter is to help you understand the social and historical roots of some of these assumptions.

EXPLORING YOUR TEACHING HISTORY

We begin this chapter from the premise that those who don't know their history as teachers and learners are condemned to repeat it. Often it's hard to put a finger on exactly why we resonate or clash with others about teaching, but when those "others" have power over our lives, these disagreements can be devastating.

Although there are surely many uncaring or ill-prepared teachers in the world, sometimes it's all too easy to pronounce someone else's teaching as mindless or cruel. Often, teachers eye each other with suspicion because they don't understand the historical origins or recognize the good intentions behind each other's teaching practices. It's also easy for any teacher—especially in an age where teaching materials and assessment techniques are a big-business enterprise—to combine various teaching approaches in a kind of mindless eclecticism, failing to understand the historical and possibly contradictory assumptions behind those approaches.

In Your Fieldwork Journal 2–1, we invite you to think back to your own days as an early adolescent. What materials and other artifacts dotted the landscape of your teachers' classrooms? As you engage in this imaginative excavation, consider the assumptions and, perhaps most important, the good intentions that may have been behind your teachers' practices.

Your Fieldwork Journal 2-1

Artifact Analysis: Revisiting Your Teachers and Textbooks

If you happen to be lucky enough to have lived in the same place for most of your life, or if your parents have saved some of your old things, you might want to *do a little archeological excavation*. Go up to your attic or storeroom and dig out any of the writings that you produced for your English teachers in middle or junior high school, as well as any textbooks or other materials you may have saved. Perhaps you used workbooks or worksheets. You may have an old literature anthology, grammar workbook, or writing textbook from this time in your life. If you're like most of us, however, you've long ago lost track of such artifacts from your past life as a student. In this case, jot down what you can remember about the classroom structures, assignments, textbooks, and other materials your teachers used, just as Noshin did in the previous example.

Now, do a mini-study of these artifacts

Consider what assumptions may have been behind your teachers' practices and teaching materials. Analyze any textbooks or materials you gathered or remembered. What seem to be the assumptions behind these published or teacher-created materials? You might want to create a double-entry journal like the accompanying sample. In the left column, jot down a description of the textbook, assignment, or other artifact from your days as a young adolescent. In the right-hand column next to each description, make a list of your teachers' "Assumptions About Literacy Learning." That is, what beliefs about reading, writing, oral language, and/or listening seem to underlie their choices of materials or teaching strategies?

When you are finished, think about the similarities or differences between your current beliefs about the teaching of literacy and your former teachers' beliefs.

Textbook, Teaching Material, Assignment	Assumptions About Literacy Learning
Grammar Workbook Page: "Parts of Speech." This is set up as a matching exercise where the names of the parts of speech are at the top and a list of definitions are below. Students are supposed to write the letter of the correct part of speech next to the matching definition below.	• Knowing the names of the parts of speech will make a person a better writer. • Memorizing definitions is important to the development of writing abilities. • Writing is an orderly process that begins with a knowledge of words, then sentences, paragraphs, and finally, longer pieces.

FROM TEXTS TO POLITICAL CONTEXTS: LITERACY LEARNING THEN AND NOW

Often, in her university classes, Susan asks her preservice teachers (who range in age from their 20s to their mid-50s) to make a list of the various approaches and materials they can remember from their own experiences as students in English language arts classes. As they share their memories of school, she makes a list similar to the one in Table 2–1

Looking closely at this table, you can see a kind of shift in the assumptions about literacy and its teaching over the years. In the first half of the 20th century, teachers seemed preoccupied with the *products* of student learning. Gradually, this preoccupation turned to a more *learner-centered* focus on the social, emotional, and intellectual development of individual students. Eventually, their concerns expanded to include the social (and sometimes political) contexts that influenced this development. Although approaches like spelling bees and sentence diagraming may have lingered from one decade to the next, we gradually began to see teaching approaches like journals, writing groups, independent reading programs, and inquiry projects in the English language arts classroom. The appearance of these approaches signaled some basic shifts in our assumptions about teaching, learning, and literacy.

English Language Arts From Mid-Century to the Millennium

TABLE 2-1 Teaching Artifacts and Approaches

1950s	1960s	1970s	1980s
• sentence diagraming	• sentence diagraming	• sentence diagraming	• sentence diagraming
• parts of speech	• parts of speech	• parts of speech	• parts of speech
• quizzes, essay & multiple choice tests on literature	• quizzes, essay & multiple choice tests on literature	• quizzes, essay & multiple choice tests on literature	• quizzes, essay & multiple choice tests on literature
• spelling bees	• vocabulary cards	• research papers (on teacher-selected topics)	• grammar worksheets
• "college-bound" literature lists	• language workbooks	• grammar worksheets	• sentence combining exercises
• research papers (on teacher-selected topics)	• "college-bound" literature lists	• "SRA" kits	• grammar mini-lessons
	• research papers (on teacher-selected topics)	• sentence combining	• collaborative inquiries
	• grammar worksheets	• "framed" paragraphs	• service learning projects
	• "SRA" kits	• "The Writing Process"	• "The Writing Process"
		• prewriting and prereading activities	• prewriting and prereading activities
		• peer writing groups	• peer writing groups
		• collaborative inquiries	• negotiated grading in assessment conferences
		• free-choice independent reading of "young adult" paperbacks	• free-choice independent reading of "young adult" paperbacks
		• literature and reading circles	• "I-Search" projects
		• "I-Search" projects	• literature and reading circles
		• collaborative learning activities	• word processors used in writing activities
			• grammar & spell checkers
			• computer-assisted writing programs

You'll notice that the sheer number of approaches and materials seems to grow with each decade. Indeed, teaching materials, high-stakes assessment programs, and a burgeoning educational consulting market have proliferated over the past 50 years. This commercialization of the educational enterprise makes it all the more imperative for us to become critical consumers of the many ideas and approaches available to us today. As a way of developing a more critical stance, this chapter will examine some of the classroom approaches and artifacts over the past half-century, attempting to put our own beliefs about literacy teaching in the middle grades into historical perspective.

OUR SHIFTING VIEWS OF LITERACY AND ITS TEACHING

As we explore the major changes in our thinking about literacy teaching from roughly the middle of the 20th century to the beginning of the 21st, it's important to remember that these shifts are not neat, tidy, or clearly bounded by historical periods. That is, what we might call the *text-* or *product-centered* approaches such as sentence diagraming and memorization of grammar rules are still alive and well in some classrooms today.

> What examples can you find in your personal experiences, classroom discussions, or conversations with teachers of the current tensions in literacy teaching?

Historically, there has been a constant tension between a preoccupation with standardized testing and teacher accountability and a concern for students' personal growth and development. As a result, even today, high-stakes testing, state standards, and teacher accountability, with their heavy attention to the *products* of learning, often coexist in a sort of schizophrenic relationship with more process-centered, social, or sociopolitical approaches, which situate student learning and achievement within the context of complex social and political forces. Perhaps it's helpful to think about English language arts teaching over the past half century in terms of five major shifts: (a) *literacy as text*, (b) *literacy as cognitive process*, (c) *literacy as personal growth*, (d) *literacy as sociocultural process, and* (e) *literacy as sociopolitical practice* (see Table 2–2).

The categories in Table 2–2 give us a language for examining our own views and understanding the assumptions behind the materials and methods in most classrooms. They should not, however, be used to stereotype individual teachers. Instead, we hope that they will serve as a frame for examining the often rough and uneven ways in which English language arts teaching has evolved through the latter half of

TABLE 2-2 Approaches to Literacy Teaching

Aspects of the Learning Climate	Product-Centered	Process-Centered		Social/Contextual	
		Cognitive/ Developmental	Personal/ Expressive	Sociocultural	Sociopolitical
Focus of Curriculum	**Literacy as Text** • Part-to-whole approach to reading, writing, and grammar • Stress on correctness in grammar, spelling, and handwriting • Reading as decoding • Oral language as memorizing or answering teacher questions • Assessment through tests, quizzes, workbooks, formal writing	**Literacy as Cognitive Process** • Cognitive stages of literacy development • Writing and reading as thinking processes • Language as a way of learning across the curriculum • Assessment of processes as well as products • Prereading and prewriting strategies • Emphasis on revision • Portfolios for error analysis and assessment	**Literacy as Personal Growth** • Stress on self-expression and discovery • Student choice in topics and reading materials • Learning to write by writing • Wide variety of "young adult" literature • Oral language as a way of learning and sharing • Individualized, qualitative assessment through portfolios	**Literacy as Sociocultural Process** • Community-building • Collaborative learning activities • Peer and teacher-pupil conferencing • Stress on "authentic" audiences for student writing and talk • Curriculum and assessment negotiated between students and teachers • Literacy as cultural understanding and tolerance	**Literacy as Sociopolitical Act** • Classroom as democracy • Emphasis on social justice and/or community action • Critical analysis of published texts and popular culture • Assessment and grading negotiated with students

Aspects of the Learning Climate	Product-Centered	Process-Centered		Social/Contextual	
		Cognitive/ Developmental	Personal/ Expressive	Sociocultural	Sociopolitical
Responsibilities of Teacher	• Dispense knowledge • Correct student errors • Keep records • Produce good citizens • Develop cultural literacy • Administer tests and quizzes • Monitor student progress on independent learning activities	• Develop "higher order" thinking skills • Develop strategies for reading, writing, and speaking in a variety of contexts • Make learning strategies explicit • Develop metacognitive awareness • Give substantive feedback to students • Teach stages of and strategies for reading and writing processes • Recognize developmental patterns in student ability and error	• Create safe classrooms • Celebrate personal expression and growth • Promote personally relevant independent language activities • Legitimize student texts • Expand the canon and curriculum to include a variety of cultural and social perspectives • Promote student choice • Read and write along with students	• Create classroom community • Foster student collaboration • Expand contexts for students' reading, talking, and writing • Promote cultural tolerance through literacy • Expand the canon and curriculum to include a variety of cultural and social perspectives • Set goals collaboratively • Teach grammar and usage "in context"	• Create a democratic classroom where all voices can be heard • Recognize influence of race, class, gender and other sociopolitical aspects of learning • Teach critical and political skills • Empower students as members of a democracy • Create opportunities for students to use literacy as a form of social action
Teaching Approaches and Materials	• Lecture • Whole class discussion • Programmed instruction • Formal speaking, reading, writing, and research activities • Workbooks • Book reports • Vocabulary cards • Spelling bees • Grammar handbooks • Reading machines • Programmed learning kits • Research papers	• Cross-curricular projects • Learning logs • "Think alouds" • Guided reading and writing activities • Sentence combining • Framed paragraphs • Slotted sentences • Portfolios for analyzing drafts, revision processes, and patterns of error in writing	• Reading and writing workshops or learning centers • Informal language experiences • Sharing circles • Student-authored publications • Informal research (or "I-Search") • Response journals • Writer's notebooks • Personal folders • Classroom libraries of young adult paperbacks • Portfolios for qualitative analysis of student learning	• Authentic audiences and purposes beyond the classroom • Project learning • Use of Internet, electronic mail, and other communication technologies • Peer response groups • Collaborative inquiry • Multiculturalism • Young adult books • Dialogue journals • Reading/writing circles • Portfolios for student-teacher conferencing • "Development" and "Showcase" portfolios for demonstrating growth to others	• "Social action," "service learning," or "community action" projects • Reading, writing, and talking about politically relevant topics • "Antibias" or "antiracist" curricula • Multiculturalism as cultural critique • Exploration and critique of popular culture • Use and critique of Internet, electronic mail, and other communication technologies • Portfolios as opportunities for demonstrating growth and negotiating grades

the 20th century. Most of us probably incorporate aspects of all five perspectives to one degree or another in our teaching. The point is not to see any one perspective as necessarily better or worse than the others, but to understand our ideas about literacy and its teaching as they developed over the past half century.

Literacy as Text: Product-Centered Approaches

Around the mid- to late 1960s, *texts*—their production and comprehension—were the centerpiece of the English language arts classroom. For Susan, the text that set the course of her entire junior high school experience was the standardized test. Given at the end of the sixth grade, this was the benchmark by which students would be sorted into the **A, B,** and **C** classes in the school's first experiment with "homogeneous grouping." Because this was her first brush with standardized tests, she got stuck on the first few items, never finishing the examination. As a result she was relegated to the **B** class for the first year of junior high school.

For a different set of reasons, Margaret was also placed in the **B** class. She had gone to a tiny rural elementary school, which had not given the standardized tests upon which students could be tracked. In addition, her administrators assumed that since she had gone to a rural school, she wouldn't be prepared to compete with children from the city.[1]

The '50s and early '60s were highly competitive times, where classroom practices like spelling bees and the public sharing of everything from class rank to individual grades were commonplace. This focus on competition wasn't all bad; for academically successful students, a certain degree of competition actually enhanced learning. For kids like Susan and Margaret who were marginalized to the B track, however, their resistance to this competition often surfaced in antisocial and disruptive ways. Susan quickly mastered the art of becoming the "class clown." At first, her homeroom teacher gave her "write-offs," then eventually moved her desk into the cloakroom as a way of controlling her distracting attempts to amuse her classmates.

Junior high school students in the '50s and '60s sat in rows, often working silently on independent activities. Sentence diagraming and workbooks were commonplace. Writing, if it was taught at all, typically focused on product-centered goals such as developing good handwriting and correct grammar, usage, or spelling. No research had yet been done on the thinking processes in which real writers engage, so writing instruction was dominated by a classical "building blocks" assumption that students should first learn words (vocabulary) before developing the ability to produce phrases, sentences, paragraphs, and finally, longer pieces of writing. If you happen to have a workbook or

> Can you see evidence of a "building blocks" approach to language study in your personal experience and classroom materials?

---

[1] Upon reading this thinly veiled rationale for why "we were so smart but nobody knew it," we had to laugh. We thought about cutting these paragraphs altogether, but we left them in, not only because they convey some of the competitiveness of our junior high school experience, but also because it's interesting that the bad memories of being relegated to the "middle" track are still with us today.

grammar handbook from the '50s or '60s, or even a more modern version, you'll probably see evidence of this building-block approach, where punctuation and grammar at the sentence level are treated in the early chapters and rules for paragraphing and organizational structures for longer pieces of writing come later.

At the same time, reading instruction was dominated by what might be called a "decoding" perspective, where teachers often presented students with short bits of texts in workbooks or readers and tested their comprehension of these reading materials. Unless teachers read aloud to students from stories or novels, or unless a school was fortunate to have class sets of anthologies, reading usually focused more on the study of these short contrived texts than it did on longer pieces of literature.

Often, if literature was taught at all, teachers, in the tradition of "New Criticism" (Brooks, 1947; Ransom, 1979), conducted discussions and gave tests and quizzes on the "correct" understanding of whatever the class was reading. Textbooks usually included a series of questions after each selection for teachers to use in assessing whether students understood what they read or, more likely, whether they read at all. Book reports were also common. Oral language opportunities consisted of oral book reports, large group discussions, an occasional assignment to memorize and present a short piece of literature, or a chance to compete in a spelling bee. Occasionally, students would stay after school to practice for skits or assemblies. Talk was usually reserved for *demonstrating* rather than *creating* knowledge.

> Do you see evidence of "reading-as-decoding" or New Critical approaches in today's English language arts classrooms?

Lest we paint an entirely dismal and oppressive picture of the junior high school English classroom at mid-century, we need to point out that, in many ways, we both flourished in this atmosphere. Margaret was good at answering questions about her reading and managed to use the same book report on *Across Five Aprils* (Hunt, 1964) three times from the sixth to the eighth grade. Always an extrovert, Susan loved to "perform" the poems she memorized and compete in spelling bees. Both of us were adept at diagraming sentences and enjoyed being tested on our reading. After all, we both became English teachers, so our own teachers must have done something right. Now that we've become teacher educators, however, we are struck by how many horror stories we hear from teachers in our workshops and classes about feeling "stupid" in class discussions and receiving papers that were viciously "red-penned" by grammar-obsessed teachers.

This product-centered view of literacy came out of the behaviorist notion that the mind is a "black box," inaccessible by any means (Skinner, 1976). This school of thought maintains that only behaviors can be empirically measured. As a result, teachers were pushed to produce "behavioral objectives" in which their goals for students had to be phrased in terms of easily measurable outcomes.

> Consider the limitations of evaluating students solely on their classroom behaviors.

In addition, since the launch of *Sputnik* by the Soviets in 1957, Americans were consumed by what became known as the "space race," and students were under tremendous pressure to excel in science and mathematics. It's not surprising that in an era of fierce national competition, standardized testing grew so powerful. Tests provided a set of neatly hierarchical and objective scores on which students could be judged against one another and placed in tracks according to "ability."

Although this text-centered view may seem altogether superficial and rigid, it's important not to dismiss its importance entirely. As teachers, we all bear the responsibility of teaching students how to craft and polish their writing, understand literary devices, learn appropriate grammar and usage conventions, master the arts of performing and publishing, and pass the standardized examinations they will surely face. If we fail to prepare them for these tasks, we have ignored one of our primary responsibilities as teachers.

When we focus too heavily on texts, however, it's easy to lose sight of individual differences among students and the way social issues such as race, class, and gender complicate their literacy practices. It wasn't until the early 1970s that educators began to question the individualistic, competitive view of literacy education, opening up the mind's "black box" and daring to speculate on the unique and varied thinking processes that lie beneath the surface.

Process-Centered Approaches

In the early '70s, classrooms were slowly beginning to change in appearance and structure. Within what has been called the *process movement* were two major views of literacy: literacy as *cognitive process* and literacy as *personal growth*.

Literacy as a Cognitive Process. In a few innovative classrooms, teacher-centered arrangements like desks in rows began to be replaced with circles of desks or small tables to accommodate collaborative learning projects. Occasionally, students were invited to depart from the standard canon of literature and choose from an array of what came to be called *young adult novels* or "YA" books.

During the famous Dartmouth Conference in 1966, an internationally renowned group of literacy scholars and researchers had assembled for the purpose of reflecting on the past and future of English teaching. The early work of the conference participants had already begun to filter into professional conversations about teaching (Dixon, 1967). The early '70s heralded what promised to be an exciting new era in the teaching of English, where a text-centered view, dominated by New Criticism, prescriptive grammars, and classical approaches to writing was challenged by a student-centered approach that focused on the unique abilities and needs of individual learners.

Books like *Teaching as a Subversive Activity* (Postman & Weingartner, 1969), *Uptaught* (Macrorie, 1970), and *Hooked on Books* (Fader, 1966) became the new staples of college methods courses in the '70s. Writers like Postman and Weingartner, Macrorie, and Fader argued passionately for the need to depart from traditional focus on correctness and conformity—to let students read freely from books written especially for them, choose their own topics in writing, and have a say in direction and content of their own learning. Despite the urgings of a few revolutionaries, though, the innovations of the '70s were slow to filter down into real classrooms. In most English classrooms sentence diagraming, workbooks, and desks in rows were still pretty much the order of the day.

> How are literacy and its teaching portrayed in the popular media?

Harris (1991) has written about this stark contrast between the "progressivist" rhetoric of the early '70s and the daily realities of most schools. He argues that this "heroic view" (p. 631) of Dartmouth as the catalyst for progressive education in America was inaccurate. In fact, there was a noticeable difference between the basic philosophies of the American and British participants at the conference—a difference that persists in the profession today. Harris argues that the British educators at Dartmouth largely supported a "growth model," informed by developmentalists such as Piaget (1950, Piaget & Inhelder, 1969), Vygotsky (1962), and Bruner (1960). This view celebrated the personal experiences of students and the expressive nature of language. In their zeal to beat the Russians in the space race, the Americans, on the other hand, were struggling to define English as an academic discipline. Inspired by the work of linguists such as Chomsky (1957) and literary critics such as Frye (1957), they were attempting to establish the legitimacy of English as a formal subject of study with distinct bodies of knowledge and subsets of skills to be mastered. This tension between knowledge and skills on one hand and personal growth on the other remains with us today.

By the early '70s, a group of writing researchers, inspired by the work of scholars such as Piaget (1950; Piaget & Inhelder, 1969), Vygotsky (1962), and Bruner (1960), began to peer inside the "black box" of literacy to explore how real readers, writers, and speakers created and comprehended language.

The earliest studies of writing were based on analyses of texts. Braddock (1975) discovered that, contrary to popular wisdom, published writers did not always have what English teachers called "topic sentences" in their paragraphs. Hunt (1970) discovered that students' sentences grew larger and more complex as they grew older. As a result, approaches like sentence combining slowly began to replace sentence diagraming, as teachers tried to give students practical ways to build the complexity and length of their sentences by creating and combining what they called "kernel sentences" in different patterns.

A group of early writing researchers (Emig, 1971; Flower & Hayes, 1977; Perl, 1979) argued that, contrary to the classical building-block assumptions, writing is a messy, often recursive process that proceeds in different ways for different writers. More experienced writers, for example, tend to make larger, more global revisions, in contrast to novice writers who typically revise at a surface level, rarely moving beyond cosmetic changes of words or phrases (Flower, 1979; Sommers, 1980). As this research gained a foothold in American education, we began to hear now-familiar phrases like "teach process not product." Although grammar handbooks still lined the shelves and windowsills of most middle and junior high school classrooms, posters of the stages of the composing process—from prewriting to revising—gradually began to appear.

> Did your teachers pay more attention to the processes or the products of your literacy learning?

In some classrooms, early adolescents would pull up chairs in pairs or small groups to give each other feedback on texts in process, and it became fashionable to turn in a series of "messy" drafts before final products were completed. What came to be called the *Writing Across the Curriculum* (WAC) movement grew out of the idea that writing could be used not just as a way of demonstrating knowledge but also as a way of learning in all subject areas. Eventually, teachers beyond the English classroom were urged to use writing as a regular way of encouraging more active learning of their course content.

> Consider the myriad ways in which writing can be used in all aspects of the school curriculum.

Inspired by Rosenblatt's landmark work, *Literature as Exploration* (1995, originally published in 1938), researchers from a "reader response" perspective (Beach, 1974; Holland, 1973; Purves & Ripperre, 1972) discovered—again, no surprise to many teachers—that each

> What does it mean to teach from a "reader-response" perspective?

student had a unique and individual response to literature. Teachers began to understand that literary reading (as opposed to informational reading) offered what Langer (1995) would later call a "horizon of interpretive possibilities" in contrast to a "steady reference point" of "correct" interpretation. Tests and quizzes on literature were sometimes replaced or supplemented by "guided response" activities where students were led through a series of strategies designed to capture their unfolding responses as they read. The traditional "questions at the back of the book" started to reflect a developmental orientation, beginning with literal questions about literature and moving toward more interpretive levels.

> How important are oral language experiences in students' literacy learning?

At the same time, definitions of literacy were being expanded beyond the traditional triad of reading, writing, and language study. Barnes (1975) from the United Kingdom showed how oral language, like writing, could be a way of learning and not just a way of demonstrating knowledge. As a result, the traditional research paper sometimes gave way to informal collaborative inquiry where students explored a topic of interest with a group of their peers. Heathcote (1970) and Moffett and Wagner (Moffet, 1968; Moffet & Wagner, 1992) introduced the importance of drama in the English classroom. Oral language activities ranging from panel discussions, public speeches, and debates to creative dramatics, oral interpretation, and readers' theater entered the literacy classroom. This approach was especially exciting and engaging for middle school students, whose keen sense of adventure and need for social interaction and physical activity were not yet dampened by the increasing peer pressure of high school.

Despite a flourishing body of research and the exciting work of innovative teachers, however, large-scale studies of how literacy was actually taught in the '70s and '80s revealed a rather bleak picture. Britton and his colleagues (1975) from the United Kingdom reported that there were few opportunities for adolescents to engage in what he called "expressive" or "poetic" writing; instead, most students wrote for a narrow audience of teacher/examiners. Similarly, Applebee (1981), in his large-scale survey of students and teachers in the United States, concluded that few writing projects longer than a paragraph were assigned by English teachers. Other content-area teachers in his study relied almost solely on multiple choice and fill-in-the-blank tests.

Later, in his study of American literature classrooms, Applebee (1993) discovered that, despite growing interest in expanding the canon of literature available to secondary students, teachers still clung to the traditional Eurocentric canon and held to the principles of New Criticism in their teaching. Although such studies were crucial to our understanding of the teaching practices of the times, it's interesting that those including the middle grades tended to lump together early and older adolescents in their discussion, reflecting little or no recognition for the unique needs and abilities of early adolescents.

Nevertheless, during the '70s and early '80s, a great many teachers gradually moved from a focus on products to a focus on the processes behind them. In some classrooms, student-created learning logs and journals replaced workbooks and worksheets as teachers recognized the value of informal, exploratory writing and self-selected reading. Teachers sought to find authentic audiences for student writing beyond themselves and engaged students in brainstorming, drafting, and revising as well as regular goal-setting and evaluation conferences throughout the composing process. Standardized tests were still present in many states and, largely as a result of the cognitive process movement, state and local curricula were often based on hierarchies or taxonomies of skills that were expected to develop as students moved through the grade levels.

Eventually, we began to realize that the strong focus on skills and knowledge, made even more pressing by the push to become an intellectually superior nation, had blinded us to important affective and personal aspects of literacy teaching.

Literacy as Personal Growth. Largely inspired by the early work of cognitive psychologists, advocates of a student-centered curriculum argued passionately for the benefits of student choice and "authentic" literacy practices. One approach promised teachers a way to provide students with choice and personally meaningful literacy experiences while still maintaining a comfortable structure and routine. This approach became known as *workshop teaching*.

Atwell's landmark work, *In the Middle* (1987), provided middle school teachers with concrete examples of early adolescents exercising choice in reading, writing, and oral language within a flexible setting. In a workshop arrangement, students often worked individually or in small groups, whereas teachers acted more as guides or facilitators rather than the sole arbiters of students' learning. Teachers learned to move among groups of students, conferring with individuals or giving suggestions to groups as they worked on a variety of projects. Perhaps because of their need for constant movement, change, and choice, early adolescents seemed uniquely suited for workshop models of literacy learning. Even today, it is more common to see workshop teaching in a middle than a high school classroom.

With the aim of developing students personally and intellectually, teachers and researchers began to focus on the affective and aesthetic as well as cognitive dimensions of language learning. In the late '70s, Rosenblatt wrote *The Reader, The Text, The Poem* (1994, originally published in 1978), noting the differences between "aesthetic" and "efferent" reading. Literature, she argued, should be read aesthetically (with a near-total absorption in the reading process); yet, in classrooms, students often read literature efferently (from the Latin *effere*, "to carry away") for the purpose of remembering bits of trivia for a test or quiz. Based largely on the work of humanistic psychologists such as Rogers (1969) and the work on aesthetic reading by Rosenblatt (1994, 1995), teachers acknowledged the complex interplay of personal response, motivation, and authenticity in literacy learning. Atwell (1987), Graves (1983), Calkins (1986), and Murray (1985), among others, urged teachers to give students choices in their reading and writing activities and to encourage the development of "authentic voice" in writing and personal response in reading.

> How is workshop teaching uniquely suited to the middle school classroom?

In some classrooms, as a result of the reader-response movement, reading workbooks were replaced by more personal "response journals," and the competitive forum of the large group discussion was offset by opportunities for small circles of students to talk informally about paperback young adult novels. Teachers began to install book racks or set aside areas for classroom libraries of these paperbacks for students' independent reading. With the publication of Hinton's *The Outsiders* in 1967, a healthy market emerged for books written especially for teenage readers. Today, although YA novels are supposed to be for both middle and secondary students, they are typically viewed as more appropriate for early adolescents. Perhaps because they face less pressure for college preparation, middle school teachers are more likely than high school teachers to embrace adolescent literature and independent reading programs.

In the early '70s, the Assembly on Literature for Adolescents (ALAN) was created within the National Council of Teachers of English to help teachers discover and evaluate the burgeoning supply of literature for young adults. *The ALAN Review,* Carlsen's *Books and the Teenage Reader* (1980), Fader's *Hooked on Books* (1966), and *Your Reading* (an annotated bibliography of young adult books published and updated regularly by the National Council of Teachers of English) helped teachers to expand the canon of literature available to students beyond the traditional. At the same time, the Bay Area Writing Project and its offshoot, the National Writing Project, offered hands-on staff development and a support network for teachers interested in implementing a process-centered approach to writing in schools across the nation.

> What "intelligences" do your middle school students seem to draw upon? Do their school experiences seem to support the development of these intelligences?

In the early '90s, student-centered approaches to literacy were enriched by the work of Gardner (1993) and his theory of multiple intelligences. Anyone who has taught in the middle grades can attest to the tremendous range of preferences and abilities among early adolescents. Perhaps no other period of development captures students at so many different points on the intellectual and social spectrum. It is no wonder that Gardner's work was so relevant to teachers in the middle grades, inspiring them to look beyond the logical and linguistic (the intelligences most valued in schools) and discover the vast wealth of other capacities in young learners. Especially during this personal growth movement, artistic, spatial, kinesthetic, and other "alternative" intelligences began to be represented in the middle school English language arts classroom. It was not uncommon for students to include drawing or other artistic representations in portfolios and journals as teachers discovered the need for allowing all students choices in representing their learning in a variety of ways beyond the logical and linguistic.

Beginning in the '80s, rigid developmental sequences and hierarchies of skills were challenged by the work of K. and Y. Goodman and the "whole language" movement. This movement started in the elementary grades and gradually worked its way into the middle and (occasionally) the high school classroom (Goodman, 1986; Goodman, Goodman, & Hood, 1989). Although the movement is far more complicated than we can describe here, it is founded on the notion that literacy skills are best developed as learners encounter whole texts rather than the "manufactured" atomistic stuff of the workbooks, quizzes, and basal readers of the '60s. Rather than relying on standardized tests and quizzes or rigid taxonomies of skills that students are supposed to master at certain age levels, the whole language movement encouraged teachers to become "kid watchers" and researchers in their own classrooms, developing curricula and evaluation materials sensitive to the unique groups of students they served. Perhaps because some middle school teachers have an elementary background or because the middle school is not as rigidly segmented by subject matter areas as high school, it seems that middle school teachers have been more accepting of whole language than secondary teachers, though not perhaps quite as accepting as their colleagues in elementary settings.

Considering the rather rigid and simplistic text-based views of literacy teaching being advocated by politicians and test makers today, this learner-centered perspective seems too good to be true, as, in a sense, it still is. Gradually, though, some limitations of this personal growth approach became apparent. First, although teachers experienced the satisfaction of offering students choices and inviting their unique personal perspectives into the literacy classroom, it became difficult to assign grades or to assess their progress without appearing to squelch their creativity and enthusiasm. Second, even though techniques like personal sharing and collaborative learning worked well in relatively homogeneous classrooms, the increasing cultural diversity of our schools made such approaches complicated for children of different cultures, especially those who spoke English as a second language. Finally, we began to realize that, considering the incredibly social nature of language, there was really no such thing as the "individual" response to literature or even what came to be called "personal" writing. Language learning occurred not in a vacuum, but in a complicated web of social relationships. As the next section will discuss, we are both created by and the creators of our language acts.

Social/Contextual Approaches to Literacy Teaching

Literacy as a Sociocultural Process. Eventually, as approaches like workshop teaching began to bring students and teachers into closer collaboration, it became apparent that literacy was not simply an isolated activity where students' reading, writing, and oral language processes operated independent of the social contexts surrounding them. Although the goal of most English language arts teaching still focused heavily on the development of individual language skills, we began to recognize that social, cultural, academic, and other experiences all influenced the development of those skills. Through the work of Vygotsky (1962), we began to realize that what students could do on their own was only a small part of what they could do with the help of peers, teachers, and other adults. Vygotsky's "zone of proximal development" referred to the spectrum of language activities that individuals could accomplish with the assistance of more able individuals in their social realm.

A movement known as *constructivism* promoted the idea that students should be viewed not as passive learners but as active in constructing their own knowledge, often in social interaction with teachers and more able peers (see Hiebert, 1991). In contrast to more private, individualistic approaches to literacy learning, students in constructivist classrooms discovered the power of engaging in such collaborative activities as writing conferences, peer response groups, literature circles, and collaborative inquiry. This social view of language stood in stark contrast to the assumptions of the '50s and '60s that students should be taught and tested independently, without outside help. Fifty years ago, it was considered "cheating" to collaborate with others on tests and papers. By the mid- to late 1970s, collaboration on everything from writing to research projects became the order of the day. Such collaborative approaches became even more popular in the middle grades where early adolescents' need for social interaction is paramount.

> How does constructivist teaching differ from more "individualized" models?

At the same time, as more and more children of diverse cultures and languages began to enter the public schools, it became painfully apparent that the experiences of young women and children of color were not represented in textbooks, classroom libraries, or even standardized tests. The term *multiculturalism* entered our vocabularies as we strove to make our students more tolerant of difference through their reading, writing, listening, and talking. In its early days, multiculturalism became associated with building cultural tolerance. Teachers and students began reading and writing about the holidays and traditions of particular cultural groups. For example, literature by African American, Latino/Latina, and Asian writers, among other racial and ethnic groups, began to make its way into some classrooms. In the '70s and early '80s, however, literature by women and writers of color was still hard to come by, and most teachers continued to teach from a primarily White European canon.

> What challenges do we face as our classrooms become more diverse?

Our views of the "individual" language learner were challenged by anthropologists and psycholinguists (Heath, 1983), who argued that race, culture, and class profoundly influenced the ways in which students used language and, consequently, the impressions their teachers developed about them. Scholars such as Smitherman (1986) and Labov (1972) popularized the notion that the language of some African American children, in contrast to popular stereotypes, is rich with nuance and complexity and not, as many teachers suspected, a sign of laziness or sloppiness. As a result of such work, teachers began to question the legitimacy of Eurocentric approaches to grammar and language study that had long been the mainstay of American public education. "Correctness" began to be viewed within the context of the varied cultural and social expectations that students encountered in their daily lives.

A view of literacy as sociocultural process went a long way in promoting the value of collaboration in the English language arts classroom and encouraged an understanding and tolerance of diversity. In the latter part of the 20th century, however, we were confronted by difference and diversity in ways we had never imagined. Understanding the vital role of literacy in a democratic society, we began to believe that students could use literacy, not only to understand, but also to transform the world around them.

Literacy as Sociopolitical Practice. As scholars such as Luke (1988), Edelsky (1994), and Willinsky (1990) began to make their mark upon the field of literacy education, teachers were urged to move beyond the goal of developing individual students' cognitive and social skills toward a greater awareness of the role of literacy in a democracy. For the past several decades, whether represented by the individualized learning approaches of the '50s and '60s or learner-centered approaches such as reader response and the process approach to writing, English language arts teaching had been largely focused toward developing the skills and capacities of individual learners. This highly individualized view of literacy has recently been criticized on many fronts.

> Are all of our teaching decisions inherently political?

In a more politically situated approach, students are challenged to use their literacy as a way of promoting social change. On one end of this spectrum, English language arts teachers might engage students in a service learning curriculum, in which they participate in service projects aimed at helping others or improving community life. On the other end of the continuum, teachers might create an antibias, antiracist, or social justice curriculum, in which students work collaboratively on social and political issues such as the environment, crime, and political reform. When literacy is viewed as a sociopolitical practice, it is not enough to simply include multicultural literature or promote tolerance of others in the classroom. We are challenged today as never before to make issues of race, class, gender, and injustice explicit aspects of our literacy teaching.

Through the influence of movements such as postmodernism, feminism, and cultural studies, we are also urged to become more sensitive to the ways in which issues like race, class, gender, and other sociopolitical factors influence the literacy practices of students. As Edelsky (1992) has argued, every curricular choice, from textbook selection to assessment practices, has political implications:

> Many people, especially in the United States, think of politics only as dirty and "backroom stuff." As a result, we regard it as not polite to engage in controversial arguments or politics; we don't want to politicize.... The schools, because they are public schools, supposedly do not advocate any particular position. But we ignore the fact that embedded in every textbook, every basal reader, and every classroom discussion is a political perspective. (p. 325)

In a similar vein, work on gender in the literacy classroom (Barbieri, 1995; Finders, 1997) has made teachers more sensitive to the fact that young girls are often socialized toward silence. Young men, on the other hand, are steeped in a tradition of competition and aggressiveness; they often demand more "air time" in class discussions and are reluctant for male peers to see them reading books or writing poetry.

In a sociopolitical approach to literacy, teachers have an increasingly difficult role to play. In contrast to their role in the teacher-centered classrooms of the '70s and '80s, they are urged to create classroom democracies where all voices can be heard and no students are silenced because of race, class, gender, or privilege. This is no easy task, since engaging middle school students in considering issues they might not have sought out on their own requires a new kind of "teacher-centeredness." In contrast to their experiences as student-centered teachers in the '70s and '80s, today's English language arts teachers cannot afford to simply step out of the way and allow students total choice in the topics and products of their learning. Sometimes, students and teachers alike must step into uncomfortable positions as the literacy classroom becomes a crucible for the divisiveness and discomfort that often accompany social change.

In addition to adopting new roles in their literacy classrooms, teachers are also challenged to compete with the ever-expanding horizon of reading, writing, talking, and interactive experiences available to their middle school students through technological advances such as the Internet. More important, they must teach their students to become more critical of the barrage of popular culture in their daily lives. This is no easy task for early adolescents, who often define themselves and others by choices in everything from fashions to music groups to popular magazines.

> What roles do technology and popular culture play in students' literacy learning?

It's important to reiterate that the move from *product* to *process* to *social and political contexts* over the past 50 years is neither neat nor clearly represented by historical epochs. Although different ideas about the nature of literacy learning have been more popular at certain historical points than others, the relationship between theory and practice has never been tidy. Often, historical shifts in practice have come more from classroom constraints than published journal articles. Text- or teacher-centered approaches have appeared and disappeared in different guises throughout the latter half of the century, just as some approaches have dropped out altogether. Our aim in this chapter has been to give you a lens for viewing what you see in classrooms—your own and those of other teachers—from a social and historical perspective.

Now, we'd like to give you a chance to place some of what you've just learned into the context of your own beliefs about teaching literacy in the middle grades. Your Fieldwork Journal 2–2 should help you to consider some of the major ideas in this chapter in a more concrete and personal way.

Your Fieldwork Journal 2-2

Cutting the Pie: Your Approach to Literacy Teaching

Now that you've read about the five approaches to literacy teaching in the past 50 years, we'd like you to try your hand at mapping out your own assumptions about literacy at this point in your career. Think about what aspects and approaches to literacy teaching you value most and least. Then sketch out a pie chart like the one in the accompanying figure, allotting the space that you think each approach deserves in your philosophy of teaching.

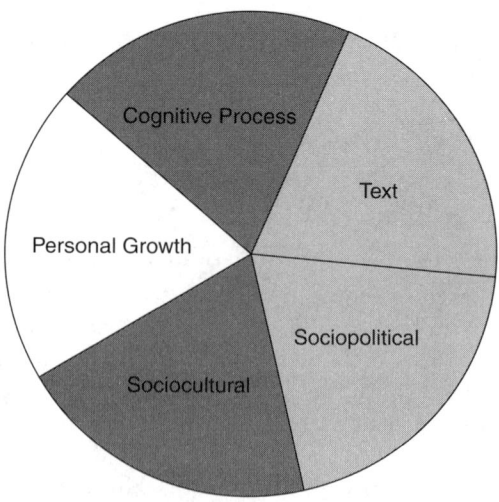

To jump start your thinking, consider the degree to which the following are important in your middle school classroom:

- **Literacy as Text:** To what extent do you think it's important for middle school students to craft and perfect their writing? To read and comprehend complex texts that they might not seek out on their own? To recognize and use literary techniques in their reading and writing? To learn about principles of correct grammar and usage? To present or perform in front of a large group? To participate in a whole class discussion? To succeed in standardized examinations?
- **Literacy as Cognitive Process:** To what extent do you think it's important for middle school students to develop metacognitive and higher order thinking skills? To draw upon a variety of strategies for composing and revising texts? To develop a repertoire of strategies for understanding and analyzing literature and nonfiction? To use both exploratory and more formal language as a way of learning?
- **Literacy as Personal Growth:** To what extent do you think it's important for middle school students to use literacy for self-expression and personal growth? To make their own choices about reading, writing, talking, and listening? To share reading and writing with others? To feel safe and respect others in the classroom community? To see themselves as competent readers, writers, and language users?
- **Literacy as Sociocultural Practice:** To what extent do you think it's important for middle school students to understand how social and cultural contexts shape language? To engage in collaborative projects? To reach out to others in the larger world through their literacy practices? To appreciate culturally and socially diverse perspectives? To read from an array of multicultural literature and nonfiction? To respond to each other's writing critically and sensitively? To use language in a variety of social and cultural contexts?
- **Literacy as Sociopolitical Process:** To what extent do you think it's important for middle school students to recognize the role of literacy in a democracy? To understand and critique the political motivations of texts from print to electronic to multimedia and beyond? To use literacy as a tool for social action and change? To become critical consumers and producers of popular culture? To recognize the influence of race, class, gender, and other sociopolitical aspects of literacy?

If you're like most of us, your pie chart contained aspects of all five approaches to literacy teaching. Few of us can afford the luxury (or the narrow-mindedness) of philosophical purity where our beliefs about teaching and learning are concerned. A certain amount of eclecticism is not only healthy but necessary in the midst of real-world concerns like high-stakes testing and increasingly diverse classrooms.

The point here is not to aim for a mindless consistency, but to consider where some of our assumptions about literacy may be undercutting others. For example, if we believe in nurturing an aesthetic appreciation of literature yet base our grades on short-answer quizzes, we are clearly at cross purposes with our own goals. As you read through the other chapters of this book, keep this chart handy. You may find yourself questioning your original choices or wondering about how they play out in the real world of the middle school English language arts classroom. Perhaps by the end of the book, you'll revisit and rework your original chart, based upon the insights and ideas you encounter along the way.

In the next chapter, we invite you to step more firmly into your role as teacher as you consider the process of planning instruction for your middle school students.

Standards in Practice

Charting the Assumptions of Your State Standards

For this exploration, we'd like you to consider the assumptions behind your statewide English language arts standards. First, find a copy of your state standards. Try the *Developing Educational Standards* Web site in the Resources section of this chapter *(http://edstandards.org/Standards.html)*, or locate a printed copy. Find the section on the middle grades, and read closely the parts that address what early adolescents should know and do. Your task is to unpack the assumptions upon which the standards are based according to the five historical perspectives on literacy presented earlier in this chapter: literacy as text, literacy as cognitive process, literacy as personal growth, literacy as sociocultural process, and literacy as sociopolitical practice.

We realize that this is a difficult task, with which teachers, teacher educators, and legislators continue to struggle. But try to tease out the ways in which a particular standard (or standards) is built from a set of assumptions about literacy and its teaching. For example, if your state standard specifies that all students should be able to "use language for literary response and understanding," what perspective (or perspectives) about literacy are represented? How might the assumptions be different if the standard were worded "reading comprehension and analysis" or "cultural and political critique" instead of "literary response and understanding"?

Don't stop with the general standards statements

Look for places where your state might specify certain tasks that students should be able to perform at different grade levels, for instance. If the standard says "literary response and understanding," but the examples of what students should be able to *do* focus mostly on knowledge of literary historical periods, recognition of genre features, and the ability to arrive at a "correct" interpretation of a literary text, then you can be pretty sure that the state is working from a text-centered rather than a personal response perspective about the reading of literature.

After you've completed this informal analysis, go back to the pie chart you just created and sketch out another chart, this time representing what seem to be the guiding assumptions of your state standards. How do your beliefs match with what your state says you and your students should be doing? Consider where you are likely to have problems "teaching to the standards" or preparing your middle school students for the standardized tests based upon them. Then consider which standards embody perspectives on literacy teaching that you can support in your classroom. In your objectives for each lesson you might want to briefly note which of the standards you are addressing. As you plan your future lessons, it's a good idea to return constantly to your state standards, asking yourself which aspects of the standards are represented in your overall goals and your daily teaching. This kind of cross-checking and informal documenting can be invaluable in conversations with supervisors, administrators, and parents. It can also help you to prepare your middle school students for the standardized tests in a way that won't diminish your overall goals for their literacy learning.

REFERENCES

Applebee, A. N. (1981). *Writing in the secondary school: English and the content areas.* Urbana, IL: National Council of Teachers of English.

Applebee, A. N. (1993). *Literature in the secondary school: Studies of curriculum and instruction in the United States.* Urbana, IL: National Council of Teachers of English.

Atwell, N. (1987). *In the middle: Writing, reading, and learning with adolescents.* Montclair, NJ: Boynton/Cook.

Barbieri, M. (1995). *Sounds from the heart: Learning to listen to girls.* Portsmouth, NH: Heinemann.

Barnes, D. (1975). *From communication to curriculum.* Harmondsworth, UK: Penguin.

Beach, R. (1974). Conceiving of characters. *Journal of Reading, 17*(7), 546–551.

Braddock, R. (1975). The frequency and placement of topic sentences in expository prose. *Research in the Teaching of English, 8*(3), 287–302.

Britton, J., Burgess, T., Martin, N., McLeod, A., & Rosen, H. (1975). *The development of writing abilities* (pp. 11–18). London: Macmillan.

Brooks, C. (1947). *The well wrought urn: Studies in the structure of poetry.* New York: Harcourt, Brace & World.

Bruner, J. (1960). *The process of education.* New York: Vintage.

Calkins, L. M. (1986). *The art of teaching writing.* Portsmouth, NH: Heinemann.

Carlsen, G. R. (1980). *Books and the teenage reader: A guide for teachers, librarians, and parents* (2nd ed.). New York: Harper & Row.

Chomsky, W. (1957). *Syntactic Structures.* The Hague: Morton.

Dixon, J. (1967). *Growth through English.* Urbana, IL: National Council of Teachers of English.

Edelsky, C. (1992). A talk with Carole Edelsky about politics and literacy. *Language Arts, 69*(5), 324–329.

Edelsky, C. (1994). Education for democracy. *Language Arts, 71*(4), 252–257.

Emig, J. (1971). *The composing processes of twelfth graders.* Champaign, IL: National Council of Teachers of English.

Fader, D. (1966). *Hooked on books.* New York: Berkeley Medallion.

Finders, M. (1997). *Just girls: Hidden literacies and life in junior high.* New York: Teachers College Press.

Flower, L. (1979). Writer-based prose: A cognitive basis for problems in writing. *College English, 41,* 19–37.

Flower, L., & Hayes, J. R. (1977). Problem solving strategies and the writing process. *College English, 39*(4), 449–461.

Flower, L., & Hayes, J. R. (1981). The pregnant pause: An inquiry into the nature of planning. *Research in the Teaching of English, 15*(3), 229–243.

Frye, N. (1957). *Anatomy of criticism, four essays.* Princeton, NJ: Princeton University Press.

Gardner, H. (1993). *Multiple intelligences.* New York: Basic Books.

Goodman, K. (1986). *What's whole in whole language?* Portsmouth, NH: Heinemann.

Goodman, K., Goodman, Y., & Hood, W. (1989). *The whole language evaluation book.* Portsmouth, NH: Heinemann.

Graves, D. H. (1983). *Writing: Teachers and children at work.* Exeter, NH: Heinemann.

Harris, J. (1991). After Dartmouth: Growth and conflict in English. *College English, 53*(6), 631–646.

Heath, S. B. (1983). *Ways with words: Language, life, and work in communities and classrooms.* New York: Cambridge University Press.

Heathcote, D. (1970). How does drama serve thinking, talking, and writing? *Elementary English, 47*(8), 1077–1081.

Hiebert, E. H. (1991). *Literacy for a diverse society: Perspectives, practices, and policies.* New York: Teachers College Press.

Hinton, S. E. (1967). *The outsiders.* New York: Viking.

Holland, N. N. (1973). *Five readers reading.* New Haven, CT: Yale University Press.

Hunt, I. (1964). *Across five Aprils.* New York: Follett.

Hunt, K. W. (1970). Syntactic maturity in school children and adults. *Monographs of the Society of Research in Child Development, 35*(1), 1–67.

Labov, W. (1972). *Language in the inner city: Studies in the black English vernacular.* Philadelphia: University of Pennsylvania Press.

Langer, J. (1995). *Envisioning literature: Literary understanding and literature instruction.* New York: Teachers College Press.

Luke, A. (1988). *Literacy, textbooks and ideology: Postwar literacy instruction and the mythology of Dick and Jane.* Bristol, PA: Taylor & Francis.

Macrorie, K. (1970). *Uptaught.* New York: Hayden.

Moffett, J. (1968). *Teaching the universe of discourse.* Boston: Houghton Mifflin.

Moffett, J., & Wagner, B. J. (1992). *Student-centered language arts, K–12* (4th ed.). Portsmouth, NH: Boynton/Cook.

Murray, D. M. (1985). *A writer teaches writing.* Boston: Houghton Mifflin.

Perl, S. (1979). The composing processes of unskilled college writers. *Research in the Teaching of English, 13*(4), 317–336.

Piaget, J. (1950). *The psychology of intelligence.* London: Routledge & Kegan Paul.

Piaget, J., & Inhelder, B. (1969). *The psychology of the child.* New York: Basic Books.

Postman, N., & Weingartner, C. (1969). *Teaching as a subversive activity.* New York: Delacorte Press.

Purves, A., & Ripperre, V. (1972). *Elements of writing about a literary work: A study of response to literature.* Urbana, IL: National Council of Teachers of English.

Ransom, J. C. (1979). *The New Criticism.* Westport, CT: Greenwood Press.

Rogers, C. R. (1969). *Freedom to learn: A view of what education may become.* Upper Saddle River, NJ: Merrill/Prentice Hall.

Rosenblatt, L. M. (1994). *The reader, the text, the poem: The transactional theory of the literary work (with a new preface and epilogue).* Carbondale, IL: Southern Illinois University Press.

Rosenblatt, L. M. (1995). *Literature as exploration* (5th ed.). New York: Modern Language Association.

Skinner, B. F. (1976). *About behaviorism.* New York: Vintage Books.

Smitherman, G. (1986). *Talkin and testifyin: The language of black America.* Detroit, MI: Wayne State University Press.

Sommers, N. (1980). Revision strategies of student writers and experienced adult writers. *College Composition and Communication, 31*(4), 378–388.

Vygotsky, L. (1962). *Thought and language.* Cambridge, MA: Harvard University Press.

Willinsky, J. (1990). *The new literacy: Redefining reading and writing in the schools.* New York: Routledge.

RESOURCES

Print

Historical and Critical Accounts of English Teaching Theory and Practice

Applebee, A. N. (1974). *Tradition and reform in the teaching of English.* Urbana, IL: National Council of Teachers of English.

Applebee, A. N. (1996). *Curriculum as conversation: Transforming traditions of teaching and learning.* Urbana, IL: National Council of Teachers of English.

Beach, R. (1993). *A teacher's introduction to reader response theories.* Urbana, IL: National Council of Teachers of English.

Eagleton, T. (1983). *Literary theory: An introduction.* Minneapolis: University of Minnesota.

Elbow, P. (1990). *What is English?* New York: Modern Language Association.

Farrell, E. J., & Squire, J. (1990). *Transactions with literature: A fifty-year perspective.* Urbana, IL: National Council of Teachers of English.

Hook, J. N. (1980). *A long way together.* Urbana, IL: National Council of Teachers of English.

North, S. M. (1987). *The making of knowledge in composition: Portrait of an emerging field.* Upper Montclair, NJ: Boynton/Cook.

Purves, A. (1973). *Literature education in ten countries: An empirical study.* Urbana, IL: National Council of Teachers of English.

Purves, A. (1981). *Reading and literature: American achievement in international perspective.* Urbana, IL: National Council of Teachers of English.

Tobin, L., & Newkirk, T. (1994). *Taking stock: The writing process movement in the '90s.* Portsmouth, NH: Boynton/Cook.

Willinsky, J. (1991). *The triumph of literature/the fate of literacy: English in the secondary curriculum.* New York: Teachers College Press.

Annotated Bibliographies

Beach, R., & Hynds, S. (1991). Research on response to literature. In R. Barr, M. L. Kamil, P. Mosenthal, & P. D. Pearson (Eds.), *Handbook of reading research* (Vol. II, pp. 453–489). White Plains, NY: Longmans.

Purves, A., & Beach, R. (1972). *Literature and the reader: Research on response to literature, reading interests, and teaching of literature.* Urbana, IL: National Council of Teachers of English.

Handbooks and Encyclopedias

Cushman, E., Kintgen, E. R., Kroll, B. M., & Rose, M. (2001). *Literacy: A critical sourcebook.* Boston, MA: Bedford/St. Martin's.

Flood, J., Jensen, J. M., Lapp, D., &. Squire, J. R. (eds) (1991). *Handbook of research on teaching the English language arts.* New York: Macmillan.

Purves, A. (1994). *Encyclopedia of English studies and language arts: A project of the National Council of Teachers of English.* Jefferson City, MO: Scholastic.

Electronic

ALA Best Practices for Junior High/Middle School. The American Library Association sponsors this Web site and features practices of middle school teachers across the nation. This is a good chance to learn what other reading, English, and language arts teachers are doing across the country.

http:/www.ala.org/aasl/learning/mspractices/html

ALAN. The Assembly on Literature for Adolescents (ALAN) was founded in 1973 as a special interest group of the National Council of Teachers of English to inform teachers, authors, librarians, publishers, teacher educators, and others of new developments in young adult literature. The Web site includes previews of upcoming presentations and access to the publication, *The ALAN Review.*

http:/english.byu.edu/alan

Developing Educational Standards. This is a comprehensive annotated list of Internet sites for K–12 educational standards, curricula, frameworks, and documents listed by state. The site provides a great resource for looking up your own state standards and related Web sites by state.

http://edstandards.org/Standards.html

ERIC Clearinghouse. ERIC contains, among other things, one of the most useful bibliographies for educators available. The online catalog includes an index of journal articles (CIJE) and ERIC publications (RIE) as well as book-length publications and reports from 1966 to the present. Extended bibliographies and access to Web sites are available by subject area.

http://askeric.org/

International Reading Association. An organization with more than 90,000 members, the IRA sponsors a host of national and regional conferences and has an extensive publications department. The site includes a number of helpful literacy links, notices of upcoming events, and access to current research, and innovative practices in the teaching of reading and literacy.

http://www.reading.org/

National Center for the Study of Writing and Literacy. Sponsored by the U.S. Department of Education, this center is a cooperative venture between the University of California at Berkeley and Carnegie Mellon University. The site provides access to publications and resources, information about current research projects, and information about interactive workshops available through the center for classroom teachers.

http://www-gse.berkeley.edu/research/NCSWL

National Research Center on English Learning and Achievement. CELA is a nationally funded center for study of the learning and teaching of literature. The site includes links to more than 600 research reports from other OERI (Educational Research and Improvement) centers nationwide. The site includes a discussion board, newsletter, highlights of current research in literature, and notices of upcoming presentations.

http://cela.albany.edu

National Writing Project. The NWP started in the 1970s for the purpose of helping classroom teachers learn how to teach the composing process to their students. Based on a grassroots model of teacher change, the organization has been holding institutes and workshops for teachers across the country for the past 30 years. The site includes access to NWP publications, presentations, workshops, institutes, and support networks.

http://writingproject.org/

NCTE. The National Council of Teachers of English Web site has a number of useful features for teachers from elementary school through college. Through the site, you can access the NCTE/IRA standards, share syllabi, access resources for new teachers, get copies of position statements, learn about profession trends, get information about grants, and keep abreast of upcoming events.

http://www.ncte.org/

Writing Across the Curriculum. Several sites deal with writing across the curriculum, but this one seems especially useful. It includes a brief history of the WAC movement, along with links to several other university and K–12 sites.

http://www.niu.edu/acad/english/wac/waclinks.html

chapter 3

Planning and Adapting Instruction for Middle School Learners

GUIDING QUESTIONS
1. How do your students' home, community, and cultural backgrounds shape their literate identities?
2. How do you plan and adapt instruction to support each of the learners in your classroom?
3. How do you recognize the needs of your classroom as a whole while still allowing for the preferences, abilities, and needs of individuals?

A CASE FOR CONSIDERATION

The Techno Trio

Raymond, Isaac, and Jimmy—the "techno trio," as they liked to be called—sat in the back of Mr. Walters's sixth-grade classroom, huddled together over a notebook, impatiently waiting for their turn at the computer. "If Sarah knew how to turn the computer on, she might be about done by now," Isaac whispered, loudly enough for the girls who were working beside them to hear. Ray chimed in, "Yeah, Sarah and Rachel say, 'Let's comb our hair and use the monitor for a mirror. That's what a computer is for, right?' They don't even know how to turn it on! Oh, duh."

    The techno trio shared a fascination for monsters and computers and a strong dislike for girls. They avidly devoured comic books and were, in fact, the proud authors of a comic book series, *Monster Mad.* They read, wrote, and drew monsters and supermonsters. Notebook after notebook was filled with storyboards for future episodes in the never-ending story of the arch monster rivals, Monster Mad and Dr. Dead.

    Although they were avid readers and writers, all three boys were failing Mr. Walters's language arts class. They did not participate in literature discussions. They did not write in their learning logs. They did not hand in daily assignments. Mr. Walters didn't think they read anything except comic books, monster Web sites, and technology manuals they needed in order to advance the production quality of *Monster Mad.*

Mr. Walters struggled with ways to support the techno trio. He struggled with ways to keep them from intimidating less capable computer users. Mr. Walters, in fact, literally struggled to keep them "in line." He resorted to taping a masking tape square around their desks with the firm instructions to "keep in your area." The trio knew they couldn't "drive" their desks beyond the taped boundary or they wouldn't be allowed to work together for five days.

Today, they were working together, staying within the lines, and trying to finish the next installment of *Monster Mad.* It was difficult, since there was only one computer in the room, and none of the trio was allowed to go to the media center because they had abused that privilege the day before. They hated to wait for their turn at the computer. Smug about their computer skills, which far exceeded everyone's in the room (even the media specialist often turned to them for help), Raymond, Isaac, and Jimmy often created a disturbance when they were expected to wait for others in their class.

Mr. Walters worked closely with their parents, creating a contract for them to earn and lose privileges at home and at school, but nothing worked. The techno trio simply refused to do anything except create monsters, which sometimes mutilated and murdered other students in the class, especially Sarah and Rachel. Although Mr. Walters wanted to give students the chance to express themselves and make personal choices, such choices often resulted in hurtful acts, such as an excerpt from "Monster Mad, Dr. Dead, and the Two-Headed Princess of Darkness" that Isaac shared aloud in class one day. It didn't take Sarah and Rachel long to recognize themselves in the thinly veiled caricature called the "two headed princess."

> It was some horrible thing. SA-RA, the two headed princess, was coming right at Dr. Dead. He never had saw anything so hidious. The two-headed creature was talking and talking, "Oh, my hair. Oh, my lip stick," the monster said. She used this to hynotize her victims. She talked ooo so much. She never did shut up. Dr. Dead couldn't stand it. For the first time ever, Dr. Dead agreed with Monster Mad. We must kill this hideous thing, he said. We must cut off their heads. We must, said MM. Let's cut them to pieces. And so we cut off their heads. Blood was everywhere. It was too bloody. Dr. Dead and Monster Mad washed their hands and went out to dinner together. On the way to the restrant, they seen SA-RAs mom. She cried and cried. So they killed the mom too. They threw her in a paper shredder and it was so bloody.

FOR DISCUSSION

- How do you think Mr. Walters should handle this story?
- Why might these sixth-grade boys and girls seem to hold such different computer competencies?
- How might you support the literacy learning of Jimmy, Isaac, and Raymond? Of Sarah and Rachel?

BEYOND PRINT: HOW WE THINK ABOUT LITERACY LEARNING

In the last chapter, we saw how views of literacy teaching have changed over the course of the past 50 years. Now, at the dawn of a new millennium, we can no longer afford to view classrooms as closed communities. Students bring to the language arts classroom different expectations for, experiences with, and expertise in literacy. Their encounters outside the classroom shape how they engage with peers, texts, and the world. In supporting the literacy learning of all students, we need to think beyond the materials we select, focusing instead on the intersections among the learner, text, and social context.

As we begin to think about creating teaching plans, we ask you to consider the incredible complexity of what it means to be and become literate as an early adolescent in today's society. Before we explore this issue, however, we need to define some key terms.

> Consider the complexity of developing literacy skills in early adolescence.

Literacy. Reading words on a printed page is only one of the many dimensions of literacy. More broadly defined, *literacy* includes the multiple ways in which reading, writing, and language interrelate with the workings of social life. Beyond the ability to create and understand the printed word, literacy in this larger sense involves using language to learn, to influence, and ultimately, to transform our personal and social worlds. As you think about this broad definition of literacy, or what has been called "multiple literacies," ask yourself: How many different ways do my students create and consume language within and outside of school? What are the difficulties my students might face with any particular materials they may encounter? How can I provide support?

Text. Like literacy, this term encompasses far more than print-based materials. The "texts" that middle school students encounter range from popular media to computer programs, Web sites, video, film, television, and other media. You need to provide ways for students to create, understand, and critique a variety of texts in multiple contexts. As you do so, ask yourself: What texts (print and beyond) are important to my students? What texts are important to my discipline and my curriculum? In what ways can I help students to build bridges between the texts they value and those I provide?

Discourse Community. Different groups have different ways of talking, thinking, and acting in the world (Gee, 1999). A child who grows up in a "soccer family," for example, learns the rules of the game in terms that reach far beyond the playing field. This child learns how to talk/think/act/dress soccer. Because social practices valued in one discourse community may not be valued in another, students must often switch their behaviors within different contexts. Students who are members of Honors Choir are expected to dress, talk, and even walk across the stage in a particular manner. Those same students may need to change "costumes" and "scripts" when they prepare for their work as an order clerk at McDonald's. In much the same way, students in different disciplines need to learn the rules of multiple communities, learning how scientists talk about experiments or how artists critique a work of art, for instance. To participate in each of these communities, students must become adept at "reading" cues and reactions that indicate which practices are valued in a community. As you help them to negotiate these different discourse communities, ask yourself: What are the multiple contexts in which my students live and work? What literacies are important in each? How can I address their real-world literacy needs in my classroom?

In order to understand the complexities of the early adolescent experience, we invite you to seek out at least one early adolescent who will start you on your journey into the world of the middle school learner. Complete the task outlined in Your Fieldwork Journal 3–1.

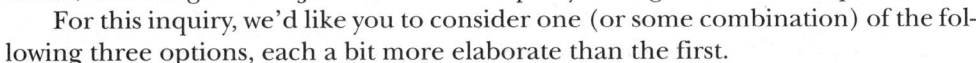

Your Fieldwork Journal 3-1

Classroom Inquiry: Adolescent Portraits

Because it may have been more than a few years since you were a part of an "adolescent culture," this project is designed to allow you to learn directly from an "insider." Your focus will be on an early adolescent's typical days, conversations, routines, and rituals. Your informant's favorite clothing, jargon, foods, reading materials, and hangouts are just a few of the topics you might decide to explore.

For this inquiry, we'd like you to consider one (or some combination) of the following three options, each a bit more elaborate than the first.

- **Option 1: Interview** someone who is between the ages of 11 and 15. This could be one of your students, someone in a classroom you're observing, a relative, or the child of a friend. If possible, take some time to make him or her feel comfortable around you before you do any serious work. Explain that you want to learn what it's like to be a teenager today, that you are collecting information on his or her views, interests, activities, hobbies, ways of getting along with others. Before you begin your interview, make a list of some open-ended questions that will guide (but not limit) the conversation. Your questions might include the following:
  - Could you describe a typical . . . (language arts class, football practice, trip to the mall, telephone conversation between you and your best friend)?
  - What are all of the things you do during a day . . . (volleyball, band, study hall)?
  - What do teenagers do for . . . (fun, lunch, entertainment)?
  - What are some ways to . . . (relax, get hired, talk with adults)?
- **Option 2: Observe** one or more early adolescents at the video arcade, a sporting event, a restaurant, a music store, or the library, for instance. Choose an unobtrusive location and "stop, look, and listen." Pay attention to the words and actions of the person (or persons) you're observing. Notice who and what is present. What happens when one person enters or leaves the scene? Who talks and who listens? What goes "underground"? What gets "center stage"? What seems to be going on "backstage"?

  If you can't take notes unobtrusively, make sure you allow time immediately after your observation for this purpose. You might want to create a double-entry

> **Double-Entry Journal: Adolescent Portraits**
>
> **Observations**
>
> In this column, write what you directly observe, such as:
>
> 1. **People:** Note number of people in the scene, their activities, dress, age, appearance, race, gender, body language, facial expression, tone of voice.
> 2. **Turf:** Describe the setting in detail, visual details, layout, size, organization, arrangement.
> 3. **Activities and material possessions:** Note things that stand out for you in some way. For example, what is taken for granted? What do these activities suggest that one should value?
>
> **Reflections**
>
> In this column, write down any hunches, hypotheses, or questions you may have about your observations. For example:
>
> 4. Do you notice any assumptions about adolescents that may be emerging in your feelings, reactions, ideas, insights, things that strike you or stand out for you?
> 5. What do you think is considered appropriate or ordinary, and what is considered inappropriate or out-of-the-ordinary within and across groups?

journal in which you record your observations on one side of the page and your reactions, impressions, and speculations on the other side, as in the illustration above.

- **Option 3: Create a mini-case study** of an early adolescent. Perhaps you are already making observations in someone else's classroom over a period of time or have been keeping a teaching journal. Combine two or three sources of information (e.g., interviews, observational notes, journal entries, student writings, or other student-created artifacts) and create a descriptive portrait of your informant. What are the multiple discourse communities in which she or he operates? What literacies seem to be important to him or her? What are some of the different "rules" that operate in this particular adolescent's life? Include quotes wherever possible. Remember as you do so that this is one individual. Be careful not to stereotype an entire group or make hasty generalizations such as "typical of all 12-year-old boys. . . ." To avoid stereotyping, it may be helpful to share your portrait-in-progress with someone else. In the conclusion of your case study, discuss some implications for literacy teaching in the middle school classroom.

PLANNING FOR ALL STUDENTS

Understanding the multiple discourse communities in which our students live and work provides for a more responsive classroom. As Literacy Lesson 3–1 demonstrates, in order to support students, we must begin to tap into the range of experiences, abilities, and expertise each of them brings to the classroom.

Literacy Lesson 3-1

Three Students, One Plan

As a way of considering the remarkable diversity of the middle school classroom, we'd like you to consider how you might adapt your teaching for three of the students you met in the Case for Consideration at the beginning of this chapter. As you examine these "mini-case studies," imagine that these are your students. Think about the special experiences, preferences, and abilities that each brings to the classroom, and consider how you can design a curriculum that allows each student to succeed.

Isaac

You already know a little about Isaac. He seems to spend most of his school time trying to disrupt learning. He's the class clown, and he loves attention. If you leave the room, he will immediately start "driving" his desk across the room, visiting with his best buddies. When you are in the room, Isaac still "drives" but a bit more subtly. Isaac says he hates girls, but you often find him sending anonymous electronic "I like you" messages to them. He's computer savvy and is often called upon to help out the other students in the room. He makes a big fuss when asked to help but is proud of his skills. He has created a sign that he occasionally hangs over his desk: "Isaac's Computer Support Network. One question/One dollar. If I have to get up, it will be an additional dollar. Girls get one free answer cause they need it." In a group task, he may eventually settle down but only after a lot of prodding and personal attention. He is an avid reader and highly competent writer, but he rarely does what you ask, except when given a chance to share one of his monster stories. Then he is engaged and on task.

Isaac rejects all teacher or peer input except when it is offered by Jimmy or Ray. He is disinterested in every book or story suggested unless it has a monster in it. Often he is rude to classmates, and he never holds back his dislike for others' work. On the other hand, he does offer high praise when he thinks it's merited. In spite of his many negative behaviors, you've noticed that sometimes Isaac can be helpful, compassionate, and engaged.

Sarah

Sarah sits at her desk, trying to hide behind the long hair that covers her eyes and most of her face. Sarah does not speak in class unless called upon. When she does respond, she seems to be "paying by the word," because she answers most direct questions with a one- or two-word response. She is silent during whole class discussions, never raising her hand except during independent work time. When you crouch beside her desk, you can barely hear her. Sarah is always prepared with her assignments as long as they do not involve talk. You can occasionally hear her whispering to her best, and only, friend, Rachel. She often enlists Rachel to ask questions for her. In class, Rachel will sometimes say, "Sarah wants to know. . . ." Because Sarah is so quiet, you don't know much about her. Her standardized test scores indicate that she will face many challenges with "grade-level" materials. She regularly places an order from your class book club for "self-help" teen books about such things as dancing, make-up, and hair styles. Even then, Rachel often brings Sarah's book order to the front of the class. On occasion, Sarah leaves a note under your desk calendar: "Please don't give me my book order during class time. Leave me a note and I will come after school." During independent reading and writing time, Sarah is always busy working, but when anyone walks past, she puts her arm over her work to shield it. Although Rachel is clearly her best friend, Sarah is alone most of the time in the hallways and the lunchroom. When asked to share her writing with her classmates, she whispers, "How much will my grade go down if I just turn it in? I could do something else. I really don't want to."

Rachel

Rachel is much more outgoing than Sarah. You wonder how these two can be considered friends. Rachel is loud and bold. She interacts with other students freely, often acting as an advocate. She takes things into her own hands and has been known to let Isaac "have it" when he starts in on some student's work: "Isaac, you just shut up. Who do you think you are, the writing police? Just because it didn't have enough blood or killing in it, you don't like it." She appears to thrive in a group, quickly jumping in, telling others what to do, where to sit, how to get started. She seems to have a strong sense of self and views herself as a highly competent reader and writer, which she is. But her skills may not completely match this self-assessment, and although you are glad that she thinks so highly of herself, you worry that her positive self-image may prevent her from being open to further learning. She pushes others to improve their writing in a thoughtful manner, but is quite content with her own writing in first-draft stage. Her parents are proud of her, and they call you on occasion when they worry that Rachel's grades don't reflect her keen abilities. Of all the students in your class, Rachel is one of your biggest challenges. You would never admit it publicly, but you find it difficult to like her. Her father is a university professor, and her family has given her the luxury of international study and travel. Occasionally, Rachel will correct you in class with statements such as, "My dad is a professor and he says. . . ." or "When I was traveling in Russia, I learned. . . ." She is an avid reader of British literature and world history. You thought she might have some social problems, but her peers elected her to be the editor of the class anthology.

As you can see by the mini-case studies in Literacy Lesson 3–1, the middle school classroom is a dynamic ecosystem. Isaac, Sarah, and Rachel bring different levels of expertise, expectations, and preferences where literacy is concerned. Although you can't design foolproof plans, you can at least anticipate possible obstacles and opportunities that these three students and their classmates might face. Consider, for example, how you might accommodate the needs of all three students as you design the following literacy activities:

- free-choice independent reading time
- collaborative writing groups
- whole class discussions

These are just a few of the activities you might sponsor in your classroom, but they give you a rough idea of the different challenges and opportunities each poses for students like Sarah, Rachel, and Isaac. Whereas Isaac and Rachel will probably thrive in a whole group discussion, the same activity will be tortuous for Sarah. You'll also have to plan some strategies for guiding the discussion so that Rachel doesn't dominate it and Isaac doesn't derail it with rude and inappropriate comments. Collaborative activities pose yet another challenge. Imagine these three students in a small group task. Who would vie for leadership, and who would withdraw? Who is likely to pull everyone off task, and who will be worried about grades and outcomes? Should you allow students to select their own groups? If so, what if shy students like Sarah don't get chosen? If *you* select the groups, what are your criteria for making your selections? Similarly, if you allow students to choose books for independent reading, how will you help Isaac to move his reading choices beyond monsters and gore? How do you get him to read silently, given his propensity for disrupting things? How do you help Sarah to demonstrate her understanding without placing her in the glare of the whole group (or even small group) discussion?

These are just a few of the questions you face in the early stages of your planning. As if this weren't enough, you must create a climate where each of these unique students can somehow come together as a community of learners. In Your Fieldwork Journal 3–2, we ask you to think about the context in which you teach or will be teaching.

Your Fieldwork Journal 3-2

Describing Your Teaching Context

This experience can serve as an introduction to an instructional unit you may be planning. At the very least, it will start your thinking where all good teaching begins—with a real group of students in a real classroom—if you are either currently teaching or you are in an observational placement prior to student teaching. If not, perhaps you can visit a classroom and try your hand at this observational activity.

- **Select a school:** This might be one of the schools in your local area or the middle school that is hosting your student teaching or field placement. Describe this setting in as much detail as possible. If you're having trouble finding information, visit the school or district Web site or call the district office.
- **Identify the community:** Indicate geographic location, size, primary employers, per capita income, average years of education among residents, problems/issues within the community, community support for education, socioeconomic levels, and ethnic diversity.
- **Identify the school:** Include information about the school name, mascot, support for a middle school philosophy, support for community-based education, socioeconomic levels of students' families, and problems at this middle school such as the presence of gangs or drug and alcohol use. Explore the following questions by contacting the district office or Web site and talking with other teachers in the building.
  - What percentage of students are on free or reduced lunch programs?
  - What is the racial and ethnic makeup of the school?
  - Who decides what and when courses will be taught?
  - How involved are parents in their children's education?

- Is there a curriculum guide? How closely are teachers expected to follow it?
- Do teachers have common planning time? Do they work in teams for thematic planning?
- Overall, what voice do teachers have in school policies, procedures, and practices?
- **Focus on one class (your own, if possible) and describe the students: in terms of age, grade level, gender ratio, ethnic diversity, socioeconomic level:**
  - Do any students have IEPs (Individualized Educational Programs)?
  - What abilities and disabilities might you encounter?
  - What support services are available for these students?
  - Does your school operate on an "inclusive" model where individuals are placed in the classroom to assist students with special needs, or do students spend some part of their day in a resource room?
  - Do any students speak English as a second language? What services, if any, are provided for these students?
  - What are the social dynamics of this classroom?
  - Do you notice any pattern in terms of gender, race, social class, or ability?

As a way of understanding how the community and school context influences your planning decisions, consider the following description written by Evan, a preservice teacher in a suburban middle school. Notice how Evan has forced himself to look beyond the obvious in describing what at first glance may appear to be a "homogeneous," White, upper middle class setting.

Eastvale Middle School is located in a newly renovated, very modern building. The building was refurbished last year, as teachers and students (seventh and eighth graders) were temporarily housed in a nearby elementary school. The hallways are bright and cheery, matching the personalities of the teachers I have met thus far. The spacious library has plenty of room for students to spread out and several computers for their use. There is also soothing, quiet music from a "light hits" radio station continually being played through the hallways. The bell system is actually not a bell at all, but three soft tones that signal the end of each 40-minute period. The principal says that the tones are so students don't view the end of a period as a harsh, abrupt stop to one subject and the beginning of another.

Team teaching is the norm at EMS. One team consists of the English, math, science, and social studies teachers. Collaboration with the art teacher is also common. The resource teacher is in constant contact with the content teachers, giving them feedback not only about students' work but also about what is happening in their often incomprehensible day-to-day lives. The members of my team meet informally every day and formally when needed. Judging from their rooms, my teammates are firm believers in displaying student work. Projects most recently completed occupy every spare inch of wall space.

My host teacher's room is situated as such. Jackie designs units so that there will be some sort of artifacts to hang on the back wall when they are finished. The room itself is a little small for how many seventh graders she has, but with desks in traditional rows, the students don't feel cramped. Huge windows and billowing plants give the room a more spacious feel. Jackie's loud, cheerful voice keeps most students highly engaged. She also gives students a lot of freedom. She allows students to come in during her lunch period to work or talk. She has them make out their own passes when leaving the room. She treats students with a great deal of respect, and they reciprocate that, feeling perfectly comfortable to come up and talk to her in a friendly way.

At a glance, the students at EMS are racially homogeneous, with white students making up the majority. That, however, is basically the only way in which my students are homogeneous. The range of socioeconomic status in the Eastvale school district stretches from wealthy to near poverty, with each and all between represented in Jackie's classes. Many students who are financially disadvantaged come from homes where at least one parent is alcoholic, siblings are dropouts or have run away, or parents simply don't have the time between jobs to spend going over schoolwork.

The students represent a vast array of ability levels as well. Eastvale's commitment to inclusion is evident in Jackie's classes. There are four students with IEPs. Each IEP is necessary because of severe reading and writing deficiencies. Other students possibly should be considered for an IEP. Several students have poor reading and/or writing skills. One boy's reading level, according to Jackie, is not higher than third grade.

One boy recently transferred from another school, where he was the head of his class. Since coming to Eastvale, he has done absolutely no work. . . . Another boy needs constant reminders to keep him from sleeping through every class. He appears completely uninspired by whatever the class is engaged in, but is seldom openly disruptive. Yet another boy has recently come off of a two-week suspension for possession of drugs. . . . Divorce, abuse, and alcoholism are common themes among the struggling students in Jackie's class.

Six students in my classes have been labeled as "gifted." Unlike my own middle school experience, the gifted students are not put on a pedestal in Jackie's classes. Each student is treated with the same respect in the classroom.

As I think about it, the girls in the classes do not stand out as gifted, nerdy, disciplinary problems, etc. There are some girls who are very bright and there is one with an IEP. Discipline has not been an issue with them thus far in my experience. They seem to try hard and work well together, often acting as leaders when put in groups that include both sexes. I think this is a perfect example of the beginning of the physiological changes in boys and girls. Girls generally mature faster and earlier than boys do. The differences will be much more evident in a couple of years when they are in ninth grade.

Nearly all of the students were extremely eager to talk to me and "check me out." They seemed enthusiastic about having me in their classes. In my few initial visits, I feel that I have definitely been accepted into their world.

This is a thoughtful and detailed description of the classroom where Evan will soon be teaching. At the same time, Evan needs to consider some assumptions before beginning his student teaching placement. Notice, for instance, that he seems to associate only the students whom he calls "financially disadvantaged" with such problems as alcoholism and divorce; yet, we know these problems know no racial, economic, or social bounds. In addition, whenever he talks about "problem students," he focuses on the males. His female students, by contrast, are described as hardworking and congenial. Although this may well be the case, as teachers, we need to look hard beneath the surface to make sure that our girls are truly untroubled and our boys are the ones most in need of our attention. As Barbieri (1995) wrote of her early days as a teacher,

> If I thought in terms of gender at all back then, my concern had been for the boys. How could I get them to love poetry? How could I find more contemporary novels to hold their attention? And what about writing? Were they doing enough reflecting? Were they stretching themselves? When I look back, I realize I expected the girls to read and write; I expected the boys to need my extra attention and encouragement. As I read some of the student journals I've saved from those years, I am filled with remorse. My girls were calling out to me from their own "underground." There were issues on their minds, turmoil in their lives, and questions in their hearts that I had been unwilling or unable to hear. (p. 7)

Writing, and perhaps sharing, a description of your students and school is a good way to challenge your assumptions about the classroom where you are or will be teaching. As you read between the lines of your writing, you can often "hear" the subtle voices of students like those Barbieri describes—students whose voices may be understated but who most need your extra help and attention all the same.

STARTING TO PLAN

Once you have the information about whom you will be teaching, you can begin to plan. There are three main aspects to planning: goals, support for learning, and assessment.

Goals

Begin with your goals for your students at this particular time in their lives and this point in the school term. Remember that goals (the *why*) are always intertwined with the activities and content (the *what*) of your lessons. Although most of the time your goals should guide what you ask students to do, there are times when the content of your teaching is prescribed by circumstances beyond your control. In that case, you have to find a way to accomplish your goals within these constraints. Where goals and activities are concerned, "you can't have one without the other," as the old song goes.

Consult your school's curriculum guide.

Most middle schools have a curriculum guide that provides some parameters for your teaching. You need to understand that not everyone is equally on board with this document. It may have been created by "outsiders" (someone in central administration, for instance) and thus may be not accepted by the majority of teachers in the building. Often, unless the teachers who use it have had a hand in its development, the curriculum guide sits in a drawer unnoticed. In other cases, your principal or department chair may have a stake in seeing that all teachers follow this guide. It may list specific texts or broad grade-level goals. You may discover, for example, that all seventh-grade students are expected to read the novel *Nothing but the Truth* by Avi (1998), while Wakatsuki Houston's *Farewell to Manzanar* (2000) is taught in the eighth grade. Such decisions are often made according to what resources are in the book room and which teachers have laid claim to particular books at certain grade levels. Whatever the case, part of learning the culture of your school involves distinguishing between what you must teach and where you have some leeway.

Even if in the worst case you are told exactly what you must teach and when, you will need to create a list of goals to best support your learners. If you are expected to teach a particular novel to your fifth-grade students, for example, don't simply write a goal such as "Teach Lois Lowry's novel, *The Giver*" (2002). Think about what your students will be better able to know and do after encountering this novel. Rather than focusing on what you will teach, begin by considering *what students will learn*. As a way of keeping students' learning foremost in your planning, start all of your goal statements with the phrase "My students will . . ."

- make predictions from what they have read.
- support opinions with textual references.
- learn to tell why they like or dislike certain aspects of a film, while acknowledging different points of view.
- become aware of and use different communication modes, such as dance, art, signs, and music.
- evaluate the reliability of electronic texts.

At the same time as you are thinking about goals, you must keep in mind that students need to feel a shared sense of ownership in classroom activities. You'll need to balance carefully what you feel is important to learn, what your curriculum guide mandates, and what your students want to learn.

Think about planning in terms of the "rule of three" (Stevenson & Carr, 1993, p. 32). That is, try to plan a third of the unit yourself, invite your students to plan another third, and plan a third in collaboration with them. If you are in a student teaching situation, this will not always be possible. Your host teacher will already have established routines, grading procedures, and policies before you get there. It would be unwise and presumptuous to think you can change the basic parameters of the classroom in the few short weeks you will be there. Even then, think about the ways students can become more involved in your teaching decisions.

Consider the "rule of three."

If you have your own classroom, you'll need to structure carefully the ways in which you invite students to make choices, by deciding in advance what is important for you to control and what aspects can be in their control. For example, you may feel the need to control the physical arrangement, grading system, and particular goals for your students' literacy development. Your curriculum guide may mandate that certain pieces of literature are taught at a particular grade level, or your state tests may be coming up, and you need to teach particular types of writing or strategies for reading. Beyond these "givens," consider what aspects of your curriculum can be in your students' control. Let's say you have to teach the format of a persuasive letter. Can students choose the topic and audience for their letters? Can you make sure that letters actually get sent, so that the activity has authenticity and purpose for them? There is nothing wrong with closing down choices for students as long as (a) you have a

Strike a balance between student and teacher control.

good reason for doing so, and (b) you open up something else every time you close something down. For example, if a writing topic is fixed, give options for form; if form is fixed, allow choices in topic.

Although you need not worry about this exact equation (one third teacher controlled, one third student controlled, one third negotiated), you should always consider how to involve your middle school students in classroom decision making. We often think about motivation as if we can somehow give it to our students. We might be able to anticipate it, based on knowledge of our students' interests, but much of the time motivation follows naturally when students feel some control over what happens in the classroom. When students see a real need for certain knowledge or skills, and when they have an immediate use for something, they will often be highly motivated. In addition to the motivation that shared decision making offers, your students will learn to become better problem posers and problem solvers as they begin to take control of their own learning.

Support for Learners

At the same time as you are identifying your overall goals, you should be thinking about activities to support your students and difficulties they might encounter. Part of providing support involves assessing the difficulty and appeal of the materials you plan to use in light of the abilities, preferences, and needs of your particular students. As the following sections show, assessing your students should go hand in hand with assessing the materials and resources you plan to use.

> Look beyond test scores.

Assessing Your Students. Scores on standardized tests and grade-level reading scores offer an initial glimpse of the kind of materials and resources your students can understand and access. We need to caution you, however, that these scores may be useful in terms of anticipating which students *might* need additional support, but they are only one measure that reflects reading and writing in a testing situation.

Interest inventories can provide more qualitative information about the types of materials you might include in your lessons. They also provide additional information about the expertise of your students and their families, which are resources you might tap. Interest inventories can be handed out in the first few days of school. You might ask students to share them with you in a private conference, with a peer, or with the whole group. An interest inventory might include these questions:

When I have to write, I . . .
When I have to read, I . . .
Talking in class makes me feel . . .
Working in a group makes me feel . . .
Writing in a journal is . . .
My idea of a good time is . . .
School is . . .
I wish teachers . . .
To me, books . . .

I like to read about . . .
I like to write about . . .
On weekends, I . . .
I'd rather read than . . .
I'd rather write than . . .
To me, homework . . .
Computers make me feel . . .
I am at my best when . . .
I don't know how . . .
I would like to be . . .
For me, studying . . .
I wish I could . . .
I'd read more if . . .
When I read out loud . . .
My favorite place to read is . . .
My favorite place to write is . . .
My favorite book of all time is . . .

Assessing Materials and Resources

There are several ways to assess materials and resources. In the case of print-based materials, you may want to do a readability test to determine text difficulty. Several formulas provide a quick and inexpensive means of anticipating if a particular text may prove difficult for some students. For a more thorough understanding of the many tests available, you may want to turn to some of the reading texts such as Vacca and Vacca (1998). Like standardized tests, readability formulas are only one measure of reading ability; they assess possible reading difficulty, based on the lexical and syntactic complexity of the text.

The problem with any test of readability, however, is that it doesn't capture all of the difficulty that a text might pose. Hemingway's *The Old Man and the Sea* (1999) might get a relatively "easy" rating in terms of its overall length and its linguistic and syntactic complexity. To a typical early adolescent, however, this novel is likely to be obtuse, psychologically complex, and deadly dull. As one of Susan's students once said of the main character in Hemingway's masterpiece: "Do you think he's gonna catch that fish today? I don't think he'll ever catch it!" This student was sent to Susan's room for "extra help" when he was in danger of dropping out of school, and his "regular" English teacher had assigned the novel as mandatory reading.

As in Susan's case, even if you calculate that a book you are about to teach is at a fifth-grade level, don't be quick to assume that your sixth-grade students will be captivated by its content or able to grasp its complexity without additional support. Difficulty of the text in terms of vocabulary and sentence length is only one consideration. Interest in the topic and perceived usefulness are also vital elements. The "techno trio" in our initial case study, for example, can read well beyond their grade level when it comes to computer software manuals. Anything else leaves them cold.

Here are some important considerations you should follow when thinking about teaching materials:

- **Consider the subject matter.** Motivation and interest can make even a difficult text accessible to the most challenged reader. The extent to which the materials appeal to student needs and interests are important considerations. If the material is perceived to be useful, students will read it. Also, if you're planning to show a video, use a piece of art in a lesson, or invite students to visit a Web site, make sure you've covered possible parental objections. Even the most compelling videos, for example, may have a brief scene that invites parental or community censorship. Check with administrators and host teachers before you plan any whole class reading or viewing experiences.
- **Consider the language and referents.** Will textual references be accessible to middle school readers? To what extent will the language be accessible to students with different racial, ethnic, and linguistic backgrounds? Will girls and boys be equally familiar with its content?
- **Consider the style and format.** In print-based materials, attractiveness, print size, white space, cover art, length, and use of illustrations are all crucial considerations. Remember that a book, video, song, or other text must be accessible, but it can't look like it's for "little kids."
- **Consider the reactions of other students.** If a topic or text gains popularity within a classroom, it may greatly enhance a student's ability to engage with difficult materials. A student who "accidentally" leaves her copy of *Sounder* (Armstrong, 2001) on the floor after class may carry a complicated computer manual in her backpack until its cover is ragged with use.

In addition to attending to the potential difficulties that particular materials might evoke, it's equally important not to select materials that are "too easy." Don't insult your students with materials that they perceive to be too young for them. This isn't to say that children's books should be banned from your classroom. Children's books and movies can be appropriate and highly engaging texts. But if the materials are presented without a strong rationale, students may not be motivated to interact with these texts in meaningful ways.

PLANNING FOR MULTIPLE INTELLIGENCES

Will some students have difficulty in your classroom? Yes. How do you work with the vast range of interests and abilities in each of your classrooms? It is not easy, but you are not alone in this challenge. Your middle school colleagues have a tremendous wealth of knowledge and are there to help you plan and select materials to meet the needs of all learners in your classroom. Ask reading specialists, media specialists, counselors, and inclusion teachers to help you plan and adapt instruction to support your students.

> Broaden your goals to encompass multiple intelligences.

Gardner's theory of multiple intelligences (1999, 2000) may provide a useful tool to help you design lessons to support your students. Gardner is a professor at Harvard University and codirector of Harvard's Project Zero. His theory has broadened our ideas of intelligence beyond linguistic-verbal and logical-mathematical abilities to include six other intelligences that aren't commonly measured by typical standardized tests: spatial, musical,

Planning and Adapting Instruction for Middle School Learners

bodily-kinesthetic, interpersonal, intrapersonal, and (recently added) naturalist. For more information about Gardner's eight intelligences, you might want to visit the Project Zero Web site at *http://www.pz.harvard.edu/sumit/MISUMIT.HTM*.

In Literacy Lesson 3–2, Dona Ward, a middle school language arts teacher, and Amy Craig, a middle school social studies teacher, use the theory of multiple intelligences to provide support for all their students. The two teachers are planning an integrated studies unit around the novel *Orphan Train Rider: One Boy's True Story*, by Andrea Warren (1998). They begin by describing their goals for the unit.

Literacy Lesson 3-2

Planning for Multiple Successes

We selected *Orphan Train Rider* because it offers rich opportunities to connect language arts and social studies. Although it is historical, it presents issues that we think many of our students can relate to: foster care, adoption, homelessness, family loss. This book looks at the issues, concepts, and historical events that surround the time between 1853 and 1929 and the plight of the orphan train riders. It tells the story of Lee Nailing, who rode the train in 1926.

Entering the Story World

We often begin with a book talk to allow students to enter the story world through their ears rather than their eyes. We might begin with something like this:

> *Mary, Thomas, Lee. I want you all back at the house in fifteen minutes for dinner. No excuses, hear! I do declare, I sure do love those younguns of mine. It seems like only yesterday that the orphan train rolled into town and our family became complete. I'll never forget the day my Mary, Thomas and Lee arrived. Everyone from miles around came to the train station to see the children who were called "orphan train riders." Once the orphan train arrived, the children were immediately taken to the hotel where they were fed, washed and all dressed up in new clothes. When they returned, the girls had on new dresses, all alike with white pinafores over them. The boys also had on new clothes; they wore knickers that buttoned below the knee, white dress shirts, necktie and suit coats. In fact I remember Lee telling me that he never had anything new before. All he had ever worn were hand-me-down clothes from his older brothers or used clothes given to the orphanage where he used to live. . . .*

After an opening like this, we focus our book talk on a bit of historical background:

> *If I remember right, I do believe Reverend Benjamin said that between 1854 and 1930 more than 200,000 children rode those orphan trains from New York to the West. At one time the orphanages could take care of the children who had lost their parents, but immigration, the industrialization of the U.S., competition for jobs that paid low wages, people with large families just could not support their families. Reverend Benjamin said many of the children became shoeshine boys, sold matches and newspapers and did anything they could to make a little money to help the family. Some children even begged in the streets for food or money. It's been said that some parents who couldn't afford their children often would abandon their*

newborn babies in churches or just leave them in rain barrels or trash cans. Oh, I just can't bear to think about those poor younguns anymore....

Jumping In: Collaborative Planning

When we plan together, we really just jump in. We sit down together with paper and pens. We have a piece of paper and then one of us simply starts talking. We have found it beneficial for our students to be active learners in the classroom. To keep our students motivated and interested, we must actively engage them in their own learning. So we try to think of ways to get their hands-on and minds-on learning.

Traditionally, intelligence has been defined in terms of proficiency in reading, writing, and mathematics. Students who do well in these areas are "smart." However, we are aware that all of our students possess different talents, different strengths, and different ways of making meaning.

We have found when we create units that include Dr. Gardner's multiple intelligences, all of our students are more able to experience success in the classroom.... Many academic difficulties can be avoided by allowing students to work in their more strongly developed intelligence, while at the same time providing them with opportunities to develop more competency in less-developed areas.

Here's our list after a brainstorming session. It may not be pretty. It may not be grammatically correct or appear in parallel construction at this point, but we can't worry about that. We want to capture the kernels of possibilities. So we just start talking and writing and try to get it down on the page. We usually start with "Linguistic" activities. That's always easy for us. Attention to language. The others follow from there:

Brainstormed List: Planning for Multiple Intelligences

Linguistic Possible Activities
- Collect oral histories of relatives who may have lived at the time of the orphan trains.
- Write a diary entry as if you were a train rider.
- Oral presentations of research using primary documents, laws, and regulations.

Logical-Mathematical Possible Activities
- Calculate a farmer's monthly income into today's economic terms.
- Calculate the cost of feeding a child for one year then and now.
- Draw or locate a map that traces the train's journey.
- Calculate the time it would take to travel from New York to our school on the train.

Visual/Spatial Possible Activities
- Draw the train arriving at the station.
- Create a collage of the time period.
- Draw Lee or another character.
- Research period clothes and create drawings of them.
- Something with maps and/or geography of train trip.
- Size and space in the train cars; comfort and discomfort of space.
- Illustrated scenes selected by students.
- Make an exhibit that depicts something about the orphan trains.

Planning and Adapting Instruction for Middle School Learners

Musical Possible Activities
- Find actual songs from the period.
- Write a song from Lee's perspective.
- Find a piece of music that captures the emotions of the train riders.
- Popular songs that carry similar themes of homelessness, loneliness, etc.

Kinesthetic Possible Activities
- Select a scene to act out.
- Research sports played in back yards at the times.
- Make a demonstration of all of the hard work that some of the orphans had to do in their new homes.
- Show some of the farming techniques.
- Demonstrate farm tools and techniques.
- Something with the city life they left.
- Build a diorama of the story.
- Set up a model train set.
- Can we do an actual train trip?

Naturalist Possible Activities
- Investigate the local farming communities.
- Interview farmers.
- Research how to care for chickens (as Lee learned the hard way).
- Research cooking during the period.
- Find out about the weather and how that would have affected the trip.

Intrapersonal Possible Activities
- How did Lee manage his feelings?
- Set yourself in Lee's place.
- Through diary or journal entries, reflect on fears faced.
- Interview local child protective services person.
- Personal stories—*Try to imagine* the feelings and points of view of the orphans. How easy or difficult would it be to get along in a totally new family?

Interpersonal Possible Activities
- Cooperative group to investigate peer relationships among the orphans.
- How did the orphans learn to fit into the new community?
- E-mail learning partner in New York.
- Explore from multiple points of view how orphans were viewed at that time.
- Interview family members about how they came to live here.

Dona and Amy's brainstorming session demonstrates one way to begin the process of planning. Gardner's categories may be useful to help you include a broad range of activities. We need to point out, though, that there is much overlap in Gardner's categories. For example, drawing a map, can include linguistic, logical, spatial, and perhaps even interpersonal components. It helps to look at Gardner's categories as rough frameworks that allow you to think about the multiple ways in which your students make meaning and the multiple ways that you might support them in the process.

ORGANIZING LESSON PLANS

Consider multiple audiences and purposes for lesson plans.

In the early stages of your planning, think about your lessons in terms of multiple purposes and audiences. Certainly *you* will be the primary audience for your daily teaching notes and informal writings such as the list that Amy and Dona created. Your formal plans, on the other hand, are likely to be read by a variety of audiences: your principal, a team teacher, mentor teacher, or a substitute teacher. For this reason, you should think about creating at least three different kinds of plans: weekly calendars, daily lesson plans, and formal instructional (or unit) plans.

Weekly Calendar

Sometimes called "bird's eye" or weekly plans, these brief overviews help you to see your upcoming days or weeks of teaching "at a glance." Many veteran teachers keep weekly plans in "plan books" that have small boxes for each day of the week and can be purchased at office and school supply stores. These books work well for experienced teachers, but for a number of reasons, we don't recommend them for teachers in their first few years. A sample page from one veteran teacher's weekly planner is presented in Figure 3–1.

Although this teacher's weekly planner may seem disorganized to an outsider, it's typical of the way that many veteran teachers plan and orchestrate instruction. This particular middle school teacher has almost 20 years of experience. Brief notes about activities, quotations, and ideas for journal work are all that she needs to remind herself of what she will be doing each day. After nearly two decades of teaching, you'll probably carry many of your teaching ideas in your head as well. Once you've been teaching for several years, your weekly teaching calendar can be fairly sketchy, since you will often be the only person consulting it. Considering the fact that you will be working with a host teacher and possibly a teaching partner, however, you should make these brief descriptions clear enough so that someone else can easily decipher what is supposed to happen each day.

Weekly calendars that will be shared with others—what we call "elaborated calendars"—should include at least four components:

- a brief description of the lesson (no more than a phrase or short sentence)
- a list of handouts/materials (if any)
- an outline of activities (use bullets and white space for ease of reading)
- evaluation (if formal evaluation is planned for that day)
- assignments for the next day (if any)

For several reasons, hand-writing your daily plans into a notebook like the one in Figure 3–1 is probably not the best way to proceed in your first few years of teaching. Because you've not yet mastered the art of anticipating whether activities will run short or spill over into the next day, and because there are inevitable disruptions in your weekly schedule (such as fire drills and assemblies), word-processing your weekly calendars makes more sense. This not only allows you some latitude in shifting activities from one day to the next, but it also creates a record of your daily teaching that you can refer to and revise in case you teach the same class again next year.

FIGURE 3-1 Page From a Veteran Teacher's Weekly Planner

THURSDAY	FRIDAY	Week of .... to ....
date	date	Remarks/notes/comments
your writer's your inspiration entry	Keypoint 1/2	• **Folder Work** review sheet ○ complete sentences ○ correcting run-on sentences ○ subject/verb agreement
the grade level earned and explain & respecting it.	Opening Task Day sub plan Materials for	Character in Action Reading/Response A Sense of Purpose (Tie in with discovering talents that lead to purpose in life.)
procedures my need to Grade	Procedures Other half grade conferencing	ELA standards review sheet (lesson #) Practice sheet for reading comprehension (multiple choice)
talent bit.	Closure	Quotes: "We must overcome the notion that we must be regular. It robs you of the chance to be extraordinary and leads you to be mediocre." —Uta Hagen
grades choose comments	Assessment	"It is talent that creates opportunity." —Eric Hoffer

Reprinted by permission of Mary McCrone.

FIGURE 3–2 Day From Weekly Calendar in Text Form

> Day 15
> Inquiry Stations for *Roughing It* (90 min)
>
> **Materials:**
> - Internet addresses for information on Mark Twain
> - Paper
> - Sample cartoon strips
> - Art supplies, including loose-leaf paper, pens, art paper, colored pencils, markers
>
> **Activities:**
> - *Learning Stations Options* (50 min)
> - Author study: Internet search on Mark Twain in the library (list of questions and Internet sites in appendix)
> - Drama: Write and perform trial scene for a reporter who is accused of writing lies
> - Art: Create a cartoon strip
> - Reading and Writing Workshop: Choose a piece from your folder to work on
> - Catchup: Required for students who were absent this week
> - *Sharing* (20 min) Students are encouraged to share or perform their work
>
> **Assessment:**
> Work from each station will be added to students' binders for review

There are many different formats for weekly plans. You might keep a running "bird's eye" in text form such as the one in Figure 3–2. Or if you prefer, you can create a chart for each day of a teaching week and enter the information in that format (see Figure 3–3). Some spreadsheet or lesson-planning software programs may make the task of weekly planning even easier. Whatever format you choose, make sure that your weekly plans are accessible at a glance. You'll need them for those quick conversations with your host teacher or administrator about upcoming lessons. It's also good for a last-minute reminder of your activities and materials as students are streaming in your door between classes.

Especially if you're student teaching, it's a good idea to have an updated weekly plan for a minimum of one week in advance. That way you can have a conversation with your teaching partner and/or host teacher about upcoming lessons in time to make changes before your daily lesson plans are finalized for the next week.

Daily Lesson Plans

Your daily lesson plans include many of the same components as your weekly plans; however, they are more elaborated in terms of the goals and rationale behind your choice of activities and lesson evaluation.

FIGURE 3-3 Weekly Calendar for a Poetry Unit in Chart Form

Day 1
Introduction to Poetry
	Materials:
	• May Swenson, *Poems to Solve*
		Activities:
		• Create groups of 4 (5)
		• Students write "bio-poems" (20)
		• Volunteers share (10)
		• Discuss (10)
		  • Swenson's use of metaphor and imagery
		  • Differences between prose and poetry

Day 2 Poetry	Materials: • May Swenson, *Poems to Solve* • Emily Dickenson poems	Activities: • Teacher reads poems aloud, while students read silently • After each poem, students point out examples of metaphor and imagery (15) • Students begin writing their own "poems to solve" (20)
Day 3 Music Poem	Materials: • music CD • CD player • blank paper	Activities: • As instrumental music is played, students write one sentence on a piece of paper • They fold the paper back, exchange with someone else, and write another line until the paper is filled (15) • Students unfold their papers and share "group poetry" aloud (10) • Discuss similarities between music and poetry (20)
Day 4 Collaborative Editing	Materials: • group poems from previous day • blank paper • scissors • tape	Activities: • Create groups of 4 • Groups "edit" group poems by cutting lines into strips and pasting them on new sheets of paper. Students can add or delete lines in order to create a cohesive and meaningful poem or poems. • Groups share final poems
Day 5 Poetry Workshop	Materials: • copies of poem "Yellow Delicious" • samples of students' poetry and short stories	Activities: • Read "Yellow Delicious" aloud • Discuss techniques for writing strong, effective poems (15) • Students write poems independently (30)

A typical daily lesson plan should include the following:

- a description of your lesson objectives (often tied directly to your state standards or district benchmarks)
- a list of materials/handouts
- a description of activities, more elaborate than the description in your weekly plans, often with a brief rationale embedded in the description. (Particularly if you are teaching in a block schedule where classes are 80 or 90 minutes long, it's a good idea to include a rough time frame for each activity you plan.)
- a description of how you will evaluate whether you have achieved your goals for this day

As an example, take a look at the daily lesson plan in Figure 3–4. Just remember that your daily plans should be clear enough to let your host teacher, mentor, or a substitute teacher know exactly what you expect of students that day, what you will be doing in the lesson, why you have chosen the activities you have, and how you will evaluate whether you have met your goals. In most schools, as a beginning teacher, you will be expected to have available for your principal or mentor a detailed daily plan for each day you teach at least two days in advance (in case you are absent and your host teacher or a substitute needs to cover for you).

> Keep plans on hand for substitute teachers.

Veteran teachers often keep up to a week of plans that any substitute teacher could use in getting students through an unexpected period of absence. These "generic" plans do not follow exactly what you have been teaching, but can still provide valuable learning experiences no matter what unit or lesson you are currently teaching. A list of which students in each class can help with routine procedures (like taking the class roll) and a menu of writing options with explicit instructions about how writing is to be shared can get a substitute teacher through what might have been a wasted week or class period.

Formal Instructional (or Unit) Plans

These more extensive plans are designed to be shared with others and are more detailed than the list of materials and activities in the weekly calendar. These formal long-range plans serve multiple purposes. First, they give you (and your host teacher if you have one) a place to articulate your goals, sequence instructional activities, create and choose materials and texts, and evaluate student learning over an extended period. Second, you may decide to include this formal plan (or one like it) in your employment portfolio to share with administrators or hiring committees. Although many veteran teachers do not create formal unit plans such as these, our hope is that, as a beginning teacher, you will find this kind of extensive planning and reflecting useful as a way of "rehearsing and rehashing" your ideas prior to your first days of teaching. As you develop this plan, it's a good idea to share drafts and ask for feedback with a teaching peer, your host teacher, or team partner.

FIGURE 3-4 Sample Daily Lesson Plan

Day One: Getting to Know You

Objectives Students will . . .
- Speak to each of their classmates in the room, as well as their new student teachers (New York State Standard 4.1).
- Learn one new fact about each classmate.
- Become familiar with the personalities of their student teachers.

Materials
- Pens
- Gridded index cards

Procedures
- Hand out index card. Each student gets one card.
- Explain directions (1 min).
- "Fascinating Facts" activity (20 min).
  - Students walk around the classroom, interviewing their peers and teachers to learn one "fascinating" fact about each person.
  - Students record this fact with the person's name in a box on the index card until all the boxes are full and they have spoken to everyone in the room.
    - (rationale) This activity helps us learn the students' names and gives us an idea about each student's interests and experiences. The students have a chance to move around the room and socialize. They must also take risks and speak to people to whom they may have not talked all year.
- Students return to their seats and are assigned a partner.
- Each student begins by introducing his or her partner with a "fascinating fact" about that person. Other classmates can volunteer additional information about that person if they like.
  - (rationale) This allows the whole class to listen to and appreciate the experiences and interesting qualities of their peers. It also contributes to the development of community, which has been partially disrupted by the presence of two new adults in the room.

Evaluation: Observe for enthusiasm and students' interest in one another. If students display a negative attitude through comments and/or disinterest, we will have to incorporate new ways of building community in the classroom. We are not formally grading this activity.

INTERDISCIPLINARY PLANNING

One of the ways middle schools are different from elementary and high schools is in how teachers work together to plan and implement instruction. Middle schools often operate with a school-within-a-school structure. Teachers of academic areas such as language arts, science, social studies, and math share the same group of students, creating a team or family of teachers and learners. This small group of teachers works collaboratively to create learning experiences integrated across the disciplines they teach. Often, they are assigned common planning times where they decide what and how to teach particular concepts. For example, you might be assigned to work in teams of four (one English, one math, one social studies, and one science teacher).

The shared planning time in the middle school structure allows teachers to create integrated learning experiences for their students and time to discuss and deliberate on the dynamics and diverse needs of students on their team. For instance, one teacher may notice that an individual student appears to have lost interest, is tired, or is less attentive than usual. At the regular team meeting, others in the team may then be encouraged to attend to this particular student or share information that will help others to serve his or her needs.

There is no one standard way in which middle school teachers are teamed. At some middle schools, teachers are paired. You may be paired with a social studies teacher or a science teacher rather than a team of four. Many times, teachers use their team meeting time to share concerns about individual students and do not actually plan teaching together, or they may plan to teach around a particular topic across disciplinary boundaries without establishing fully fleshed-out interdisciplinary units. Some teams may concentrate on four or five large projects a year, rather than planning all units in an interdisciplinary way.

Whether you plan independently, with a teaching partner, or on an interdisciplinary team, you'll need to consider the unique needs of early adolescents as you begin planning over the long term.

LONG-RANGE PLANNING WITH MIDDLE SCHOOL STUDENTS IN MIND

Much of the time, teachers use the term *unit plan* to describe plans that typically cover 2 to 6 weeks. The term *unit* refers to a systematically organized block of instruction. Here are a few steps to think about before you write your formal plans.

Sketch Out Your Overall Goals

Although you probably have a good idea about *what* you're going to teach, it's helpful to stop at the beginning of your planning and think about *why*. Why, after all, should students write a personal narrative, read *Anne Frank: The Diary of a Young Girl* (2000), or participate in literature circles? *Our* "teacher-centered" reasons aren't enough to make these activities worthwhile. What do our students care if *The Diary of a Young Girl* is mandated by the school curriculum or your host teacher wants you to try your hand at literature circles? These activities must be clear and meaningful to students. If you can't "sell" your choices to students at the outset, you will lose many of them before you've even started. It's up to you to point out the relevance of what you're doing. For example, a personal narrative can be a way for them to share their experiences with important audiences of friends and family. *The Diary of a Young Girl* can help them to make meaningful connections with the plight of oppressed people in their own times, and literature circles can be an alternative to large group discussion.

The goals you choose should address the question: In what ways will students become better language users and thinkers than when they started this work? It's a good idea to create a first draft of what you want your students to accomplish before making any final decisions about your overall goals. While you're at it, look over your statewide standards and proficiencies for middle school students. Make sure that these are consistent with your unit goals and the objectives for each day of instruction in your daily plans. Your preliminary goals for a long-range plan might include a statement like this:

> Create student-centered goals that are consistent with statewide standards.

My students will
- understand and use the conventions and rules of language in scientific report writing.
- produce historical texts for different age groups.
- make critical judgments about journalistic texts.

In the beginning of your planning, these goals should serve as a flexible basis for teaching decisions. As you work on other aspects of your unit, you will need to return regularly to your statement of goals. Your unit plan should demonstrate an alignment between what you want the students to accomplish (goals), what the students *do* to accomplish the goals (activities), and *how well* the students *accomplish* the goals (evaluation).

Identify Relevance and Usefulness

As you plan, place individual activities within a topic or focus that is useful and relevant to early adolescents. A unit of study can be powerful if middle school students view it as relevant to their lives. Relevance for early adolescents depends on real and immediate purposes for literacy with real and immediate audiences.

Units should be planned with an end date and/or culminating activity in mind. Avoid the "endless unit" syndrome. Although you might be thoroughly enthused about a topic, some of your students will not. Nine weeks of reading, talking, and writing about myths and legends, for example, may seem like a holiday for you, but it may seem like torture to some of your students. A 6-week writing/reading workshop, culminating in a whole class anthology, may seem to allow for students' interests and experiences, but some students will need more support.

> Avoid the "endless unit" syndrome.

We recommend 3 to 4 weeks as the maximum for any thematic unit. We have probably all had the experience of waiting until a night or two before a semester project is due to begin it. Middle school students are no different. If you want them to remain engaged and on task throughout several weeks, realize that they need nudging, prodding, and support. Plan for several "checkpoints" along the way to make sure that students are staying on task and your teaching goals are being met.

Choose an Organizing Framework

If you are planning several consecutive days of instruction, it's often a good idea to organize thematically. Themes can range from topics like "beauty through the ages" to "loss of innocence," "overcoming obstacles," or "love, hate, and violence in modern society."

Depending on your goals, you might decide to organize an instructional unit around particular genres (poetry), texts (novels or plays), or language forms (the research paper). If you are in a workshop setting or will not be engaged in whole class teaching for several consecutive days, you may simply want to plan for 15 or 20 days of instruction, arranged according to a structure that makes the most sense for your situation. Three days a week may be devoted to workshop instruction, in which students work independently while you confer with individuals or groups about their work-in-progress. The remaining 2 days each week can involve teacher-led activities. Your formal plans can include a section in which you detail exactly what will happen on workshop days, followed by daily lesson plans that focus on teacher-led days.

Design a Culminating Activity

Deciding on a culminating event at the beginning of your plan serves several purposes. It prevents the unit from going on too long to sustain the interest of your middle school students. It promotes coherence for the unit, and it makes designing the activities much easier for you. The culminating activity needs to be relevant to the topic, your teaching goals, and students' lives. It may consist of a product (such as a class newspaper, wildlife habitat, or model community), performance (a class play, skit, or an evening with parents), presentation (an exhibit, panel discussion, or radio show), or field trip (to a museum, park, or business).

Your culminating event may involve individual, small group, or whole class activities. It can be an occasion for evaluating learning or an opportunity to celebrate student accomplishments. Particularly in the middle grades, it's important to design a culminating activity that promotes cooperation over competition. When products or performances are cast as competitions, there will always be winners and losers. Middle school students often learn best when activities are physical. Hands-on or even "bodies-on" experiences allow students to make strong and vital connections to what they are learning.

Investigate Materials and Resources

Explore the resources you have available. If possible, contact your media specialist or librarian early to help you secure appropriate materials such as books, magazines, newspapers, or videos. Other materials might include visual art, music, or computer software. Your department may store literature anthologies, grammar handbooks, paperback novels, or other equipment and materials in a specific location.

Consider the resources that might be available in your community. You might call upon a variety of people and organizations in planning for instruction. Invite these people to serve as subject matter experts, audience members, mentors, and learning buddies. Parents often have valuable knowledge and expertise that might support your unit goals. Contact your community librarians to see if they can locate hard-to-find materials through an interlibrary loan program or if they allow teachers to take out large numbers of books to use over several weeks of an instructional period.

Include Evaluation

Make a rough sketch of your grading and evaluation procedures. Although evaluation and response should be ongoing, formative parts of your long-range planning, final grades are typically based on how well a student has learned a set of concepts or the quality of a final project, product, or performance. Grading is always complicated. Middle school students often invest an incredible amount of energy and make tremendous leaps in learning, yet they may fail to show these strides in the finer details of a completed project. As you sketch out the rough details of your grading and evaluation system, remember the two places in an instructional plan where you need to specify your system in detail:

- **The "evaluation" component of daily lessons.** Each daily lesson must have an evaluation section that describes exactly how you'll know whether your daily objectives have been met. Evaluations may be informal journal entries or discussion prompts that allow you to provide additional instructional support. You do not need to plan a quantifiable evaluation (a test or quiz) for each day; in fact, giving daily grades can be demoralizing and detrimental to many students. Consider ways to make qualitative evaluation a part of your daily teaching. For example, at the end of a lesson, you might note,

    Students will be assessed largely on participation today. We will look for attentiveness during Story Time and during discussions and for the ability to stay in character during the debate. Journals will be collected and read for evidence that students have made sense of their reading.

- **The overall grading and evaluation system.** Often, it's a good idea to prepare two descriptions of your overall grading scheme: one to hand out to your students and a more detailed version to share with your university supervisor, host teacher, or teaching partner. Your grading system should immediately let students know how grades will be determined and the relative "weight" of each graded component (i.e., what percentage each component will carry). Finally, the grading system should be consistent with overall goals and daily activities. Figure 3–5 offers an example of a grading system for a unit on multiculturalism created by a preservice teacher.

Describe Techniques, Strategies, and Procedures

Sketch out a description of ongoing techniques, strategies, and procedures. Say, for example, that you expect certain days of the week to be devoted to what you call "learning centers." Or, perhaps you plan to set up a system of dialogue journals in which students share responses to class readings with a peer on a regular basis. Somewhere near the beginning of your unit plan, you need to describe the exact parameters for these regular activities and procedures. Here is a description of story time from an instructional unit created by two preservice teachers using the novel *Dragonwings* (1999) by Yep:

> **Story Time**:
> Periodically, students will participate in "story time," during which one of us, or one of the students, will read aloud a children's book that relates to the unit topics. These students composed their own children's works as a social studies project and are familiar with the genre. Story time will emphasize the impact of oral storytelling (a vital part of the Chinese and Chinese immigrant cultures), while giving struggling readers the opportunity to practice their oral expression in a less-threatening environment.

FIGURE 3-5 A Grading System for a Multicultural Unit

> This grading system is designed for a 4-week unit plan centered on the theme of multiculturalism. There will be in-class activities, such as poetry reading and current events discussion, as well as individual projects. A contract system looked good in theory, but I could too easily picture students taking the easy way out and contracting for the C option. So finally I decided to make it simple, and divide the unit into five parts, each representing 20% of the unit grade.
>
> I. **Journal** (20%). Evaluated by number of entries, thoroughness of the entries, and overall work it appears to represent. Individual entries will not be graded. Entire journal will be graded on an A–F scale, according to a rubric provided to students.
> II. **Homework** (20%). (Not including vocabulary assignments). Most assignments will be collected and graded on an A–F scale. Missing assignments will result in a lowering of the homework average at my discretion. At the end of the unit, I will take into account the graded assignments as well as ones that were either checked off as done or not done to determine a letter grade.
> III. **Vocabulary** (20%). This includes quizzes and the homework assignments specifically linked to vocabulary. The quizzes are graded on a 0–100 scale. Individual vocabulary assignments will not be graded, but the overall average can be lowered if vocabulary homework assignments are not completed.
> IV. **Individual Project** (20%). There will be an oral presentation and a written component. This will be graded on an A–F scale according to a rubric negotiated with students.
> V. **Participation** (20%). Each day, students are expected to contribute to class activities. They might do this by contributing to discussion, volunteering to share something they've written, participating actively in small group work, or simply being quiet and attentive. All students start out with a grade of A for participation. If students are disruptive or off task, they receive a warning. After this warning, they receive a check in the grade book. At the end of the unit, participation grades can be lowered at my discretion.

Describing ongoing techniques, strategies, and procedures in the beginning of your instructional plan allows you to craft more fluid daily plans later in the text. Consider how much easier it is to write an abbreviation "Story Time" in a daily plan, without the need to continually define what you mean for each day of instruction.

FORMALIZING LONG-RANGE PLANS

Once you've followed these preliminary stages, you're ready to write out a more formal description of your long-term plans.

Why write formal plans? It's true that some excellent teachers claim not to rely on elaborate planning. You might look at a host teacher's weekly plan book and be astounded at what appears to be utter chaos. But don't be fooled into thinking that good teachers have no need for planning. You can bet that most experienced teachers have engaged in planning, whether they've taken the time to write out those plans or not.

We see many purposes behind making formal written plans, but here are the two most important. First, formalizing your plans serves as a "writing-to-learn" experience for beginning teachers. As you craft your objectives, you are forced to think in concrete terms about what you want students to do, feel, believe, or think as a result of your teaching. Writing a description and a rough time frame for your activities forces you to grapple with exactly how you expect to orchestrate each aspect of a lesson and how long each aspect will take. Making sure you write an evaluation component for every lesson gives you a quick idea of whether you have built in enough checkpoints to determine that students are doing quality work.

The second most valuable aspect of formalizing your plans is that it allows you to "show what you know" to mentor teachers, supervisors, and would-be administrators. It's one thing to be organized; it's another to convince your supervisors and administrators that you're organized. You'll be surprised at how impressed building principals and host teachers are when they see that you can produce clear, communicative, and thoughtful plans. In more than one case, our preservice teachers have landed jobs after their student teaching placement ended because, among other qualities, they were able to demonstrate good organizational skills through well-crafted written plans.

In Literacy Lesson 3–3, we ask you to think critically about a draft of a unit plan. It's clearly beyond the scope of this chapter to include an entire long-range instructional (or unit) plan for your consideration. Instead, in the next few pages, we'd like to present some excerpts from a plan in progress. This interdisciplinary unit was designed by teaching teams of preservice science and English teachers. At this preliminary draft stage, the unit has many strengths but, like all drafts, it could be even stronger with revision. As you read through these excerpts, consider how the draft might be strengthened in terms of the questions we pose. Whenever you come to a place where you have questions or suggestions, you might want to write them out on a Post-it note and paste it in the text of the excerpt. When you've finished, plan to discuss your notes with a partner or larger group, or write a short summary of what information you need to include in your own future instructional plans

Literacy Lesson 3-3

Life on the Prairie: Then and Now

Introduction

This integrated studies unit will focus on prairies. Tall grasses and other herbaceous plants cover prairies. These areas are home to various animals, including prairie dogs and other rodents, bison, wolves, and insects. Different types of prairie are identified by the soil moisture and type. Prairies in Indiana originally consisted of black soil prairies and sand prairies. The black soil prairies were rich in nutrients and were therefore used for agricultural purposes. Remnants of these prairies are scarce. They are usually found along old railroad tracks or pioneer cemeteries. Prairie fires stimulate the growth of prairie plants. Lightning and Native Americans originally started these

fires. Today, trained professionals set fires so that prairie plants can continue to thrive. In Indiana and elsewhere, nature preserves have been set up to protect prairie communities. Additionally, numerous efforts throughout the United States aim to restore prairie land.

> What questions do you still have about the community and region where this school is located?

The topic of prairies was chosen for several reasons. First, Benton Central Junior High School is located in a region that was once prairie. Second, this topic can easily be used to cultivate an understanding of the environment locally and globally. Beyond the environmental issues surrounding this topic, the study of prairies can be linked to history, literature, agriculture, meteorology, and biology. Finally, this topic will be of interest and relevant to the students' lives since land is naturally of concern to this farming community.

> Does this topic seem relevant to the lives of most early adolescents? How can this plan be made interesting to students whose families are not involved with farming?

Social Dynamics

We assumed we would have 25 students in our classroom. We would place them in five groups of five students. We titled the five groups: Pioneers, Literature, Animals, Plants, and Farmers (agriculture). The students would each get to pick the top three groups in which they would want to participate. For the first two choices the students would have to write a reason why they want to be in the group. For the last choice they would just write down the name of the group. We would collect all of the students' choices and group them, hopefully giving them their first or second choice. We would assign groups based on students' reasons for wanting to be in each group.

> Do you get a sense of the kind of students who will be in this classroom? What questions do you have? Is the process for assigning groups workable? What problems might the planners encounter?

All teams will be working in the same area at all times unless they do work outside of class time. Each student will choose a more specific topic within their group and will add the information they find out about their topic to the culminating activity. They will use writing, research, and hands-on activities to do the final culminating project. The students will have a rubric to consult, and we will give examples when needed. As teachers, we will sit down with the different groups while they are working on their activity and help the students when they have questions. Hopefully, though, they can help each other with their problems.

> Is this description of the research process clear enough for you? Would bullets, white space, or headings help you? What do the writers mean by "hands-on" and "student-centered"?

If some students don't do their part on the project, we will need to talk to those students to help them understand that they are part of a team; if they don't do their part, then their team won't get the work done.

> How will the planners ensure that each student is participating?

At the beginning of the unit we will explain to students how the unit will proceed and what our expectations are. We want this to be a hands-on learning experience for students and more of a student-centered classroom. We may point them in a direction, but we want the students to use their imagination and explore new areas. We will have various checkpoints to find out what the groups are doing to make sure they are on track. In the end we will have them evaluate their group. If they had a good or bad team, they can tell us and we will make sure that we take that into consideration when we give students their grades. We will also welcome

> What might those checkpoints be, and how will students be made aware of them? Are there more systematic ways to grade group participation than asking students if they were on a "good or bad team"?

the students to come and talk to us if they have any problems with their group members at any time.

Unit Objectives

- For students to gain a better understanding of their surroundings
- For students to gain a better awareness of prairies
- For students to learn about issues that are going on with prairies today
- For students to develop creativity and research skills
- For students to understand changes in land use over time and the history of agriculture
- For students to understand why people settled in their communities
- For students to understand why certain plants and animals live in this area
- For students to learn about prairie conservation and what they can do to help

> Are there practical ways of attaining these goals? Do they imply a good balance of all the language acts of reading, writing, talking, and listening? Are there workable ways of evaluating whether they have been met? Will students be able to understand them in personal terms?

Calendar of Events and Activities

(Authors' Notes: The next section of the "Prairie Plan" includes a 4-week calendar of events and activities. We have included just the first week. Also, since this unit plan is in a preliminary draft stage, the planners have not yet sketched out detailed daily lesson plans. What follows are their descriptions of the culminating activity and grading system).

> Would an "outsider" such as a host teacher, administrator, or substitute teacher be able to understand what is happening each day from this weekly calendar? What activities are too vague? For this first week, do the teachers seem to be sequencing activities in a logical way?

Weekly Calendar—First Week of Prairie Unit

Day 1	Day 2	Day 3	Day 4	Day 5
Introduction and initiating grouping activity.	Field trip to Wolf Park, Battle Ground, IN (half day). Learn about how the prairie ecosystem depends on every member. Learn how every living thing in that ecosystem, including humans, must work together.	Group research. Students will break into assigned groups and go to library to research their animals. Research should focus on the habitat of their animal.	Video Day—*Little House on the Prairie*. Compare life depicted in the video to life in our time.	Technology on the Prairie—today's advances, inventions, and technological advances that altered life on the prairies.

Culminating Activity: Prairie Life Presentations

This will be the culminating activity for the unit on prairies. Divide students into their groups. Have each group choose a wild animal typically found in a prairie. These animals may include prairie dogs, mice, hawks, spiders, or snakes. Find out the characteristics of the animal's shelter, including what materials the animal uses to build it. Find out what techniques the animal uses and how long it takes to build the shelter.

Have the students collect representative materials from the environment similar to those the animal would use to construct the shelter. (*Caution:* Do not harm wildlife or disturb actual shelters.) Build models of each animal's shelter to scale, if possible. Have the students describe the shelter and the animal that uses it. Each group will have 5 to 7 minutes to present their habitat to their peers in a celebration of their learning. Discuss the time it took to replicate the shelters and compare it to the time it takes the animal to build it. Compare the similarities and differences in the shelters and the kinds of habitats in which the animals live. Conclude by discussing the consequences of habitat loss for each of the animals. Which animals are most vulnerable to loss of materials for creating shelter? After sharing in class, animal habitats will be displayed in the glass cases in the media center.[1]

> Do these culminating activities attend to middle school students' needs for activity, closure, and hands-on learning? Do the activities stress collaboration and team building over individual competition?

> How will the planners make sure that each group stays on time and on task?

Project Evaluation and Checkpoints

We will assign 200 points for the entire 2-week unit, including the final project. Of those 200 points, roughly 100 will be in the final project, as it will reflect much of what they learned. The other 100 points will represent the 50 points' worth of work they do each week. We still have to determine which assignments will be weighted heavier than other assignments, but we have a general idea.

The final project's points will be distributed as follows: 20 points for the mechanics of the presentation of the material, 20 for relating the project to the community, 20 for the quality of information presented, 20 for visual aids, and 20 for the organization and flow of the material being presented.

> Is 50% of the grade too much weight for the final project? How will the 50 points for weekly work be assigned? Are the outcomes aligned with the topic, goals, activities, and assessments?

The mechanics area involves vocal aspects and physical gestures associated with speeches. Community involves the group's attempt to relate this information to students and parents in the Benton Central area. Visual aids, as the name implies, refers to whatever aids the students use in their presentation. Organization and flow deals with the information itself and how it is divided and presented. There will be only one grade per group; there are no grades for the individual. It is important for students to learn to work as a team. One grade for the entire team will reflect this importance.

> What about students who do more than their share or students who refuse to participate? What are some specific ways in which the planners might measure and reward participation among group members?

---

[1]From Project Wild Activity Guide, 1992. Western Regional Environmental Education Council, Inc.

	Criteria	Comments
Topic/Content Excellent Good Fair 1 2 3 4 5	Provides evidence of research into the school context and local community. Multiple connections establish a "realistic fit" between topic and context. Provides a clear rationale that explains how such a unit is useful and relevant.	
Outcomes/Activities Excellent Good Fair 1 2 3 4 5	The outcomes are clearly connected to the topic. The outcomes clearly communicate learning expectations in science, English, and technology that make use of the local community and reflect Indiana proficiencies. The learning of science, English, and technology are integrated through community-based learning activities. Students learn in collaborative groups. The activities support the outcomes.	
Culminating Activity Excellent Good Fair 1 2 3 4 5	Culminating activity is relevant to the topic, outcomes, students' lives, and local issues. This activity clearly integrates learning about the community with understanding science and English and the use of technology. The culminating activity is an opportunity for the students to celebrate their learning and to make a contribution to the community.	
Evaluation and Grading Excellent Good Fair 1 2 3 4 5	Provides a list of things to look for that reflect student success. Describes how often the teacher will use the progress checklist. The grading rubric provides for student input and the teacher's standards. The negotiated rubric reflects the unit topic, outcomes, and activities.	

GRADING RUBRIC FOR THE UNIT PLAN

If you have read over the examples in Literacy Lesson 3–3 and still find yourself with questions about what to include in your own formal instructional plan, you might want to consider the following.

Rubric for Evaluating a Three-Week Instructional Plan

Introduction:
- **Is a complete description of students and school provided?**
- **Overall Goals and Rationale**
  - Are these sufficiently and clearly explained?
  - Are they congruent with daily activities, graded projects, and daily evaluation methods?
- **Description of Techniques, Strategies, and Procedures (if included)**
  - Are these described thoroughly and congruent with overall goals?

Weekly Calendar:
- Are components of the calendar clear and understandable to a naive reader?
- Are activities planned in a logical sequence?
- Is enough time allotted for various activities?

Daily Lesson Plans:
- **Materials and Handouts**
  - Are these listed in each lesson plan?
  - Are they included in an appendix?
  - Are they clear and understandable for middle school students?
  - Are they error free?
  - Are they inviting and substantive?
- **Objectives**
  - Are these clearly stated for each lesson?
  - Are they congruent with overall unit rationale and goals?
  - Are they congruent with the "evaluation" criteria for each lesson?
  - Are connections made with the state and/or district standards?
- **Procedures**
  - Are these clearly explained (with rationale embedded in description of activities)?
  - Are they well organized and coherent?
  - Are they congruent with goals?
- **Evaluation**
  - Is this clearly stated?
  - Is it congruent with daily goals?

Overall Evaluation and Grading System:
- Is this clearly explained and understandable to students?
- Does it explain how unit grade will be derived from individual graded components (i.e., what percentage each component will carry)?
- Is it consistent with overall goals and daily activities?

Overall Instructional Plan:
- Does it provide a good balance of reading, writing, and oral language experiences?
- Is it well organized and coherent?
- Are texts chosen to represent diverse cultural and gender perspectives?
- Is the plan free of error and neatly prepared?

PLANNING FOR CHANGE

Tess, a teacher 3 weeks into her first student teaching placement, posts this message to the members of her listserv. She has just been discussing different techniques for classroom management:

> *Another strategy that has become a staple of my openings is "Here's the plan for today. . . " This has immensely helped me solidify in my mind the things I want to cover during the lesson so I don't have to cheat back to my lesson plan. (Do you find that you rely on your lesson plans much?) It also helps the students understand that there are many things they need to pay attention for during the class.*

Later that week, Mary Ellen responds:

> *Tess asked if we use our lesson plan/teaching notes very often. What do the rest of you do? While teaching, I have seldom looked at my notes. It seems that careful planning has inscribed the plans into my head so I don't need the notes too often. If I were lecturing on literature, I would need to refer to notes often to get the "right" information or interpretation, but since I am discovering meaning along with the students, I don't need many notes in advance. We'll see if this proves true in the future as well.*

Soon afterward, Tess replies,

> *Back to the discussion about using notes—I have discovered that practice and planning really ARE key to success! I have begun using a highlighter to make it easier for me to see things that I need the plan for: quotes to refer to, terms that need to be defined, questions that need to be written on the board. This makes things run more smoothly, and as I highlight I also rehearse the lesson! I also paperclip any other information, like groups I have made or reminders, to the day's lesson so I don't have to flip through my binder. These things have all made teaching run more smoothly. . . . Thanks, Mary Ellen! I hope you are all having a great time!!!*

As Tess observes, "practice and planning really ARE key to success." The careful process of planning does more than simply make you "look good" to host teachers, supervisors, and administrators. As Mary Ellen points out, it "inscribes" your plans into your mind and, ironically, helps you to teach without resorting to what Tess calls "cheating back to your plans."

There's an old saying that "the only certainty is uncertainty and the only constant is change." This is never more true than in planning lessons for a middle school classroom. There will always be interruptions. Even your most carefully planned lessons are in danger of going astray in a moment of adolescent crisis. A fire drill will sound just at the moment you begin the poetry celebration you planned as a culmination to your 3-week unit. In short, if it *can* go wrong, it *will* (especially if there are audiovisual or computer components).

For these and so many other reasons, it's important to design your lesson plans as a guide rather than a script. You need to create flexible plans that can be changed at a moment's notice. Don't lock yourself into a scenario that students might not be able to follow. Anticipate the time needed for group projects or rearranging the classroom and add 10 to 20 minutes. Anticipate the time needed for a whole class discussion, and have a backup plan if your "compelling" questions only elicit 10 minutes of talk in an 80-minute period. Think about possible difficulties that you or particular students might face, and always plan for alternatives.

Remember that, much like a work of literature or a written script, teaching plans are only words on a page. Hopefully, the process of crafting them has taught you much about the what, why, and how of your teaching; but the deadliest thing you can do is to adhere slavishly to a written plan when a teachable moment presents itself. When that moment arrives, it's often best to grasp it enthusiastically, knowing that all the time you've spent "inscribing" your plans into your head was not spent in vain. The more time you spend in preparation, the more likely you will know what is essential in a particular lesson and what can fall behind for another day. You can always "sneak back" into that trusty lesson plan when those moments of uncertainty surface again, as they inevitably will.

Standards in Practice

Making Your Competencies Visible

The Interstate New Teacher Assessment and Support Consortium (INTASC), a program of the Council of Chief State School Officers, has developed a set of standards for licensing new teachers. The standards were developed to be compatible with the advanced certification standards of the National Board for Professional Teaching Standards (NBPTS), the set of standards introduced in Chapter 1. You might also want to check to see what your state uses for criteria in assessing teaching knowledge, dispositions, and performances that beginning teachers should possess when entering the classroom.

INTASC Standards

INTASC members decided that the proper benchmark for determining teacher licensing standards should represent the kinds of understandings and abilities teachers should have in order to teach diverse students responsibly from their first day of employment as a licensed teacher. The standards are expressed in the form of 10 principles, articulating the common core of teaching knowledge. The complete list can be found at *http://www.ccsso.org/intascst.html#draft*. This Web site includes a detailed explanation of the knowledge, dispositions, and performances required for teachers. INTASC has developed specific standards that address English language arts teachers. The principles include the following:

Standard One: Subject Matter
Standard Two: Student Learning
Standard Three: Diverse Learners
Standard Four: Instructional Strategies
Standard Five: Learning Environment
Standard Six: Communication
Standard Seven: Planning Instruction
Standard Eight: Assessment
Standard Nine: Reflection and Professional Development
Standard Ten: Collaboration, Ethics, and Relationships

INTASC requires performance assessments in which teachers demonstrate their competencies in each of these standards. In the following example, we have selected one of the INTASC ELA model standards. We ask you to consider how you might make your competencies visible to others. Although you could use all of the standards as a guide for creating a teaching portfolio or other form of demonstrating your competencies as a teacher, we will concentrate on Standard 7 (Planning) for this particular exercise. The following excerpt of Principle 7 was taken from the Council of Chief State School Officers Web site.

INTASC Principle Seven: Planning Instruction

Principle #7: The teacher plans instruction based upon knowledge of subject matter, students, the community, and curriculum goals.

Knowledge
- The teacher understands learning theory, subject matter, curriculum development, and student development and knows how to use this knowledge in planning instruction to meet curriculum goals.
- The teacher knows how to take contextual considerations (instructional materials, individual student interests, needs, and aptitudes, and community resources) into account in planning instruction that creates an effective bridge between curriculum goals and students' experiences.
- The teacher knows when and how to adjust plans based on student responses and other contingencies.

Dispositions
- The teacher values both long-term and short-term planning.
- The teacher believes that plans must always be open to adjustment and revision based on student needs and changing circumstances.
- The teacher values planning as a collegial activity.

Performances
- As an individual and a member of a team, the teacher selects and creates learning experiences that are appropriate for curriculum goals, relevant to learners, and based upon principles of effective instruction (e.g., that activate students' prior knowledge, anticipate preconceptions, encourage exploration and problem solving, and build new skills on those previously acquired).
- The teacher plans for learning opportunities that recognize and address variation in learning styles and performance modes.
- The teacher creates lessons and activities that operate at multiple levels to meet the developmental and individual needs of diverse learners and help each progress.
- The teacher creates short-range and long-term plans that are linked to student needs and performance, and adapts the plans to ensure and capitalize on student progress and motivation.
- The teacher responds to unanticipated sources of input, evaluates plans in relation to short- and long-range goals, and systematically adjusts plans to meet student needs and enhance learning.

As you read over these principles and standards, consider what you could do to demonstrate your emerging competency in planning instructional lessons and units. Consider what artifacts (print, media, electronic) from your teaching notebook, your fieldwork journal, or other sources might provide evidence of your competency in instructional planning for the diverse needs of your middle school learners. Remember that, according to the INTASC standards, evidence of planning goes well beyond the formal and informal written plans we have discussed in this chapter. Although it will surely be important to include samples of exemplary instructional plans and teaching materials in your portfolio, you might consider other evidence of your planning as well. For example, the "adolescent portrait" and the description of your teaching context that you were asked to create earlier in this chapter could serve as evidence of your ability to look beyond surface details in planning for the unique needs of all of your students within their particular community and school.

As you continue through the other chapters of this book, it's a good idea to refer continually to the INTASC standards in developing your teaching portfolio.

REFERENCES

Armstrong, W. H. (2001). *Sounder.* New York: Harper Trade.
Avi. (1998). *Nothing but the truth.* Magnolia, MA: Peter Smith Publisher.
Barbieri, M. (1995). *Sounds from the heart: Learning to listen to girls.* Portsmouth, NH: Heinemann.
Frank, Anne. (2000). *Anne Frank: The diary of a young girl.* Hudson, MA: Pathways Publishing.
Gardner, H. (1999). *Frames of mind. The theory of multiple intelligences.* New York: Basic Books.
Gardner, H. (2000). *Intelligence reframed: Multiple intelligences for the 21st century.* New York: Basic Books.
Gee, J. P. (1999). *Social linguistics and literacies: Ideology in discourse.* Bristol, PA: Taylor and Francis.
Hemingway, E. (1999). *The old man and the sea.* Broomall, PA: Chelsea House Publishers.
Interstate New Teacher and Support Consortium Principles. Retrieved August 1, 2001, from the World Wide Web: *http://www.ccsso.org/corestan.html*
Lowry, L. (2002). *The giver.* St. Paul, MN: EMC/Paradigm Publishing.
Luke, A. (1988). *Literacy, textbooks and ideology: Postwar literacy instruction and the mythology of Dick and Jane.* Bristol, PA: Taylor & Francis.
Stevenson, C., & Carr, J. (1993). *Integrated studies in the middle grades: Dancing through walls.* New York: Teachers College Press.
Vacca, R. T., & Vacca, J. L. (1998). *Content area reading: Literacy and learning across the curriculum.* Reading, MA: Addison-Wesley.
Wakatsuki Houston, J. (2000). *Farewell to Manzanar.* Austin, TX: Holt, Reinhart & Winston.
Warren, A. (1998). *Orphan train rider: One boy's true story.* New York: Houghton Mifflin.
Yep, L. (1999). *Dragonwings.* Hudson, MA: Pathways Publishing.

RESOURCES

Print

Alvermann, D., Hinchman, K., & Moore, D. (2000). *Reconceptualizing the literacies of adolescents' lives.* Hillsdale, NJ: Lawrence Erlbaum.

Alvermann, D., & Phelps, S. (1997). *Content reading and literacy: Succeeding in today's diverse classrooms.* Needham Heights, MA: Allyn and Bacon.

Atwell, N. (1987). *In the middle: Writing, reading, and learning with adolescents.* Portsmouth, NH: Heinemann.

Five, C. L., & Dionisio, M. (1995). *Bridging the gap: Integrating curriculum in upper elementary and middle schools.* Portsmouth, NH: Heinemann.

Moore, D., & Alvermann, D. (2000). *Struggling adolescent readers: A collection of teaching strategies.* Newark, DE: International Reading Association.

Reif, L. (1992). *Seeking diversity: Language arts with adolescents.* Portsmouth, NH: Heinemann.

Schurr, S., Lewis, S., LaMorte, K., & Shewey, K. (1996). *Signaling student success: Thematic learning stations and integrated units.* Columbus, OH: National Middle School Association.

Stover, L. (1996). *Young adult literature: The heart of the middle school curriculum.* Portsmouth, NH: Heinemann.

Tchudi, S., & Mitchell, D. (1989). *Explorations in the teaching of English.* New York: HarperCollins.

Vars, G. (1993). *Interdisciplinary teaming in the middle grades: Why and how.* Columbus, OH: NMSA.

Electronic

Middle Grades Middle School Network. The National Association of Elementary Principals sponsors this site, which provides links to middle grade resources.

http://www.naesp.org/SpecialProjects/mgn.htm

Project Zero Web Site. This site contains information on the theory of multiple intelligences by Howard Gardner and includes some excerpts from *The Project Zero Classroom: New Approaches to Understanding,* a publication based on Project Zero's 1996 Summer Institute presentations.

http://www.pz.harvard.edu/sumit/MISUMIT.HTM

***RTE*'s List of E-mail Discussion Groups.** The editorial staff of the journal *Research in Teaching English (RTE)* has compiled a listing of educational discussion listservs. You can subscribe to one that interests you by clicking on the highlighted address and following the instructions provided at this Web site.

http://www.ncte.org/rte/rtediscuss.html

Teaching Ideas at the NCTE Web Site. This site links to teaching ideas selected from NCTE publications or submitted directly by teachers. Teachers share ideas, strategies, problems, solutions to problems, and in the process create a rich resource for the community at large.

http://www.ncte.org/teach?

chapter 4

Including Middle School Learners With Disabilities

Written With Teresa Taber, *Purdue University*

GUIDING QUESTIONS

1. Who are the support personnel in the middle school to assist you and your students?
2. How do you adapt instruction to support each of the learners in your classroom?
3. How might you tap your students' social, physical, and academic competencies to support their peers?

A CASE FOR CONSIDERATION

Mr. Carlisle's First Days

Steve Carlisle is a new eighth-grade language arts teacher at Adams Middle School. He had completed a successful student teaching semester with ninth-grade students and feels well prepared for teaching middle school language arts.

During the orientation week, he is given his class roster and for the first time reviews the names of the 125 students he will teach each day. His room is ready. He has set up the desks in working groups of six; he has created a conference area in one corner and a cozy author's circle in the other. He bought an attractive large tray to place on the shelf by the door where students will place their written masterpieces. As his first day of teaching approaches, he feels ready and excited.

Following his first day of school, Mr. Carlisle discovers his classes are not what he envisioned. Almost immediately he realizes that his groupings of desks, although pedagogically sound, makes his room wheelchair inaccessible. He notes that two of his students seem inappropriately mobile. He suspects that one is not able to read. He feels overwhelmed and unprepared.

Steve doesn't want to appear incompetent on his first day, and besides, as a newcomer to the community and school, he has no idea where to turn for help. He leaves school that day less excited for the second day to begin and completely unsure of his ability to teach all the learners in his classroom.

Ms. Perkins, the special education teacher, approaches Steve in the teacher's lounge the next morning. She asks him about his first day and mentions that she will stop by after school to give him copies of the instructional objectives for the students with disabilities who are in his classes and to answer any questions he might have about particular students. Mr. Carlisle realizes he doesn't even know what questions to ask. He doesn't know where to begin. He doesn't want to appear incompetent to Ms. Perkins or the other teachers, but he has no idea what to do to support these students or how to teach them language arts.

FOR DISCUSSION

- What are the main issues that Mr. Carlisle will need to address?
- What role should the special education teacher take in Mr. Carlisle's classroom?
- What role should Mr. Carlisle take in this situation?

Teachers entering the classroom for the first time often do so with a romanticized idea of the students they will teach, the layout of their room, and the specific methods they will use to teach their students. Mr. Carlisle is not unusual, and neither is his teaching situation. Teachers are expected to teach a variety of students in their classes. Today's classrooms consist of students with various learning needs from various backgrounds and cultures. This includes students with disabilities. In Mr. Carlisle's case, three of his students have a learning disability, one has mental retardation, and one has a physical disability.

Who are these students with disabilities? Because of their disabilities, these students learn or behave in ways that may be significantly different from the majority of students in a class. These students may experience learning disabilities, behavior disorders, physical or sensory disabilities, autism, and/or mental retardation. Although these students typically require some level of support or modification in order to learn, they can learn. Teaching these students is the responsibility of all teachers in a building. This chapter will include an extended Literacy Lesson focused on Mr. Carlisle. We will follow Steve Carlisle as he learns how to support all of the learners in his classroom. Through his experiences, we'll learn where to find support and how to adapt instruction for our students with disabilities.

Teaching students with disabilities in regular education classrooms is becoming more common across the country as school administrators and teachers begin implementing components of the law that govern the education of students with disabilities. This law, known as the Individuals with Disabilities Education Act (IDEA), mandates that students with disabilities be taught in the least restrictive environment (LRE) with maximum opportunities to be educated alongside their nondisabled peers (IDEA, 1997). Specifically, this law (see *www.nichcy.org*) states that the LRE is

> the presumption that children with disabilities are most appropriately educated with their nondisabled peers and that special classes, separate schooling, or other removal of children with disabilities from the regular educational environment occurs only when the nature or severity of the disability of a child is such that education in regular classes with the use of supplementary aids and services cannot be achieved satisfactorily.

In other words, the law begins with the assumption that all students with disabilities are members of regular education classes. Students with disabilities may be removed from the regular education classroom and taught in other school or community settings only when an Individual Education Program committee (of which regular education teachers are members) documents and determines that a student's educational goals and objectives cannot be achieved satisfactorily, even with the use of modifications.

INDIVIDUALIZED EDUCATIONAL PROGRAM

All students with a disability who receive special education services must have an Individual Education Program (IEP). This legal document and the information it contains serve as the framework for the provision of instruction to a student with a disability. The IEP contains information regarding:

- a student's academic, social, behavioral, and communication strengths and weaknesses
- long-term annual goals
- measurable, short-term instructional objectives
- the provision of related services such as speech therapy or occupational therapy
- the frequency of these services
- a program of study and transition plan if the student is age 14 or older
- the settings in which the student will receive instruction in the LRE
- a description of the modifications needed and considered

An IEP is written on an annual basis and includes input from members of an IEP committee. Members of an IEP committee include: the parents of the child with a disability, at least one regular education teacher, at least one special education teacher, a representative of the local education agency, and, whenever appropriate, the child with a disability.

In Literacy Lesson 4–1, you'll see how committee members determine what modifications and adaptations might best serve two students as they move from seventh grade to eighth grade.

Literacy Lesson 4-1

IEP Meetings for Eighth-Grade Educational Placements

Jason

During an IEP meeting at Adams Middle School last spring, the committee considered LRE placement options for Jason, a student with a reading comprehension learning disability. Members of his IEP committee noted that Jason had been following the regular education program for seventh graders with modifications made to accommodate his specific learning needs. Ms. Robbins, the seventh-grade English language arts teacher, began the IEP meeting by stating that Jason had been successful in her class. She explained the modifications that worked well for Jason previously. Specifically, she recommended that next year's English teacher adapt written assignments specifically regarding length requirements and standards for assessments for Jason. In addition, she noted that his eighth-grade teacher would need to evaluate all textual materials to determine difficulty level and make alternative selections when necessary. In addition, Jason would require additional time for reading assignments. As a result of these suggestions, members of the IEP committee confirmed that the LRE for Jason to learn English language arts would be Mr. Carlisle's eighth-grade English class during the next school year.

Beth

In another IEP meeting, the committee considered educational options for Beth, a student with severe mental retardation and physical disabilities. Because Beth would be in the eighth grade next year, the IEP committee considered her placement in eighth-grade English class to address her specific educational objectives. Her IEP objectives included learning to read color words and numbers to 20, learning to write these same words, and learning to compose sentences with at least 4 words. After reviewing each of her IEP objectives and considering a variety of modifications, the IEP committee determined that to meet her educational needs, an eighth-grade English class would be a more restrictive placement for Beth. Instead, instruction in a mix of special and regular education classes were identified as the LRE that would provide maximum opportunities for her to be educated alongside her nondisabled peers. Beth would not be in Mr. Carlisle's class.

Whereas instruction in the LRE is legally mandated, the philosophy of inclusion is not. However, components of the inclusion ideal should be incorporated to the greatest extent possible into the provision of instruction to students with disabilities. Implementing inclusive practices involves ensuring that students with disabilities (a) are members of chronologically age-appropriate grades and classes, (b) attend the same schools as their siblings and the other children in their neighborhood, (c) receive support as needed across school and community settings, and (d) are actively engaged in learning within the context of classroom activities.

As Mr. Carlisle attempted to implement inclusive practices, he knew he would need support. He understood that he needed to tap the expertise of each of his students, but he didn't know how to begin. In Literacy Lesson 4–2, Mr. Carlisle begins the process of envisioning a more inclusive pedagogy.

Literacy Lesson 4-2

Talking With the Special Education Teacher

When Steve Carlisle and June Perkins meet after school, the new English teacher has many questions about his students with disabilities and how best to teach them.

Steve: Hi, June. I'm really glad we are finally able to sit down together and discuss the needs of the students with disabilities in my classes. The first thing I need to know is who are the specific students with disabilities who have IEP objectives?

June: Well, Steve, at the moment you have five students with disabilities taking eighth-grade English.

Steve: At the moment?

June: Yes. There's a possibility one more student with a disability will be assigned to your class after her IEP meeting next week.

Steve: Oh, that's right. Emily. I received notification last week of her IEP meeting. I'll be there. So, tell me about the students with disabilities who are in my class already.

June: The first three, Jason, Todd, and Maria, each have a learning disability, and the disability is different for each one. Jason experiences significant problems with reading comprehension. Todd's is primarily in math; however, he demonstrates difficulties in organizational skills. Maria experiences significant impediments in note taking and organizational skills.

    Your fourth student, Larry, has mental retardation and is working on his IEP objectives within the context of the eighth-grade English curriculum. Primarily, he is learning to read functional reading materials like grocery labels and street maps that will help lead to independent living. Your fifth student is Paul and, as you already know, he is legally blind and uses a guide dog to get around the building.

Steve: Wow, I don't know how I'm going to do this. I have to tell you I feel overwhelmed and unprepared. I have no idea what to do. I've had no training!

June: Not to worry. That's why I'm here. As the special education teacher, I go wherever my students are being served. In this case, your classroom is where they are receiving educational services. I will be meeting regularly with you to develop modifications for each of these students.

Steve: Will you also be helping me teach each day?

June: At the moment, no. The IEP committee decided that none of these students require daily direct one-on-one support from a second adult while in this class. However, I will make frequent visits to your class to help you get started teaching, and I promise that I will provide support to you and the students throughout the year. Sometimes it will be in the form of collaborative meetings, and sometimes it will require me coming into your class to work with students. I'll help you select appropriate materials and adapt instruction to support these students.

Steve: That's a relief. But, where do I start?

June: Let's take a look at the specific modifications identified by the IEP committees last spring for each of these students, and I'll give you some ideas of how these may be implemented. When we meet next week for Emily's IEP meeting, you'll see how placements and modifications are decided. In the meantime, I will place a list of modifications used in the past with students in your box for you to review before the meeting.

Mr. Carlisle and Ms. Perkins spend the next hour reviewing specific modifications for his students and sharing ideas for how the modifications can be implemented on a regular basis.

An IEP committee typically meets once a year to review a student's previous educational progress and develop new instructional goals and objectives. Although the special education teacher usually leads the IEP meeting, all members are expected to participate actively in discussions and decision making. What happens in a typical meeting? Let's consider the example in Literacy Lesson 4–3. Your Fieldwork Journal 4–1 will help you identify support personnel in your school.

Literacy Lesson 4-3

Emily's Plan

At Adams Middle School, as Emily's IEP meeting begins, Ms. Perkins introduces each member. In addition to Ms. Perkins, the special education teacher, those in attendance include Mr. Carlisle (the regular education teacher), Mr. and Mrs. Arnold (Emily's parents), Emily, the physical therapist, the speech and language pathologist, and the school counselor. Following introductions, Ms. Perkins reviews Emily's current level of functioning, which includes her strengths and weaknesses in the areas of academic, social, motor, and communication skills.

During the review of Emily's current level of functioning, Mr. Carlisle learns that Emily is a 13-year-old student with cerebral palsy who uses a wheelchair. According to her test scores, previous educational progress, and teacher and parent observations, Emily has numerous academic and social strengths. She has participated in a grade-level curriculum for her entire school career and plans to attend college one day. Her areas of weakness are her motor and communication skills. In order to provide maximum opportunities for Emily to be educated alongside her nondisabled peers, modifications were provided to accommodate her motor and communication needs in previous years.

As Emily's IEP meeting progresses, Ms. Perkins leads the team through the decision-making process for determining Emily's instructional goals and objectives, needed modifications and supports, educational placements in the LRE, additional settings or activities that would provide Emily with opportunities for interaction with nondisabled peers, and ways to evaluate her performance on IEP objectives.

The IEP committee identifies six objectives. In addition to continuing her education in regular academic subject areas over the next school year, Emily's teachers will work with her on (a) improving oral communication skills, (b) enhancing written expression skills (which include addressing her need for improvement in fine motor coordination), (c) decreasing the time it takes for her to transition between classes, (d) improving her dressing skills, (e) using public forms of transportation, and (f) increasing her skills in using a motorized wheelchair.

While each objective is being identified, Steve Carlisle begins thinking about the types of modifications that might support Emily in his class to work on each objective. He notes that he will need to think about modifications for oral and written communication skills. He writes a note to talk to June about how to adapt writing utensils and perhaps gain more access to the computer. He also jots down that he will need to think about his room arrangement and seating chart to make Emily feel comfortable and competent in maneuvering around his room from writing conference center to the group sharing area.

As you see from Literary Lesson 4–3, an IEP committee must make decisions concerning what, where, and how instruction will take place. Students with disabilities benefit both educationally and socially from receiving instruction with their nondisabled peers in a variety of school and community settings. In order to receive this benefit, the IEP committee must consider several questions:

- What is the student's current level of performance?
- What are the student's areas of strength and weakness?
- How does the student's disability interfere with academic and social learning and with communication, motor, behavioral, and social skills?

When these questions are being answered, members of the IEP committee also review student test scores and data that report the student's previous progress. By the time a student is in middle school, the committee also addresses the question, "What recommendations need to be made in order to facilitate this student's transition from school to post-school activities?"

The IEP team determines what objectives can be taught in regular education classes without modifications, and which objectives or set of objectives may require modifications and supports to teach in regular education classes? Emily, for example, may not need modifications in the writing assignments in her eighth-grade class, but she may need more access to computers to aid in her written communication skills. She may need modifications in oral activities to accommodate her speech difficulties while stretching her to expand her competencies in this area.

Your Fieldwork Journal 4-1

Learning From Support Personnel

Teaching all middle school students is the responsibility of all teachers in a building. Yet, you may feel a little like Steve Carlisle and not know how to get started or who is in your building to support you and your students. It would be helpful to find out who the support personnel are and how they can assist you and your students. Select a teacher, administrator, or support service provider at a local middle school and find out more about how they work with each other to provide for the needs of all middle school learners. Here is a list of questions to begin your interview:

1. Do all students with disabilities participate in inclusive settings in this school?
2. How does the school administration work with teachers to ensure an appropriate caseload for each teacher? To ensure that a single teacher is not assigned an overwhelming number of students with disabilities? Who makes sure the number of students with disabilities is considered to be in "natural proportion"?
3. What do you think is the most effective and appropriate educational model for serving students who experience various disabilities?
4. Who provides guidance to regular education teachers in the areas of: data collection, behavior management, instructional strategies, and social skills development?

You may want to come up with two or three more questions to learn more about the particular responsibilities of the person you are interviewing: administrator, special education teacher, related service provider, or regular education teacher.

After you have completed your interview, it may be valuable to share with your teaching colleagues what you have learned.

Once you know who your support personnel are and which of your students have IEPs, you will be ready to begin the process to actively engage the students in literacy learning within the context of classroom activities.

MODIFICATIONS

The type of modification developed for a student depends on the goal of instruction. Modifications considered for students should be age-appropriate and allow for increasing amounts of independent interactions with nondisabled peers. For example, Emily, a 13-year-old student with poor fine motor coordination, may use a large grip or Velcro strap to hold a pencil instead of being required to use the large pencils and crayons typically used by elementary-age children when writing. The ability to write independently would allow Emily to work on writing projects with her peers without having to rely on an adult or peer to write for her.

Modifications generally fall into four categories: activity modifications, instructional modifications, material modifications, and environmental modifications. Modifications may be made to accommodate learning, cognitive, behavioral, physical, and/or sensory deficits.

Activity Modifications

These changes are made to an activity to allow for active student participation. Activity modifications may include allowing a student who is nonverbal to respond by using a switch to activate a computer or an augmentative communication device. Partial participation (allowing students to participate in an activity to their maximum level, as opposed to denying access to the activity because the student could not complete the activity) would also be considered an appropriate activity modification.

Instructional Modifications

These require a change in the delivery of instruction. A teacher may modify instruction by using large and small group instruction along with peer-mediated and individualized instruction. The delivery of instruction may also be modified by shortening the length of a lesson and/or decreasing the rate at which instruction is delivered. A teacher may also use a simpler vocabulary during instruction, use visuals, and provide a student with additional opportunities to practice learned skills within and across lessons. To assist with note taking, the teacher may provide copies of the overheads and class notes, or class discussions could be recorded.

Materials Modifications

Materials may be modified in several ways to allow student learning and participation to occur. Modifying the format of materials such as using real objects and/or manipulatives instead of pictures, will adjust the cognitive demand and make the materials more functional and concrete for the student. Teachers may also alter the motor or sensory requirements of materials by changing their size, highlighting specific parts, and using a computer or other assistive technology to access materials. If a student is unable to use textual materials through traditional means, worksheets, handouts, and tests may be adapted to include more spacing, fewer items, and bold or highlighted directions and key concepts.

Environmental Modifications

> Considering the needs of Jason, Todd, Larry, Maria, Paul, and Emily, what are some considerations for their learning that may require modifications? What types of modifications might be needed for each student?

These modifications may be made to accommodate student behaviors and physical and sensory needs. Teachers may use visual daily schedules for a student who is working on self-management skills, proximity seating for a student who uses a wheelchair in order to sit with his/her peers, or lamps instead of overhead lighting to reduce the glare for a student with a visual impairment.

What forms might these modifications take for an individual student? Mr. Carlisle would need to make several modifications to support Emily. Once Emily's IEP objectives were identified, for example, the IEP committee began discussing the modifications necessary to ensure that Emily learns each objective and can actively participate in each of her classes. The IEP committee considers objectives and modifications appropriate for Emily to actively participate in class activities and master each of her specific objectives beyond the scope of Mr. Carlisle's class. Whereas Steve Carlisle needs to be aware of and support all of Emily's objectives and modifications, he will attend to those that specifically address oral and written competencies. Here are two objectives that Mr. Carlisle will need to be aware of, monitor, and support.

> *Objective 1:* When presented with an opportunity to engage in conversation during lunch and in classes, Emily will ask a question to engage a listener in a conversation during 75% of opportunities for 3 consecutive weeks.

Modification: Emily will learn to use an electronic augmentative communication device that is preprogrammed with age-appropriate vocabulary enabling her to ask desired questions to others and engage in conversations.

Objective 2: During writing exercises, Emily will write sentences and paragraphs following an outline writing at least three sentences per day for 6 consecutive weeks.

Modification(s): Emily will use a laptop computer with a modified keyboard and switch to engage in writing activities in her classes.

The IEP committee identified a few additional modifications that would enable Emily to become a more active participant in her classes. These modifications included having a table instead of a desk in each of her classrooms to accommodate her wheelchair and use of a laptop, widening the aisles of desks in classes, providing a copy of the lecture notes or allowing tape recording of lectures, and allowing Emily to take tests either with her communication device or on the computer.

Since Mr. Carlisle's class is divided into general daily activities, corresponding modifications for each activity are indicated per IEP objective and her general class participation needs. According to a schedule analysis, in order to accommodate her writing IEP objective, Emily will require a material (M) modification during all activities in which writing is required. In Emily's case, use of a laptop computer for writing and either lecture note copies or a tape recording of lectures would be the modifications implemented. To address her IEP objective of engaging in conversations, the modifications would include a material modification (an augmentative communication device), an environmental (E) modification (widening the aisles to navigate her wheelchair closer to her peers or teacher), and possibly an instructional (I) modification in which students would break into small groups for discussion.

Once Emily's IEP team identifies the modifications she will require to participate actively in her classes, members then address the issue of supports. In other words, will Emily require a second adult to assist her in her classes? Do the academic and special education teachers need to consult regularly to develop modifications? If so, how often? Will peers be used to support Emily in her classes?

SUPPORTS

In order to ensure the effectiveness of instruction in the LRE, various levels of support may be implemented. A student may require different types of support for different IEP objectives and different settings. Even within a single setting, the type of support may change over time or incorporate various types. Supports available to a student include consultative support, collaborative teaching, individual support, and peer support.

Consultative Support

This kind of support involves the special education teacher jointly planning with the regular education teacher in determining the need for modifications for a student. Planning time may be regularly scheduled, or teachers may meet more informally during lunch or on an as-needed basis. With this level of support, the special education teacher is not present in the classroom daily. However, the special education teacher maintains regular contact with students as specified by the IEP. For example, Mr. Carlisle and Ms. Perkins meet every Tuesday morning during their second period planning time to review the next week's lesson plan, identify the IEP objectives that will be addressed for the students who are served in the regular education class, and discuss needed modifications for each student.

Collaborative Teaching

This is also known as *co-teaching* and involves settings in which the regular and special education teacher share the responsibility for providing instruction to all students during a segment. Formal planning occurs regularly throughout the school year. This planning includes jointly developing lesson plans and modifications for all students in the class. Schools frequently provide this type of support by reassigning a teacher from an existing special education class to rotate between regular education classes throughout the day. For example, Mrs. Fenske, another special education teacher, collaboratively teaches with Mr. Wilson during the first 2 hours of each day in their math and language arts classes. During the 4th and 5th hours, Mrs. Fenske collaboratively teaches with Mrs. Johnson during language arts and social studies.

Individual Support

This kind of support involves providing one-on-one support to a particular student so he or she can participate in a specific setting. Support may be required for academic, behavioral, and/or physical reasons. Although the primary responsibility is to work individually with the student with a disability, the support person should do this within the context of small group activities with nondisabled students to prevent isolation from the rest of the class. For example, Mr. Carlisle provides individual support for Jason during individualized reading time. Since Jason has difficulty with reading, Ms. Perkins assists him at times in actively participating, sometimes partially, in the same physical setting in group reading activities in which his classmates are participating. In addition, Mr. Carlisle works with Jason's classmates in demonstrating supports they can provide. Occasionally, while Jason is being supported by his peers or independently participating, Ms. Perkins assists other students or the classroom teacher. Under this type of support, related service professionals (e.g., speech and language pathologist, occupational therapist, physical therapist) are frequently scheduled to provide services to particular students while participating in general education settings. While providing support to the classroom teacher, related service providers are often able to serve several students on their caseload simultaneously within the regular education classroom.

Peer Support

This kind of support is vitally important and requires delicate support from significant adults to do it well. Peer support is often used in conjunction with other models of support. Although never a substitute for the teacher, peers assist the student with a disability in a variety of ways. In academic settings, peers guide and encourage involvement in various components of lessons and materials. Within instructional formats, they can provide opportunities to practice skills. Peers also encourage students in the use of their augmentative communication systems and assist in transitions from one school setting to another.

In order for the student with a disability to engage in a structured manner with classmates and for the nondisabled students to share the responsibility of providing support, peers should be rotated on a regular basis. Teachers may also facilitate peer relationships by reformatting the manner in which information is presented in their classes. Use of hands-on, experiential learning and heterogeneous small groups tend to foster peer collaboration and the development of peer relationships. The student with a disability is provided with the same materials as other students in a class (e.g., workbooks, handouts, notebooks, supplies) and is expected to participate actively in class activities. Peer supports are often assigned to students not only in classroom settings but also in the school cafeteria, field trips, and after-school activities.

> What practical considerations come to mind when you think about providing supports for students like Jason, Larry, Todd, Maria, Paul, and Emily? In what ways might Jason, Larry, Todd, Paul, Maria, and Emily support their peers?

Supports are often modified over time to lead toward independence. As the IEP meeting continues for Emily, for example, committee members discuss whether Emily requires additional support during her school day. All members agree that peer support should be used during all of her classes as well as during some of the transitions between classes. Because Emily demonstrates significant motor and communication challenges, the team decides that for the first 3 weeks, individual supports will be provided in each of her classes. After the first 3 weeks, support will be shifted to consultative. In her social studies class, a co-teaching (collaborative) model will be used.

Because the time it takes Emily to transition between classes is a concern, the location of her classes is an issue. Team members want to ensure that Emily's classes are located in proximity to her previous classes. Thus, the time it will take for her to move between classes should be decreased. Because at least two teachers in each academic area teach eighth graders, the team chooses between classes in each academic area and provides Emily with a schedule that accommodates her needs.

> How can you evaluate whether supports and modifications you have initiated are actually supporting your students?

When a student's IEP indicates that he or she needs to learn skills that cannot be taught in a regular education class, even with the use of modifications and supports, the committee must consider another step in the LRE decision-making process. In which special education or community settings will IEP objectives be taught?

INTERACTION WITH PEERS

When students receive instruction in settings other than the regular education classroom, the IEP committee must consider another question, "What additional settings or activities will provide opportunities for interaction with nondisabled peers?" Opportunities for interaction may occur during lunch, recess/break, assemblies, dances, field trips, plays, school programs, sporting events, clubs, extracurricular activities, homeroom, hallways, walking together between and to classes, and transportation to and from school and activities.

In Emily's case, the IEP committee identifies transportation to and from school and activities as an additional opportunity for her to interact with her nondisabled peers. Because Emily uses a wheelchair, a school bus equipped with a lift is required. Although the only buses with lifts are mini-buses, the school system agrees to use one of these buses to transport Emily and several of her neighborhood peers to and from school and other activities. Emily's committee decides that she should participate in community-based instruction during the assemblies/clubs/computer period two times per week to address the objectives on the use of public transportation and navigating her wheelchair in a variety of settings. On the 3 days she remains in the school building, she would meet with the drama club on club day and receive instruction in computer class.

As a means of encouraging peer interactions, some schools implement a peer support system in which students without disabilities are paired with students with disabilities for extracurricular and integrated activities throughout the school (e.g., clubs, breaks, homeroom, lunch, athletic practice, band). Typically, students with disabilities would then be included in general education classes that their peer support partners attend. In doing so, students with disabilities have access to an immediate support network for social interactions and academic assistance.

In Literacy Lesson 4–4, we'll see Steve planning for Emily and the other students in his classes.

Literacy Lesson 4–4

Providing Social and Academic Assistance

Steve Carlisle learns early in the year that many of his students do not seem connected to literature in ways he would like. In fact, many enter the room reporting, "I hate reading." He wants to create a learning opportunity that engages all his students in reading and motivates interaction with the texts in meaningful ways. He also wants to create opportunities for all students to work together, especially early in the year so they learn to depend upon each other for social and academic support. Since all teachers have been asked to organize some sort of mini-showcase for the upcoming Parents' Night, Steve decides to organize and videotape students reading as a sort of "Beatnik Café." He knows from his team meetings that his students are studying the 1950s in an exploration strand for another class. Dramatic readings with accompanying music might be just the thing to engage students, and they can work collaboratively to create the stage, organize music, and set the whole thing in motion. His eighth graders will have a real audience of parents and siblings for their performances.

"Will any students have difficulty in selecting and presenting poetry and short stories?" Steve asks himself. Clearly, yes. But this activity accommodates the vast range of interests and abilities in each of his classes. He decides to make available difficult and more accessible reading materials. Length of reading materials can be equally as varied. He builds in peer support for Emily by inviting students to read with partners and small groups. He already has planned to build in support for Jason by inviting him to serve as video technician. Although he will be challenged by the oral reading, Jason can lend expertise in videotaping. Steve realizes that he needs to build in modifications for Todd and

Maria, who demonstrate difficulties in organizational skills. He designs a step-by-step guide to help them select materials, rehearse in the company of their peers, and be ready to perform for the video camera. Actually, he knows that this early in the year all students will benefit from such support structures. For Larry, who has mental retardation and is working on his IEP objectives within the context of his eighth-grade English curriculum, and for Paul, who is legally blind, he will need to order special textual materials from interlibrary loan.

Steve thinks about the ways in which this Beatnik Café can tap students' interest and expertise. He knows he can count on Larry to run the lights. Emily, who loves to tell him about her CD collection, with peer support can be part of the group that organizes the music. Several students will surely sign up to bring in dark glasses, props, and any other costumes or visual materials, he thinks. Steve starts to sketch out ways to organize the event and to plan ways to solicit his students' counsel in designing this dramatic event.

Just as Steve Carlisle plans to support the students in his classroom, you'll want to think about the ways that you can build in support for your students.

CONSIDERATIONS FOR SUPPORTING EACH LEARNER IN THE MIDDLE SCHOOL CLASSROOM

- **Middle school students need positive social interactions with peers and adults.**
  - In what ways might peers, support personnel, parents, and/or community members contribute to students' learning experiences?
  - How do we set up supports that tap the expertise of each learner?
- **Middle school students need physical activities to develop and showcase their competencies.**
  - When and how do we infuse nonlinguistic opportunities to support learning?
  - What are some alternatives to paper-and-pencil activities and exams?
- **Middle school students need opportunities for self-definition, creative expression, and a sense of competence and achievement in their learning experiences.**
  - How might a teacher build in opportunities for students to support their peers?
  - How do we design age-appropriate modifications to support the learning of each student?
  - How do we set high standards for performance that are reachable for individual students?
- **Middle school students need opportunities that promote meaningful participation in families, school, and the larger world.**
  - How might each student receive positive recognition from peers or adults?
  - How do we make learning activities real and relevant to students' lives within and beyond the classroom?
  - How might students contribute to social and academic activities within and beyond the classroom?

As you think about your own planning and implementing, you will want to plan for all students in your classroom. Once you know your students and the support people in your building, you can better implement literacy learning activities that will meet the needs of your students. Your Fieldwork Journal 4–2 offers some practice in this critical area.

Your Fieldwork Journal 4-2

Adapting Instruction to Support All Learners

We'd like you to think about planning a lesson in terms of some students you met in this chapter. You already know a lot about Emily's disabilities but little about her interests. That is perhaps too often the case for students who are "labeled." Be certain to know your middle school students well beyond any academic or behavioral labels.

Emily

Emily loves music. Although she does not sing, she has an extensive CD and video collection of music, including pop, classical, country, and Latin. Emily is a serious student who plans to attend college to prepare for a career in music history. Because of her inattentiveness to dress and at times hygiene, Emily has a difficult time making friends. She is consciously aware of this need and has been making tremendous progress with the help of her parents and teachers. She works closely with an eighth-grade peer named Ronda who has helped her to integrate into lunch hour social activities. Ronda has also signed them both up for Mr. Carlisle's drama club to serve on the props and make-up crew.

Larry

Larry is a 13-year-old young man who loves to be the center of attention. He has a pleasing personality, and his teachers and peers enjoy being around him. However, at times, Larry doesn't know when to stop seeking attention. He is occasionally reinforced when others laugh at what he says, and so he frequently makes comments or repeats jokes when they are no longer funny. In addition, he will often interrupt conversations between others to gain attention. This can be annoying to others, but since Larry tries so hard to be pleasing to others, his teachers and peers refrain from correcting him.

Academically, Larry is working on a variety of skills. Because Larry experiences a moderate level of mental retardation, his academic objectives are focused learning and maintaining functional skills that will increase his independence as he gets older. Presently, he can recognize and read approximately 120 functional sight words and is now beginning to focus on reading those words in context, such as reading the movie section of a newspaper, washing instructions on the labels of garments, the TV program guide, and basic instructions for completing vocational tasks. Some of his other learning objectives include identifying various types of jobs in the community, using a calculator to determine the costs of various items purchased at a drug store, appropriately engaging in conversations with peers and teachers (refraining from interrupting), and working cooperatively in a group with peers. Because Larry requires instruction on these skills in numerous settings for maintenance and generalization, he attends the following classes: consumer math, language arts, computers, music, physical education (PE), and two segments per day in either the community or the resource room for one-to-one instruction.

Maria

Maria is an attractive, tall, 13-year-old who has numerous friends in school and her neighborhood. Maria is easily distracted by others during lunch, PE, and group assignments and between classes. She is especially distracted by boys who often tease her and call her a "bubble-headed girl." Even her girlfriends often refer to her as an "airhead" because she often forgets where she put things, and her locker is a mess. This teasing seems to bother her at times, although she is well liked and appears to be quite popular.

In addition to being distracted, Maria is extremely unorganized and has difficulty with note taking. Both of these characteristics are a result of her learning disability and directly affect her ability to understand and retain information. Prior to being officially identified as having a learning disability, Maria had low self-esteem because she thought she was dumb. She struggled daily to keep up with assignments and frequently received low grades. When Maria was tested, results confirmed the presence of a learning disability and also indicated that she had an above average level of intelligence.

Encouraged by these results, Maria began working with a special education teacher to learn strategies that would assist her in learning. Now, as long as she receives a few modifications and reminders for note taking, she does extremely well academically.

Support for Maria, Emily, Larry, and Their classmates

As noted in Chapter 3, the classroom context is a dynamic ecosystem, and you can't ever design foolproof plans. You can, however, anticipate how a literacy lesson might unfold. You can anticipate the needs and possible obstacles that some of your students will encounter. Effective teachers consider the strengths and weaknesses of their students and plan modifications and additional supports for specific difficulties that students are likely to experience.

Use these sample questions to help you anticipate the ways in which you might need to modify lessons to support the learning of your students.

Examining Teaching Plans

1. *Goals and Objectives:* Do I need to adapt goals for particular students? Do I need to consult with support personnel to modify my lessons and make the learning opportunities more appropriate for some students?
2. *Selection of Materials:* In what ways do I consider the abilities, interests, development, and backgrounds of my students? Do I need to accommodate some students' needs through the selection of alternative materials?
3. *Activities and Procedures:* Does this lesson provide support, practice, and models? Does it support learners with time to rehearse the skills? Do I need to consult with support personnel to help me design some of the activities? Do I need to consult an IEP for any modification in these activities?

4. *Extensions and Adaptations:* What difficulties are students likely to encounter, and is further support provided? Do I need to adapt instruction for particular students? Do I need to adapt (a) the learning environment, (b) the materials, or (c) the teaching strategies to support particular learners? Are modifications age-appropriate for and respectful of the learners?
5. *Evaluation:* Do I plan for success for all students? Do I need to modify assessments for some students to match their particular learning goals for my class? Do I need to adapt (a) the testing environment, (b) the assessment materials, or (c) the assessment strategies to support particular learners?

With these questions in mind, think about some lessons you have planned or are in the process of planning for a middle school setting. Focus on one of the plans and anticipate the ways in which each of these students might need additional support. How might you need to adapt it for the unique needs and interests of Larry, Maria, and Emily? Write a modification for each.

After you have tried to anticipate the ways you might adapt your plans, it may be valuable to work through some teaching plans together with some of your peers.

In addition to designing activities and supporting student learning, regular classroom teachers like Mr. Carlisle need to collect data to evaluate how well a student is meeting her or his IEP objectives. In other words, you'll need to think about how you will measure and document student progress. Although this may seem like a tremendous job, it's what we need to do for all of our students.

EVALUATION OF STUDENT PERFORMANCE

An IEP committee must consider how student performance on IEP objectives will be evaluated. For students with disabilities, regular education teachers will need to collect data to determine if a placement is appropriate and student learning is occurring. For example, one of Emily's IEP objectives is that she ask questions and engage in conversations using her augmentative communication device. Data might be collected on the number of questions Emily asks during a class period or on the length of her conversations using her communication device.

The individual responsible for data collection is generally based on the type of support provided to a student. For example, in classes where co-teaching exists, general and special education teachers are responsible for the data, depending on who is working with the student at any given time. If a paraprofessional is present, he or she may collect data. In addition, peers may be trained to collect data on student learning. However, in classes where only one adult is present, that adult is responsible for collecting data on student learning.

When discussion turns to data collection, beginning teachers like Mr. Carlisle may express concern with two issues. First, beginning teachers may be unfamiliar with how to collect data on IEP objectives. Second, beginning teachers may not be sure they will have time to collect data. Be assured that you will not be the sole person responsible for data collection. As part of the collaborative planning process, teachers work together to collect data. You will work closely with the special education teacher and other teachers on the team. Mr. Carlisle, for example, worked with Ms. Perkins to review the data collection form with him and demonstrated during class how to record progress on Emily's, Jason's, and other students' IEP objectives.

A sample lesson plan in Mr. Carlisle's class and the data collected on four of Emily's IEP objectives are presented in Figure 4–1.

FIGURE 4–1 Lesson Plan and Data Collection Format

Lesson Plan for 8th Grade English

Student: Emily Arnold   Special Education Teacher: Ms. Perkins
Weeks of: September 4–25   Regular Education Teacher: Mr. Carlisle

Objectives   **Dates**

Wheelchair navigation
                            P
                            P
                            P
Engage in conversation
                            V
                            V
                            I
                            I
Transition between classes
                            V
                            V
                            V
                            V
Writing
                            V
                            V
                            M
                            M

Key: I   Independent
       V   Verbal Prompt   √   Correct
       M   Model   OR   X   Incorrect
       P   Physical Guidance   O   No Response
       NR   No Response

Adapted from *A Guide to the Instruction of Students with Disabilities in the Least Restrictive Environment*, by S. A. Brozovic, T. A. Taber, P. A. Alberto, & M. A. Hughes, 1999, unpublished manuscript, Atlanta: Georgia State University. Used with permission.

This combination lesson plan and data form provides teachers with a "quick glance" at what instruction will take place for the whole class, and it highlights a student's specific IEP objectives. This form could be used during collaborative planning meetings between teachers to identify lessons and modifications or individually for general planning.

Emily's IEP meeting concludes with a final review of the decisions made and all members signing the IEP document. Mr. Carlisle feels a great sense of relief following his first experience in an IEP meeting. In Literacy Lesson 4–5, you'll see a more comfortable Mr. Carlisle who now knows that he is not alone in teaching his students; rather, he is part of a team of educators who is responsible for the education of all students in the school.

Literacy Lesson 4-5

A Day in Mr. Carlisle's Class

After three months in his first teaching job, Mr. Carlisle doesn't exactly feel like a pro, but he feels more confident in his abilities to support all of the students in his class. His class is running smoothly and is much more organized now than during the first few weeks. No longer does he panic when a student experiences difficulty in learning. Every week, he and Ms. Perkins meet to review student progress and plan for modifications that might be needed during lessons over the next week. In addition, Ms. Perkins helps in the brainstorming process for identifying modifications that may benefit students without disabilities who may be struggling with the curriculum material.

Over the past week, students began studying about the Middle Ages in social studies and science class. As part of a thematic unit, activities that incorporate the Middle Ages theme are addressed in the eighth-grade English class. Mr. Carlisle decides to work on his students' research and writing skills. In prior weeks, students learned to use the Internet to locate information about topics of interest in addition to using the library to locate books. Today's activity is for students to research medieval castles. Students are asked to draw and describe castles and then to write about what it was like to live in a castle during the Middle Ages.

In their weekly meeting, Mr. Carlisle and Ms. Perkins identify specific modifications to guarantee the active participation of each student with a disability. Many of the modifications identified for students are used on a regular basis and thus require little planning. Larry, for instance, will spend his time drawing castles rather than writing about them. Jason's Internet search is supported by working with a partner. However, modifications for Paul, the student who is blind, require advance planning to obtain critical materials from outside sources such as recordings for the blind and texts in Braille.

Mr. Carlisle knows how to order materials for Paul. Ms. Perkins introduced him to the Recordings for the Blind and Dyslexic. He knows how to order materials, but more important, he knows Ms. Perkins, the media specialist, the guidance counselor, and many parents. He also feels a little more comfortable with what his role will be in teaching students who experience disabilities.

In this chapter you have been introduced to data collection to monitor and evaluate student progress. In the next chapter, we ask you to consider how ongoing evaluation can be a regular part of your planning and teaching. As you think about the processes of planning and adapting instruction for your middle school students, you'll want to think through how you'll approach response, evaluation, and grading in your middle school classroom.

Standards in Practice

The Council for Exceptional Children has created a set of standards for beginning teachers. Although this set of standards applies to special educators, you may find these guidelines useful for you to learn how special educators can support you and to learn more about disability-specific knowledge and skill bases (e.g., learning disabilities, emotional and behavioral disorders, visual impairment).

The CEC home page can be found at *http://www.cec.sped.org/index.html*

Standards of Practice for beginning teachers are located at the following Web address: *http://www.cec.sped.org/ps/perf_based_stds/common_core_4-21-01.html*

Select one activity below and prepare to share with your classmates.

1. What does this set of standards implicitly advocate for all teachers? Looking at the 10 standards, how might you characterize the role of the English language arts teacher? Write a paragraph or two on the ways in which this list could serve as a set of standards for all classroom teachers.
2. Use the Council for Exceptional Children Web site as a starting point or those at the end of this chapter. Search for additional internet Web sites that can be accessed as resources for literacy teaching and learning.

REFERENCES

Brozovic, S. A., Taber, T. A., Alberto, P. A., & Hughes, M. A. (1999). *A guide to the instruction of students with disabilities in the least restrictive environment.* Unpublished manuscript, Georgia State University, Atlanta.

Individuals with Disabilities Education Act Amendments of 1997, Public Law 105-17, 105th Congress, 1st session.

RESOURCES

Print

Bender, W. (1997). *Understanding ADHD: A practical guide for teachers and parents.* Upper Saddle River, NJ: Merrill/Prentice Hall.

Dunn, P. (1995). *Learning re-abled: The learning disability controversy and composition studies.* Portsmouth, NH: Boynton/Cook.

Falvey, M. A., Grenot-Scheyer, M., Coots, J. J., & Bishop, K. D. (1995). Services for students with disabilities: Past and present. In M. A. Falvey (Ed.), *Inclusive and heterogeneous schooling: Assessment, curriculum, and instruction* (pp. 23–39). Baltimore, MD: Paul H. Brookes.

Friend, M. (2002). *Including students with special needs: A practical guide for classroom teachers.* Needham Heights, MA: Allyn & Bacon.

Lang, G., & Berberich, C. (1995). *All children are special: Creating an inclusive classroom.* Portland, ME: Stenhouse.

Lee, C., & Jackson, R. (1992). *Faking it: A look into the mind of a creative learner.* Portsmouth, NH: Boynton/Cook.

Murphy, S. (1992). *On being L.D.: Perspectives and strategies of young adults.* New York: Teachers College Press.

Pierangelo, R., & Crane, R. (2000). *The special education yellow pages.* Upper Saddle River, NJ: Merrill/Prentice Hall.

Sailor, W. (2002). *Whole-school success and inclusive education: Building partnerships for learning, achievement, and accountability.* New York: Teachers College Press.

Smith, T., Polloway, R., Patton, J., & Dowdy, C. (2001). *Teaching students with special needs in inclusive settings* (3rd ed.). Needham Heights, MA: Allyn & Bacon.

Uphan, D., & Trumbull, V. (1997). *Making the grade: Reflections on being learning disabled.* Portsmouth, NH: Heinemann.

Electronic

Council for Exceptional Children. The CEC is the largest international professional organization dedicated to improving educational outcomes for individuals with exceptionalities, students with disabilities, and/or the gifted. This Web site includes policies, practices, and standards regarding exceptionalities.

http://www.sped.cec.org

National Information Center for Handicapped Children and Youth. The NICHCY is the national information and referral center that provides information on disabilities and disability-related issues for families, educators, and other professionals. The special focus is children and youth (birth to age 22). The Web site includes publications, personal responses to specific questions, and links to other Web sites.

http://www.nichcy.org

Recordings for the Blind and Dyslexic. The RFB&D is an invaluable educational resource for those with print disabilities. Established in 1948, this service provides recorded textbooks and other textual materials to those who cannot effectively read standard print because of a visual, perceptual, or other physical disability.

http://www.rfbd.org

chapter 5

Integrating Assessment

> Keeping track is a matter of reflective review and summarizing, in which there is both discrimination and record of the significant features of a developing "experience." It is the heart of intellectual organization and of the disciplined mind.
>
> —John Dewey, *Experience and Education*, 1938

GUIDING QUESTIONS

1. How can you assess your instructional goals and practices in teaching reading, writing, oral language, and listening?
2. How might you encourage middle school students to set and assess their own learning goals?
3. What approaches might you take to standardized and high-stakes tests?

A CASE FOR CONSIDERATION

Managing the Mess

Ellen Barton was student teaching at Carmel Middle School. She came to her student teaching seminar with a large cardboard box overflowing with brightly colored folders, decorated with magazine pictures and letters. "All about Me" was the title of the red folder on the top. After carrying this huge box up three flights of stairs, Ellen entered the college classroom, beaming and breathless. "My first project," she announced. "I'm so proud of my sixth graders. Look how cool these folders are! This is my first assignment—students' illustrated autobiographies. Look how pretty these are. The students were all so into it. Look. I am so proud of them!"

After working for two weeks, Ms. Barton's sixth-grade students had each handed in a 7- to 10-page book with at least three chapters. "I have 165 students, and all but five students handed theirs in on time," Ellen reported to her peers in the student teaching seminar. After several students "oohed" and "ahed" over the illustrated books, one asked Ellen, "How long do you think it will take you to grade all of those?"

Ellen stopped abruptly. She hadn't really thought about the amount of time that she would spend on each of the projects. Even though her mentor teacher had warned her not to make the assignment due only 1 day before the 9-week grades were due, Ellen had fully expected that she could grade these in one night, average the grades into the 9-week average and have report cards ready to turn into Mr. Overly, the principal, by 3:00 the next afternoon. The next day was, after all, an in-service day designed for just such things. She stopped short and asked her cohort group, "If I spend 5 to 10 minutes on each, how long will that take me?" Her teaching cohort began brainstorming ways to help Ellen get through the grading period:

"Do you have a rubric?"

"No."

"Do you have a list of expectations or something?"

"No."

"Have you read these in earlier drafts?"

"Yes, I've read most of them, and I have signed forms that at least one of their parents have read them and edited them."

As Ellen spoke, she began to realize that she had been so excited about the students' attractive covers and neat illustrations, she hadn't formulated any specific criteria for grading.

After the student teaching seminar that night, Ellen began by scanning the projects. Some were exactly what she had expected, although what she had expected was still a vague concept in her mind. Apparently it was not clear to some of her students either. She struggled to create a grading rubric to help her with this tremendous task—a tool that would encourage her students, yet help her to evaluate the quality of their writing. The rubric alone took her more than an hour. It was almost 10:00, and she hadn't even looked at the projects yet.

FOR DISCUSSION

- Given the benefit of hindsight, how might Ellen have designed an assessment system that was manageable, yet allowed her to set appropriate standards of performance?
- How can assessment both nurture growth and measure achievement?
- What kind of assessment tools would you use if you believe reading, writing, listening, speaking, viewing, and thinking are *equally* important?

Although this may sound like a beginning teacher's nightmare, it actually happened to one student teacher in Margaret's methods seminar. As you might imagine, Ellen did not meet the principal's deadline. After staying up until past 2:00 A.M., Ellen simply couldn't read any more of the *All about Me* reports. She worked furiously all the next day and did finish grading the projects, but she had not even begun to record them in the electronic grade book before Mr. Overly came in to ask why her grades were not on his secretary's desk. Embarrassed, Ellen tried to explain about the projects. Mr. Overly didn't seem interested in her explanation and attempted to hurry her along, complaining, "I can't send any of the grade cards over until I have them all. Get them to me ASAP."

Beginning teachers like Ellen need support and guidance in many areas, but one that is perhaps most difficult is setting appropriate standards for each group of students, then finding a manageable way to assess those standards while still maintaining a healthy personal life. Ellen's dilemma is the focus of this chapter.

ASSESSMENTS! ASSESSMENTS! ASSESSMENTS!

Many of us hold on to painful memories of assessment. We have stories of how embarrassed or humiliated we felt because of some grade or score that our teachers, parents, or peers felt was too low. We may even have painful memories of grades that were deemed too high for our peer group. Some of us can remember teachers who rearranged the seating chart after each test with the highest-scoring person in one row and the lowest in another. Healthy competition is often cited as the rationale for this practice. Surprisingly, students are often as embarrassed to be in the smart row as they are to be in the dumb row.

It would be good to remember that the word *assess* comes from the Latin word *assidere* which means "to sit by," to determine the value or significance of something. This definition stresses our responsibility not only to be in charge of certain aspects of the assessment process, but also to be patient and observant—to *stop, look, and listen* as our students teach us about their unique competencies and needs.

> Use both formative and summative evaluation in your classroom.

We design assessments for a variety of purposes and audiences. Assessments can both inform decisions and convey information. In addition to giving students and parents an idea of student progress, assessments can inform our daily teaching and program development. Unfortunately, we often reduce our notions of assessment to summative evaluation, ignoring the important role of formative assessment in students' literacy development. We would do well to remember *assessment*'s Latin root, recognizing that we must *sit by* our students every step of the way.

There are three major components of our duty as teachers: (1) to plan and structure learning experiences, (2) to facilitate the moment-to-moment orchestrations in our literacy lessons, and (3) to monitor student progress. Assessments are not limited to the third responsibility but come into play in all three roles. As we monitor our students' learning, we must also continually evaluate our planning and teaching during each phase of a lesson.

Whereas all three functions are vitally necessary for the English language arts classroom, our focus in this chapter will be on the third dimension: monitoring

Integrating Assessment 113

FIGURE 5-1 Purposes of and Audiences for Assessment

Purposes of Assessment

To assess teacher effectiveness
To document growth
To reflect on experiences
To examine teaching and adapt strategies
To inform teaching and program development
To provide student feedback and guidance
To engage in dialogue that supports growth and reflection

Audiences for Assessment

Teachers
Students
Parents
Administrators
School support personnel
Policy makers
Community members

student progress in both formative and summative ways. In doing this, we may find ourselves disrupting traditional notions that assessment comes *after* teaching and learning have occurred. We must also be more conscious of the audience for our evaluation methods. Report cards are perhaps intended mostly for parents, whereas standardized test scores are important to parents, community members, and school administrators. Informal comments on written work or oral conferences are intended primarily for students. In designing assessment tools, we need to think through two key questions: "Whom is it for?" and "What is it for?"

A few of the purposes and audiences for assessment are presented in Figure 5–1.

INTEGRATING ASSESSMENT

As much as we'd like to believe it's not the case, assessments often drive curriculum. Like it or not, we will sometimes be expected to *teach to the test*. Discussions of assessment historically have been at the center of attempts to transform teaching practices. Most recently, since the late 1980s, there has been a particularly strong drive to change and improve educational practices through increased emphasis on testing. Many of these efforts have focused on rather decontextualized skills and contrived testing situations. Wiggins (1989) has argued, however, that we should "test those capacities and habits we think are essential and test them in context" (p. 41). In other words, assessments should be designed to evaluate how well students can use skills in real-life contexts rather than testing isolated or discrete skills.

> Are your tests and other assessment techniques authentic and integrated with your teaching goals?

Critiques of traditional assessment methods and strategies are now commonplace. Educational reformers call for the replacement of multiple-choice and fill-in-the-blank tests with more authentic tests characterized by Brown (1989) as essential—not needlessly contrived and decontextualized, not atomized tasks.

According to Brown, authentic tests assess students' habits and repertoires, not mere recall or plug-in skills. Gardner (1991), drawing on a huge body of research in fields that range from mathematics to literature, from astronomy to history, demonstrates that traditional testing situations do not necessarily develop skills beyond the paper-and-pencil testing situation. Gardner sets a mission for schools to move students toward deep understanding, which he defines as the ability to make appropriate decisions in applying and adapting knowledge in new contexts. In a study of conceptions of literacy assessment from 1985 to 1990, Finders and Graham (1991) argue that discussions of teaching and assessment are often distinct from one another and are rarely integrated in a meaningful way; similarly, distinctions between formative and summative assessment strategies are seldom made clear and explicit by teachers in the literacy classroom.

CONSIDERATIONS FOR ASSESSMENT IN THE MIDDLE SCHOOL CLASSROOM

It's probably unfortunate but true that, as children advance through the middle grades toward high school and higher education, grading and assessment become more remote from their personal lives. Yet, this need not be the case, especially in early adolescence, where enthusiasm and motivation are often fragile and tenuous. Think about the following list of considerations, based upon these four precepts of the National Middle School Association whenever you design assessment tasks for your middle school students.

- **Middle school students need positive social interactions with peers and adults.**
  - In what ways might assessments involve peers, parents, and/or community members?
  - How do we set up assessments that balance academic rigor and social comfort?
  - In what ways can we collaborate with students in creating assessment goals and grading rubrics?
- **Middle school students need physical activities to develop and showcase their competencies.**
  - When and how do we infuse nonlinguistic opportunities to showcase learning?
  - When is it important to allow students time to talk, draw, or perform?
  - What are some alternatives to paper-and-pencil tests?

- **Middle school students need opportunities for self-definition, creative expression, and a sense of competence and achievement in their learning experiences.**
  - How do we facilitate students' comfort while expanding their range of competencies?
  - How do we integrate instruction and assessment?
  - How do we set real and reachable standards for performance that give students a sense of accomplishment?
- **Middle school students need opportunities that promote meaningful participation in families, school, and the larger world.**
  - How might students receive positive recognition from peers or adults?
  - How do we make assessments real and relevant to students' lives beyond the classroom?
  - How can performance assessments promote students' involvement in social and political activities in neighborhoods, communities, and the larger world?

PERFORMANCE ASSESSMENT OF AUTHENTIC LEARNING TASKS

A recent movement toward *performance assessment* seeks to engage students in authentic learning experiences that are close to the kind of real-world experiences they will experience outside of classroom contexts. The assumption behind performance assessment is that typical paper-and-pencil tests cannot yield rich understanding of the wide range of products and processes students need to master to become literate in our complicated world.

Although we are pleased to see this movement toward performance and authentic assessment, we think that many obstacles remain. Our conceptions of assessment still rely for the most part on a linear curricular model that does not allow for the kind of educational transformation that Wiggins or Gardner advocate. It appears that even though our assessment practices may have changed, as a profession, we have not shifted our bedrock assumptions about the multiple purposes of assessment.

> Assessment should be recursive and not linear.

In a linear model of curriculum, teaching and testing might look something like Figure 5–2. In this linear model, we begin by articulating our goals and philosophy. Next, we design a lesson, using strategies and techniques that fit the guiding principles of the goal statements. Finally, we test students' abilities to meet curricular standards. Literacy Lesson 5–1 contrasts this linear model with a more recursive and ongoing model of assessment.

FIGURE 5–2 A Linear Model of Assessment

Write Unit Goals → Create Learning Activities → Assess Learner Outcomes

Literacy Lesson 5-1

Assessing Processes as Well as Products

Martha is a sixth-grade teacher in a rural middle school. During the first few weeks of class, she decided to try a community-building activity that she hoped would develop her students' skills as researchers and language users. She divided her class into small groups. She asked them to research the necessary supplies and expenses of owning particular classroom pets. Students would then draft letters to the administration, asking for permission to purchase a pet of their choosing for their classroom and requesting money for the project.

The Traditional Assessment Scenario: A Linear Model

In a linear model of assessment, although students might work on this project for several weeks, Martha would base their grade on the quality of their final product, the letter to the administrator. This is a typical example of the limits of summative evaluation. Students' levels of interest, collaboration, research practices, even the real-life desire to acquire a pet for the classroom could potentially fulfill the criteria of "authentic" instruction. In the course of their learning, students would use oral language and listening skills in group work, investigate sources of information in the library and beyond, and compose multiple drafts of their letter. Yet, without a sensitive, ongoing assessment system based upon processes as well as products, all of these valuable learning experiences would be cast aside as little more than "additional" projects and activities leading toward the ultimate goal—the letter to the principal. It's not hard to see what's wrong with this picture.

An Alternative Assessment Scenario: A Recursive Model

In contrast to this linear model, assessment should be based on a recursive model that allows for student involvement in the process and ongoing formative assessment. This is just what Martha did. She began by sharing some of her goals and ideas, then invited her students to become active participants in setting up the goals at every step of the way. She didn't expect her students to take total control of the curriculum, but she wanted to make them active partners in setting up activities and assessing their own needs and strengths. In this brief summary, you can see the recursive and ongoing nature of her assessment system:

A Recursive Model of Assessment

- Martha and her students negotiate unit goals, which are posted in the room.
- Students work in teams, researching various pets, keeping progress logs.
  - √ Assessment Checkpoint: Weekly conferences with teams and brief check of progress logs (Martha keeps anecdotal records and awards √, √+, or √− for logs).
- Teams write 1- to 2-page reports of progress and share reports with larger group.
  - √ Assessment Checkpoint: Martha confers with each team and sets future goals. Reports are assessed informally (√, √+, or √−).

> - Teams make oral presentations on the merits and drawbacks of different pets. Class votes on pet to be selected.
>   √ Assessment Checkpoint: Grades of A–F are awarded to the oral presentations of teams, based upon a class-created rubric. Class members write informal notes to teams after each presentation.
> - Students draft individual letters to the principal. Each student confers with (and receives written response from) at least three classmates during the drafting process.
>   √ Assessment Checkpoint: Grades of A–F are awarded on individual letters, based upon number and quality of revisions and quality of the final letter.
> - Letters are delivered to the principal for response.
>   √ Final Grades: These are based upon Martha's assessment of all aspects of the project, including progress logs and reports, oral presentation, drafting process, and final letter to the principal.

Think for a moment of all the skills and processes Martha's students drew upon during the course of this project: *social skills* (using the conventions of conversation and cooperating with other students in small groups); *research skills* (selecting appropriate print and nonprint resources; finding, summarizing, and synthesizing information); *mathematical skills* (calculating the cost of buying and maintaining their chosen pets); *problem-solving skills* (identifying problems, brainstorming, establishing steps to solve the problem); *oral language and listening skills* (creating and participating in a group presentation); *writing skills* (writing informally in progress logs and persuasively in final letters, supporting opinions with facts, adapting writing to a real audience); and *language skills* (editing and proofreading for standard spelling and usage).

Much of the vast array of knowledge required to successfully complete this project would not be visible in any draft of a letter. It remains our challenge to create formative and summative assessment systems to capture the competencies that often lie beneath the surface of our classroom tasks. Wiggins (1989) has argued:

> How can you assess your students' varied abilities?

> Rather than seeing tests as after-the-fact devices for checking upon what students have learned, we should see them as instructional; the central vehicle for clarifying and setting intellectual standards. The recital, debate, play, or game (and the criteria by which they are judged)—the *performance* is not a checkup, it is the heart of the matter. (p. 42)

In a day where calls for more testing and high-stakes accountability are commonplace, we cannot afford to ignore Wiggins's notion of placing assessment at the *heart of the matter*. Unfortunately, however, even the most well-intentioned teaching ideas can be circumvented by unimaginative minds. Portfolios may be mere containers for

student work; performance assessments may be just another meaningless project. Brown (1989) characterizes performance assessments in the following ways:
Performance assessments

- are essential and authentic
- are contextualized
- assess skills in use—require applications, analyses, judgments
- assess students' habits and repertoires
- are enabling, engaging, and educational
- integrate instruction, learning, and assessment (pp. 31–33)

In the next section, we present some possibilities for assessment that provide a window for understanding your students' needs and help you to design meaningful ways for them to engage with you, their peers, and the larger community.

BEYOND PAPER-AND-PENCIL TESTS: TOOLS FOR ALTERNATIVE ASSESSMENT

Learning Logs as a Form of Assessment

Just as Martha does in Literacy Lesson 5–1, you may ask your middle school students to keep a learning log in which they record their reactions, state their opinions, and explain their learning processes. In the learning log, middle school students can reflect on their own learning processes, assess their progress, and begin to take on responsibilities for their own learning. Students can record questions, make predictions, and judge the merits of a literary work. Learning logs can begin with simple prompts: "I learned. . ." "One thing I wonder about. . ." "What I still want to learn more about is . . ." Students can use the log to prepare for conferences with you or each other. You can use the learning log to check their progress on particular projects, document growth over time, and evaluate the depth of their understanding. The learning log is also useful to inform your teaching decisions. Unfortunately, due to its overuse or perhaps *abuse* in English language arts classrooms, many students have come to see the journal or log as one more meaningless exercise. Particularly when journals or logs are used in the literature classroom, they can prove cumbersome and intrusive for students who prefer to read aesthetically, immersing themselves in the momentary act of reading.

> **Language Study in Context**
>
> Students can keep track of "skills to work on" in their learning logs. Each time they make an error in a piece of formal writing, instead of correcting the error, you can place an *X* in the margin next to the line where the error occurs. If you see a pattern of error (for example, forgetting to use a comma in a series), you can circle the *X*. Give students extra credit for correcting errors.

Mary McCrone has invented a solution to this dilemma in her seventh-grade classroom. She requires students to stop each day after reading their independently chosen novels and write no more than three sentences. In these three sentences, they let her know about something they are thinking, feeling, or imagining at this point in their reading. Mary periodically reviews the reading journals, awarding them a √, √+, or a √−, depending upon her judgment of whether and how well students have been reading. Notice how much information you might glean from Tessa's reading response journal in Figure 5–3.

FIGURE 5-3 Tessa's Reading Journal

> The Wind In The Door Madeleine L'Engle 53-99 9-22
> I feel like Progo is an interesting idea. A drive of dragons and a cherubim don't mix to me, but Ms. L'Engle put the two together and came out with an interesting believable character.
>
> The Wind In the Door Madeleine L'Engle 100-176 9-23
> I think that knowing who you are has a lot to do with life and that your true name is kind of like your calling; its what you are meant to be or do.
>
> A Wind In The Door Madeleine L'Engle 177-208 9-24
> I remember back in the first book where both Murry children and Cal worked together and I think in this one it will be mostly just Cal and Meg.
>
> ✓+ Excellent insights M.

In these few sentences, Tessa has managed to critique Madeleine L'Engle's ability to create characters, to develop a philosophical stance toward the novel ("your true name is kind of like your calling"), and to make an intertextual connection with another of L'Engle's books. Both responses (Tessa's and Mary's) took only a few moments, but each has value in helping Mary to assess Tessa's progress in her independent reading. Best of all, such journal entries can be a starting point for Mary's regular reading conferences with Tessa.

Graphic Representation as an Assessment Tool

Some early adolescents may demonstrate knowledge more effectively in graphic forms. Charts, graphs, and time lines represent just a few ways that students may

FIGURE 5-4 Graphic Visual From Inquiry Project

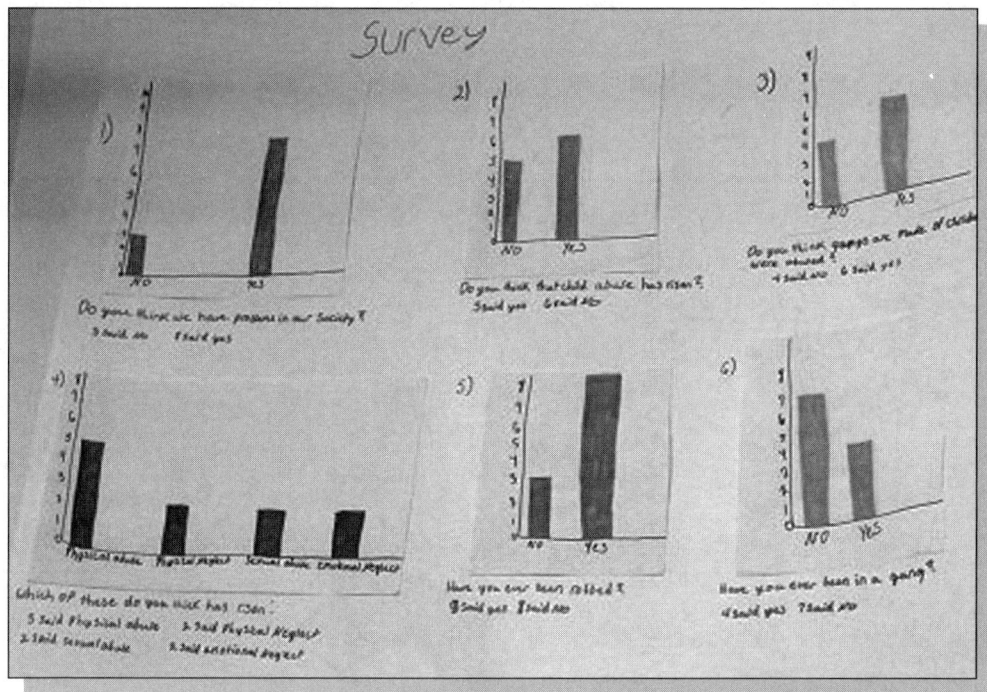

demonstrate their understandings. Drawings, cartoons, and other artwork can showcase how they are interpreting literature and how they compare different aspects of events, characters, or settings. Graphic representations can help early adolescents enter a story world, make predictions, and render judgments. Notice, for example, the literacy skills required to create Figure 5–4, a visual display of a survey that students conducted with their classmates about violence in society.

Assessment Conferences

> **Language Study in Context**
>
> If you hold regular writing conferences with students, choose one draft in progress and look for patterns of error or other issues (e.g., spelling, punctuation, transitions between paragraphs). Choose two "skills to work on" in future drafts and write these on a special "skills" page of students' writing folders. Check their progress on these skills each time you discuss new drafts.

Conferences and interviews may be used as formal or informal assessment tools. They can be led by you, your students, or groups of students and can focus on reading, writing, speaking, or language study. In group or individual conferences, students can share different aspects of their learning logs or portfolios as a way of helping you see their development over time. You could ask them to create a one-page self-assessment of their weekly or monthly goals, or they could write periodic entries in their learning logs about their strengths, needs, and progress over the course of the grading period.

Sometimes it helps to create a brief set of prompts for students to bring with them to an evaluation or goal-setting conference (see Figure 5–5).

FIGURE 5-5 Self-Evaluation Rubric

Name_____

Week_____ to Week_____ (include dates since last evaluation conference)

The goals that I have worked on for the past 3 weeks are:

I have done the following to achieve these goals:

My best piece of writing for the past 3 weeks is (give title and dates of all drafts):

I think it is the best because (state at least three specific reasons):

I have read the following (books/chapters) for independent reading:

Based on the work described above, I believe that I deserve a grade of _____

Assessing Small-Group Work

When students are working together in groups, they may be assessed both individually and as group members. You will want to focus on both social and academic competencies in designing tools to assess group projects. Teachers and students can collaborate on identifying check points to match project and group goals.

One quick way of assessing daily group work is to allow a few minutes at the end of the class period for each participant to make a list of all group members present and note what each member contributed on that day. These notes can give you a quick view of students who may be contributing a great deal or those who have opted out of group work. If particular students are not mentioned by others in the group, it's a good bet that they aren't devoting their full attention to a project. Periodically, you may also ask students to fill out anonymous rating sheets on other group members as a further check on individual and group progress.

As a way of acquainting your students with helpful and unhelpful discussion behaviors, you could hold a *fishbowl* discussion in which a small-group of students talks about a piece of literature or a current topic. The discussion group meets in the center of the room, while the remaining class members sit on the outside of the circle, noting what they think are the most and least helpful comments made by participants in the smaller circle. Students' observations can then be turned into a rubric by which you, or they, can rate group participants.

You might consider periodically placing a tape recorder in the middle of a small-group discussion. Ask students to take the tape home and transcribe a small portion of the discussion. Later, they can analyze the transcript to determine the helpfulness or unhelpfulness of each person's comments.

Assessment of Performances and Demonstrations

Performances and demonstrations are usually formal presentations in front of an audience, such as public speeches, readers' theater presentations, broadcasts, plays, or skits. Demonstrations and performances needn't always be polished or formal, however. Informal activities involving hands-on demonstrations, drama, music, or other visual or performing arts can make learning visible to you and your students. For example, students might give short informative presentations to a small group of their peers, create presentations for parents' night, or make informal presentations about their work as a regular part of your class.

One group of seventh grade students in a city school decided to investigate possible community service or social action projects in which they might become involved, using a variety of sources from electronic to print. As part of their collaborative inquiries, students were required to write a five-page paper and create a visual for a *share fair* to be held at the end of the 4-week period. One group explored the topic of *Violence in America* and depicted the results of their project in the striking visual in Figure 5–6. Their grade was determined by the quality of their final paper and the quality of their presentation and visual display. Criteria for the visual display included clarity, content, and visual attractiveness.

Assessing Student Participation in Large Groups

As an informal assessment tool, you might ask students to bring in what one middle school teacher refers to as *magic questions* or *real questions*. These are discussion questions to which answers can't be found in the book. Obviously, literal-level questions like "Who was Bill's nephew?" don't fit the category of real questions. Students are encouraged to ask their peers what they are wondering about or what they think is just or unjust. Students might be asked to make judgments or speculate on causes. As you assess the depth and kind of questions students pose, you can make immediate pedagogical decisions to further support students' understanding.

Integrating Assessment 123

FIGURE 5-6 Student-Created Visual for Share Fair

Some teachers have used discussion leading as an assessment of students' preparation and understanding of the subject under study. If you decide to grade discussion leadership, you'll want to be sure to give time to prepare for this, including time for rehearsals and class discussion about what constitutes good leadership qualities. If your classroom has the kind of open forum in which middle school students are encouraged to share, respond, and respect their peers, a discussion led by middle school students can be an effective assessment strategy. Discussion leaders can be selected on a rotating basis and evaluated on criteria such as poise and presence, fairness, and knowledge of subject matter.

Assessment of Inquiries and Investigations

Inquiries and investigations are important ways to integrate the language arts and to cross disciplinary boundaries. Inquiries allow students to connect their literacy practices to their own lives. These investigations may take a variety of forms. They may involve critically examining an Internet chat room for teenagers, researching the historical setting of a novel, or investigating an issue within a neighborhood or school. Inquiries treat students as active investigators of a social scene.

Beach and Myers (2001) note that inquiry activities allow students to acquire various social practices that include using literacy to understand real-world concerns, issues, and dilemmas. According to Beach and Myers, this shift in the English curriculum from traditional studies to an inquiry model makes space for students to critically examine story, virtual, and lived worlds. This critical examination leads students to a deeper understanding of complex relationships and events and helps them to question injustices in the world.

Inquiries and investigations allow students to participate actively in their school and community and to make both better places to be and work. Inquiry projects can be informal and personal; for example, you might ask students to investigate a relationship they have with an important person by keeping a journal of their interactions with this person for a period of time. They can also be more formal and collaborative. Students might research an important social problem, do something to address that problem, and document the outcomes of this work orally, visually, and in writing. In Literacy Lesson 5–2, one middle school teacher implements a performance evaluation of her students' year-long inquiry projects.

Literacy Lesson 5-2

Performance Final Examination

Mary McCrone decided to try something a bit different for the mandatory "final examination" held by all seventh- and eighth-grade teachers in her city school district. Instead of a paper-and-pencil test, she created a performance assessment. Students had been working all year on the theme of "Making a Difference." They culminated the year by working on individual or collaborative inquiry projects in which they were required to demonstrate—through reading, writing, and oral language—how they could "make a difference" in their school, family, community, or the larger world. Some students chose topics close to home like helping the elderly or preventing animal cruelty, while others explored broader issues like the environment or violence prevention.

Evaluating and grading the examination was a bit tricky, but after some thought, Mary came up with a system. With the help of her teaching team, she set up four rooms, each proctored by a different homeroom teacher from her team, plus two community volunteers. Other interested parents and community members were also invited, but only the three proctors gave students a written evaluation of their work.

For the weeks prior to the examination, Mary monitored the progress of each group and collected various artifacts of their research, including lists of sources consulted, informal progress logs, and other materials. These raw materials constituted part of their final grade. Each group was required to create a table display and make a 4- or 5-minute presentation based upon their work. On the day of the examination, students were

Integrating Assessment

placed into groups according to rather broad topics which Mary had chosen in advance. For example, on the door of the examination room titled "violence free" was a sign that read "We stand for helping our homes, schools, and communities be violence free." Topics included "street violence," "gun violence," "irresponsible driving," "teen violence," and "hate crimes." On the day of the examination, Mary posted the agenda on her classroom door (see "Agenda for Performance Examination" below) and rotated among the

---

Agenda for Performance Examination

Good Morning,
   Thank you for proctoring this performance exam.
   Schedule:

8:00 - 8:15   Homeroom / Attendance
8:15 -   Parents and students go to classroom labled with their topic.
              (If a student comes unprepared, he/she should report to the conference room in the office to receive a written test.)
8:30 - 9:00   Set up table displays in classrooms and practice performances.
9:00 - 10:00 Performances and presentation of table displays
              (Refreshments all .50 for charity)
10:00 - 10:15 Making a Difference Committment Ceremony
              (Every student swears to make a difference by ———.)
10:15 - 10:30 Clean-up.

Reprinted by permission of Mary McCrone.

classrooms, enjoying the work of her eighth-grade students while the invited respondents gave feedback to each group.

As with most middle school events, the morning was not without its humorous moments. Katie Splinter, a social studies teacher on Mary's team, began to regret her decision to proctor the "animal cruelty" presentations for the exam, when she saw live birds, dogs, and other pets being brought in as "visual aids" for student demonstrations. One girl even brought a visiting (and unsuspecting) grandmother to take care of her pet dog while she made her presentation.

In another room, a group of young women decided to investigate community-based agencies where teens could volunteer their services in improving their neighborhoods and city. They created a pamphlet, detailing the names and contact information for these agencies and made an oral presentation on their project, "Getting Socially Active" (see the photo below and the illustration on p. 127).

Getting Socially Active

By Shannon Nolan, Mallory Hohm and Jenny Aiken

COMMUNITY SERVICES

*Loretto   469-1991
Program and Housing Information
700 E Brighton Av.
Syracuse NY 13205

*Meals on Wheels   478-5948
300 Burt St.
Syracuse NY 13202

*Rescue Mission   432-8560
112 East Manlius
East Syracuse NY 13057

*The Salvation Army   475-1688
677 S. Salina St.
Syracuse NY 13202

*Thrifty Shoppers   492-0802
410 W. Seneca Trnpk
Syracuse NY 13207

*Motivational Learning Center
200 Gifford St.   472-3700
Syracuse NY 13202

*Clothes and Stuff   472-7205
120 Gifford St.
Syracuse NY 13202

*Auto Donation Center 423-8247
167 Richmond Av.
Syracuse NY 13204

*Westcott Community Center Inc.
826 Euclid Av.   478-8634
Syracuse NY 13210

EDUCATION INFORMATION SERVICES

*Friends for Life   468-6798
2010 W. Genesee St.
Syracuse NY 13219

*Project Save   476-2120
157 Fellows Ave.
Syracuse NY 13210

*Syracuse Association for the
Education of Young Children.
3175 E. Genesee St.   449-3632
Syracuse NY 13224

VOLUNTEER SERVICES

*Francis Corps   426-0481
110 Walnut Pl.
Syracuse NY 13210

YOUTH SERVICES

*Boy Scouts of America 463-0201
Hiawatha Council Inc.
113 Twin Oaks Dr.
Syracuse NY 13206

*Girl Scouts   437-6531
Central NY Council
6724 Thompson Rd.
Mattydale NY 13211

*Boys and Girls Club
- 375 W. Onondaga 472-6714
  Syracuse NY 13202
- 210 Hamilton   468-0521
  Syracuse NY 13204
- 201 Shonnard   475-5069
  Syracuse NY 13204
- 2100 E. Fayette   424-8643
  Syracuse NY 13224

✲ Portfolio Assessment

Portfolios are much more than a collection of student work. They help students document and reflect upon their progress over a period of time. Student self-assessment should be an important outcome of portfolio evaluation. For example, progress logs, self-assessment forms for writing, and brief written updates about independent reading progress can be included in a student's portfolio. You may ask students to problem solve or problem pose by asking them to identify their next steps and set future goals.

The portfolio may include both written and electronic artifacts. Many middle school students may already be savvy about ways to enhance and expand their portfolio with technology. Others may need support. The portfolio may be a box, a notebook, or a Web site. Whatever form the portfolio takes, middle school students can take on much of the responsibility for managing and assessing it. They may select those pieces within their portfolio that need further work or response from you. Students can keep portfolios of work-in-progress or design more elaborate *performance portfolios* for the purpose of sharing their work with teachers, classmates, or other interested adults. See the Resources section at the end of this chapter for more valuable information on portfolios.

GRADING: THE FINAL ACT

All of the strategies presented in the last few pages may be used to inform your teaching and to document student growth. Some of them will turn into numbers or letters in the grade book and some will not. As we've noted throughout this chapter, grading and assessment are not synonyms. Whether your students are engaging in self-assessment, peer assessment, or teacher assessment, you will eventually need to establish a set of criteria for grading. Depending on your purposes, those criteria may include growth in social and academic competencies or changes in attitudes or behaviors. Above all, your grading criteria should never be hidden from your students. Success in meeting your criteria depends upon student understanding and, in many cases, student input into the process.

Creating a Grading Rubric

A grading rubric or grid is a useful tool for both you and your students. The rubric makes clear what students are expected to accomplish and the standards upon which their work will be judged. In designing a rubric, begin by considering expected outcomes, which can later become strands of the rubric. For example, one outcome that we anticipated for this chapter is that beginning teachers who are reading this book will expand their understanding of clear and useful assessment. Second, we hoped that your assessments would not only guide your grading and evaluation practices, but inform your teaching as well. Let's say we could step out of the

Integrating Assessment

pages of this book and evaluate one of your lessons-in-progress, according to these goals. As one strand of our rubric, we might select "the ability to write clear and useful grading criteria." That strand could then be part of a rubric used to grade your lesson plans (see Figure 5–7).

FIGURE 5-7 Sample Grading Rubric

Criteria	Exceeds expectations	Meets expectations	Does not meet expectations
Students will write clear and useful grading criteria.	• The criteria are clearly connected to the topic and written in ways that are both accessible and useful to middle school students. • The criteria clearly communicate learning expectations that attend to multiple language arts. • The criteria are explicitly aligned with mandated standards. • The criteria allow room for negotiation and attend to the interests and expectations of early adolescents. • The activities support the criteria. • The assessments are logically aligned with the criteria.	• The criteria are somewhat connected to the topic and appropriate for middle school students. • The criteria communicate learning expectations that attend to multiple language arts most of the time. • The criteria sometimes align with mandated standards. • The criteria sometimes allow room for negotiation and attend to the interests and expectations of early adolescents. • The activities sometimes support the criteria. • The assessments are sometimes aligned with the criteria.	• The criteria are disconnected from the topic and/or are inappropriate for middle school students. • The criteria fail to communicate learning expectations that attend to multiple language arts. • The criteria seldom or never align with mandated standards. • The criteria seldom or never allow room for negotiation and attend to the interests and expectations of early adolescents. • The activities seldom or never support the criteria. • The assessments are seldom or never aligned with the criteria.

BEYOND TRADITIONAL TESTS AND QUIZZES

Recently, Pam, a member of Susan's student teaching seminar, voiced this concern over the listserv:

> *I have a dilemma (funny, I must have had many this semester because I know how to spell* dilemma *now). I'm supposed to give a "test" on Tuesday. I would rather give the students a take-home project in place of a test, but the last time I did that only five kids turned in anything. . . . That project was part creative, part process paper, and there were more than ten choices, so I was very disturbed when I only received five projects. However, when I gave an essay "test" on* The Color of Water, *everyone took it and anyone who was absent came the very next day to take it. I don't plan on giving a multiple-choice test or anything like that, just an essay to write in class where students are allowed to use their notes and are given a full block to write. If I make them write in class, at least they're writing, right? It seems when I send something home, it falls by the wayside. If I connect the word "test" to anything, they really pay attention. I have a student who hates to write and whines about it every single time. However, he took the essay test without complaint. That made my life so much easier. What do you think I should do?*

> Avoid the "teach-then-test" pattern.

Pam's concern is perhaps familiar to all of us. Our daily class activities can be creative, engaging, and inviting, but if we follow them with a traditional test, we risk undercutting our teaching goals. Giving a test on *The Color of Water* (McBride, 1997) may have resulted in greater attendance or fewer complaints, but chances are that students didn't learn anything more about the novel as a result of taking the test. In fact, many of them may have focused on memorizing trivia rather than forming deeper or more critical understanding. It's easy to fall into the trap of a "teach-then-test" pattern because it's so comfortable and familiar to teachers and students alike. In the few remaining pages of this chapter, starting with Your Fieldwork Journal 5–1, we'd like you to consider some alternatives.

Your Fieldwork Journal 5–1

Alternatives to Traditional Testing

If you happen to be teaching in a middle school, see if you can find a list of competencies students are supposed to master at a particular grade level. Such competencies are often listed as part of statewide assessment documents.

If you can't find such a list, look at the following list of competencies from the New York State standards (see *http://www.ncte.org/standards* for a full listing) and ask yourself this question: How might you design an assessment tool that doesn't involve a paper-and-pencil test? Choose one or more of these competencies and, in a double-entry journal, list as many forms of assessment you can think of that avoid the teach-then-test pattern. To jump start your thinking, we've provided an example of what we mean, using the New York State standards. Brainstorm several assessment techniques that might be useful in demonstrating some or all of your own statewide or schoolwide standards (see accompanying figure).

Integrating Assessment

Meeting Competency Requirements

Competency	Assessment Techniques
Acquire information from a variety of print and nonprint sources.	• Students keep logs of resources consulted. • Periodic "progress conferences" are held with students. • Periodic checks on notes in a learning log are conducted. • Final product is assessed on an A–F scale by means of a rubric, focusing on the ability to back up assertions with evidence.
Make connections to prior reading and personal experiences.	
Understand how language is used to influence others.	
Write for different purposes and audiences.	
Adapt speaking to different audiences and purposes.	
Use language, both oral and written, while working with others to learn and solve problems.	

In Literacy Lesson 5–3, you will see how one middle school teacher designed an innovative and successful assessment strategy that avoided the typical teach-then-test syndrome in his literature classroom.

Literacy Lesson 5-3

Cartoon Quizzes

One day, Ben Clardy, a teacher in the Fayetteville-Manlius school district in New York, decided to let his ninth-grade students try their hands at a different form of assessment. He asked them to express their ideas about a piece of literature in the form of a cartoon. Ben describes his process as follows:

> As a teacher who wants to push close readings of the text in the classroom, I struggle with students who, in a class discussion, are unable to recall a moment in the text with anything but the weakest of detail. In the past, I had students who could talk about the way they saw a scene, but they were never able to get their vision

across to the other members of the class. I saw their frustration have a negative impact on the class as a whole. It was with these incidents in my mind that I designed the cartoon quiz. The idea was simple enough: students were asked to draw a cartoon (either a strip that could include a few panels or one larger single picture) of an important incident from the reading. I assured them that their artistic ability (or lack thereof) would not impact the grade and that I was looking to see that they had read the text carefully. They had ten minutes to do the assignment.

Every student saw the chapter differently. There were seven figured men talking to women with one leg. There were stick figures, fat-headed snowmen with bubbles above their heads, packed with dialogue. The perspectives included overviews, first person, and the ever-popular missing wall that gave a kind of diorama of the scene. A few students in the class were accomplished artists, and they saw the quiz as a badge of honor. They included shading, a landscape that disappeared and a protagonist that looked a lot like themselves. Students were asked to write a short paragraph explaining the action of the cartoon on the back of the page or underneath the cartoon. The writing they did was, in most cases, precise and specific. Their writing supported the picture, as opposed to being a substitute. While most students chose one particularly memorable scene, a few made choices to focus on scenes that stood out for them.

Grading the quiz was fun. I constructed a rubric that I shared with students, emphasizing detail, accuracy in terms of the events in the story, and the relative importance of the scenes students selected. In the context of the quiz, students had to have a level of recall and familiarity with the text to create the cartoon. The students who read the novel without an eye for detail were unable to generate a cartoon that represented the complexity of the story. Initially, I graded based on how the scene was represented by the student, looking at the cartoon as a representation of the key images and ideas within a particular section. I shifted my grading rubric to include the student's "eye for detail," which came to include giving students credit for correct placement of characters, recreation of dialogue in the cartoon, and pulling in elements of the text that may have been more subtle. Students who are careful readers and have a memory for the specifics of a scene were able to represent the moment in the cartoon as clearly as it had happened in the text. The quiz had credibility in the sense that there were students who, because they had not read, failed the quiz. In turn, the students who read but were less likely to do well on a quiz that asked specific questions were able to choose the scene they wanted to work with and (literally) draw out the meaning.

Reading the quizzes allowed me to see that the work done in the cartoon was, for the students, a way to represent the literature that they had read for the class in a genre they had not assumed would be used to respond to literature. Students created meaning (for the story) as they created the cartoon. The "cartoonists" represented the information they had read in a new way. Representation operates on the assumption that the literary text is the basis for a new (and in this case visual) text.

Think about the literacies that one of Ben's students brings to his rendering of the jailhouse porch scene in *To Kill a Mockingbird* (Lee, 2001) in Figure 5–8. Beyond

FIGURE 5-8 Cartoon Quiz on *To Kill a Mockingbird*

133

his sophisticated understanding of cartoon devices, this student's drawing reveals a familiarity with Harper Lee's novel and a recognition of overriding themes and character motivations (the law as "absent once again," Atticus as "challenging the mob once again"). His reference to foreshadowing demonstrates a knowledge of literary devices and his ability to predict events in a story. Cartoon quizzes may allow less-verbal students a chance to demonstrate their understanding and reading competencies in an innovative way.

COLLABORATIVE RUBRICS: ASSESSMENT AS A TEACHING TOOL

Unless students have some rather specific criteria to indicate whether they have done a good job, many early adolescents will fall back upon vague "I liked it" or "I think maybe it could be better" comments. On the other hand, giving your students criteria that are too detailed can turn all projects and assignments into uniform fill-in-the-blank activities that allow students to be successful without thinking deeply or doing much real work. It is a difficult balancing act. Students need to know before a project begins what the criteria for evaluation are so they are not simply guessing what is in your head. Many students are adept at this guessing game and work only to please you with no real attempt at independence; others don't have a clue about what you want.

> How can your students have a voice in your assessment and grading procedures?

Collaborative rubrics, as their name implies, are negotiated by teacher and students as an integral part of instruction. Negotiated assessment can build a sense of shared ownership and responsibility for classroom experiences and for learning. There is no one correct way to develop the collaborative rubric. Many teachers have their students come to class the second or third day of a project with a list of things they think are important to accomplish. Students may work in small groups before sharing with the whole class. You can then create a grid on the overhead, asking students to look at the task and generate a list of what they should be doing to accomplish it. If the task is extensive, the rubric may need to be revisited and revised to stay in line with how the project is developing. This ongoing negotiation continually creates learning opportunities for students and teachers; it helps to close the gap between instruction and assessment and shows students that assessments need not always come last.

Collaborative rubrics perform many functions. First, they demystify teacher expectations. Students often fail to understand our expectations, no matter how clearly we think we've defined a task. As a result, many students move forward with a project without a clear idea of what's expected of them. By working with you to design the criteria, middle school students will have firsthand knowledge of what is expected of them. As they have a hand in identifying what constitutes good work, early adolescents can become more adept at posing problems rather than simply solving those that you identify. Consider the oral language and listening skills that went into creating the rubric in Figure 5–9 for a public speaking assignment in one eighth-grade classroom.

As students collaborate on drafting the rubric, you can gather information about what students think is important. If there is a mismatch, students can use this information to correct any misconceptions they may bring to the work.

FIGURE 5-9 Grading Rubric

Public Speaking Assignment

                                                         Inadequate   **Excellent**

Preparation:
1. Were all notes and short assignments handed in on time?   1 2 3 4 5
2. Does the speech show evidence of careful research?   1 2 3 4 5
3. Does the presentation appear polished and rehearsed?   1 2 3 4 5

Comments

Clarity:
4. Are the speaker's main points clear and understandable?   1 2 3 4 5
5. Are controversial claims backed up with evidence?   1 2 3 4 5
6. Are concrete examples provided for abstract statements?   1 2 3 4 5

Comments

Organization:
7. Does the speech follow a recognized organizational scheme (problem-solution, chronological, topical)?   1 2 3 4 5
8. Are transitions used to signpost for the listener?   1 2 3 4 5
9. Are overviews and summaries presented?   1 2 3 4 5

Comments

Presentation:
10. Does the speaker maintain eye contact and use appropriate gestures?   1 2 3 4 5
11. Is the presentation well prepared without appearing "canned"?   1 2 3 4 5
12. Is the speaker neatly dressed and poised?   1 2 3 4 5

Comments

Overall Average _____   **Final Grade** _____

As Ellen in the opening Case for Consideration learned the hard way, without a clear idea of where you are going, you'll most likely end up somewhere else. By making standards explicit, you can be sure to align your instruction with your assessment. In addition, you can align your lessons with local and national standards.

Negotiating a grading rubric makes students feel a real sense of shared responsibility over the learning activities. It is important, though, that negotiations are true negotiations. Although you may have a clear sense of where the project or performance should be headed, you must make sure that a good many aspects are still open for negotiation.

Attending to the language of how the rubric is written is vital. Students must recognize it as their own. Your main goal should be to make your students feel like learning partners. With so much classroom time devoted to setting standards collaboratively, the eventual process of grading usually becomes much less overwhelming and time consuming.

THE DILEMMA OF HIGH-STAKES TESTING

Amy, a student teacher in a rural middle school, wrote this message to the members of her student teaching seminar:

> *I was thinking long and hard about the ELAs [the New York State eighth-grade competency examinations] and their relation to my eighth graders. I know that the tests are different between eighth and eleventh grade, but Mr. Campbell and I got into a very interesting discussion about the tests in general. I made two points to him, one being that the whole "critical lens" idea contained in part 3 of the high school test is not even defined right by the test makers. Call me crazy, but my definition of a critical lens is a discourse under which to read a piece of literature. For example, you could read* Jane Eyre *from a feminist perspective or a postmodern perspective. Those are critical lenses. What this test is asking students to do isn't even close to that. All they want to know is "Have these students read anything?" and "Can they compare two pieces of literature with a quote framing their response?" Personally, I think the questions themselves are ridiculous. The grading system for that test . . . Please! That is for a whole other e-mail. I know I am rambling, but I have a touch of a cold and the Nyquil is starting to set in so forgive me.*

Like it or not, as Amy observes, standardized testing is a present (and pressing) reality. Your middle school students and their parents will need guidance in understanding and preparing for the different tests the state and school district require them to take. As Amy so accurately points out and as we've said many times already, tests are often misguided, misunderstood, and misused. Before you can help students and their families understand the tests, you'll want to examine them yourself. Standardized tests may be used for school accountability, to guide the curriculum, and to identify students for special programs. Such multiple purposes often create tensions and the potential for misuse of individual scores.

Integrating Assessment

It's important to understand that during middle school, test scores may carry greater consequences than in the earlier grades. Students, parents, and guidance counselors may be looking at high school courses through the lens of middle school test scores. In some states, scores serve as *gateways,* and students do not progress without meeting a particular score. Although we do not agree that a test should govern the curriculum, we understand that the stakes can be quite high and that you need to support your students in meeting the standards implicit these tests. Unfortunately, as professional decision makers, we often find ourselves in a quandary when standardized tests do not match our views of appropriate content. That said, we cannot afford to ignore standardized tests; nor should we want to do so. We can teach the test without teaching *to* the test.

> Consider the consequences of high-stakes tests for middle school students.

You should address some considerations in preparing students for standardized tests. First, before you introduce them to the test itself, give your students meaningful opportunities to learn the content to be tested. If the test asks them to take a quotation and use it to analyze a piece of literature, give them lots of opportunities to write about quotations from a text in their journals as a prereading or a postreading strategy. Give them chances to talk about their responses and to hear the responses of others. Eventually, you can move them toward the more formal task of analyzing literature through the "literary lens" (or quotation) that Amy mentioned previously.

We need to consider issues of motivation as we help students to become test savvy. Some students will refuse to do their best if they are not motivated to learn in the first place. In addition, we should use multiple assessment tools, so that students become familiar and proficient with a wide variety of strategies to showcase their competencies. Especially in the early phases of test preparation, we should focus more on student learning than on test scores, being constantly mindful of the need to make adaptations and modifications in materials and/or testing environments for students who need them. Finally, and perhaps most important, we must develop our *public relations* skills as we help parents and students to interpret the meaning of test scores.

> Prepare your students for standardized tests with authentic activities throughout your curriculum.

As a way of helping you think further about the issues involved in standardized testing, the task in Your Fieldwork Journal 5–2 focuses on the standardized tests in your state or school district.

Your Fieldwork Journal 5–2

Artifact Analysis: Examining Your State or District Tests

If possible, secure a copy of the standardized tests given in your state or school district. Depending on the time of year, current test booklets may not be available, but you may be able to locate previous years' tests by contacting a guidance counselor, English teacher, or building administrator. If a copy of the test is not available, you may find the answers to the following questions through an interview with one of these persons. You can also find some information about your state tests at the Web site "Developing Educational Standards," *http://edstandards.org/Standards.html.*

Once you get to the site, simply click on your state and visit the links. If the links are outdated, a simple keyword search on one of the recognized Internet search engines like Lycos, Google, or Excite will probably lead you to sites that describe your state standards and perhaps provide samples of the English language arts tests given in previous years.

However you acquire the test (or the standards associated with it), begin to analyze what is required of students:

- **Read the introductory materials.** What purposes do the test makers suggest the tests serve?
- If they are available, **look specifically at samples of the English language arts or reading tests.** What forms of reading and writing are expected of students (e.g., answering multiple-choice questions, writing a one-paragraph persuasive essay, analyzing a short piece of literature, supplying evidence from reading to support an argument)? Which of your students will have trouble with the various forms of reading and writing expected of them, and how can you prepare them to manage their difficulties?
- **Consider the environment in which the test is administered.** Will students have unlimited time in which to complete the test? Are adaptations possible for students with special needs? How can you approximate the actual testing situation without creating needless anxiety or dampening your students' motivation?
- Finally, **choose one part of the test and consider what specific skills** in reading, writing, listening, speaking, and language study your students will be expected to master. For example, the New York State Grade Eight Intermediate-Level Examination in English Language Arts has a *listening* component that requires students to listen to a text read aloud and answer 25 multiple-choice questions afterward. Students hear the speech twice and may take notes, after which they are expected to answer the questions. In analyzing a task like this, you might want to make notes in a chart such as the accompanying example on the next page.

If you are working in a classroom or workshop setting, individuals or teams might want to split up the work of this task in some way. For example, the New York State Grade Eight Intermediate-Level Examination in English Language Arts has three tasks. After individuals or small groups have analyzed each task, you may want to discuss in the larger group how to design test preparation sessions on the various tasks and language arts activities that may lead to the competencies students eventually need to develop.

Integrating Assessment

"Listening Task": Grade Eight Intermediate-Level Examination in English Language Arts

Language Lenses

Skills Needed	Reading/ Viewing	Writing	Talking/ Listening	Language Study
	reading test directions	writing notes quickly and accurately	listening for factual information	understanding the vocabulary of test prompts and suggested answers
	comprehending the proper form for noting answers (i.e., writing numbers in spaces, underlining, etc.)	deciding what is important to note	understanding and remembering the "gist" of the oral reading	
	reading and comprehending multiple-choice prompts		anticipating possible questions to follow	
	reading and comprehending possible answers			

In an era of high-stakes testing, it's all the more important to look beyond numerical scores to discover the hidden competencies that often lie behind traditional measures of ability. Standardized test scores are often used to identify students for special programs. Even though these scores may serve to identify how well students can perform in one context, they may miss other sources of student competencies. This is a lesson that Gary Zmolek, a teacher in a rural Iowa school, learns in Literacy Lesson 5–4. Gary tells the story in his own words.

Literacy Lesson 5-4

Multiple Pathways and "Cultural Blinders"

The South Tama County Community School District embraces five small communities, the Meskwaki Settlement, and the surrounding rural areas. The population of Tama is about 3,000, the population of Toledo is about 2,500, and the population of the towns of Chelsea, Montour, and Vining is under 500 each. The Settlement has somewhere between 500 and 1,000 inhabitants. The district breakdown is as follows:

Total K–12	1,694
Native American	245
African American	2
Asian Pacific American	15
Hispanic and Hispanic American	172
European American	1,250

The main industries are (a) farming, (b) agribusiness (Pioneer Seed Corn and, until recently, a packing plant, the reason for the Hispanic influx; the packing plant closed but will reopen), and (c) the Meskwaki Casino. The casino is the largest employer in the county and creates by far the most wealth. As an indication of economic status, 44% of students are on reduced or free lunch.

I was just finishing my third year of teaching in a new program, my third year at the middle school. I had finally overcome the insecurity of my first few years in a new school and a new position. Furthermore, I had the excitement of the neophyte. As the gifted education coordinator and enrichment teacher, I had successfully launched a new program model. The students seemed to love it. One nagging and continuing concern was my difficulty in identifying Native American students for the program. About 12% of the school-age population is labeled "gifted." Test scores created quandaries. I could find no convincing pattern of high ability. An individual might have a really high score on a subtest but score lower in other areas. Achievement was not a helpful indicator, either. There might be really interesting ability score data, but the basic skills tests didn't match up or students' grades indicated they were underachieving. This was in the early 1980s, and there was a good deal less literature about underachievement and giftedness. The gifted program was still new enough that I felt I needed to have numbers on my side. What if I misidentified someone?

The new program model promised to be a big help. It emphasized multiple pathways to identification and a truly multifaceted understanding of giftedness. An important part of the identification process under this model was the personal interview. This was supposed to reveal what the tests could not. Following the general nature of questions suggested in my training to teach the model, I had been happily interviewing Morgan, an intense, handsome seventh-grade boy who was the first of two Native American students I hoped to identify from the class. Sitting in on the interview at my request was the Native American paraprofessional counselor.

Morgan's responses were terse but communicative. He was obviously tense. I couldn't tell if he wanted to be identified for the program or not. I asked him, "What are some of your strengths?" I knew that one of the possible hallmarks of the gifted child was an awareness of abilities above the norm. Morgan sat silent. I rephrased the question slightly, "What are some of the things you can do a lot better than other people your age?" Still no response. Instead, after a long, painful silence, Morgan lowered his gaze and looked at the floor. I tried to move on to some other questions, but the interview was over. Morgan left the room without a goodbye, and I sat perplexed with the paraprofessional.

"Do you know what you asked him to do?" she said. Her tone was friendly, the voice of someone who is going to point out a blunder you could not have realized you were going to make. "You asked him to tell you his strengths. In other words, you asked him to boast, and that is something we learn very early never, ever to do. He wanted to answer you out of respect, and because I'm sure he wants to get into the program. But he just couldn't. The taboo is so strong."

After teaching in my district for 9 years, I assumed I knew enough about the local Native American tribal ways to avoid such a difficulty. I realized how much my cultural blinders interfered with my task to identify Morgan's abilities without asking him such a question, which required a self-emphasizing answer. Considering the fact that I rather than Morgan had blown the interview, Morgan was identified and stayed with the program until he decided to finish high school at Philips Andover and then went to Dartmouth College.

Fortunately, Gary had a caring and sensitive paraprofessional counselor to help him remove his cultural blinders, and Morgan was afforded the educational opportunities he so deserved. Unfortunately, many students like Morgan fall through the cracks of gifted programs and other special opportunities. It's probably not hard to figure out that all children have special gifts and each child should receive enriching and challenging learning opportunities, especially those who are not always successful in a performance-centered curriculum. Gary's story reminds us that it is important to look far beyond those things that are most easily captured by a numerical score.

The content and format of any assessment system and its performance demands should be carefully aligned with your teaching goals. Special accommodation for students with disabilities should be given appropriate attention, so that all students have a fair opportunity to achieve success and their test scores accurately reflect what they can do rather than what their disabilities may hide.

> Make sure your assessment measures are culturally fair.

In this chapter we have focused on the multiple ways that assessment may serve you and your middle school students. We tried to present a variety of formal and informal assessment techniques that should help you to enhance your students' knowledge, evaluate their progress, and tailor your teaching strategies to meet their complex and varied needs. As your students are given more responsibility for their own learning, you can reduce the anxieties that often accompany assessment. Contrary to what we read in the popular press, more difficult tests don't create good teaching or enhanced learning. Your challenge is to design fair and sensitive assessment tools that allow your students to negotiate all literacy skills demanded of them in our fast-paced and ever-shifting world.

Standards in Practice

Assessing Student Performances

The Interstate New Teacher Assessment and Support Consortium (INTASC) model core standards for licensing teachers represent those principles that should be present in all teaching, regardless of the subject or grade level taught. The standards are intended to serve as a framework for the systemic reform of teacher preparation and professional development. Principle 8 addresses competencies in using formal and informal assessment tools. A detailed description of each of the standards can be found by visiting the INTASC Web site at *http://www.ccsso.org/intascst.html#draft*. We have included a brief excerpt of Principle 8 (assessment). This principle includes three subcategories: knowledge, dispositions, and performances. For a full understanding of the INTASC standards for assessment, be sure to visit the Web site and examine all of the ways in which INTASC recommends that teachers should handle assessment in their classrooms.

> **Principle 8:** The teacher understands and uses formal and informal assessment strategies to evaluate and ensure the continuous intellectual, social and physical development of the learner.

Once you have thoroughly examined Principle 8 and all of its subcategories, consider these possibilities as you begin to develop your assessment practices

1. If you are beginning a student teaching placement, you may want to discuss with your mentor teacher different ways of monitoring student learning and teacher effectiveness. Keep a running list of the different assessment practices your host teacher uses on the left side of a double-entry journal. Later, when you have some time to reflect, note in the right-hand column the INTASC criteria that are being addressed. As you begin your student teaching, use the INTASC standards to add new assessment practices to your preliminary list.
2. If you are currently tutoring or teaching in a middle school, you may want to examine your own assessment strategies in light of the INTASC performance indicators under Principle 8:
    - The teacher appropriately uses a variety of formal and informal assessment techniques (e.g., observation, portfolios of student work, teacher-made tests, performance tasks, projects, student self-assessments, peer assessment, and standardized tests) to enhance her or his knowledge of learners, evaluate students' progress and performances, and modify teaching and learning strategies.
    - The teacher solicits and uses information about students' experiences, learning behavior, needs, and progress from parents, other colleagues, and the students themselves.
    - The teacher uses assessment strategies to involve learners in self-assessment activities, to help them become aware of their strengths and needs, and to encourage them to set personal goals for learning.
    - The teacher evaluates the effect of class activities on both individuals and the class as a whole, collecting information through observation of classroom interactions, questioning, and analysis of student work.

- The teacher monitors his or her own teaching strategies and behavior in relation to student success, modifying plans and instructional approaches accordingly.
- The teacher maintains useful records of student work and performance and can communicate student progress knowledgeably and responsibly, based on appropriate indicators, to students, parents, and other colleagues.

Create a section for your professional portfolio in which you document the different types of assessments you use, as well as your growing understandings about assessment in general. You may want to include some assessment artifacts that you designed or assisted in preparing, along with a reflective commentary on how these artifacts and approaches meet the INTASC standards.

3. If you bring a greater amount of experience with assessment to this chapter, you may want to try to complete the task that is actually used in the INTASC portfolio. Select examples of how three students responded to your assessment tool. (These examples should represent three different levels of performance. One student's work should represent an understanding of ways of responding to the task that *meet your criteria* for successful performance. The second example should represent understanding that *did not meet your criteria* for successful performance. The third should represent understanding and ways of responding that in some way *exceeded your criteria* for successful performance.) Remove students' names from their work to protect their anonymity, then write an explanation of the following:
   - How you determined and responded to the three levels of performance on the assignment
   - How the assessment of your students matches your teaching goals
   - How this assessment will guide your future instruction
   - What you have learned about assessment, what you would keep the same, and what things you would try to change or improve

REFERENCES

Beach, R., & Myers, J. (2001). *Inquiry-based English instruction: Engaging students in life and literature.* New York: Teachers College Press.

Brown, R. (1989). Testing and thoughtfulness. *Educational Leadership, 46*(7), 31–33.

The Council of Chief State School Officers. (1992). *Model Standards for beginning teacher licensing and development: A resource for state dialogue.* Retrieved August 5, 2002, from http://www.ccsso.org/intascst.html#draft.

Finders, M., & Graham, P. (1991). Commissioned research report by American College Testing. *Teaching composition: A review of current instructional practices 1985–1990.*

Gardner, H. (1991). *The unschooled mind: How children think and how schools should teach.* New York: Basic Books.

Lee, H. (2001). *To kill a mockingbird.* New York: Harper Trade.

McBride, J. (1997). *The color of water: A black man's tribute to his white mother.* Madison, WI: Turtleback Books.

Wiggins, G. (1989). Teaching to the (authentic) test. *Educational Leadership, 46*(7), 41–47.

RESOURCES

Print

Applebee, A. (1994). English language arts assessment: Lessons from the past. *English Journal, 83,* 40–46.

Brown, R. (1989). Testing and thoughtfulness. *Educational Leadership, 46* (April), 31–33.

Capper, J. (1996). *Testing to learn—learning to test.* Newark, DE: International Reading Association.

Dana, T., & Tippins, D. (1993). Considering alternative assessments for middle level learners. *Middle School Journal, 25,* 3–5.

Gill, K. (1993). *Process and portfolios in writing instruction.* Urbana, IL: NCTE Press.

Graves, D., & Sunstein, B. (1992). *Portfolio portraits.* Portsmouth, NH: Heinemann.

International Reading Association. (1999). *High-stakes assessments in reading: A position statement of the International Reading Association.* Newark, DE: International Reading Association.

International Reading Association and National Council of Teachers of English Joint Task Force on Assessment. (1994). *Standards for the assessment of reading and writing.* Newark, DE: International Reading Association.

Lewin, L., & Shoemaker, B. J. (1998). *Great performances creating classroom-based assessment tasks.* Alexandria, VA: The Association for Supervision and Curriculum Development.

Lustig, K. (1996). *Portfolio assessment: A handbook for middle level teachers.* Westerville, OH: National Middle School Association.

Perrone, V. (Ed.). (1991). *Expanding student assessment.* Alexandria, VA: Association for Supervision and Curriculum Development.

Reif, L. (1990). Finding the value in evaluation: Self-assessment in a middle school classroom. *Educational Leadership, 47*(6), 24–29.

Schurr, S. (1999). *Authentic assessment using product, performance, and portfolio measures from A to Z.* Westerville, OH: National Middle School Association.

Stiggins, R. J. (2001). *Student-involved classroom assessment* (3rd ed.). Upper Saddle River, NJ: Merrill/Prentice Hall.

Sunstein, B., & Cheville, J. (1995). Assessing portfolios: A portfolio. *Iowa English Bulletin.* Urbana, IL: NCTE Press.

Tchudi, S. (1997). *Alternatives to grading student writing.* Urbana, IL: NCTE Press.

Wiener, R., & Cohen, J. (1997). *Literacy portfolios: Using assessment to guide instruction.* Upper Saddle River, NJ: Merrill/Prentice Hall.

Wiggins, G. (1994). Toward better report cards. *Educational Leadership, 52*(2), 28–37

Winograd, G. (1994). Developing alternative assessments: Six problems worth solving. *The Reading Teacher, 47,* 420–423.

Yancie, K. (1992). *Portfolios in the writing classroom: An introduction.* Urbana, IL: NCTE Press.

Yancie, K. B., & Weiser, I. (1997). *Situating portfolios: Four perspectives.* Logan: Utah State University Press.

Electronic

ERIC Clearinghouse on Assessment and Evaluation. The ERIC Clearinghouse on Assessment and Evaluation provides balanced information concerning educational assessment and resources to encourage responsible test use. The site is extensive and offers information on topics ranging from student evaluation to professional standards.

http://ericae.net

Learning Record. The Learning Record (LR) gives helpful information about involving teachers, parents, and students in the assessment of student work. This site provides a balanced approach to assessment, emphasizing public accountability for student progress based upon standards-referenced (as opposed to norm-referenced) evaluation methods.

http://www.learningrecord.org/

National Center for Fair & Open Testing (FairTest). This advocacy organization works to end the abuses, misuses, and flaws of standardized testing and ensure that evaluation of students and workers is fair, open, and educationally sound.

http://www.fairtest.org

National Coalition of Education Activists. The NCEA is a multiracial network of families, school staff, union and community activists, and others organizing for equity and fundamental changes in local school districts. Its purpose is to support activists in their efforts to develop, promote, and implement progressive school reforms, to provide a counter to the right, and to fight racism and other forms of institutional bias. NCEA was incorporated in 1991.

http://members.aol.com/nceaweb/

North Central Regional Educational Laboratory. NCREL is one of 10 not-for-profit Regional Educational Laboratories. The organization is dedicated to helping schools and students reach their full potential. Search the keywords "alternative assessment" for links to useful resources on approaches to alternative assessment techniques.

http://www.ncrel.org

Parents for Public Schools. This national organization of grassroots chapters is dedicated to involving parents in more meaningful roles as decision makers in their children's education.

http://www.parents4publicschools.com/

chapter 6

Language Lenses: Integrating the Language Arts in the Middle Grades

GUIDING QUESTIONS

1. What does the phrase *integrated language arts* mean to you?
2. How are reading, writing, talking, and listening alike, yet different?
3. How can you create experiences with language that help all students to succeed?

A CASE FOR CONSIDERATION

A Constant Voyeur

Mary McCrone is a seventh- and eighth-grade teacher at Roberts school, a K–8 building in the city school system of Syracuse, New York. Although her building includes children from the primary grades, there are approximately 170 seventh and eighth graders who, along with their middle school teachers, occupy the entire top floor of the building. This "school-within-a-school" has adopted many aspects of the middle school model such as team advisement, 80-minute block scheduling, cross-curricular planning, and team teaching.

Students stay with the same English teacher for the entire 2 years of middle school, so Mary will have her seventh-grade students again next year. In fact, she teaches all 170 middle school students in the school on a 6-day schedule. On days 1, 3, and 5, she teaches the seventh-grade students, while on days 2, 4, and 6, she teaches eighth-grade. This arrangement is possible because her students have math and science every day but take English and social studies on a rotating basis. On days when a group isn't with Mary, they are with their social studies teacher. The following story is from Mary's seventh-grade classroom. She tells it in her own words.

At eight o'clock in the morning the school is buzzing with a familiar mixture of sounds. I hear voices in the hall, collectively. The agitated hum of adolescence. Busses pull away. The crossing guard yells to a motorist. A bell rings. Announcements begin. My eighth-grade homeroom has gone to its first period, and I await my first seventh-grade class of the day. For now, all noise stops at my door. Room 303 is silent, except for my soft classical music that floats from the corner. That music will strive all day to help me maintain an atmosphere of peace. Now it is my companion as I quickly rummage through my desk for my attendance cards. Another bell rings and students begin to prance, saunter, leap, stroll, and drag into my classroom. "Good morning," I say, momentarily looking up from an overstuffed desk drawer. They kind of ignore me, which is okay for now, because I am rabid to find these stupid attendance records.

By the time I am victorious, students are seated at their tables. Some have started to copy what's on the overhead screen. Some are chatting and some are staring into space, waiting for my invitation to begin. One boy has his nose in a book, one girl is frantically finishing a note, and one girl has already fallen asleep. I scan the room. They are all so different, yet even before I look up to greet them, I know which class they are. The sound of them. Their patterns of movement. They have group characteristics as well as individual ones. I walk from behind my desk and slip through the maze of tables, couches, chairs, plants, bookshelves, lamps, and computers to the destination of my wind chimes. I run my fingers across them and, magically, all becomes quiet. (Surprise!) I welcome them again and begin to review what is on the screen (see accompanying figure).

The opening task gets their attention. Some "oooh" and "ahh." Some hide in their notebooks. Some roll their eyes. "Mrs. McCrone, you need to stay 'out of the business'!" I assure them that I don't want to be "IN the business," that they can keep this writing private if they like. Heads bow in unison. The music plays. I find my writer's notebook, have a seat on couch, put my feet up on the coffee table, and begin writing. Even though there are 25 kids in the room, I momentarily get lost in the memory of my first crush. We write separately, yet the sound of our sliding pens and

---

OPENING TASK

KEY POINT: One purpose for real-life writing is to record memories.

AGENDA: March 30–Day 3

1. opening procedures: task and silent reading
2. choice: Literature Circle—the poem "Oranges" (Gary Soto)
   OR Reading/Writing Workshop
3. closure: class meeting; follow-up choices

OPENING TASK: Write about a time when you had a crush on someone, or write about a character in a movie you have watched or a book you have read who has experienced a crush.

pencils makes us one. After about 10 minutes, some kids are bursting to share, while others would die first. As I finish my writing, I scan them. I feel a sudden pang for those students who have never been "crushed out" on anyone or, worse yet, have never had anyone be infatuated with them. I realize that this topic will evoke very different memories, thoughts, and self-perceptions.

My eyes skip from face to face as we read the poem. I am a constant voyeur with my students, watching them from the back of my head or out of the corner of my eye to see their unrehearsed reactions. Today we are reading the poem, "Oranges," by Gary Soto (2000). It's about a young man on his first date with a girl. He walks to her house with a nickel and two oranges in his pocket. Together, they walk through city streets on a winter day until they come upon a drugstore. Soon, they are standing before the candy counter, and he tells her to pick out something. When she chooses a candy that costs a dime, he doesn't say a word. Instead, he places his only nickel and an orange on the counter. There is a moment of suspense as he waits to see if the shopkeeper will trade these for the dime candy the girl has chosen. The poem ends on a happy note as the girl unwraps the candy, he peels the orange he has left, and they continue on their first walk together.

We are halfway through, and I can almost see the individual "movies of the mind" that they are creating as they read. The films dance in front of them and over their heads. Some visions hold them close, like a first hug, as it dawns on them that this is exactly what this poem is about—first love. As I continue my peeking, I am jerked to a halt by one student who is (of course) not paying the slightest bit of attention. "He hasn't loved a girl yet," I think. "There is no movie for him." Another student seems almost to be crying. "OK, whom does she have a crush on now?" I take a deep breath as I realize that it's now up to me to think of a way to get all these different students to respond to this poem.

When we prepare to teach anything, we have so many decisions to make. Is this primarily a literature lesson? Do I want to focus on reading skills or appreciation? What about writing? Is the lesson going to inspire a creative piece because we are going to reach down into their gut and pull it out? Or, do we need to focus on organization, grammar, spelling, punctuation, sentence structure? OR should the previous OR be an AND? What about style, organization, and audience? Maybe we'll concentrate on their speaking skills—let's see, formal or informal? With audiovisuals or not? Probably we have to bring in Howard Gardner's eight intelligences and let them act, draw, build, blah, blah, blah. . . . Maybe we should let them use this as a journal piece? Or, do we get this to publication in their folders? Should they work in groups or alone? Should they make the choice, or should I?

One of the hardest decisions has to do with the language experiences I offer. Some of my kids are born readers, preferring to bury themselves in a good book; others would rather die than be caught reading. Some love to write in journals or diaries, while others find them too "touchy-feely." Some of my students are natural performers and sharers. Put them in a group and they're in heaven. Others sit shyly on the sidelines, preferring to write or read silently in the privacy of their own thoughts. And, let's face it, nobody likes to study grammar. As a language arts teacher, I know you can't please all students all of the time. But how can you at least create enough variety so that all students have an equal chance to succeed?

FOR DISCUSSION

- What are your own strengths and preferences where different language arts are concerned? As an early adolescent, how would you have preferred to respond to a poem about first love?
- If you were teaching this poem to this particular group of middle school students, what kind of language activities might you design to allow all students a chance to succeed?
- What can you tell about the ways in which Mary sets her class up to allow for her students' diversity?

INTEGRATING THE LANGUAGE ARTS: TEACHING FOR DIVERSITY

For roughly a year, Mary and Susan have been working on a collaborative teaching and research project with Mary's seventh-grade students. Although they have taught seventh grade as a team for most of the past semester, Mary taught the lesson described here during a week when Susan was not there. What Mary had planned to be a 1-day experience ended up taking on a life of its own and stretched out over several days.

We're sure you'll agree that Mary's class load of 170 middle school students is daunting enough, but the diversity of these students makes her life as an English teacher even more complicated. For the rest of this chapter, we will do something a little unusual. Instead of profiling the experiences of different teachers in our literacy lessons, we will present an extended lesson that Mary taught over the course of several days.

In this chapter, we ask you to consider the different ways that language can be put to use in classrooms like Mary's and to accept the premise that, regardless of how similar the students in any classroom may appear on the surface—particularly at the middle school level—*there is no such thing as a homogeneous classroom*. Not only does each student come from slightly different racial, cultural, and family backgrounds, each has also developed particular preferences and predispositions toward different language acts, from reading and viewing to writing, talking, listening, and language study. Your constant challenge as a middle school teacher is to provide ways for reluctant readers, writers, and language users to succeed alongside those who seem to be more eager and flexible.

We'd like to begin by introducing you to the concept of *language lenses* that forms the organizing framework for the following chapters in this book. After this introduction, we'll bring you back into Mary's classroom for a look at how students themselves can learn to view their literate acts through these lenses. We hope that this chapter will provide you with a set of tools to assist you in helping students like Mary's in your current and future classrooms. Let's begin, though, with some common misconceptions that seem, at least on the surface, to work against the idea of integrating the language arts.

CHALLENGING SOME MYTHS ABOUT LANGUAGE

Somewhere in your teacher education program or on the pages of professional journals you've probably encountered the phrase *integrated language arts*. Although we believe this is an excellent idea (we wouldn't be writing this chapter if we didn't), we need to point out that integrating doesn't mean throwing reading and viewing, writing, talking, and listening activities together haphazardly or assuming that one language form is the same as all the others. Creating an integrated curriculum must be done mindfully, just as you would sequence a good lesson or unit plan. Although your particular students and circumstances will dictate many of your decisions, *you* bear the ultimate responsibility for deciding exactly how and in what form different language acts will support and enrich each other. This is a difficult process, especially when your administrators, colleagues, or former teachers may have been operating on some myths about language that seem to argue against an integrated approach to English language arts teaching. Let's consider three of the most common.

Myth: Speech Is an Inferior Form of Language

As Britton (1970) once said, "Talk is the sea upon which all else floats." This is true in two senses. On the one hand, talk is our first language. From the moment of birth, we are immersed in talk. Our fledgling attempts at communication are in the form of sounds, which later become words and eventually the longer utterances we call oral language. We have been talking longer than we've been writing or reading, and much of our thinking, conscious or otherwise, is accomplished through talk.

On the other hand, just as fish are the least likely creatures to be aware of water, young people in schools are not often taught how to make oral language work for them in their learning processes (see Hynds & Rubin, 1990). In addition, English language arts teachers, most of whom are not trained as speech or drama teachers, are sometimes reluctant to bring oral language into their classrooms. Even if teachers are comfortable with oral activities, there is often a misconception that writing is more formal and therefore more appropriate for the English classroom than talk.

Oral language includes pauses, repetition, slang, and other evidence of informality. It "leans upon" context in a way that writing does not. That is, you might say to a friend, "Get that!" as you gesture toward something that is blowing away. Your nonverbal behaviors assist your talk. Sometimes they're quite literally worth a thousand words, or at least a few. If you were writing about the same incident, you might say: "Get that napkin! It's blowing away!" Notice how much more formal and explicit the written sentence is.

Because of the formality of most writing done in schools, the mistaken belief is that students who "write as they talk" fail to write in cogent, coherent ways. This simply isn't true. As Elbow (1985) has pointed out, talk not only helps the development of writing skills, it's essential to that development. And talk, like writing, can be permanent (try to take back something you said when you thought no one was listening) or what Elbow calls evanescent and inconsequential, like singing in the shower or "practicing" a conversation in a private moment.

As you help your students to become writers, you need to engage them in this kind of informal "talking to learn." Brainstorming informally with teachers and peers in pairs or groups helps students to develop and create ideas for writing. Later in the process, peer- and teacher-student conferencing can help them to craft and polish their writing. Finally, reading their writing aloud to others not only builds confidence, but also lets them "hear" their words as others may perceive them. Thus, contrary to our former beliefs, oral language is not an inferior form of language, but an integral aspect of literacy learning.

Myth: Learning to Read Must Precede Learning to Write

For years, it was assumed that elementary school children had to learn to read before they could be taught to write. As a result, many children prior to the 1970s were denied the opportunity to play with written language through what's known today as "invented spelling." As we've explained earlier in this book, both of our elementary school teachers focused on reading, with perhaps a little attention to writing in the form of copying words from lists or printing the alphabet. Today, however, young children in a great many elementary classrooms are encouraged to interweave drawing and "invented spelling" (their fledgling attempts at sounding out and spelling words) as part of their early writing processes.

Today, reading/viewing and writing are often taught in tandem, not in some kind of arbitrary sequence. This same principle holds true for middle school students. Some still need to draw before (or during) writing; others become writers before they discover the power and pleasure of reading and viewing. Although the processes are different, reading/viewing, writing, talking, and listening can enrich and enhance each other. It's your job to find a way to make all of these language activities work together.

Let's say you have an avid writer who hates to read. Encouraging that student to "read like a writer" (Smith, 1984), with an eye to a published author's techniques, may allow you to turn an enthusiasm for writing into a love of reading. Another student may shy away from reading or writing but produce elaborate drawings or cartoons. This student's attraction to drawing may be a key to thinking skills just waiting to be tapped and transformed into literate behaviors. Through talking about their art or illustrating their own writing, students may develop other literacies. In an integrated approach to English language arts, students should always be shuttling from among a variety of language experiences that support and enrich each other.

Myth: Fluency in One Language Interferes With Fluency in Another

In fact, one supports the other. Perhaps you have students in your classroom whose family members speak Spanish or Hmong or a dialect of Chinese. For years, America was seen as a "melting pot" where teachers were supposed to turn students quickly and permanently away from their home language to help them to master English. If you have ESL learners in your classroom, it is not your responsibility to eradicate their first language, often called "L1" by linguists.

In fact, research consistently bears out the fact that children who are supported in two or more languages can actually develop superior language competency to that of monolingual students. Occasionally providing reading materials in a student's home language or allowing the use of L1 in the context of informal logs or journals gives students whose first language is not English the opportunity to read and write with fluency without always having to "translate" ideas from or into an unfamiliar language. This isn't to say that ESL learners should never have to speak, write, or read in formal English. A good literacy program supports the development of both languages, fostering a kind of back-and-forth process, where one language "teaches" the learner about the other.

We need to point out that by asking you to *integrate* the language arts, we are not assuming that all language processes are the same. In fact, different thinking and linguistic processes underlie each language act. Reading is not writing, is not talking, is not listening. More important, students view these processes very differently. Some love to write and share in large groups; others, like some of Mary's students, "would rather die first." Some will write, but only in the privacy of journals or notes to trusted friends. Others won't write at all, preferring to lose themselves in a good book or chat with classmates. Some students are natural performers; others shrink from group discussions or oral performance.

All of these students will be sitting side by side in your classroom. What's a middle school teacher to do? The trick is learning to create lessons with enough diversity of language choices that students of all stripes can succeed and prosper. This means helping them to view their learning through what we will call "language lenses."

LANGUAGE LENSES

Perhaps a metaphor will help you to envision the integration of language arts in a more concrete way. First, consider these four aspects of English language arts teaching: (a) reading and viewing, (b) writing, (c) talking and listening, and (d) language study. Think of each aspect of language learning as a *lens* through which you might view all of the other possibilities available to create a lesson, a unit, or an entire curriculum. Lenses may be tinted particular colors or may have surfaces that seem to transform what the viewer sees. Think, for example, how the color and thickness of an eyeglass changes your view, or how objects look when seen through a multifaceted lens. Each **language lens** changes the appearance and array of the other language options in some way. The possibilities for supportive language activities change when viewed through different language lenses.

Before explaining this concept in more depth, we'd like to define a few key terms. According to the *NCTE/IRA Standards for the English Language Arts* (1996),

> we use the term *text* broadly to refer not only to printed texts, but also to spoken language, graphics, and technological communication. Language . . . encompasses visual communication in addition to spoken and written forms of expression. And reading refers to listening and viewing in addition to print-oriented reading. (p. 2)

By this definition, reading can encompass all manner of "texts" from printed materials to film and other media, including visual art, television, and different forms of electronic communication. Similarly, "writing" can include drawing, photographing, and producing computer graphics, among other forms of nonprint representations.

To further clarify our notion of language lenses, we'll begin with an example. Suppose you want to focus your students' attention on reading and viewing. Maybe they seem to be struggling readers, or you have been spending a lot of time on other types of language activities in the past several weeks and want to focus more particularly on reading and viewing. When seen through the lens of reading and viewing, the other language arts available to you take on new dimensions and possibilities.

Focus On
Reading and Viewing

Language Lenses: Integrating the Language Arts in the Middle Grades **153**

Just as a lens may highlight certain aspects of an object over others or even change the shape and array of a set of objects, the lens through which we view different aspects of language learning renders new possibilities for how we use them. Notice in Figure 6–1, for example, the ways in which the possibilities for talking/listening, writing, and language study take shape when seen through the lens of reading and viewing.

You might bring the other three aspects of language learning into your reading and viewing instruction in several ways. If, for example, your students are reading literature, you can engage them in a variety of oral language experiences such as book clubs where five or six students meet regularly to talk about a group-selected novel. At various points in their reading, you might ask different students to role-play events or scenes alluded to but not directly presented by an author. Or, you could invite a librarian in to model

FIGURE 6-1 The Lens of Reading and Viewing

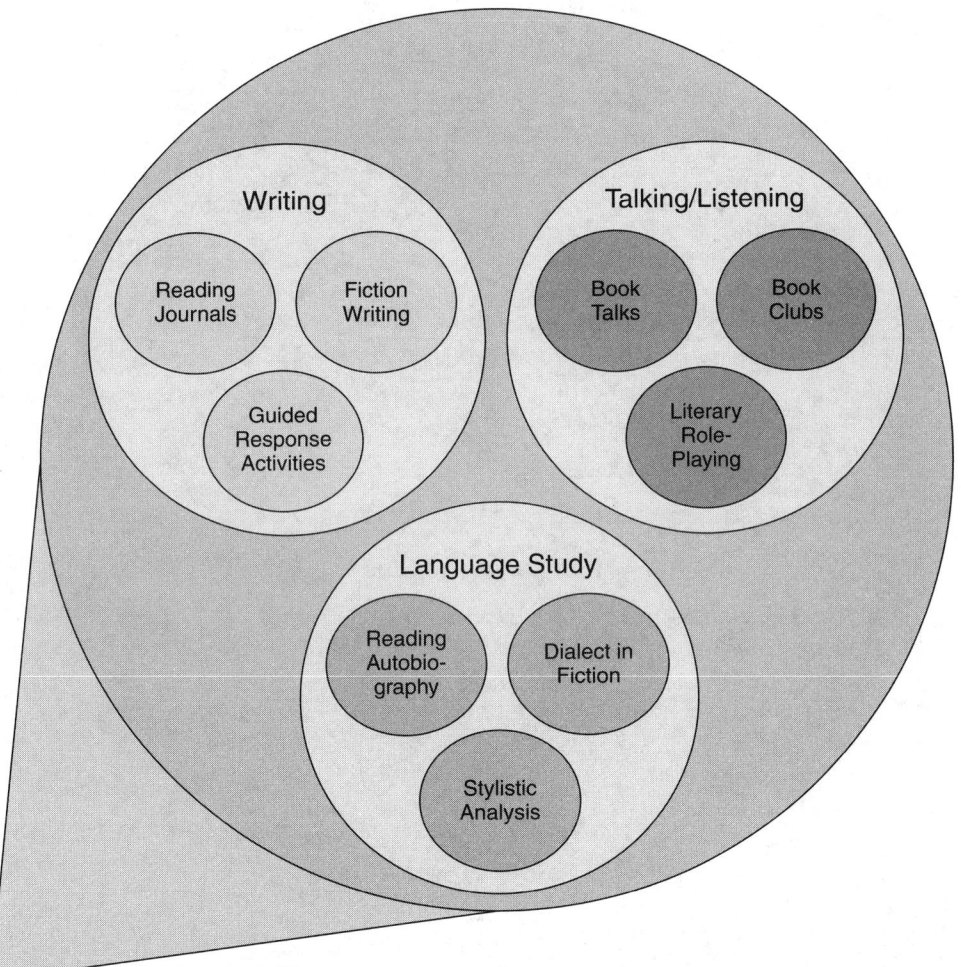

the art of book talks, where readers create lively, dramatic renditions of favorite books, designed to entice their classmates into reading the same book.

Your students might begin writing their own fictional pieces, writing informally about their reading and viewing in logs or journals, or following guided response opportunities.

You might want to focus specifically on the study of language by asking students to write memoirs about their own histories as readers, studying the use of dialect in published fiction, or analyzing a writer's style by comparing several pieces by the same author across different genres.

Focus On Writing

Now try switching your language lens to writing. Notice how the options and possibilities for other aspects of language learning shift and change, as depicted in Figure 6–2.

FIGURE 6-2 The Lens of Writing

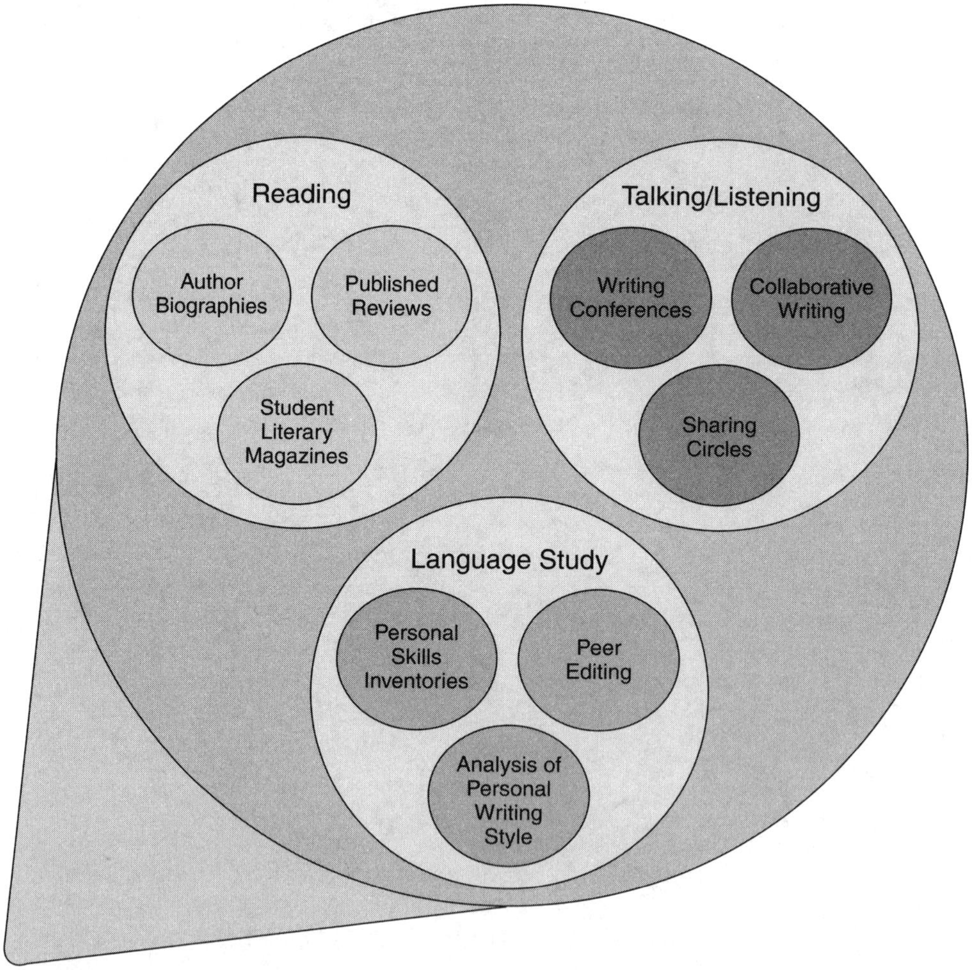

Perhaps you decide to begin a *writing* unit by examining the work of published writers and engaging in some informal research. Your students might read several works by a favorite writer, read a biography of that author, or engage in some informal research about him or her. In the process, they could read published reviews by literary critics or even other teenagers on literature listservs (see the address for the NCTE listserv at the end of this chapter). You might want to wrap up a unit on fiction writing by helping students to publish an anthology of their best pieces.

Talking and listening could be used to support writing in the form of teacher-student or peer conferences, collaborative writing projects, and regular opportunities for students to read work-in-progress to each other in sharing circles.

Finally, you can focus students on their own language processes by helping them to analyze patterns of error and keep personal "skills-to-learn" inventories in their writing portfolios. Periodically, students might exchange papers and respond to or edit each others' work. Finally, they might compare their own stylistic preferences with those of published authors through regular analysis of their writing with your help or the help of their peers.

Now let's shift the lens again to focus explicitly on talking and listening (see Figure 6–3).

Focus On
Talking and Listening

Although much oral language in the English classroom is informal and exploratory, students can try their hands at writing or scripting of oral language activities, preparing manuscripts or outlines for formal speeches, debates, or dramatic performances of student writing.

The reading of literature lends itself naturally to performance through activities such as readers' theater, choral reading, oral interpretation, and dramatic enactments. More informally, students can talk about their reading and viewing in pair-shares, small groups, or larger forums such as literature circles, where volunteers meet in a comfortable place to read and talk about a piece of literature while other class members are working on independent projects.

Language study takes on a new richness as students explore different facets of oral language. Perhaps they might want to conduct a bit of informal research by taping and analyzing the conversational patterns in a social gathering or a workplace setting. The study of slang and regional usage patterns helps students to understand that language is constantly changing and often bonds people together on the basis of neighborhood, family, or age group. Students might also be urged to study the dynamics of group discussion by sitting in a circle and watching a small group as they note "helpful" and "unhelpful" discussion patterns in a "fishbowl" arrangement.

Finally, let's say that you want to focus explicitly on the study of language (see Figure 6–4). Students might begin their study of language by researching and writing about the origins of words or the history of family names. If they have been studying different aspects of an author's style or have been reading literary or film criticism, they might be encouraged to write critical reviews of their own, paying particular attention to the language of writers or the visual "language" of film makers.

Focus On
Language Study

Each day might start off with a bit of oral language as students present mini-lessons in groups or individually on various aspects of style, grammar, and usage. As a regular part of writing instruction, students could work in collaborative teams of "editorial experts," where each team is responsible for a particular skill, such as subject-verb agreement, and all drafts must be analyzed by different "expert groups" before

FIGURE 6-3 The Lens of Talking and Listening

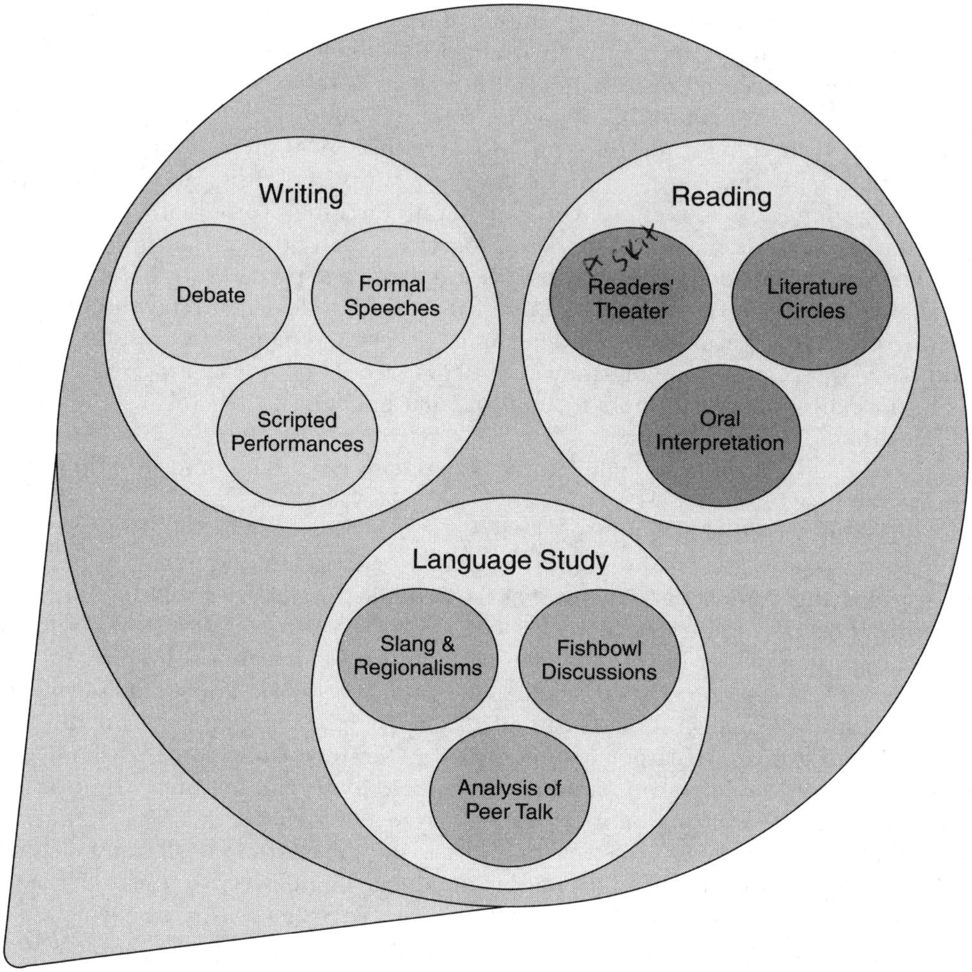

- **Writing**
  - Debate
  - Formal Speeches
  - Scripted Performances
- **Reading**
  - Readers' Theater
  - Literature Circles
  - Oral Interpretation
- **Language Study**
  - Slang & Regionalisms
  - Fishbowl Discussions
  - Analysis of Peer Talk

being handed in. Small groups of students could become "dialect detectives," taping and/or studying the language of people in different occupations such as restaurant workers, computer programmers, or mechanics.

Reading and viewing can be enlivened by asking students to examine how published authors use language or by studying their own reading preferences and keeping regular personal reading inventories. Finally, principles of grammar, vocabulary, and usage can be taught by asking students to focus explicitly on structures peculiar to certain authors whose work they have been reading.

To more fully understand the concept of language lenses, try this brief classroom inquiry project in Your Fieldwork Journal 6–1.

FIGURE 6-4 The Lens of Language Study

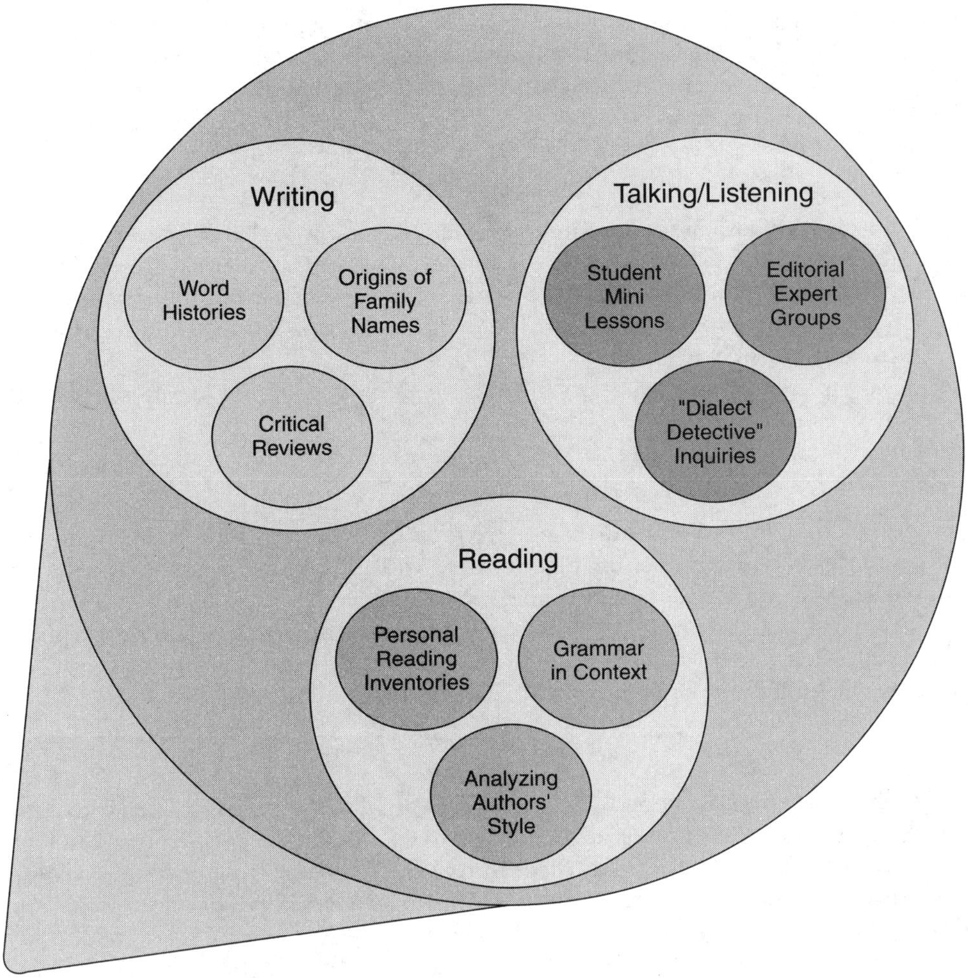

[Diagram: A large teardrop-shaped area labeled containing three overlapping circles: "Writing" (containing Word Histories, Origins of Family Names, Critical Reviews), "Talking/Listening" (containing Student Mini Lessons, Editorial Expert Groups, "Dialect Detective" Inquiries), and "Reading" (containing Personal Reading Inventories, Grammar in Context, Analyzing Authors' Style).]

Your Fieldwork Journal 6-1

Classroom Inquiry: Viewing a Lesson Through Language Lenses

Now that you've learned a bit about language lenses, find a lesson plan that you have created or one on which you are currently working. First, decide if your overriding goal can be captured in one or more of the language lenses presented earlier in this chapter. Maybe your main goal involves reading or oral language. Don't worry if you can't narrow everything down to one lens. Teaching is messy and not easily captured in simple diagrams like those you've just seen.

Begin with the lens that seems most salient in this particular lesson, then examine the language activities you have created. If your goal is reading and viewing, look for any examples of writing, listening, talking, or language study that you could use in the service of your goals for reading and viewing. Underline and label any instances such as these with abbreviations ("W," "T&L," "LS"). Don't forget, by the way, that different language acts can take on different guises. Drawing or artistic representation, for example, can be an important part of the writing or reading process. When you're done, ask yourself the following questions:

- Does my lesson focus too heavily on one language lens to the exclusion of others?
- Can struggling readers be given options to use informal writing, talking, or other forms of language to develop their reading and viewing skills?
- Do the writing experiences I provide include a range of opportunities from informal to more formal?
- Have I missed important opportunities for talking, listening, or language study in this lesson?
- Can students' reading and viewing experience include their own choices as well as mine?

Remember that every lesson does not have to incorporate options from all four lenses. At the same time, identify places where you can expand your offerings to include options that help all language learners to succeed.

When you've finished with this informal analysis, write a paragraph or two about what you've learned. Or perhaps better yet, revise this lesson with an eye to expanding the language possibilities available to your students.

At this point, the concept of language lenses may still be a bit fuzzy to you. After all, this whole business of integrating the language arts sounds good, but as you have probably guessed, it can get pretty dicey in real classrooms with real students. Sometimes, though, our students can help us with this process if we share our goals and allow them to shape their own learning experiences.

In Literacy Lesson 6–1, Mary McCrone does just that. As the lesson begins, her students have just finished writing about their first crush and are now getting ready to choose whether they want to gather together for "literature circle," to explore Soto's poem in more depth, or to participate in what Mary calls "reading/writing workshop." Those who choose reading/writing workshop work quietly outside the circle individually, in pairs, or small groups on independent reading, writing, or inquiry projects.

Literacy Lesson 6-1

Decisions, Decisions

One of the hardest things about teaching, for me at least, is striking the balance between letting the students construct their own learning and knowing when to step in with my expertise and facilitate. Because this poem is about a pretty personal topic, I'm glad I am presenting it in a voluntary literature circle. Some kids might need to opt out.

I stand, walk, ring the chimes again, and without a word, open my record book. "When I call your name, please tell me if you are doing reading/writing workshop or joining us in literature circle for the poem, 'Oranges.' " I give them a trailer for the poem and promise that if they want to share what they've written, they can do so in literature circle. I start reading names. There is a bustle of movement. "Can I go to the library today to finish my research?" "Can I get online?" "How long is the poem?" "Where are you going to sit, Mrs. McCrone?" "Can I go to the bathroom?" Finally we are settled. I have 15 students lounged around me in the couch area, 9 students sprinkled around the room reading silently, working on writing pieces (oops, that one child is asleep again), and 3 students in the library. There are 60 minutes of class left. We begin.

We get to the last line of the poem—the one that talks about the young man's orange, "so bright against the grey of December that someone might have thought I was making a fire in my hands" (Soto, 2000, p. 339). There is a pause, then Danielle says, "That reminds me of my parents. I bet they fell in love like that." Tim says, "Yeah, nobody had any money in the days—not like now." Then Bruce yells from somewhere on the floor of literature circle, "I think they were black; what he did was so 'ghetto.' "

Some kids talk about a time when they liked someone. We tease each other about who is going out with whom. I relate stories of my first love (which, of course, really put them in a tizzy). We dissect why the boy told the girl to buy anything when he knew he didn't have much money. We put all the metaphors of the weather and time of day under a microscope. We create the voice of the girl, remarking how silent she is in the poem. What was she thinking and feeling anyway, and just how do we know? We take turns pretending to be the saleslady, acting out the look on her face when she saw the orange and the nickel on the counter. Then we write:

Jomell: I think the boy really liked the girl because of the way he went to her house in the winter, but then it didn't seem like winter.

Katy: I liked how the girl put makeup on to see him. She must think he was going to ask her out.

Alicia: The poem made me sad. I used to like somebody, but now he goes with someone else.

Shaliah: When people are young, love is so sweet. But I don't think it's that way when they get older. People just fight.

Brooke: I would like to be that girl, and have a boy do that for me. Now, boys don't buy you anything. Not even when you go to the movies.

Tim: That's how my mom and dad must have met, or something like that. Sometimes we drive by a little store on a corner where they used to live.

Some students draw pictures of porches with one light brilliantly on, of girls with too much rouge, of two oranges on a counter, of candy on a shelf, of a cold day, lit by a small fire. Because I am blessed with block scheduling, they are all still sitting in front of me. Waiting. Looking. OK, I guess it is my turn. So I say, "Now it's time to go deeper. Now it's time to learn more about communication and how we can connect this piece of writing with our lives."

They still sit there, rather empty. They have just written, discussed, created art, and I am asking for more. But, they are used to this from me. So one boy yells out, "Class meeting." My students know that whenever they want choices in what they do, they can call for a class meeting and I will try to negotiate their choices with them. Ben's announcement breaks the quiet moment, and we all laugh a little. So I say, "The class meeting concerning where we go next with the poem 'Oranges' is now in session." Corny, I know, but it works.

I have to think fast. I reach back into my (not so distant) memory and remember that Susan had asked me to write something she calls a "Case for Consideration" for the book she has been writing. In typical style, I haven't done it yet, though we've both been thinking about the concept of "language lenses" for some time now. I pull out the diagram she gave me a few weeks ago, and before I know it, I'm standing in front of the overhead projector.

"I'm going to let you create the possibilities for what you want to do next with the poem we just read." I decide for the moment not to get into explaining what a "language lens" is, since I'm not even sure I know what it is myself yet. Instead, I draw four circles on the transparency: "reading," "talking and listening," "writing," and "language study." I have to explain what language study is for a few minutes. Even though I teach grammar and usage some of the time and even though I try to teach kids how to be aware of the ways in which language works, I usually do it in ways that don't overwhelm them—in the context of informal conferences or mini-lessons.

After a brief explanation that language study can include everything from examining a published writer's technique to improving their own grammar and writing style, I say, "All right now, let's fill up each of these circles with things we might do in response to 'Oranges.' Anybody have any ideas?" The silence almost kills me, as usual. But suddenly Tara steps up to the plate. She crawls over several people and stands by the projector next to me. I am impressed that this 4-foot-tall blond is so gutsy all the time. "What about reading choices?" she asks. Silence. I tap my overhead marker against the side of the machine. "I want to read more poems like this. Can we find poems about falling in love or liking people?" She grabs the marker from my hand (they do that sometimes) and writes "find poems" in the reading circle. A couple other girls grab the marker and scrawl "write our own poems" in the circle I have labeled "writing."

The boys sit on the sidelines, waiting for the next choice. Interesting, as this poem is written from the male perspective. Another hand. Pat: "How about if we read other stuff and compare it to characters in movies? People are always falling in love in movies." Sounds good, I say, and I grab the marker from Theresa, writing "compare characters" in the "reading" circle, though I realize this could be a writing choice as well. Another student asks if we can figure out how the author wrote the poem and then try to write like the author. Inside I'm thinking, "Wow, someone really wants to do that? Cool!" This is the only entry so far in the "language study" circle.

"Time to move on," I say. Tara moves us to the writing circle. "What if we pretend we were these two kids and wrote letters to each other after the date?" Her best friend Maggie says, "Yeah, then we could do a reading of the letters and act it out." Selwyn looks like he is ready to say something, but he would never volunteer, so I say, "Selwyn, what's on your mind?" He smiles shyly and says, "I want to write about why people fall in love, about love in general." Everyone laughs. Selwyn is always our class philosopher. In large groups, he masquerades as a nonwriter and a reluctant reader, yet he just finished reading *Care of the Soul* (Moore, 1994) for independent reading and is working his way through *Tuesdays with Morrie* (Albom, 1997).

"That sounds good, Selwyn. Why don't you see what you can find?" I say. Tara moves on, "What about talking and listening?" Time is ticking away. Brittney, our resident actress, pipes up: "Listening sometimes happens without words. Maybe we could do a play without words about this poem. Act out all the looks and stuff. Remember the last readers' theater we did? We could put all this stuff together, all our writing, and do one of those again." Brittney is satisfied with this category, and so am I.

We go on for a bit, adding options to the different circles. Then Tara says, "Language study looks pretty empty." Some kids chuckle uneasily; then there is nothing. Silence. Heads down. So I say, "What if you picked another poem like this one and taught it to us as a language study option?" I don't think they care at this point, but heads nod. Jessica asks, "Can we use the board and overhead?" "Yes," I say. That creates interest. Kids will do almost anything if you let them use chalk or transparencies. Then I say, "How about if I work up a mini-lesson on the writing techniques that I know are used in this poem." They groan, but agree, because they know I'll do it anyway. "Are we done?" I ask, feeling guilty because I know I am rushing them.

They take my question as a cue to be dismissed. I run for my chimes. I won't see them for 2 days and I am suddenly frustrated. "Think about these choices, make up new ones if you like, and come to class on Wednesday ready to tell us what you are doing." I'm struggling to be heard over the sounds of backpack zippers and chairs and rising conversations. "I wish I was better at this closure stuff," I moan to myself. "Goodbye. Have a good lunch." Then they are gone. I am invisible to the stragglers, and I wonder what this poem will do to their hearts, souls, and minds while they are away from me. I guess a little incubation time never hurts.

As you can see by Mary's story, nothing ever works seamlessly, especially when you have to make so many spur-of-the-moment decisions. Since she barely understood the concept of "language lenses" herself, she didn't even try to teach it to her students. Her instinct told her that this abstract concept was something she and her students could do without for the moment.

By drawing circles on a transparency and asking students to think about the different language possibilities available to them, she was making them conscious of their options for integrating reading, writing, talking, listening, and language study in a concrete and nonthreatening way. After some time to think, she introduced the idea of language lenses and helped her students to look through those lenses in creating their own language activities. The next phase happened 2 days later.

Literacy Lesson 6-1 (continued)

It's Wednesday. I am ready for them. I have set up a table strewn with markers, newspapers, magazines, poetry books, construction paper, drawing pencils, and so on. It is the last period, unfortunately. We rotate our schedule, so now I get them after lunch and after what we call "study and support" time. The last time we met was the beginning of the school day when they were still waking up. This isn't the best time, but we'll roll with it. They enter in a fury of conversation, arguments, a little slapping, and exhaustion.

I sigh to myself but smile and greet them. It takes a little bit more to settle them down. They can't hear the music or the chimes. "Just keep smiling," I say to myself. They eventually calm down and begin to write down the agenda. A moment of suspense for me. I know some are walking in with more than I sent them away with last time, some come with less, some with nothing. Today's agenda looks like this:

Agenda

KEY POINT: All of our communication skills overlap. We are never using just one.

AGENDA: April 1–Day 5

1. opening procedures
2. lens activity time
   OR reading/writing workshop
3. performance plans

OPENING TASK: Write down your choice of activity in response to "Oranges," or write about what you accomplished during reading/writing workshop last class.

I begin by explaining that each of the circles we drew last time represents what we'll call a "language lens." I am grateful for the 2 days of thinking that led me to the explanation I'm about to give. It's funny how teaching something forces you to learn it yourself. I tell them that although we began by reading the poem "Oranges," there are many other kinds of language activities we can create whenever we "put on our reading and viewing lenses." Reading and viewing can lead to everything from written responses to oral performances to studying a published author's style. I explain that just as a pair of sunglasses seems to change the color of a landscape or a kaleidoscope seems to create a new "picture" every time we move it, our reading and viewing lens brings into focus a variety of options for other language activities.

"Today," I explain, "we're going to look at the reading of 'Oranges' through all four language lenses. As you think about what you'd like to do next with the poem, think about each of the lenses. Try on different language lenses and see which seem to suit you best. Are you more of a writer than a reader or vice versa? Do you like to talk and perform? Look through your favorite lens and create an option for yourself. Or better yet, try a lens you don't usually use. Take risks. Try something different for a change. You can work with a partner or a group if you'd like."

After a few minutes of settling in, they write. I hop from student to student and put in my two cents about their choice. I coax students without a choice. I listen to why students who were not technically part of the last literature circle want to join us in the activities. This all takes about 20 minutes. We are ready to begin.

Now, you have to have some tolerance for chaos, noise, and constant movement to proceed. It is the end of the day after all, and I am questioning my own tolerance levels. I am kind of wishing that I was just passing out dittos. A period-long, silent test would be nice, I think. But, I shake off those fantasies and begin to arrange the kids.

We do what I call a "four corners." I put up signs around the room: *Reading and viewing lens, Writing lens, Talking/listening lens,* and *Language study lens.* (I'm so clever!) I ask them to move to the category of the project they chose. All but three students get up and move. The three left behind are opting out for other work, and I ask them to find a space. Then I survey the results. They're always interesting. Let's see, we have eight in the reading and viewing, four in the writing, six in talking/listening, and zero in the language study corners. Guess I'm the only one for that category.

I give them time to discuss their ideas and ask them to find a space in the room where they can work together. Some will choose to do the activity with a classmate or two; some will work alone. Ten minutes later, we are settled. I announce that they have the rest of the period to work. One group asks to work in the library so that they can do a literature search. One group wants to use the Internet. Their quest has taken them to searching song lyrics to compare to the poem. One student has crawled under my classroom stage with a piece of drawing paper and a flashlight. Forget the classical music. A student puts a tape of "15A" in the boom box and we let each song fuel our work. When the period is over, the room is a mess, I am exhausted, and they are cranky. Some are done, and others will continue for homework. "Presentations on Friday!" I announce.

Two days later, I simply write PRESENTATION DAY on the overhead. They come in, laden with props. Some have sob stories about why they didn't finish. I give them 10 minutes to rehearse, get their materials together, and generally get organized. Then I call them, table by table, to the couch area. Some sit on the soft furniture, some pull up chairs, some sit on the floor. I ask who wants to go first. Many hands are raised. Good sign. I sit back and enjoy the show which includes:

- A collage of pictures of couples of all ages, with a poem about love through the years.
- Two letters written by the characters in the poem.
- Clips from three movies about young love, with commentary on how the emotions were like the ones in the poem.
- A humorous poem about how embarrassing it can be to like someone.
- A copy of a love letter that was written by a student's parents, all written in song titles from the '60s. Pat talks about how his parents fell in love.
- A readers' theater of Jessica and Alicia's love poems, mixed with other poems they have found.
- A poster about safe sex (don't ask).
- An essay called When Love Dies, in which a student writes about his parents' divorce.
- One group, not ready, saved for next time.

Because time is running out, I agree to do my mini-lesson next time. By the end of class, I am amazed at the dimensions of this one work of literature. I am amazed at how much these young people understand about the intricacies of love, and I am shocked that they, for the most part, worked so hard and learned so much.

We want to stress the fact that Mary is a veteran teacher with many years of trial-and-error under her belt. These lessons may seem to have been planned on the spot, but they aren't quite that spontaneous. Mary has honed her instincts about what works with her students and has carefully paved the way for such "teachable moments" to unfold. Choice—or rather negotiating options—is a regular part of her curriculum. Most of her lessons "integrate" the language arts, so her students are already comfortable with the idea that writing can spring from reading and viewing or that oral performance can be a regular part of language study.

You may decide that a concept as complicated as language lenses can be a part of your teacher toolkit, but that right now, it's too difficult for your students to grasp. That's fine. You know your own comfort zone. If the "lenses" concept works for your students, as it did for Mary's, that's great. If it doesn't, put it in the back of your mind and be willing to pull it out later when you've strengthened your confidence and sharpened your teaching practices. As you read the remaining chapters of this book, we'll return often to the concept of language lenses, so you'll become better acquainted with the idea as time goes by.

MAKING A FIRE IN OUR HANDS: ONE FINAL THOUGHT

After reflecting for some time on the myriad ways her students combine reading and viewing, writing, talking, listening, and language study, Mary was still left with a nagging feeling that teaching English language arts involves far more than just language. Her reflections are important for all of us to ponder. Again, we present Mary's own words:

Obviously, I found the concept of lenses to be a great help. Although we were focusing on reading at first, we quickly ran the gamut of other possibilities from writing to talk and listening, extended reading, and even (with a little help from me) language study. The idea of language lenses helps me to put my choices for language learning in focus and helps to ensure that I am teaching evenly, giving equal air time to all facets of what I teach.

But I think something less tangible lurks beneath the language activities in my classroom; just like a lens, that "something" colors everything students do. I think that Bruce and Danielle and Tim and Phillip bring it with them to class every day. It has to do with their own experiences, past and present, their personality and their family life, their neighborhoods and their friendships. It has to do with what they did or didn't have for breakfast that morning, who hugged or didn't hug them as they walked out the door. It's small enough to fit in a pocket or a pencil case next to the white-out. However, some kids wear it on their sleeve.

At the end of the year, as I leave the building, final exams bursting from my book bag, I stop, lean against the fence, and watch the girls' softball game. "Hi, Mrs. McCrone," Danielle yells to me as she waits to bat. I watch them. I think of that certain "something" that lies beneath all of the language activities I provide. The something that students bring with them every day. And I continue my walk home. I realize as I do so that every day we teach, it is a combination of their needs and our choices. If we work together, some days we'll get it right. And, just like the boy and girl in the poem, we can make "fire in our hands."

Language Lenses: Integrating the Language Arts in the Middle Grades

Standards in Practice

NCTE/IRA Standards

Locate a copy of the *NCTE/IRA Standards for the English Language Arts (1996)*. For an explanation of the standards, as well as a table of contents for the volume, an annotated listing of each standard, and chapter excerpts, consult the NCTE Web site at this address: *http://www.ncte.org/standards*.

To begin, look over the list on page 3 of the *Standards for the English Language Arts*. At first glance, what do the NCTE and IRA seem to believe about integrating the language arts? What evidence do you find that the standards support (or fail to support) an integrated approach?

Next, we'd like you to practice looking at the standards through the four language lenses presented in this chapter. For this particular exercise, you will be focusing only on the first standard, but it would be useful to think about all 12 standards in this way.

> **Standard One states:** Students read a wide range of print and nonprint texts to build an understanding of texts, of themselves, and of the cultures of the United States and the world; to acquire new information; to respond to the needs and demands of society and the workplace; and for personal fulfillment. Among these texts are fiction and nonfiction, classic and contemporary works.

Obviously this standard asks teachers to look at instruction through the lens of reading and viewing. Its intent appears focused on providing a variety of reading and viewing genres, as well as spanning a broad spectrum of historical and cultural perspectives.

- Begin by reading the "Standards in Detail" section on pages 27–46.
- Next, brainstorm a list of different kinds of reading materials and activities suggested by this first standard. For example, the section titled "Standards in Detail" suggests reading Katherine Patterson's *Lyddie,* a story about textile workers in 19th-century New England.
- Finally, refer back to Figure 6–1 ("The Lens of Reading and Viewing"). Draw a similar diagram and fill in each of the smaller circles with possibilities for integrating writing, talking/listening, and language study with the kinds of reading experiences suggested by this standard. For example, in reading Patterson's novel, students might create a 19th-century newspaper (for the "writing" lens), perform a readers' theater of women's letters from the period (for the "talking/listening" lens), and so on. If possible, share your diagram with others when you're done. If you're working with a larger group, you might want to divide up all 12 standards among your group members and follow a similar process with each one.

REFERENCES

Albom, M. (1997). *Tuesdays with Morrie: An old man, a young man and life's greatest lesson.* New York: Doubleday.

Britton, J. (1970). *Language and learning.* Harmondsworth, England: Pelican Books.

Elbow, P. (1985). The shifting relationships between speech and writing. *College Composition and Communication, 36*(3), 283–303.

Hynds, S., & Rubin, D. L. (1990). *Perspectives on talk and learning.* Urbana, IL: NCTE.

Moore, T. (1994). *Care of the soul: A guide for cultivating depth and sacredness in everyday life.* New York: Harper Perennial.

Smith, F. (1984). Reading like a writer. In J. Jensen (Ed.), *Composing and comprehending* (pp. 47–56). Urbana, IL: NCTE.

Soto, G. (2000). Oranges. In *The language of literature, grade nine* (p. 339). Evanston, IL: McDougal, Littell.

Standards for the English Language Arts. (1996). Urbana, IL: National Council of Teachers of English/International Reading Association.

RESOURCES

Print

Resources Relevant to the NCTE/IRA Standards

The standards themselves are detailed in the publication *Standards for the English Language Arts.* (1996). Urbana, IL: National Council of Teachers of English/International Reading Association. Vignettes describing how the standards play themselves out in a variety of middle school settings are available from the Standards in Practice series of NCTE and IRA: Wilhelm, J. (1996). *Standards in Practice 6-8.* Urbana, IL: NCTE.

Two publications of interest to middle school teachers from the NCTE/IRA Standards Consensus Series are: *Motivating Writing in Middle School* (NCTE, 1996) and *Teaching Literature in Middle School: Fiction* (NCTE, 1996).

Assessment issues related to the NCTE/IRA standards are presented in: International Reading Association and National Council of Teachers of English Joint Task Force on Assessment. (1994). *Standards for the Assessment of Reading and Writing.* Newark, DE: International Reading Association.

Resources on Integrated Language Arts Relevant to Middle School Teachers

Anders, P. L., & Pritchard, T. G. (1993). Integrated language curriculum and instruction for the middle grades. *Elementary School Journal, 93*(5), 611–624.

Beane, J. A. (1993). Problems and possibilities for an integrative curriculum. *Middle School Journal, 25*(1), 18–23.

Beane, J. A. (1997). *Curriculum integration: Designing the core of democratic education.* New York: Teachers College Press.

Flurkey, A. D., & Meyer, R. J. (Eds.). (1994). *Under the whole language umbrella: Many cultures, many voices.* Urbana, IL: NCTE and Whole Language Umbrella.

Gaveleck, J. R., Raphael, T. E., Biondo, S. M., & Wang, D. (2000). Integrated literacy instruction. In M. L. Kamil, P. B. Mosenthal, P. D. Pearson, & R. Barr (Eds.), *Handbook of reading research: Volume III* (pp. 587–607). Mahwah, NJ: Lawrence Erlbaum Associates.

Pearson, P. D. (1994). Integrated language arts: Sources of controversy and seeds of consensus. In L. M. Morrow, J. K. Smith, & L. C. Wilkinson (Eds.), *Integrated language arts: Controversy to consensus* (pp. 11–31). Needham Heights, MA: Allyn & Bacon.

Powell, R., & Skoog, G. (1995). Students' perspectives on integrative curricula: The case of Brown Barge Middle School. *Research in Middle Level Education Quarterly, 19*(1), 85–115.

Smagorinsky, P. (1991). *Multiple intelligences in the English class.* Urbana, IL: NCTE.

Tchudi, S. (Ed.). (1993). *The astonishing curriculum: Integrating science and humanities through language.* Urbana, IL: NCTE.

Wilhelm, J. (1996). *You gotta be the book.* New York: Teachers College Press.

Wixson, K., Peters, C. W., & Potter, S. A. (1996). The case for integrated standards in English language arts. *Language Arts, 73*(1), 20–29.

Electronic

NCTE/IRA standards. The standards can be accessed at the following Web site:

http://www.ncte.org/standards

chapter 7

Reading and Viewing in the Middle Grades

GUIDING QUESTIONS

1. What different print and nonprint "texts" do middle school students encounter each day?
2. How would you define *reading* at the dawn of the millennium?
3. How are reading and viewing alike and yet different?

A CASE FOR CONSIDERATION

Making Room for Poetry

Brendan is approaching his first student teaching placement in a suburban middle school. After consulting with his host teacher, he decides to create a unit on poetry for his eighth-grade students. As you can see in this excerpt from his unit plan, several issues trouble him as he prepares for his first teaching experience:

> Campbell Middle School is a suburban, or perhaps it might be more accurate to say rural, school. One might presume this would mean a fairly homogeneous student population consisting mainly of white, middle class students. Indeed this was my naive assumption on my first visit to the school. We all know the code words. "Inner city" is taken to mean poor and black, and "suburban" means white and middle class. This is what I naturally assumed upon pulling into the parking lot of Campbell Middle School for my first classroom visit with Mrs. Martin and her eighth-grade English class. One look at the school confirmed my suspicions. . . . Most of the kids are white, neatly dressed (some look like they stepped out of the pages of a J. Crew catalog), and "into" school. . . . But after my first visit and my first conversation with Mrs. Martin, I understood that my assumptions were not in the least bit accurate. Campbell Middle School, in fact, consists of a very diverse

student body. . . . Those J. Crew models might be in some way learning disabled, and those receiving the reduced and free lunches are among the most gifted. . . .

After deciding to teach a unit on poetry, my task was to find appropriate materials and activities. . . . My initial worry was not being able to find age-appropriate materials to work with. I don't want to have them working on simple elementary poems; they will just tune out. Nor do I want to work with poetry that is so obscure and remote that they will grow frustrated and resentful.

Fourteen is a difficult age. Kids are burgeoning adolescents. They are no longer children and hate to be thought of as such (in my experience, at least). They are starting to date. They worry about their experience and what peers think of them. One teacher said to me that it is all about being cool in junior high. But coolness is an ever-shifting definition. In researching this unit and the emotional and social development of the ages I will be working with, I found that adolescence is a period in life marked by an awareness of death. Kids begin to think about it for the first time. They start to become more existential in their thinking, but at the same time they listen to the Back Street Boys, throw spitballs at one another, and make crude jokes. In many ways they are still children; in others they are more complicated than ever before in their young lives. Considering all this, how then does one choose appropriate poetry? I don't want them rolling their eyes in boredom, nor do I want them tuning out because the selections I have chosen have zero relevance to them and what they are experiencing. Luckily for me, however, poetry seems like an ideal unit for us to work on together. There are volumes of poems and an endless list of poets on which I can draw. The difficulty has been in narrowing my selections.

As a student teacher, I didn't want to insert myself and my unit in a jarring or obtrusive way. I didn't want my unit to feel "tacked on." Above all, I wanted my unit to relate to what Mrs. Martin and her students have been doing all along. . . . They have just come off a unit on creative writing. I felt my job then was to relate poetry to the work they have done already. . . . I don't want the students to think that they are done with their short stories, that these will be stuffed away in a folder or in the bottom of their lockers never to be seen or heard from again. I especially don't want my instruction to be a side-show—a student teacher coming in two thirds of the way into the school year only to disappear again like some magic act after 6 weeks. I want my instruction to be as seamless as possible, and I think a way to achieve that is to relate it back to what the students have been doing all along. . . . So, how do I connect two seemingly unrelated genres in a meaningful and cohesive way?

As Brendan's comments indicate, decisions about teaching reading (and, we will argue, viewing) in the middle school classroom are far more complicated than simply deciding on which texts to choose. As what he calls "burgeoning adolescents," his students are developing unique tastes and preferences for not only *what* they read, but also *how, whether,* and *with whom.* To complicate matters for Brendan, his relationship with a creative, experienced, and well-loved host teacher constrains his choices even further.

FOR DISCUSSION

- Of the poems with which you are familiar, which would be most appropriate for middle school students and why?
- What forms of resistance to reading in general, and poetry in particular, might you expect, even among a seemingly "homogeneous" student population like the one in Brendan's student teaching placement?
- Do you worry about other people (parents, a host teacher, principal, or department chair) as you plan your students' reading and viewing experiences? If so, how do you deal with these constraints?

READING AND VIEWING IN NEW TIMES

Let's begin by examining our assumptions about what counts as "reading" in today's world. You'll notice that the title of this chapter covers "Reading and Viewing." This choice comes out of a belief that students in the 21st century need to become "active, critical, and creative users, not only of print and spoken language, but also of 'visual' language," according to the *Standards for the English Language Arts* (National Council of Teachers of English 1996, p. 5). Traditional notions of reading based upon printed materials are no longer appropriate, as we understand that today's students must develop "multiliteracies" (New London Group, 1996), enabling them to adopt new ways of talking, feeling, acting, listening, and responding within and outside of our classrooms (Gee, 2000; Luke, 1988).

> What is your definition of "reading" for the 21st century?

In this book, then, we define *reading* in rather broad strokes, including not only the reading of print-based materials, but also of electronic texts, video, film, television, and other media that surround middle school students at the dawn of the millennium.

As we define it, the term *reading* can involve many different varieties of texts from Instant Messaging posts to Internet sites, video games, television, and film, to name a few.

READING AND VIEWING FOR MULTIPLE PURPOSES

Consider the many texts and techniques for reading and viewing in the middle school classroom. The chart in Figure 7–1 represents only a few of the many options available.

Reading and Viewing in the Middle Grades 171

FIGURE 7–1 Texts and Techniques for the Reading and Viewing Classroom

political documentaries	newspaper editorials
literary fiction	nonfiction
music videos	movies
advertisements	electronic texts
silent reading	film critiques
learning logs	dramatic "spin-offs"
response guides	scene improvisations
reading/viewing journals	oral interpretation
critical essays	readers' theater
reviews	choral reading
book talks	cartoon illustrations
character sketches	imaginary dialogues
rewrites or parodies	multimedia presentations
inquiry projects	montages
author/director studies	Internet-based research
film production	scripts
class anthologies	oral reports on reading
literature circles	book clubs
television closed captioning	

In the following entry for Your Fieldwork Journal 7–1, we ask you to use this preliminary list as a springboard in considering how these texts and techniques might be used for a variety of reading and viewing purposes.

Your Fieldwork Journal 7–1

Reading and Viewing for Multiple Purposes

First, take a look at the list in Figure 7–1. Feel free to add your own texts and techniques for reading and viewing to this preliminary list. Now, create a chart like the one we've done for multimedia presentations on page 172. Pick one of the texts or techniques from Figure 7–1 and experiment with the different purposes it might serve in your teaching of reading and viewing. We've selected multimedia presentations as an example, but you should feel free to select other texts and techniques from Figure 7–1. When you've finished this exercise, you might want to share some of your ideas with others.

Purposes for Reading and Viewing				
	Reading and Viewing to Explore	**Reading and Viewing to Learn About Reading and Viewing**	**Reading and Viewing to Connect and Transform**	**Reading and Viewing to Showcase**
Techniques for Reading and Viewing	How might students explore ideas and express themselves through the reading of literature, nonfiction, film, or electronic texts?	How might students become better readers of print and nonprint texts?	How might students use reading and viewing to connect with others and make an impact on their world?	How might students share or demonstrate what they have learned through reading and viewing?
Multimedia Presentations	Students read self-selected books, keeping track of their responses through multiple genres of writing, drawing, and so on.	Students explore how the same story is presented in multiple media (e.g., film, novel, documentary, etc.).	Groups of students create and share multimedia presentations based upon their responses to "book club" selections.	After completing inquiry projects, individuals or groups create multimedia presentations to showcase what they've learned.

READING AND VIEWING WITH MIDDLE SCHOOL STUDENTS

What's important to know about teaching reading and viewing to middle school students? First, because of their high need for activity and intellectual stimulation, middle school students quickly tire of skills-based "comprehension" activities that focus on contrived texts and "testable" experiences. Similarly, few are intellectually ready for the meticulous rendering of literary interpretation and the kind of close reading that have become the staple of many high school literature programs. They need chances to read books, stories, and poems that are full of compelling action, to share their choices and opinions in the comfortable forum of their peer group, to discover reading's dramatic potential, and to read nonfiction texts with depth and insight. Because they are moving toward high school (and in most cases, high-stakes testing), many middle school students *do* need help with reading comprehension. It's important to remember, though, that they need a particular kind of help to *think deeply* about important issues *while* they are developing reading skills. As teachers, we do not have the luxury of teaching them to think *after* we've finished teaching them the basics of decoding, comprehension, and critical analysis. This is all the more reason to offer multiple ways of responding and showcasing what they have learned through print as well as nonprint media. Middle school students respond particularly well to the incorporation of drawing, dramatic enactment, visual representation, music, film, video, and electronic texts into their reading and viewing experiences.

Whether they are "reading" fiction, film, music videos, or electronic media, middle school students are at a crucial period of developing identities, tastes, and preferences that will carry them into high school and adulthood. To teachers, they may seem hopelessly stuck on a steady diet of Harry Potter, Britney Spears, Spike Lee, or *Teen People*. However, these obsessions and binges are often the seeds of students' developing identities as readers and critical viewers.

> How can you balance choice and challenge in the reading and viewing experiences you design?

Sharing reading materials and ideas through book clubs or dialogue journals and having a great deal of choice in selecting (or abandoning) particular texts are crucial at this stage. At the same time, too much choice in texts and topics can be ironically limiting, considering the fact that they will soon be expected to read, view, and understand materials about people, ideas, cultures, and topics that are often remote from their personal experience. More important, it is crucial for early adolescents to develop a critical sense of the content of the many texts that bombard them, the way in which these texts are marketed to young people, and their impact on society at large.

CONSIDERATIONS FOR READING AND VIEWING WITH MIDDLE SCHOOL STUDENTS

It would be impossible to list "best practices" for the reading and viewing classroom, since every middle school, community, and group of students have particular constraints that shape what those practices might be. Instead, we offer some considerations for you to explore in creating opportunities for reading and viewing in your classroom. The following list is loosely based on the recommendations for early adolescents by the National Middle School Association that we paraphrased in Chapter 1. As you review your own lessons and unit plans, you might want to periodically review these questions and considerations.

Considerations for Reading and Viewing in the Middle School Classroom

- **Middle school students need positive social interactions with adults and peers.**
  - When is it important for students to read and interact with texts freely and privately as opposed to publically?
  - In what ways can teachers become collaborators with students in their encounters with print and nonprint texts?
  - How can we balance middle school students' need for greater autonomy with the need for greater social interactions?
- **Middle school students need physical activities to support the development of reading and viewing skills.**
  - How can reading and viewing become active, rather than passive pursuits?

- How do we support physical activities that prepare students for reading and viewing?
- When is it important for students to draw, talk, demonstrate, or perform their responses to texts?
- **Middle school students need opportunities for self-definition, creative expression, and a sense of competence and achievement in their reading and viewing experiences.**
  - How do we facilitate students' choices of texts, while expanding their range of competencies with unfamiliar texts?
  - How can students create their own print and nonprint texts for other students to read, view, and enjoy?
  - How can we provide opportunities for reading and viewing that are not graded or evaluated, along with those that are?
- **Middle school students need reading and viewing opportunities that promote meaningful participation in their families, school, and the larger world.**
  - How do we connect students' lives outside the classroom with their reading and viewing experiences?
  - How do we help them to become critical consumers of the texts that surround their daily lives?
  - How can reading and viewing promote students' involvement in social and political activities outside the classroom?

DIFFERENCES BETWEEN LITERARY AND NONLITERARY READING

It's probably safe to say that the person who revolutionized the teaching of literature to adolescents was Rosenblatt. In her landmark work, *Literature as Exploration* (1995, originally published in 1938), she heralded what would become a truism for teachers over the past several decades: There are as many individual responses to literature as there are readers of literature. Rosenblatt (1994) made us aware of the differences between what she called "efferent" and "aesthetic" reading. Taken from the Latin word *effere* ("to carry away"), efferent reading is for the purpose of gathering information to be used at some later time. Much reading in schools, Rosenblatt argued, is efferent reading, as opposed to the near-total absorption in the reading act, or "aesthetic reading" that literature requires.

> How can you provide both aesthetic and efferent reading opportunities?

Reading nonfiction requires a different stance from that used in literary reading. When we read information, we maintain what Langer (1995) calls a "point of reference" (p. 30). Literary reading, on the other hand, involves exploring what Langer calls "horizons of possibilities" (p. 26). For example, on the day the twin towers of the World Trade Center were destroyed, we all read or viewed the news reports, grasping for the details. The exact language of the reporters and newscasters did not register with us. Reading a poem is very different from this sort of nonliterary reading. Poetry and other literature invites us to explore a variety of possible meanings, personal and aesthetic as well as intellectual. As middle school teachers, we must remember these differences as we teach reading and viewing.

INVITING STUDENTS' RESPONSES TO LITERATURE: STANCES VERSUS HIERARCHIES

For many years, and even today, some literature anthologies follow each literary selection with a list of questions, ordered in a hierarchy, beginning with "literal," and proceeding through some variant of "interpretive" and "inferential" levels. Yet we know this isn't how real reading happens. Think of the last book or story you read. Did you begin by noting a list of literal details and then proceed neatly toward the other levels of the hierarchy? Of course not! Maybe you said something like "This book stinks. I'm going to put it down!" (an interpretive, evaluative level). Or maybe you read the first few pages and thought, "This is a typical murder mystery" (an inferential stance).

> Remember that reading strategies are messy, overlapping, and recursive.

In contrast to the idea of reading *levels,* we'd like you to consider the intellectual *stances* that readers move through at various phases of their reading. You might begin a lesson from a connecting or extending stance, for example, asking students to make predictions from illustrations or cover art as a way of introducing a text. Or you could ask them to take a few minutes and freewrite about their first understandings. One rule of thumb in dealing with aesthetic reading, however, is that it's best to allow students to *experience* the text on their own terms before leading them into rigidly teacher-directed activities. Feel free to modify the order presented in Figure 7–2, depending upon the particular text and students you are teaching.

FIGURE 7-2 Stances for Reading and Viewing

Experiencing—In this stance, readers are simply gathering their first impressions of the book, movie, visual, or aural representation. They may be creating mental images, following random associations, forming a kind of gut response to an author's words or a filmmaker's images. They might be completely oblivious to events around them, as they immerse themselves aesthetically in what they are reading or viewing. Especially in the early phases of **experiencing**, they may be unable or unwilling to verbalize their response because they are so deeply engaged in forming their initial impression.

Connecting—In this stance, readers are thinking about similarities and differences. They might be comparing a movie with a book or holding characters and plot events up against their own lives. Perhaps they are rereading, rethinking, revising their initial impressions, looking closer at language and image, changing or enriching an earlier impression.

Extending—In this stance, readers are making broader connections between the text and other texts, ideas, or events in the world beyond. As part of an **extending** stance, they might be pondering what might come next or even creating their own classroom "literature," film, or artistic representation. As an extension of their reading and viewing, they may also be researching ideas and dramatizing or performing texts.

As a way of making these stances more concrete, you may want to think of your own reading process as you began this chapter. In the **experiencing** phase, you were probably focused on gathering impressions of what the chapter might be about. Perhaps you were underlining words or phrases with a highlighting pen or just trying to grasp the gist of the chapter without bothering about specific details. Brendan's story in the Case for Consideration at the beginning of the chapter might have set up a **connecting** stance, where you were judging his experience against your own. The exercise in Your Fieldwork Journal 7–1 on "Reading and Viewing for Multiple Purposes" was designed to bring you into an **extending** stance, where you created new understanding about your own teaching. As readers, we shuttle imperceptibly among these three stances. They do not occur in a lockstep order and are not mutually exclusive. Connecting and extending often occur simultaneously and are often a part of our first experiences with a text. It is important, however, to consider what stances you invite in your reading and viewing lessons.

STRATEGIES FOR COMPREHENSION AND UNDERSTANDING

Regardless of the myriad innovative ideas for teaching reading and literature that have sprouted in our professional conferences and in journals, the one staple of the middle or high school English language arts class seems to be the teacher question. How many of our own English language arts teachers have followed each literature lesson with those teacher-created questions, and how many of us have dutifully crafted them in our own lesson plans, assignments, and examinations, only to look out at a blank sea of student faces when we pose those "no-fail" queries about *our interpretations* of *their* reading?

> Ask no question to which you already know the answer.

The best advice we can offer is to avoid what Mehan (1979) has called "known information" questions, or those to which we already know the answer. Literal questions immediately after reading can do more to stifle discussion than they can to promote it. We will cover the art of conducting whole class discussions more thoroughly in Chapter 9. For now, however, we'd like to ask you to consider ways to develop your students' understanding and response without relying on a steady diet of known information questions that set up a "one-correct-answer" atmosphere in your reading and viewing classroom. We'll begin by proposing six basic reading strategies that you might use in encouraging your students to read a variety of texts from fiction to nonfiction to visual and electronic (see Figure 7–3).

To make these strategies more concrete, think again about your own reading of this chapter. You might have scanned the headings or opening questions in an attempt to **predict** the chapter content. As you read the vignettes about other teachers' classrooms, you were probably making **connections** or asking **questions** like "Has this ever happened to me?" or "What would I do in this situation?" You might have been **visualizing** what someone else's classroom looked like or **evaluating** the worth of an idea. Throughout the whole process, you were probably **clarifying** unfamiliar ideas by making notes in the margins, writing down questions you intend to ask in class, or rereading key passages. As with the stances for

FIGURE 7–3 Strategies for Reading and Understanding

> **Predicting:** Figuring out what might happen next, what a text might be about, how it might end, or what might happen at some future time.
>
> **Visualizing:** Creating "mind pictures" of characters, setting, story events, or other aspects alluded to but not directly presented.
>
> **Connecting:** Making associations between texts and related ideas, texts and personal experiences, texts and other texts.
>
> **Questioning:** Posing questions about plot, characters, information, or issues raised during reading or viewing.
>
> **Clarifying:** Reviewing, rereading, researching, or searching out resources to assist understanding.
>
> **Evaluating:** Forming opinions about the quality of texts, motivations behind characters' actions, and other issues raised during reading and viewing.

reading, these strategies are not neat and tidy. They are messy, recursive, and overlapping. Good readers use them in varied ways. Unfortunately, not all of our students have them at their command. As a way of thinking about how you might help your students to be more strategic readers without destroying the aesthetic stance so necessary for literary reading, try the following artifact analysis in Your Fieldwork Journal 7–2.

Your Fieldwork Journal 7-2

Artifact Analysis: Stances and Strategies in Your Reading and Viewing Lessons

We'd like you to consider the stances and strategies presented here as they pertain to your own teaching. First, find a lesson or unit plan involving reading and/or viewing that you've already taught or one you're currently planning. Think about the three *stances* of experiencing, connecting, and extending in Figure 7–2, then ask yourself:

- Are students allowed to experience a text on their own terms before moving into a connecting or extending stance? If not, do you have a good reason for your choices?
- Do you seem to prefer one stance over the others in this lesson? That is, do you rely heavily on personal connections, rarely asking students to extend their original interpretations into the realm of larger ideas or issues?
- Conversely, do you plunge students into an extending stance too soon? Do you, for instance, push them to find a "theme" for everything they read before they've fully experienced the text?

Now, think about the *reading strategies* you set up in this lesson (see Figure 7–3).

- Do you begin with literal questions or prompts designed to help students clarify what they've read? If so, consider whether these questions actually clarify ideas, or whether students feel "put on the spot" or encouraged to search for trivial answers rather than forming more global impressions of what they read.
- How often do you ask students to make connections between their reading and their own lives? Other texts? The larger world?
- How can you encourage students' curiosity and engagement by asking them to predict, generate their own questions, or follow up on ideas they are reading about with some additional research?
- How can you encourage multiple ways of responding, including visualizing or visual representation in your reading lessons?
- Do you encourage students to move beyond grasping the ideas in a text toward more critical understanding that requires them to evaluate the worth of those ideas and their larger implications?

STRATEGIES FOR CRITICAL READING AND VIEWING

In her marvelous book, *Critical Encounters in High School English: Teaching Literary Theory to Adolescents* (2000), Appleman observes:

> What could poststructuralism, new historicism, deconstruction, Marxism, and feminist literary theory possibly have to do with the average adolescent, just struggling to grow up, stay alive, get through school, and make the most of things? Why it sounds almost like I'm suggesting that passengers taste truffles as the *Titanic* sinks. It sounds as if I'm promoting a sort of theoretical fiddling while the Rome of our sacred vision of successful public education burns.... Nothing, however, could be further from the truth.... [C]ontemporary literary theory provides a useful way for all students to read and interpret not only literary texts but their lives—both in and out of school. In its own way, reading with theory is a radical educational reform! ... Literary theories augment our sometimes failing sight. They bring into relief things we fail to notice. Literary theories recontextualize the familiar and comfortable, making us reappraise it. They make the strange seem oddly familiar. As we view the dynamic world around us, literary theories can become critical lenses to guide, inform, and instruct us. (p. 2)

In his large-scale study of literature teaching in the United States, Applebee (1993) revealed that, despite the broad expansion of literary critical theory in the past few decades, two approaches still dominate American schools: New Criticism and Reader-Response Criticism. With its text-based focus on literary devices, "close reading," and definitive interpretations, New Criticism remains popular in many high school and middle school classrooms. On the other hand, Reader-Response Criticism, with activities designed to foster students' highly personal and individual responses to literature, is perhaps more conducive to teaching on the middle school level. Unfortunately, both reader-focused and text-focused approaches have overshadowed many other valuable approaches to literary reading that Appleman and others have begun to bring to the fore. Although it's beyond the scope of this book to present either current literary theories or their complex implications for adolescents' reading, we'd like to offer just a taste of how you might introduce your own students to the practice of looking at texts through what Appleman calls "critical lenses." Remember, though, that Literacy Lesson 7–1 offers only a glimpse of the complicated topics discussed in Appleman's book and other sources included in the Resources section at the end of this chapter (see "Links to Young Adult Authors").

Literacy Lesson 7-1

Popular Culture Through Critical Lenses

Let's say you want to introduce students to view aspects of their popular culture through a variety of critical lenses. You might begin by asking students to bring in some popular magazines, catalogs, video clips, or other texts marketed to teenagers.

You'd be surprised at how many of your students carry catalogs for everything from sports equipment to video games in their purses and backpacks. After you've collected several of these advertising artifacts, ask students to meet in small groups and analyze the "language" of advertisements through the following lenses:

> **Reader response:** Describe what personal associations or emotions these advertisements evoke in you and from where your feelings might be coming.
> **New criticism:** What techniques do these advertisers use to achieve their goals? These might include camera angles, word play, metaphor, juxtaposition of objects, and emotional or logical appeals. What might be the primary themes, arguments, or messages of each advertisement?
> **Feminist criticism:** How are males and females portrayed in each advertisement? In what ways do advertisers play upon our traditional notions of what women and men are, desire, or are supposed to be?
> **Marxist criticism:** How do these advertisements play upon people's desire for wealth and power? What symbols of wealth and power do advertisers depict?
> **Historical criticism:** What do these advertisements reveal about the social, political, and material conditions of our historical epoch?

Language Study in Context

Ask students to keep a running list of verbs, nouns, adjectives, and adverbs associated with different kinds of products in advertisements. Talk about what images and emotions these images conjure and what associations advertisers are appealing to in their language. For example, what does it mean when words like "sleek" or "sexy" are used in automobile advertisements?

INVITING ALL READERS

As we've discussed earlier, a growing number of middle school classrooms are based on a model of inclusion. Students with disabilities or special needs are included in the regular classroom, often with the assistance of a teacher's aide or resource specialist. It's likely that you will have students with physical, emotional, or learning disabilities in the same classroom with students who are not labeled. One of your

> **How can you invite all students to join the "Literacy Club"?**

greatest challenges will be finding a way to invite all students, regardless of ability, preference, or desire, to become members of what Smith (1984) calls the "literacy club."

Struggling readers, for example, might need some prereading enrichment before tackling a futuristic novel like Lois Lowry's *The Giver* (1994). Students who are resistant toward or confused by poetry might begin by circling every reference to colors in a poem like Gary Soto's "Oranges" (1990), then writing or talking about what those color references evoke in them. For students who are turned off to reading, you might want to entice them into the literacy club through aspects of their popular culture such as Internet sites, videos, popular music, and other forms of nonprint media.

> **Learn to "read" cultural differences.**

It's also important to be aware of cultural differences that influence and constrain students' reading and viewing processes. Often, teachers misinterpret the active, oral communication style of some students, as for example, a sign of disrespect or disinterest. On the contrary, students may have internalized the "call-response" pattern of communication in African American churches, where members of the congregation participate actively and vocally (Labov, 1972). When students call out responses without being formally recognized by teachers or move around the room without permission, we must realize that their behaviors do not necessarily signal disrespect. We must also be sensitive to early adolescent girls who are afraid of participating in a discussion for fear of looking "too smart" and boys who avoid traditional literacy activities like keeping journals (too personal) or reading poetry (too feminine). Depending upon their cultural backgrounds, some of your students may have parents who believe that being "seen and not heard" is a sign of respect and that the best way of learning is silence.

> **Consider the importance of "wait time."**

Research has demonstrated that a certain degree of "wait time" will often encourage shy or reluctant students to participate in a class discussion or performance. Asking students to take a moment to jot down their ideas, talk with a partner, or simply think about their response will sometimes provide all the encouragement that a shy or reluctant student needs to enter the class activity. Placing students into familiar "home groups" for collaborative learning activities and giving them advanced notice of when they will be expected to read aloud or change activities will also go a long way in reducing the anxiety of "going public" in the reading and viewing classroom.

Although it has become popular to base many activities on personal sharing, some students may see as many perils as potential benefits when they bring their personal experiences and reactions to the forum of a whole class or even a small group discussion. Consider, for example, the penalties of personal sharing for gay students, those whose parents may be neglectful or abusive, or those whose cultures may differ significantly from what their classmates consider to be the norm. Never force students to share private writing without a great deal of advance warning. Give students plenty of warning when you expect them to share ideas or writing, and be on hand to offer advice or counsel when students feel that their personal experiences are too risky to be shared.

TEXT SELECTION IN THE MIDDLE SCHOOL CLASSROOM

Locating Texts

If your school has a large budget (an unfortunately rare situation), you may be able to purchase class sets of paperbacks for your students' independent reading and a modern literature anthology full of engaging multicultural texts geared toward students of various backgrounds, abilities, and preferences. If you're like most teachers, however, you'll need to build a classroom library without going into substantial personal debt. Your school library should be your first stop. Most school librarians are happy to put together a cart of books for your classroom during a particular unit. For example, say you're teaching *Briar Rose* (1992), a holocaust novel by Yolen. Your school librarian could provide you with a shelf of books, newspaper articles, videos, DVDs, or books on the holocaust. Texts that your library doesn't own can often be borrowed from other libraries through an interlibrary loan program. Enterprising teachers browse used bookstores, thrift shops, and, of course, yard sales or garage sales. Sometimes local bookstores or libraries hold end-of-the-season book sales. If you're fortunate enough to attend a regional or national conference, visit the booths of publishing companies and get on their catalog or mailing lists. Once you start receiving catalogs and collecting books, you'll be surprised at how crowded your own bookshelves begin to be.

> Look for free or inexpensive materials.

During her teaching career, Susan created a small classroom library of books and stories she had scavenged over the years. Never an expert at the art of record keeping, she placed her students on an honor system. If they took out a book from her classroom library, they had to return that book or a different book (subject to her approval). This system ensured a constantly fluid supply of different books and allowed students who had fallen in love with a particular book to make it their own. Luckily, many students not only returned the books they had taken out but voluntarily brought bags of other books from home. By the end of the year, she had to find additional shelf space for her classroom library.

> Create a classroom library.

Censorship and Text Selection

In recent years, our classroom bookshelves have expanded to include literature and nonfiction representing a variety of cultural, racial, and ethnic perspectives. At the same time, formerly taboo issues like sexual identity, teenage suicide, pregnancy, and teen violence have been making their way rapidly into books targeted for teenagers. In light of the spate of lawsuits brought against teachers and school systems, only you can decide for which reading materials you are willing to "go to the mat." Some English departments form selection boards made up of parents, students, and teachers that review books and other materials to ensure that teachers are not harassed for their decisions about which texts to teach or make available to students in the classroom. Parental permission letters or contracts for students' independent reading have become commonplace (see the Resources section at the end of this chapter on combating censorship). Remember, though, that there is a difference between censorship and text selection. When you exclude

> Consider issues of censorship.

texts from your curriculum out of fear that students will be exposed to disturbing ideas or parents will retaliate, you are engaging in censorship. You should try not to operate from fear but out of reasoned choice.

> Broaden racial and cultural perspectives in your choice of texts.

For example, however limited your budget may be, try to offer variety in the racial, ethnic, and cultural perspectives in your textual choices. Don't make *To Kill a Mockingbird* (Lee, 2001) the one text that includes African American characters or *Anne Frank: The Diary of a Young Girl* (1988) the one representative text of the "Jewish experience." Consider how your African American or Jewish students must feel when they see themselves reflected in servile characters or are made to feel that racism was an unfortunate situation "dealt with" in the 1960s and that antisemitism was obliterated after World War II. If you only have time for so many longer works like novels or plays, try to collect shorter works—poems, songs, primary source documents, short stories, or picture books—to broaden the perspective that students have on cultural and historical issues. A picture book like *Rose Blanche* by Innocenti (1996) makes a powerful companion to a holocaust novel like *Briar Rose* (1992). Spielberg's film, *Survivors of the Holocaust* (1996), is a stunning documentary based upon the experiences of a group of Hungarian Jews who were children during the Nazi occupation. Similarly, *Faithful Elephants* by Tsuchiya and Dykes (1988) portrays the poignant situation of Japanese citizens during World War II and would be a good companion to a book that portrays the American experience. These shorter texts could be presented in one or two class periods and are a marvelous supplement to longer pieces of literature and nonfiction.

Organizing Instruction

When planning units, choose an organization that best supports your goals for reading and viewing. For example, if you want students to explore broad ideas, you can pull together a variety of texts that all relate to the same theme or subthemes, such as "Making a Difference" or "The Search for Identity." A *historical* approach works best when you want to focus on a particular period in history. A social studies unit on World War II can be enhanced by an English language arts unit on the Japanese internment in America. Books like *Farewell to Manzanar* by Watkusaki Houston (1983) can be supplemented with poems like Dwight Okita's "In Response to Executive Order 9066: All Americans of Japanese Descent Must Report to Relocation Centers" (1991) and a collection of primary source documents from the children of the Poston internment camp called *Through Innocent Eyes: Teenagers' Impressions of WW2 Internment Camp Life* (Tajiri, 1990).

> **Language Study in Context**
> Locate some primary source documents from the Japanese internment. Newspaper articles and editorials from the time and transcripts of congressional debates and executive orders are good sources. Ask students to pay close attention to the language used to describe Japanese Americans by politicians, journalists, and editorialists. Discuss the power of language in stereotyping racial groups and in justifying decisions like the internment of Japanese Americans during World War II.

If you want to focus on the work of particular authors, a biographical approach makes the most sense. Some modern literature anthologies include "author studies," which offer short pieces in several genres by contemporary and classic authors like Maya Angelou, Gary Paulsen, Edgar Allen Poe, and Jack London. A variety of Web sites that feature biographical sketches and author interviews are included in the Resources section at the end of this chapter.

Finally, if you're interested in reading/writing connections, organizing by genre makes sense. A unit on poetry might include the free verse of e. e. cummings alongside the heavily metered and rhymed work of Alfred Noyes or Edgar Allen Poe. Tracing similar ideas across several genres is another interesting approach to genre study. For example, students might compare the myth of Pyramus and Thisbe with the play *The Fantasticks* (Schmidt & Jones, 1992), a video of Shakespeare's *Romeo and Juliet*, or one of the many film modernizations of this famous tale.

A blend of several approaches is often a good idea. Themes like "Taking a Stand" can be traced through different genres or explored through various historical epochs. Above all, try to avoid the orthodoxy of boiling everything down to one simple theme or proceeding in a lockstep matter through each of the literary genres. Be creative, and don't let your organizational system impose itself on your common sense when planning reading and viewing experiences for your middle school students. In the next section, we ask you to consider the many ways in which you can invite your students into a supportive community of readers.

CREATING A CLASSROOM CLIMATE FOR READING AND VIEWING

Organizing for Whole-Class Instruction

For many of us, reading instruction in junior high or middle school was often in the form of whole-class reading of novels or nonfiction. Despite the proliferation of workshop models and independent reading programs in recent years (Atwell, 1987; Krogness, 1995; Reif, 1992), it seems that large-group instruction, where all students read the same text at the same time, still remains a popular (if not *the* most popular) approach. In many recent discussions of reading and its teaching, whole-class reading is often thought of as hopelessly outdated and traditional, a stifling approach that ignores the unique needs and preferences of individual students. Although it's true that middle school students especially benefit from abundant opportunities for independent, private reading or talking about their reading in small groups or book clubs, it is not true that whole-class instruction is limiting or boring. In Literacy Lesson 7–2, consider the ways in which Jennifer, a student teacher in a suburban school, skillfully manages to weave the language acts of writing, talking, listening, and viewing into her whole-group reading experience.

Literacy Lesson 7-2

No Promises in the Wind

Jennifer is teaching Hunt's novel *No Promises in the Wind* (1986) to a group of eighth-grade students at a small suburban middle school. Her students, on the surface, are relatively homogeneous. Most come from what her host teacher describes as middle class "well-to-do" backgrounds, and most are White. Among her 45 eighth-grade students, only one is African American, for example. Yet within this seeming homogeneity is subtle diversity. Many of Jennifer's students live in single-parent households, and around 10% are from lower-middle class backgrounds. Three of Jennifer's students receive services from a special education teacher, and four have been diagnosed with reading difficulties. Understanding that even in a suburban setting, there is no such thing as a "homogeneous" classroom, Jennifer decides to begin by making sure all of her students have the necessary knowledge and resources for understanding Hunt's historical fiction about a young boy and his family during the Great Depression. She begins with a bit of prereading.

Focus On
Writing

Writing to Build Background for Reading

Realizing that her students may not have family members who remember the Depression, Jennifer decides to engage her students in several informal writing tasks, using graphic organizers as a way of building background for their reading. Due to block scheduling, her class periods are 80 minutes long. On the first day, she reads the first page of the book from a handout as students students circle words or phrases that jump out at them, write comments in the margins, or underline particularly striking or confusing passages. She then asks them to fill in a first impressions chart (see below). For each prediction, they must also write down some evidence from the passage that supports their hunches.

First Impressions Chart

Impressions	Questions	Predictions

Focus On
Talking and Listening

Bringing It All Together

The next day, after a brief review of the previous day's discussion, Jennifer asks students to jot down in their notebooks anything they know about the Great Depression along with what they might have learned from their reading. When they have written for a few moments, she helps them to create a concept map on an overhead transparency that includes what they know about this period in our history (see the accompanying figure).

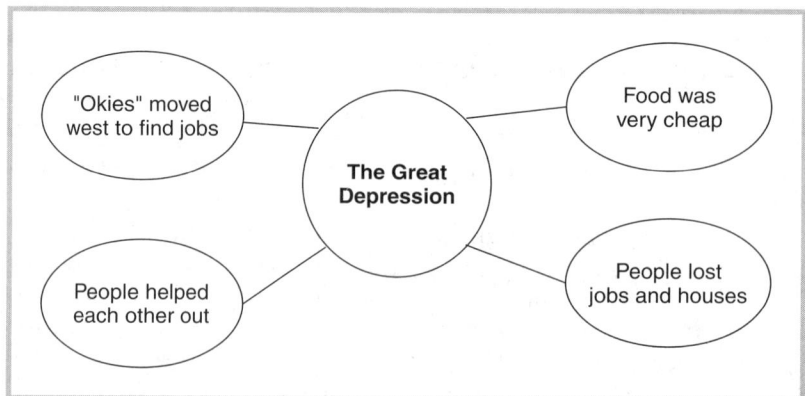

Building Background Through Film

After students discuss what they already know, Jennifer places them into small groups and shows a documentary film about the period while students "round robin" a sheet of paper in which they take turns noting important information from their viewing (see below).

Focus On Viewing

Viewing Sheet

Round Robin

Every time you hear an important fact about the Great Depression mentioned in the video, write it down on one of these lines. Then pass this sheet to the person sitting next to you in your group.

_____
_____
_____

Learning About Historical Fiction

The next day, to familiarize students with the characteristics of historical fiction, Jennifer begins a "guided imagery" (see figure below) in which she asks students to envision themselves as characters in history.

Guided Imagery

Close your eyes. Tell all your muscles to relax. You are entering a time machine that looks like the one in *Back to the Future*. You sit inside the time capsule, which has soft, plushy seats. Suddenly, the machine starts its engine and begins to speed up. You quickly realize that it is about to take you back in time to another destination. You look down at the screen: It reads "October 29, 1929." With your knowledge of this time era, you decide to relax and enjoy the ride. Besides, you have enough plutonium to get you back. You buckle your seat belt and the time machine goes faster and faster. Suddenly, there is a flash of light. Within a second you arrive on Wall Street in the year 1929. It is morning and the stock market is about to crash. As you step out of the time machine, you immediately notice hundreds of people frantically rushing to banks. They are in such a panic that they don't even see you. In fact, the mob of people almost pushes you down, but you manage to keep your ground. You move away from the crowd and stop by a newspaper stand. A show business newspaper called *Variety* has a headline that strikes you: "WALL STREET LAYS AN EGG." You suddenly remember what is in the future for these people, and you decide to return to the present as soon as possible. The year 1929 is beginning to depress you. You make it back to the time machine and start the engine. Before you know it, you are back where you started from, back in good ole Campbell Middle School. Tell your muscles to move. Now open your eyes.

What made your trip seem real?
What aspects of your trip are imaginary?

Focus On Listening

Focus On
Reading, Viewing, Talking, and Listening

Learning, Sharing, and Performing

As students move into groups to discuss their first responses to the guided imagery, Jennifer gives them a handout describing the unique characteristics of historical fiction and asks them to consider how Hunt's novel fits within this genre. She then presents each group with some primary source materials from the depression, including photographs, newspaper advertisements, and an article from *Variety* called "Wall Street Lays an Egg." Other items include a "Depression Shopping List" specifying prices of everything from a Pontiac Coupe ($565) to a box of corn flakes (8 cents).

She assigns roles to each group member, such as task organizer, recorder, timekeeper, and presenter(s), and asks them to create a chart with two columns (see the figure below). Using their novels, reading-response logs, class webs, and depression artifacts, students perform several tasks. For example, they choose at least one aspect of the setting that is factual and one that is fictional. They do the same for aspects of the plot and for the story's characters. At the end, they are asked to discuss what Hunt needed to know and do as an author to help them as readers to experience what it was like to live during the depression era. As a final wrap-up, group presenters share their graphic organizers and ideas with the class.

Collaborative Learning Chart

Facts	Fiction

Focus On
Writing, Talking, and Listening

"Reading Like a Writer": Collaborative Story Making

Over the next several days, Jennifer asks students to engage in what Smith (1984) calls "reading like a writer." In groups, they create very short pieces of historical fiction (3–4 paragraphs) that combine what they learned about the Great Depression with their knowledge of historical fiction. Group members explore various forms of collaborative writing. In some groups, each person takes turns contributing a sentence or two in a round-robin fashion. Others engage in what she calls "jump-in" writing; that is, any student is free to jump in with suggestions for plot, characters, or wording at any time. Students who are uncomfortable with such close collaboration can study the depression-era photographs and create individual vignettes, eventually combining them into one piece.

Although the series of lessons presented in Literacy Lesson 7–2, taught over several days, relies heavily on whole group instruction, we think you'll agree that it is hardly traditional and not a one-size-fits-all approach. Students constantly shift from among the language arts of reading, viewing, speaking, listening, and writing. They work collaboratively and alone, learning sophisticated reading skills, enlarging their understandings of Hunt's novel, making predictions about the outcome, and developing the necessary historical background knowledge for a rich and complicated reading. In addition, they are presented with a broad variety of evaluation and response options from visual to oral to more print-based. In the next section, you will see three different approaches to workshop teaching that allow for independent and whole group reading experiences.

Organizing for Student-Selected Reading

There are several reasons why we believe it's important to provide opportunities for free-choice reading in your middle school classroom. First, if you consider yourself a lifetime reader (and remember that some English language arts teachers don't), it's at least partly because of your private reading experiences that are not monitored or assigned by others. If you don't consider yourself a lifetime reader, ask yourself whether your own teachers' criticisms or tests may have something to do with your negative perceptions about yourself as a reader. Whatever the case, as a teacher, you need to provide opportunities for reading that "counts" (i.e., carries some kind of reward or credit when grades are due), but does not *count against* your middle school readers.

We urge you to create a system of *independent reading*, where students select their own reading and viewing experiences for at least part of their grade. Simply asking students to read so many books (or other texts) each marking period is a good way to start. Create a simple record-keeping system where you check in periodically (once a week, for example) and ask students to tell you what they are reading and how much they have completed for that week. If you want to monitor their reading a bit more closely, consider holding periodic reading conferences, in which students take 5 minutes to tell you about their independent reading and you write simple notes about their progress in a folder. Or perhaps better still, invite four or five students at a time to hold an impromptu discussion about their independent reading while at the same time giving each other suggestions for what they might read next. If you don't have time for individual or small group conferences, you might hold a sharing circle each week or every 2 weeks, where students give book talks or other informal presentations on their current independent reading experiences.

If you want to structure students' choice of response options, you might design a "menu" for students to use in deciding how to represent what they learned or experienced in their independent reading. Your menu could include choices that range from writing a critical review to artistic representation or oral performance. The idea is to open up the options for students to let you know that they have done their independent reading, while avoiding the fear of evaluation that often accompanies traditional tests, formal writing, or whole class discussion.

Organizing for Small-Group Reading Experiences

As a companion to an independent reading program, you might want to sponsor some opportunities for reading and viewing in the company of a small group of peers. For instance, you could hold literature circles in which students gather to read print or nonprint texts with or without your assistance.

Teacher-sponsored literature circles might be held on a regular basis (as often as 5 days per week, or as seldom as once every week or 2). Students could have the choice of attending a literature circle with you or working independently on other assignments. Your might also ask students to gather in small groups for student-led literature circles.

If you have access to sets of paperbacks (five or six copies of a few titles), you could create book clubs, which meet regularly to discuss common texts. Many modern paperbacks for adult readers are now being published with a list of discussion questions in the back. You could create similar lists for your students, or simply ask them to come to each book club meeting with a list of questions they are wondering about at particular points in their reading. As one way of holding students accountable, you could offer a set of options for final projects, to be handed in at the end of the reading or presented for classmates. Options might include everything from research on related issues or topics to performance of key scenes.

Organizing for Workshop Teaching

Perhaps the approach that offers the greatest flexibility for teachers who wish to combine whole class, small group, and independent reading is what is commonly called "workshop teaching" (Atwell, 1987; Reif, 1992). In Literacy Lesson 7–3, you will see three different approaches to workshop teaching, though the possible configurations are practically limitless.

Literacy Lesson 7-3

Three Approaches to Reading Workshop

Ken: A Modified Workshop

The seventh-grade students in Ken's city classroom are primarily from impoverished or working class backgrounds. Although his school has adopted many aspects of the middle school model, such as team advisement and interdisciplinary planning, block scheduling is not one of them. His class periods are 40 minutes long, leaving him precious little time for extensive group experiences, individual conferences with students, or other approaches typically associated with workshop teaching. Nevertheless, he has created a modified workshop, combining whole class, small group, and independent learning activities.

Although he combines all of the language arts in his teaching, this brief description focuses mainly on his teaching of reading. Two days a week (Tuesdays and Thursdays) are reserved for whole group instruction. On these days, Ken makes great use of video, film, and television, often asking students to critique programs and advertising geared to teens. Mondays and Wednesdays are learning center days, when students work quietly at one of six learning centers: reading, drafting, editing, free reading, conferencing, and grammar/usage. A couch in the corner of the room serves as the free-reading center, where students can relax and enjoy a book of their choosing.

Students must complete at least one independent book by the end of every marking period and keep a reading log, which they either exchange with a partner or with Ken for feedback and response. Reading logs are kept in crates and left in the classroom each day. At the Reading Center, students sit at a table with five or six other students and respond individually or collaboratively to a short text, photograph, or piece of visual art that Ken has chosen for that particular day. Students often have choices to write, draw, perform, or discuss their responses. Fridays are reserved for Sharing Circle, where students take turns either sharing a piece of writing they created or talking about something they've read that week.

As you can see, Ken's modified workshop allows him to make the most out of a 40-minute class period, offering students many opportunities to read and view a variety of texts alone and with others.

Mary: Reading/Writing Workshop

In Mary's city classroom, students are on a block schedule of 80-minute class periods. Her seventh-grade students come to her every other day and attend a social studies class on alternate days. Within this broad structure, students know that each 80-minute period will be broken up in roughly the same way. As they enter the room, they take their assigned seats at small tables with five or six members of their "home group." In this arrangement, they spend 10 to 15 minutes copying the agenda from the overhead and responding to a brief writing prompt, usually related to the day's reading. After this initial "warm-up" time, Mary calls the roll and asks students to choose either reading/writing workshop (working independently on reading and writing activities or inquiry projects in the classroom or at the library), or literature circle. Her philosophy of reading is that it can't be separated from the other language arts; students learn skillful ways of reading the work of published authors as they become writers themselves. By the same token, oral language, listening, and an understanding of various media all contribute to a rich reading curriculum.

Literature circles are always held in an area with a couch, two large padded chairs, and several pillows. As students settle into soft seats, pull up chairs, or find spaces on the floor, Mary begins by tying each day's opening task writing to the piece of literature or nonfiction she has selected. After a few minutes of sharing their writing, the students usually take turns reading the day's selection aloud. Like Ken, Mary keeps track of students' choices in her plan book. If students choose reading/writing workshop 2 days in a row, they must come to literature circle the next time it's offered.

In addition to attending literature circles, students choose independent reading books roughly every 2 weeks. They keep track of their independent reading in logs, which are discussed with Mary and the other students periodically. Roughly every month, students conduct inquiry projects, based upon some of the reading and writing they have been doing. Inquiry projects give them the opportunity to combine nonfiction, fiction, and electronic texts.

As you can see, Mary's workshop model is based upon a great deal of student choice, balanced with more teacher-structured activities. Students have chances to read, write, talk, and engage in projects independently or with others. They have regular conferences with Mary for responding to writing or reading, goal setting, and evaluation. Each year, language activities are organized around a major theme and several subthemes.

This kind of balance is crucial for middle school students, who are poised between dependence on adults and the development of their own identities and preferences.

Jerome: A Workshop in a Day

Jerome is starting a student teaching placement with a host teacher who has already established a successful set of routines and procedures in her sixth-grade classroom. He is wary of making large changes in her comfortable and predictable routine. After all, his placement is only for 11 weeks, and his host teacher must take over when he leaves. Nevertheless, she is willing for him to experiment a bit with the approach.

With that in mind, Jerome embarks on his first instructional unit on short stories. He has already chosen a theme for the unit: "Searching for Self." Within this theme, he has collected stories by writers like Maya Angelou, Sandra Cisneros, Gary Paulsen, Toni Cade Bambera, Gary Soto, and other popular young adult authors. Because he wants students to explore the differences between short stories and other genres, he plans to bring in a short video, poetry, nonfiction, and other texts for comparison. At the same time, he plans to continue with some of the procedures his host teacher already uses: "Daily Oral Language," where students identify grammar and usage problems for a few minutes at the beginning of each period; weekly vocabulary or spelling quizzes; and regular journal writing on teacher- or student-selected topics. He decides to devote 1 day per week to reading workshop.

Because most of his students have never experienced a workshop model, he prepares a handout, explaining what is expected of them on workshop day, which he plans to sponsor each Friday. For the first 3 weeks of the unit, students use their Friday workshop day in one of two ways: reading and discussing short stories together in a kind of book club arrangement or reading silently and responding privately to one of five different stories, copies of which he has placed on tables around the room. Students respond in ways that include drawing, visual representation, or oral performance, as well as more traditional writing activities. During the 4th week, his students gather in one area of the room to share what they learned about the unit theme, "Searching for Self," from their workshop experiences.

For the next 3 weeks, students use their workshop days to craft their own short stories, either independently or with others. As students work quietly around the room, Jerome holds conferences with them, helping them to generate ideas, reviewing their progress, or helping them to revise their writing. For the final 3 weeks, students are expected to work in small groups on various inquiry projects, focused on the unit theme. Toward the end of the unit, Jerome decides to expand workshop to 3 days per week, allowing more time for students to work together in the library, the computer lab, or the classroom, collecting resources and planning their final projects.

On the final workshop day, students invite their parents and other interested adults to attend a "share fair." Refreshments are served as visitors walk around the room, enjoying the many posters and displays that students have created to represent their learning for the past 11 weeks.

Considering the broad diversity of practices and procedures in these three scenarios, you may be wondering just what sets workshop teaching apart from other approaches. We think you'd agree that in a comprehensive approach to workshop teaching, reading and viewing should be only one part of a rich fabric of other language activities. What makes workshop teaching unique is that it allows for a great deal of flexibility within structure. There is no one-size-fits-all workshop model. In general, workshop approaches allow students to follow their own pace and sequence, promote a balance of student and teacher choice, and allow students to work collaboratively and independently.

Now that we've covered the different approaches to creating your reading and viewing curriculum, we come to the thorniest and perhaps most important issue: your evaluation system.

ASSESSMENT ISSUES IN THE READING AND VIEWING CLASSROOM

First, it's important to distinguish between response, evaluation, and grading. *Response* involves giving students the benefit of your personal reaction to their ideas and their work. It can encompass everything from recognizing and enlarging upon their comments in class discussions to writing in the margins of their reader-response journals. In contrast to evaluation and grading, response should generally begin with "I" statements: "I wondered about this, when you said that," "I was moved by your story about your grandmother," "I can suggest other books by that author," and so on. Your intent should be to support students in voicing and elaborating upon their ideas and insights.

> Offer opportunities for response, evaluation, and grading.

In contrast to response, *evaluation* involves judging student work against some kind of standard. It's not quite as final as grading, where students are given a summative appraisal of their work to be filed in a grade book or sent home on a report card. Evaluation can be performed in conferences with students, where you help them to see areas where they have grown or are in need of help. It can also be done in the form of comments on papers or check marks on a rubric designed for particular projects.

Whatever *grading* scheme you use, remember that students quickly learn to "read" your grading and evaluation system for evidence of how reading and viewing should proceed in your classroom. If every reading or viewing experience culminates in a multiple-choice test, students will learn to read literature efferently, making notes of "important" details to be remembered later for the test. If every reading experience begins with a vocabulary quiz, students may not be encouraged to figure out words in context. Remember that literature is not driver's education. Because it's important for inexperienced drivers to know the difference between a yield and a stop sign, an objective test on the rules of the road is probably necessary for obtaining a driver's license. Creating lifetime readers is a more delicate issue, requiring sophisticated response, grading, and evaluation procedures that mirror our true goals for students' reading in our classroom and in their lives outside of school.

Responding

One of the most popular ways of keeping track of students' responses is to ask them to keep a journal or log. Students may simply stop at various points in their reading (at the end of each class period, or the end of each book chapter) and jot down what they are wondering about, thinking, and feeling. Such jottings can be helpful if you

FIGURE 7–4 Reading Menu

> **Reader's Choice**—Perhaps there is something you are dying to write. Go to it! Choose any form that's comfortable and begin to write.
>
> **Personal Connections**—Does this text remind you of anything in your own life? Try to capture that experience as closely as you can. Choose any form you like.
>
> **Playing With Form**—Take one of the ideas in this text and write it into another form. Write a story, a letter, an essay, a dialogue, or monologue.
>
> **Futurizing**—Write about what might happen to the characters at some future time. Choose one or more characters and pick a time a few minutes later or several years later. Choose any comfortable form.
>
> **Role Playing**—Take the perspective of a character other than the speaker and write about the same incident from that character's viewpoint.

plan to conduct conferences with students (either individually or in small groups of four or five students). Mary McCrone, a middle school teacher in an urban district, asks students to write three sentences at the end of each day they spend in reading workshop. She then uses these short log entries to talk in more depth with them about the books they've chosen for their independent reading. Other teachers like to structure the experience a bit more, asking students to choose from a menu of writing options such as the one in Figure 7–4.

There's no denying that students need response to their work and lots of it. As teachers, however, we also need to protect our personal lives. When you find yourself lugging response journals home every weekend or making copious marks in your grade book, you're probably headed for burnout. As an alternative, each morning you could ask students to call out the page number and title of their independent reading book as you call the roll. A quick notation system like this gives you a quick glance at the reading tastes and progress of your students. Of course, you need to combine this system with more concrete evidence of their reading such as journals or conferences with you. If you need to know whether students are being honest with you about their independent reading, consider giving brief independent reading quizzes on a regular basis. For example, you could give students a writing prompt such as "Who is the most memorable character in your book and why?" or "What has just happened in your book and what lesson can you learn from it?" A 5-minute freewrite can give you a pretty good idea about who is reading and who is not. You can make a point to confer with students whose responses are vague or questionable.

Holding conferences with small groups of students about their independent reading and making brief notes in your plan book (check, check plus, check minus) can be a healthy alternative to writing those laborious comments in the response notebooks of 100 to 120 students.

You might also consider dialogue journals, where students write back and forth to a peer about their reading. Another idea is to collect a small number of journals each week and ask students to place a paper clip on an entry they'd most like to share with you. This entry, plus one that you choose randomly, could serve as a basis for a brief response.

Remember that a few honest and well-timed responses from you can be as valuable as a lengthy dialogue in a student's journal or the margins of a paper. Try to make a personal connection with each student about his or her reading at least once a week. It might be something as simple as a quick remark before class ("You're reading Harry Potter. Why do you think so many kids like that series?"), a comment during class discussion ("Josh, I know you like mystery stories. What do you think of this one?"), or a special act ("I brought in this book because I know you like this author so much."). The important thing is to create a classroom climate where reading and viewing are held in high regard and where students and teachers alike feel free to share their responses to everything from books to films to television programs.

Evaluation

A colleague of ours likes to distinguish between "responding" and "response" to reading. Because *response* is always necessarily private and hard to tap, teachers must create more public ways of *responding* that can be evaluated and eventually graded. Your choice of responding experiences will strongly shape the future responses of students and their reading processes and strategies. If you want students to respond aesthetically to literature, giving a factual test or assigning a literary essay on the front end will pretty much rule out this kind of response. This doesn't mean that every reading and viewing experience needs to be nebulous or highly personal. Reading a nonfiction piece on violence in America or homelessness can be followed by a formal writing assignment requiring critical analysis or an extended research project.

> Consider the difference between responding and response.

Many teachers find it helpful to create a simple evaluation rubric for more formal papers and projects. Questions like "Does the paper/presentation reveal a thorough understanding of major issues?" or "Is the language clear, lively, and engaging?" can provide a comfortable yet clear structure for giving students feedback on their work. Rubrics can include a Likert scale, which allows you to circle numbers from 1 (poor) to 5 (outstanding) and to write qualitative comments in the space below.

Regular evaluation and goal-setting conferences can also be very useful to teachers and students alike. In preparation for such conferences, students can complete self-evaluation forms that include responses to prompts such as "How many books did you read on your own this marking period?" or "Give some examples of how you have grown as a reader over the past several weeks." As you and your students discuss their self-evaluation, you can negotiate two or three goals to be completed before the next evaluation conference. Goal statements such as "Jordan will read at least two books in a genre other than mystery" or "Shaliah will read from her independent book and write in her response journal at least twice each week" can be noted in the student's reading log and discussed during the next evaluation conference.

If you don't want to grade students' class participation or informal writing in a formal way, you might consider walking around the room during silent work time and placing "check plus" or "check minus" next to the names of students who seem particularly engaged or off task. A similar evaluation system can be used to give students credit for journal entries or informal writings that are especially thought-provoking or to cue them that they are not putting enough effort into these assignments.

Grading

> Balance teacher- and student-controlled assessment.

As you construct your grading system, you should try to balance student-controlled, teacher-controlled, and negotiated grading opportunities. In the past few pages, we have discussed teacher-controlled approaches from conferences to quizzes.

Contract grading is an example of a more student-controlled activity. For independent reading, for example, you could create a contract such as the example in Figure 7–5.

In the case of formal projects and papers, you and your students may negotiate a grading rubric. If you have strong opinions about what needs to be included in grading a particular assignment, begin by writing these "givens" on an overhead transparency or a flip chart. Statements like "The paper must be seven pages long and typewritten" or "Each student must show evidence of his or her contribution to the project" can be written on the top of the list. Then, in an open discussion students can suggest items they would like included in the rubric.

Teacher-controlled grading must be handled with care and consideration. Ask yourself what is most acceptable, considering where the students are at any particular moment. You may begin a school year with a large number of teacher-controlled activities, then gradually shift to student-controlled or negotiated approaches as students prove they can handle such opportunities in a mature and conscientious way.

> Modify assessment techniques for students with special needs.

In planning your grading and evaluation system, remember to keep in close contact with resource personnel in providing alternative assessments for students with special needs and abilities. Particular students may need extra time for papers, quizzes, and projects, or they may need printed materials to be read aloud. Remember that some students may be reluctant to write about what they consider private thoughts in journals or logs, and others may find oral conferences with teachers torturous. Try to provide opportuni-

FIGURE 7-5 Grading Contract for Independent Reading

> A: Read four books for the next marking period and produce a minimum of 12 entries of at least one page in your response notebook.
> B: Read three books and produce a minimum of 9 entries.
> C: Read two books and produce a minimum of 6 entries.
> D: Read one book and produce a minimum of 3 entries.
> F: Little or no evidence of independent reading.

FIGURE 7-6 Board Game from *The Sword and the Stone*

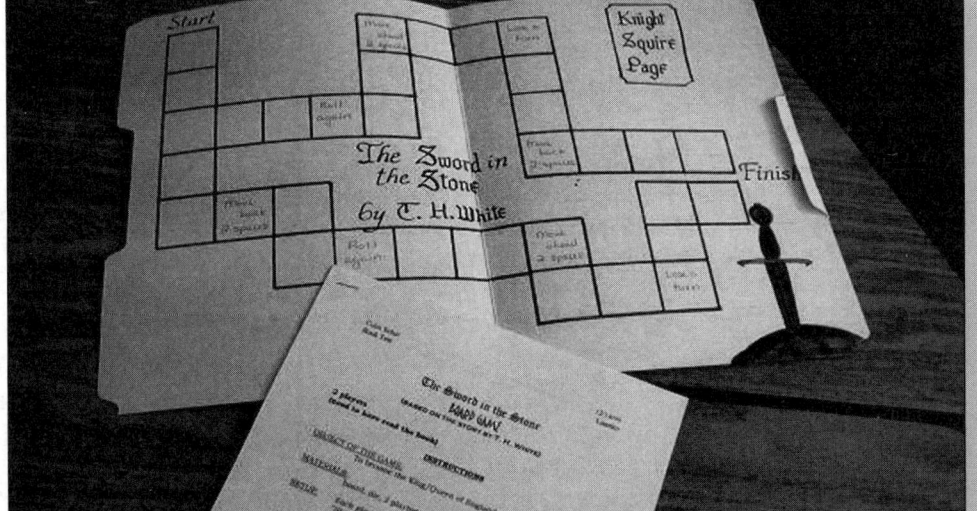

ties for all students to succeed. Draw upon multiple intelligences (Gardner, 1993) in the grading and evaluation experiences you provide. Notice, for example, the literacies involved in the board game a seventh-grade student created to represent his reading of *The Sword and the Stone* by White (see Figure 7–6).

Not only did this student use his knowledge of game construction, but he cleverly incorporated elements of the story's plot into each stage of the game.

Whatever your choices for response, evaluation, and grading in your reading and viewing classroom, remember that beyond the goal of creating intelligent, informed, and critical readers, it is also your responsibility to create citizens who will actually put these competencies to use in their daily lives beyond their years of formal schooling.

Standards in Practice

Viewing Your Reading and Viewing Lessons Through the IRA/NCTE Standards

Locate a copy of the IRA/NCTE *Standards for the English Language Arts* (1996). For an explanation of the standards, a table of contents for the volume, an annotated listing of each standard, and chapter excerpts, consult the NCTE Web site: *http://www.ncte.org/standards*.

Although all of the standards are relevant to your reading and viewing classroom, for purposes of this exercise, we suggest you look most closely at Standards 1, 2, 3, and 11. You will notice that within each standard are words or phrases that could be construed as subgoals for your reading and viewing classroom. Begin with the first standard and highlight the subgoals within this standard as we have done in this example:

> **NCTE/IRA Standard One**
>
> 1. Students read a wide range of ==print and nonprint texts== to build an ==understanding of texts==, of ==themselves==, and of the ==cultures== of the United States and the world; to ==acquire new information==; to ==respond to the needs of society and the workplace==; and ==for personal fulfillment==. Among these texts are ==fiction and nonfiction==, ==classic== and ==contemporary== works.

Now locate a reading and viewing lesson you have created or one you are in the process of creating. If you aren't currently planning lessons of your own, you might want to refer back to Literacy Lesson 7–2 on *No Promises in the Wind*. For each activity in your lesson plan, try to tie it to one or more of these subgoals from Standard 1. As an example, we've paraphrased some of the activities in Jennifer's unit. Beside each activity, we have placed the relevant subgoals of Standard 1.

- Students watch a documentary film about the Great Depression, noting important information from their viewing. (Standard 1 subgoal: [read] print and nonprint texts; acquire new information.)
- Students listen to a "guided imagery" and envision themselves as characters in history. (Standard 1 subgoal: [understand] themselves [understand] cultures.)
- Students consider the unique characteristics of historical fiction. (Standard 1 subgoal: understand texts.)
- Students view primary source materials from the depression and discuss and consider which aspects of Hunt's novel are fact and which might be fiction. (Standard 1 subgoal: [read] fiction and nonfiction; understand texts.)

When you've finished with Standard 1, you might want to do the same for Standards 2, 3, and 11. If you are working in a group, perhaps different groups can view the same lesson through different standards. If you work in a school district where state or national standards are important, it's a good idea to begin tying all of your lessons to those standards in this way.

REFERENCES

Applebee, A. N. (1993). *Literature in the secondary school: Studies of curriculum and instruction in the United States.* Urbana, IL: National Council of Teachers of English.

Appleman, D. (2000). *Critical encounters in high school English: Teaching literary theory to adolescents.* New York: Teachers College Press.

Atwell, N. (1987). *In the middle: Writing, reading, and learning with adolescents.* Montclair, NJ: Boynton/Cook.

Frank, A. (1988). *Anne Frank: The diary of a young girl.* New York: Bantam Books.

Gardner, H. (1993). *Frames of mind: The theory of multiple intelligences.* New York: Basic Books.

Gee, J. P. (2000). Teenagers in new times: A new literacy studies perspective. *Journal of Adolescent and Adult Literacy, 43*(5), 412–420.

Hunt, I. (1986). *No promises in the wind.* New York: Berkeley Publishing Group.

Innocenti, R. (1996). *Rose blanche.* Madison, WI: Turtleback Books.

Krogness, M. M. (1995). *Just teach me, Mrs. K.: Talking, reading, and writing with resistant adolescent learners.* Portsmouth, NH: Heinemann.

Labov, W. (1972). *Language in the inner city: Studies in the black English vernacular.* Philadelphia: University of Pennsylvania Press.

Langer, J. (1995). *Envisioning literature: Literary understanding and literature instruction.* New York: Teachers College Press.

Lee, H. (2001). *To kill a mockingbird.* New York: Harper Trade.

Lowry, L. (1994). *The giver.* New York: Bantam Doubleday Dell.

Luke, A. (1988). *Literacy, textbooks and ideology: Postwar literacy instruction and the mythology of Dick and Jane.* Bristol, PA: Taylor & Francis.

Mehan, H. (1979). What time is it Denise?: Asking known information questions in classroom discourse. *Theory into Practice, 18*(4), 285–294.

National Council of Teachers of English. (1996). *Standards for the English language arts.* Urbana, IL: Author.

New London Group. (1996). A pedagogy of multiliteracies: Designing social futures. *Harvard Educational Review, 66*(1), 60–92.

Okita, D. (1991). In response to executive order 9066: All Americans of Japanese descent must report to relocation centers. In Minnesota Humanities Commission/Minnesota Council of Teachers of English, *Braided lives: An anthology of multicultural American writing* (pp. 280–281). Saint Paul: Minnesota Humanities Commission.

Reif, L. (1992). *Seeking diversity: Language arts with adolescents.* Portsmouth, NH: Heinemann.

Rosenblatt, L. M. (1994). *The reader, the text, the poem: The transactional theory of the literary work.* Carbondale: Southern Illinois University Press.

Rosenblatt, L. M. (1995). *Literature as exploration.* New York: Modern Language Association.

Schmidt, H., & Jones, T. (1992). *The fantasticks.* New York: Applause Theatre Books.

Smith, F. (1984). Reading like a writer. In J. Jensen (Ed.), *Composing and comprehending* (pp. 47–56). Urbana, IL: National Council of Teachers of English.

Soto, G. (1990). Oranges. In *Braided lives: An anthology of multicultural American writing* (pp. 134–135). Minneapolis: Minnesota Council on the Humanities.

Spielberg, S. (1996). *Survivors of the Holocaust.* Dir: Allan Holzman. Shoah Foundation.

Tajiri, V. (1990). *Through innocent eyes: Teenagers' impressions of WW2 internment camp life.* Los Angeles: Keiro Services.

Tsuchiya, Y., & Dykes, T. T. (1988). *Faithful elephants.* New York: Houghton Mifflin.

Watkusaki, Houston, J. (1983). *Farewell to Manzanar.* Madison, WI: Turtleback Books.

Wilhelm, J. D. (1996). *Standards in practice grades 6–8.* Urbana, IL: National Council of Teachers of English.

Yolen, J. (1992). *Briar rose.* New York: Tor Books.

RESOURCES

Print

Resources for Readers' Workshop

Allen, J., & Gonzalez, K. (1997). *There's room for me here: Literacy workshop in the middle school.* York, ME: Stenhouse.

Bomer, R. (1995). *Time for meaning: Crafting literate lives in middle and high school.* Portsmouth, NH: Heinemann.

Conn, J. L. (1994). The Christian coalition: Behind the mask. *Church & State*, pp. 4–7.

Daniels, H. (1996). *Literature circles: Voice and choice in the classroom.* York, ME: Stenhouse.

Hagerty, P. (1992). *Readers workshop: Real reading.* Richmond Hill, Ontario: Scholastic, Canada.

McKenzie, J. (Ed.). (1992). *Readers' workshop: Bridging literature and literacy.* Toronto: Irvin.

Raphael, T., & McMahan, S. (Eds.). (1997). *The book club connection: Literacy learning and classroom talk.* New York: Teachers College Press.

General Resources on Reading

Beers, K. (1996). *Into focus: Understanding and creating middle school readers.* Norwood, MA: Christopher-Gordon.

National Council of Teachers of English. (1996). *Teaching literature in middle school: Fiction.* Urbana, IL: Author.

Robb, L. (2000). *Teaching reading in middle school (grades 5 & up).* New York: Scholastic Professional Book Division.

Schoenbach, R., Greenleaf, C., Cziko, C., & Hurwitz, L. (Eds.) (1999). *Reading for understanding: A guide to improving reading in middle and high school classrooms.* New York: Jossey-Bass.

Soter, A. (1999). *Young adult literature and the new literary theories: Developing critical readers in middle school.* New York: Teachers College Press.

Wilhelm, J. (1996). *You gotta be the book: Teaching engaged and reflective reading with adolescents.* New York: Teachers College Press.

Wilhelm, J. (2001). *Strategic reading: Guiding students to lifelong literacy, 6–12.* Portsmouth, NH: Boynton/Cook.

Including All Readers

Finders, M. (1997). *Just girls: Hidden literacies and life in junior high.* New York: Teachers College Press.

Ohanian, S. (2001). *Caught in the middle: Nonstandard kids and a killing curriculum.* Portsmouth, NH: Heinemann.

Resources for Young Adult Literature

Hurst, C., & Otis, R. (1999). *Using literature in the middle school curriculum.* Worthington, OH: Linworth Publishing.

The Lure of Young Adult Literature. (2001). (Special themed issue; articles by Cindy O'Donnell Allen et al. and Marshall George are particularly useful.) *English Journal* 90 (3).

Stover, L. (1996). *Young adult literature: The heart of the middle school classroom.* Portsmouth, NH: Boynton/Cook–Heinemann.

Resources for Combating Censorship

Anaya, R. (1992). The censorship of neglect. *English Journal, 81*(5), 1992.

Applebee, A. N. (1992). Stability and change in the high school canon. *English Journal, 81*(5), 27–32.

The Bell Curve: How a dangerous book won legitimacy. (1994, Winter). *Rethinking Schools: An Urban Educational Journal,* 1, 14, 16.

Conn, J. L. (1994). The Christian coalition: Behind the mask. *Church & State,* pp. 4–7.

Duke, D. (1993, Summer). Are fundamentalists taking over your school? How the Christian right organizes. *Rethinking Schools: An Urban Educational Journal,* 4–5.

Fawcett, G. (1993–1994). Tom didn't say anything. *Educational Leadership, 51*(4), 35–36.

Garden, N. (1994). Banned: Lesbian and gay kids' books under fire. *Lambda Book Report: A Review of Contemporary Gay and Lesbian Literature, 4*(7), 11–13.

Lee, N., Murphy, D., & Ucelli, J. (1991). Whose kids? Our kids! Race, sexuality and the right in New York City's curriculum battles. *Radical America, 25*(1), 9–21.

National Council of Teachers of English (1999). *Guidelines for dealing with censorship of nonprint materials.* Urbana, IL: Author.

National Council of Teachers of English (1982). *Statement of censorship and professional guidelines.* Urbana, IL: Author.

Noll, E. (1994). The ripple effect of censorship: Silencing in the classroom, *English Journal, 83*(8), 59–64.

On guard: Alice Walker story removed. (1994, Spring). *Rethinking Schools: An Urban Educational Journal,* 23.

On Huck, criticism and censorship. (1984). *Interracial Books for Children Bulletin, 15*(1, 2, 3).

Peterson, B. (1993, Winter). What should kids learn: A teacher looks at E. D. Hirsch's work on "cultural literacy." *Rethinking Schools: An Urban Educational Journal,* 1, 8–11.

Pollard, B. (1990, October 15). To see one's face in the mirror: Teaching black American literature. *New York Teacher,* 19.

Reed, A. J. S. (1994). Censorship and the young adult book. In A. J. S. Reed, *Reaching adolescents: The young adult book and the school.* Upper Saddle River, NJ: Merrill/Prentice Hall.

See also articles by Greenlee, Reed, and others in a special section on censorship in *English Journal, 81*(4), 1992.

Electronic

***The ALAN Review* Digital Library and Archives.** This site features entire issues of the *ALAN Review* and great articles about teaching literature to adolescents.

   http://scholar.lib.vt.edu/ejournals/ALAN

Young Adult Library Services Organization Web Site. Sponsored by the American Library Association, this site has many helpful features, including information about conferences and events, as well as several sites linking to award-winning books for young adults.

   http://www.ala.org/yalsa

Reading Online: A Journal of K-12 Practice and Research. Published by the International Reading Association. This online journal has several helpful articles for practitioners by well-known practitioners and researchers in the field of reading. A chat line and helpful ideas for integrating technology into the literacy classroom are also offered.

http://www.readingonline.org

PBS TeacherSource Arts and Literature Page. A great source of fiction, nonfiction, and information on various topics relevant to the language arts classroom. Subjects range from slavery to immigration, architecture, and music, to name a few. A great way to introduce students to print and nonprint resources for inquiry projects related to their reading.

http://www.pbs.org/teachersource/arts_lit.htm

The *New York Times* Daily Lesson Plans. Developed in partnership with the Bank Street College of Education, this site provides ways for teachers to use the newspaper to teach reading and other skills.

http://www.nytimes.com/learning/teachers/lessons

Internet School Library Media Center Index to Children's Authors and Illustrators Page. This is a good place to hook students up with information about authors and illustrators of their favorite books. The home page also provides an index to additional Internet sites featuring young adult authors and illustrators.

http://falcon.jmu.edu/~ramseyil

Lynch Multimedia Adaptations of Shakespeare's Plays. For middle school teachers wishing to give readers a "taste" of Shakespeare, this site features prose adaptations of Shakespeare's major plays alongside the original text.

http://www.lynchmultimedia.com/index2.html

Mr. William Shakespeare and the Internet. This site offers a terrific array of links to various bits of information about Shakespeare's life and times. Perhaps most useful for middle school teachers is the link to Charles and Mary Lamb's "Tales from Shakespeare," a series of prose versions of the major plays.

http://shakespeare.palomar.edu

Center on English Language and Achievement Web Site. An OERI-funded research center dedicated to promoting English and literacy achievement in schools across America, CELA's Web site links teachers to relevant research in the area of literacy education. Many of the reports focus on reading and literature instruction.

http://cela.albany.edu

The ERIC Children's and Adolescent Literature Resources Page. This site, an offshoot of the ERIC Clearinghouse on Reading, English, and Communication, features links to everything from home pages on children's and adolescent literature to bookstores and publishers featuring publications for children and young adults.

http://www.indiana.edu/~eric_rec

Reading and Viewing in the Middle Grades

KidLit Web Site. This site is designed for children and adults interested in quality children's literature. One of the best features is the "KidLit Reviews," where students can write (and publish) reviews of their favorite books.

http://mgfx.com/kidlit

Links to Young Adult Authors

A variety of Web sites feature interviews, biographical sketches, and links to the Web sites of authors whose work is directed toward adolescents and young adults. The Web sites of most major publishers (especially those who publish anthologies for middle and high school students) feature regular biographies and interviews with young adult authors. Three other sites are particularly useful:

Dmoz Open Directory Project. This has extensive links to Web sites focused on literature for young adults.

http://dmoz.org/Arts/Literature/Authors/Young_Adult

Canton Public Library Site. Also a good source of links to popular young adult authors.

http://www.cantonpl.org/ya/arts.html

Kay E. Vandergrift's Special Interest Page. An excellent resource for locating authors of children's and adolescent literature, and for picking up interesting teaching ideas.

http://www.scils.rutgers.edu/~kvander

chapter 8

A Focus on Writing

GUIDING QUESTIONS
1. For what purposes do middle school students need to write?
2. What are the multiple ways that writing can be showcased in an integrated language arts classroom?
3. What are the key components of an effective middle school writing program?

A CASE FOR CONSIDERATION

To Assign or Not to Assign

Cristina and Emily are co-teaching in an eighth-grade classroom for a 6-week student teaching placement. Although Cristina hated keeping journals during her own middle school days, she wants to assign them to her students. She writes in her professional journal:

> *When Emily and I were designing our unit, I insisted that the students keep journals. She and I agreed that I would be responsible for reading and responding to the journals. Although I hated keeping a journal as a student, I wanted to see how the students would respond if they receive a lot of personal feedback. Every time journals were collected, my students could expect a letter that was at least half a page long. My feedback was primarily praise or questions about what they had written, often asking them about their hobbies or experiences. I never gave negative feedback or corrected their writing.*
>
> *On the first day of class, Emily and I were discussing our policies and the grading rubric. I discussed the journal component with the class, explaining the rationale was that it would help us get to know the students better and would give them*

practice writing. At the end of the period, I assigned a journal entry for homework. It was to be at least a page, and the topic was "names." One girl raised her hand and commented, "You said that you wanted to get to know us through the journals but how do you expect to get to know us if you assign topics?" I didn't have a really good answer. Afraid of being wrong or of contradicting what I had said already, I skirted the question. I did not modify the assignment and to my relief the bell rang.

That night I went home and thought about the girl's comment. I knew she was right, but I didn't know how to fix it; yet the answer seemed so simple. I could let the students select their own topics. This was a simple solution but one I didn't like. If the students wrote about what they wanted, then I was not in control. How would we be able to tie their journal entries to class discussion?

Anyone who has ever taught writing in a middle school classroom has struggled with Cristina's questions: How do we invite students to write for authentic purposes? How much choice should we let students have, and when do we need to take charge? How do we make our goals coincide with theirs? And, selfishly, how do we handle the burden of all those half-page comments in the midst of our busy lives? Like Cristina, many of us believe that journal keeping can be an effective means for students to explore ideas and for us to document growth or change over time. Yet, like the eighth-grade girl in Cristina's class, students may see journals as one more thinly veiled exercise in teacher control—meaningless and contrived. It's also a good bet that, after a few weeks of those half-page responses, Cristina may come to regret assigning them in the first place.

FOR DISCUSSION

- What goals did Cristina appear to have for assigning journals, and what did she do to undercut those goals?
- How do you balance your need to develop students' writing skills and tie writing to other aspects of the curriculum with students' needs for freedom and choice?
- Considering that this student teacher had 129 eighth-grade students, what suggestions do you have for managing the "paper load"?

WRITING WITH MIDDLE SCHOOL STUDENTS

Although the focus of this chapter is writing, we believe that writing should be interwoven with other language arts to support students' confidence and competence as language users. In this chapter, we will attempt to demonstrate the ways that writing can both support and be developed through meaningful activities in all of the language arts.

Just for a moment, think back to your middle school or junior high days. Try to remember an artifact, text, or teaching material your teachers might have used to teach writing. This artifact might be a grammar handbook, a workbook, a notebook, or an empty sheet of unlined paper. Perhaps, like a good many English language arts teachers, you can't remember being explicitly taught to write. What does this artifact (or lack of it) say about your former teachers' assumptions about learning to write? The difference between a workbook and a spiral notebook is probably vast in terms of the assumptions that lie with each of them. Keep these thoughts in mind as you explore some of your own assumptions about the teaching of writing in Your Fieldwork Journal 8–1.

Your Fieldwork Journal 8–1

Writing Assumptions

Part One: Examining Your Writing Assumptions

Write for a few moments on the following prompts:

1. Writing is . . .
2. Writing is not . . .
3. If I were to create a metaphor for my own writing process, it would be . . .
4. I would rank the following aspect as most (1) to least (5) important in terms of what I hope to develop in my students:
   ____ writing as personal expression
   ____ writing as thinking
   ____ writing as crafting clear, polished, and correct texts
   ____ writing as communication
   ____ writing as socially transforming
5. Which of the following expresses your sense of the prevailing middle school students' attitudes toward writing?
   a. They hate any form of writing.
   b. They love to write stories and poems.
   c. They see it as less important now that they have computers and other technologies.
   d. _____

After you have written for a while, consider how your assumptions about writing and your own writing processes may have been influenced by the curriculum of your own middle or junior high school teachers.

Part Two: Student Survey

If you are currently teaching, ask students to respond to the first three questions in Part One. Then analyze their responses according to the following questions:

- How closely do your assumptions about writing match theirs?
- How might your writing curriculum have influenced their responses?
- Considering the diversity of the metaphors they chose to describe their writing processes, how can you reach all of the writers in your middle school classroom?

In Your Fieldwork Journal exploration, you might have unearthed a question that a great many literacy teachers struggle with: "How can I teach writing when I don't feel like a writer myself?" In our work with teachers in classes and workshops, we have noticed that some excellent writing teachers feel great inadequacies in terms of their own writing abilities or feelings about writing. Some would rather do anything than write in a journal, write letters to friends, or even answer an e-mail. Others have vivid memories of negative writing experiences in school that seem to hold them hostage even today to feelings of incompetence in writing. If you are one of these teachers, there is hope. First you need to realize that many "closet nonwriters" are out there, and some have become outstanding teachers of writing and outstanding writers themselves. This is a dilemma that Herm Card worked out over the course of his teaching career. A veteran English teacher in a rural middle school as well as a poet and successful workshop facilitator, Herm describes his own transformation in Literacy Lesson 8–1.

Literacy Lesson 8-1

Back to Poetry

For some 10 years of my teaching career, I steadfastly avoided the curriculum's reference to poetry. I had been told, essentially, to teach "what works," and I was sure poetry wasn't going to work. The reason I made that assumption was that I didn't know much about it, and cared less. Not that I hadn't taken poetry courses, or read poetry, or written poetry. I had done all three. Unfortunately, the one poetry course I had taken pretty much did me in for poetry. It was horrible. Not horrible if you were a poetry scholar perhaps, but horrible if you were a college sophomore who fancied himself an aspiring poet, a poet who had written tons of love poems and another ton of angry, dark, '60s style poems, two of which had actually been published.

The poetry course was a semester devoted to rhyme, meter, and forms, with the word "poetic" seldom uttered by the professor. Having had this experience, I was so turned off to poetry that I stopped writing it and years later, when I entered the teaching profession, avoided teaching it. I realized that I knew nothing about poetry and really felt nothing for it. I assumed I was an anomaly, the poster boy for fear of poetry.

The bottom line is that some 10 years after I began teaching, I began writing poetry again, and I began reading poetry again. Soon after, I made the seemingly daring leap into teaching poetry.

The poster boy for fear of poetry. Over the years I have discovered that was not the case. As my career has evolved for some 8 years I have been presenting workshops on teaching poetry and writing to teachers. I have discovered the trepidation I felt about teaching poetry to be relatively common among teachers. Something about poetry makes them question their ability, question their knowledge, and, more important, question themselves. Many teachers do not consider themselves poetic. Most students do not consider themselves poetic, so it's not like the odds are against us. In my workshops, the very people who claimed to have never taken a poetic breath have produced some of the most astonishingly personal, sensitive, and beautiful poetry I have ever read. It is not unusual for a piece of writing from an "I can't write poetry" claimant to send people scurrying for the tissue box. I have had workshops nearly end because no one, including me, could imagine reading next after a piece that had reduced us all to tears or gales of laughter or sent us deep into nostalgic reverie.

The point of this is that I have not taught these teachers to write poetry any more that I can or do teach my students to write it. It is not teaching poetry that we strive for as much as it is allowing our students to become aware of poetry and involved with poetry. By exposing them to poetry in as many ways as possible, by allowing them to experience poetry at a comfortable pace and level, we allow them the opportunity to be comfortable with poetry and even appreciate and enjoy the experience.

Perhaps a first step in developing our own identities as teachers who write is accepting the fact that both teaching and writing are enriched when we find the "comfortable pace and level" that Herb described, a pace and level that can support teachers and students alike to flourish and grow.

We can all probably agree that our former teachers had a great influence on our assumptions, feelings, and fears where the teaching of writing is concerned. Consider as well the role of popular media in shaping your assumptions. For years, newspapers and television have speculated on why Johnny can't write. In such public arenas, conceptions of teaching writing may be reduced to teaching and testing issues of correctness. With the arrival of computers, technology has often been touted as the answer to our writing problems.

Certainly computers can support the teaching of writing. Since the arrival of word processing, multiple drafts can be managed with more ease than middle school students are usually willing to devote to rewrites. The Internet makes the process of research more intriguing and accessible than ever before. But there are few easy solutions to the complexities of teaching writing. In fact, many have argued that computer technology only increases this complexity. Grammar and spell checks and the polished look of word-processed texts can give students the impression that drafts are perfect just as they are. The barrage of information, advertising, and propaganda on the Internet heightens our responsibility to make students critical consumers and producers of electronic media. Quite frankly, that statement strikes fear in many of us.

Current writing literature is flooded with talk of "new literacies," "technoliteracies," and "multiliteracies." With the arrival of new information and communication technologies comes an imperative that we expand old notions of a traditional writing curriculum. Texts may be face-to-face, virtual, and/or multimedia. New technologies give us rich opportunities to open up classrooms and our writing curriculum. Luke and Carrington (in press) critique literacy programs that remain traditional in a print format that is disconnected from a broader analysis of community, of environment, of the experiences and practices of globalization. The goal of a writing program is, according to Luke and Carrington, to engage children critically using both digital and print media. There is a growing attention to the need to teach students how to become critical consumers and producers of texts, to understand the multiple dimensions of literacy, and to teach critical perspectives.

Approaches to classroom study then can and should be a part of a larger critical analysis of who uses language, where, and with what power (Carrington & Luke, in press; Comber & Simpson, 2001, Edelsky, 1996; Luke, Freebody, & Land, 2000)

In short, there is no quick fix or cure-all for the cries of politicians, pundits, and policy makers about the woes of poor Johnnie or Janie. You will be pulled to teach a narrow writing curriculum, geared to improve standardized test scores. You will be pushed to teach critical literacies with a focus on larger social issues. Convincing parents, administrators, and even students that writing is complicated, messy, and often difficult is no easy task. Teaching writing is many things. It is giving students access to the conventions of edited English, at the same time that we value and respect their home languages. It is making students aware of rhetorical choices and the social and political consequences of those choices at the same time we provide opportunities for private, informal exploration. Even today, after three decades of attention to the importance of teaching processes as well as products, writing is still seen by many as the end of the learning process, a way of showcasing what students have already learned.

As this chapter will show, writing can be used to learn, to explore ideas, to rehearse and perform, and to develop language skills. Of course, writing skills are necessary for students to pass standardized tests, but this is only one small part of the purpose writing should play in the life of the early adolescent. In this chapter, we'll address strategies for writing to learn as well as learning to write.

Before we focus on the teaching and learning of writing, let's examine the ways in which writing may support multiple purposes and multiple language arts. Oftentimes, responding to literature overshadows other acts of writing in an English language arts classroom. Although book reports, essay exams, or research report writing may be integral parts of a middle school writing curriculum, other purposes may be overlooked. Think back to the language lenses presented in Chapter 6. In what ways might writing support reading? How might writing serve to support language study or talking and listening? How might writing serve the local community?

Writing-to-learn activities give middle school students a chance to make predictions, record what they already know, ask questions, and explore their views. In addition to being a tool for learning, writing can enable students to share and to showcase, to forge connections with peers and family, and to reach out to the larger community. Let's explore those purposes in Your Fieldwork Journal 8–2.

Your Fieldwork Journal 8–2

Writing for Multiple Purposes

Consider all the ways that writing may be used in a middle school classroom. The chart on the following page lists some of the many forms that writing may take in a classroom or community

Think about this list of texts and techniques for writing and see how many you can add. Then, in your fieldwork journal, create a chart like the one on page 209. Pick one of the techniques in the list and experiment with the different purposes this technique

Texts and Techniques for the Writing Classroom

journals	sketches	concept maps
applications	critical reviews	Web pages
songs	anecdotes	response papers
stories	field notes	novels
commentaries	requests	cartoons
dialogues	proposals	photo essays
editorials	charts/graphs	directions
research reports	monographs	diaries
book reports	applications	fictional
letters	puzzles	narratives
resumes	résumés	story problems
essays	scripts	autobiographies
memos	lists	drawings
poems	notes	diagrams
		e-mail messages

might serve your teaching of writing. Consider, for example, the topic of the Case for Consideration at the beginning of this chapter: the journal. Rather than serving one narrow purpose in your writing classroom, we see the journal as an incredibly flexible tool for multiple uses. After reading the example we provide in the purposes for writing chart, choose another of the writing forms and techniques from the chart above and experiment with the different purposes it can serve in your curriculum.

In addition to sharing your ideas with others, you might want to reflect on the ease or difficulty you had thinking of writing activities for each of the four purposes presented in the chart. Perhaps it was easy for you to list examples of writing to connect but more difficult to provide any examples of writing to learn about writing. If so, what might account for this difference? Just as any activity may support more than one of the language arts, a writing activity may clearly fit into more than one category. For example, although we've placed them in the category of *writing to connect and transform,* dialogue journals (journals kept by two students who exchange them on a regular basis and respond to each other's work) may fit equally well under *writing to explore.* Ask yourself if you resonate with one of these writing purposes more than others, or if you have strong positive or negative feelings about particular activities on the list. What do your feelings and preferences imply for your own teaching of writing with students at the middle school level? Do you hold positive or negative views of any of these categories or any particular activities? What are the implications for you as a middle school writing teacher?

A Focus on Writing

	Purposes for Writing			
Texts and Techniques for Writing	**Writing to Explore** How might students explore ideas and express themselves through writing?	**Writing to Learn About Writing** How might students become better producers of print and nonprint texts?	**Writing to Connect and Transform** How might students use writing to connect with others and make an impact on their world?	**Writing to Showcase** How might students share or demonstrate what they have learned through writing?
Journals and Logs	• Students keep personal **journals** or **diaries** to record experiences that might lead to future writing topics. • Students keep **learning logs** for recording their growing understanding about particular readings or topics. • Students create **dialectical notebooks** (Berthoff, 1981) to record observations and inferences about their observations of everyday life.	• Students create writing **stylebooks** that include personal skill inventories, spelling lists, and examples of techniques borrowed from published writers. • Students keep **reading journals** or **literature logs** to record responses to literary styles. • Students keep **dialect journals** to record observations about language use in multiple social contexts.	• Students trade **dialogue journals** in which they write informally to their teacher or a peer about their learning experiences. • Students keep project journals as a repository of research citations, writing ideas, interview notes, and for other data on social action or community service projects.	• Students create **writers' notebooks** in which they showcase polished writing, keep notes on future writing ideas, and reflect on their progress over the course of time. • Students keep logs of Internet addresses with evaluation of the sources of information available.

BALANCING ACTS: WRITING INSTRUCTION IN THE MIDDLE SCHOOL

Just as Cristina struggled to balance the need for student choice with her own needs to prepare students for a class discussion, teaching writing is always a balancing act. There is no list of best practices for teaching writing to early adolescents. Considering the diversity of interests, abilities, and experiences middle school students bring to the writing classroom, we look awry at any such lists. Issues of class, race, and gender also complicate issues of effective writing instruction. As we detailed in Chapter 1, we want to complicate a view that all middle school students want or need the same things. Yet, early adolescents do face challenges that entangle with any given pedagogical approach. Gender roles become more intensified; expectations increase for peer group affiliations outside the home. Attention to social and political issues becomes more salient; and standardized testing looms large as middle school students prepare for high school. Likewise in our classrooms, students have a wide range of abilities and preferences. Given all of this complexity we pose the following considerations.

Considerations for Writing in the Middle School Classroom

- **Middle school students need positive social interactions with peers and adults.**
  - When and how do we support students writing collaboratively and privately?
  - What authentic opportunities can we create for sharing and publishing students' writing?
  - In what ways can teachers and peers become partners in students' writing experiences?
- **Middle school students need physical activities to support the development of writing skills.**
  - How can we make writing an active rather than a passive activity?
  - What roles can talking, writing, drawing, and performing play in students' prewriting, drafting, and editing?
  - How can students "publish" their writing in forms other than the printed word?
- **Middle school students need opportunities for self-definition, creative expression, and a sense of competence and achievement in their writing experiences.**
  - How do we balance our responsibility to develop writing competencies with students' need for choice over topic, genre, audience, and purpose?
  - How can we create opportunities for formal and polished as well as expressive, informal writing?
  - How can we make substantive comments on students' writing without squelching their creativity and motivation?
- **Middle school students need writing opportunities that promote meaningful participation in families, school, and the larger world.**
  - How might we find authentic and appreciative audiences for students' writing outside of our classroom walls?

- How can our students use writing as a form of personal expressions, critical thinking, and communicating with others?
- How can writing promote students' involvement in social and political activities of importance to them?

Comfort and Challenge

Creating a comfortable writing classroom with students as the central focus is not as easy as it may seem. Comfort is a cultural construct. What may appear comfortable to some may create great discomfort for others. What is familiar and routine is comfortable. The routines that students may bring to your classroom may not match your expectations or the routines of their peers.

As early adolescents continue to grow and develop, they will work with people less like themselves. They may have just moved from a small rural elementary school, or they may be bussed from one part of the city to a less familiar area. The middle school will most likely draw students together who have not attended similar schools in the past.

For many early adolescents, the "rules" of school may appear to have changed now that they are no longer "little kids" in an elementary school. Forces within and beyond the school will influence how students engage with their peers at school. Collaborating in writing projects and sharing writing with others are sound pedagogical practices for middle school students, yet just as these activities provide learning opportunities, they may carry with them social tensions that we cannot afford to ignore.

Collaboration and Privacy

If you have ever spent time in a middle school classroom, you have probably witnessed incredible compassion and astonishing cruelty. Peer group interactions and strategies for collaborations are centrally important and must be guided with much care. For any number of reasons, students may be uncomfortable sharing writing with peers. Yet, increasing students' abilities to engage in positive social interactions with adults and peers is vitally important. To make such interactions and collaborations positive, we must first build a supportive classroom community. How exactly do we do this?

Simply assigning students into writing groups does not ensure positive social interactions. Lensmire (1994), for example, discusses the social tensions that surround groups in a writing workshop. Making sure students see valid purposes, not only for writing but also for the collaborative effort, is a necessary first step. But most important, we must make sure that we "do no harm" by placing students from divergent backgrounds in the same group and expecting them to work out social complexities on their own. Attending explicitly to the purposes for writing and designing instruction to support positive interactions are vital. Writing opportunities that extend beyond the classroom walls to the home and neighborhood can add relevance that makes writing more meaningful and social interactions more positive when students come together to write something that may have the potential for a real impact on their school or community. Literacy Lesson 8–2 explores one teacher's work with peer response groups.

Literacy Lesson 8–2

Making Writing Groups Work

Patricia Lopez makes peer response groups a regular part of her classroom instruction. She admits to having struggled in the past with how to place students in groups:

> *I used to just number kids off by six or seven and ask them to get into groups. This was usually a disaster. There were always boys who didn't want to sit next to girls or kids from one neighborhood who didn't want to sit next to those from another. It was a mess. Now I plan for my writing groups. First I ask each student to write me a private note, listing people they would like to work with and any individuals they might have trouble working with. I use these lists as a starting point, but I reserve the right to veto anybody's choice if I think that cliques will form or work won't get done.*
>
> *Then I follow a few rules of thumb:*
>
> 1. *Each group should have a mix of kids in terms of race and gender.*
> 2. *Groups should include quiet as well as more talkative kids.*
> 3. *When I have students with special needs or whose first language isn't English, I try to place one or two of the more "tolerant" kids in that group—people who are likely to help out others and collaborate with those who need extra support.*
> 4. *Finally, for writing groups, I try to have around three or four per group. If you have more than this, each student doesn't get a chance to share writing. If you have less, and someone is absent, students can get stuck without a group.*
>
> *From this starting place, I create my first groupings. I like for kids to stick together for several weeks so that people feel comfortable sharing their writing, but I always reserve the right to break up groups that are too rowdy or not working productively. It's interesting, but I usually don't have to break up groups once they get started. Especially in the first few weeks, I make sure that I constantly circulate around the room, sometimes sitting in on a writing group that seems to be struggling or straying off task. Later, I can hold individual writing or reading conferences while peer groups are under way.*
>
> *Next, there's the issue of how to respond to each other's writing beyond the usual "it's great" or "it sucks" language that middle school students tend to use. Sometimes I give them a page with three simple prompts and task them to: (a) listen to a writer read a piece aloud, (b) take notes for a few minutes, and (c) respond orally. The prompts are usually something like this:*
>
> 1. *One thing I noticed about your writing was . . .*
> 2. *Some questions I had were . . .*
> 3. *For your next draft you might think about . . .*
>
> *For the first few weeks, students fill these forms out each time they give oral feedback on each other's writing. Later, groups can give feedback without writing out their comments first. I collect the written comments as a check on which students may be straying off task or are unclear about how to give productive feedback. Sometimes I give a little mini-lesson on helpful and unhelpful comments just as a reminder.*

Eventually I lead students into more extensive types of response. I like to use a list of options I derived from Elbow's book, Writing without Teachers.

1. *Mirroring—paraphrase the writer's text or ideas back to him/her just as you heard them.*
2. *Movies of the Mind—describe your moment-to-moment responses, reactions, images, and feelings as you listened.*
3. *Nutshelling—sum up the writer's main point in a sentence or two.*
4. *Questioning—ask the writer questions about points you are wondering about or points that are unclear to you.*
5. *Pointing—tell the writer what words or phrases successfully "penetrated your skull" or those that were weak, hollow, or empty.*
6. *Potpourri—say whatever comes to mind after hearing the writing.*

On the first day I hand out this list, I usually cut the class into six sections and ask students sitting in each section to take one of the response options and write an anonymous response to a piece of writing I read aloud to them. I then collect their anonymous responses and read each one to the class, commenting on which responses were most and least helpful to me as a writer. The first time I place students into their writing groups, I ask them to choose one response type—usually "movies of the mind" because that's really fun for them—and to try giving this kind of oral feedback to each other. As weeks go by, they can try other ways of responding as they feel more comfortable as writers and as responders.

We only do writing response groups every week or two in my classroom so kids don't get bored with this activity. If interests begin to wane, I stop them for a while. Generally, though, with a little planning and structure on my part, the kids build their enthusiasm and confidence with a little help from their friends.

I wish I could say that these groups are an unqualified success. I have to admit there are times when students' responses are negative and not productive. There are also those students who enjoy making comments on each other's work but do little to revise their own work in terms of other students' comments. I still feel these group sessions are important. For one thing, students learn to work together. And they're only one part of my writing instruction. I always take the opportunity to hold conferences with students and make comments on some (but not all) of their written work so they have that feedback from me. The peer writing groups serve a couple of important purposes, though: They help kids to understand what it is to write for a real audience, and they make them aware of techniques that other students are using and that they might use in their own writing. For these reasons and many others, I'll continue to use peer groups in my classroom.

Just as there is a need to create opportunities for social interactions around writing, there is a vital need to respect the privacy of our students. Students need to explore their views without fear of the judgments of their peers or the evaluation of their teachers. As we set up our writing classrooms, we'll need to consider the obstacles and opportunities that imposing any structure might create for particular students. We'll want to consider how and when students should be given choices, not only about topics but about the social structure of the classroom as well. Clearly, no one structure should be considered to be the best for all students under all circumstances. We must often negotiate a fine balancing act between careful planning of writing activities and a willingness to adjust the moment-to-moment orchestration of our lessons as the social dynamics shift.

Choice and Control

Many middle school specialists would say that student choice is clearly a hallmark of any writing program. On the surface, we agree heartily with this idea. A great many early adolescents relish the idea of writing on topics of their own choosing and exploring a variety of self-selected genres. When we taught middle school, we were always delighted when a student handed over his or her personal journal or poetry notebook for us to read. Sometimes we were shocked to discover that students who contributed little in the forum of a large group activity were actually prolific writers in their private lives.

For these students, activities and projects like keeping a writer's notebook and producing so many "polished" pieces of writing per marking periods work very well. As a way of sponsoring choice without grading every piece of writing, part of your grade can be determined by a simple contract such as the one in Figure 8–1.

For students who seem paralyzed by completely open choice, it's often helpful to provide a menu of options such as the one in Figure 8–2.

Although many students flourish in an atmosphere of free choice, we must remember that choice is never really free from the tangle of the peer dynamic, especially in a middle school classroom where peer groups may just be solidifying and the stakes

FIGURE 8-1 Grading Contract

Twenty percent of your grade for the next 6 weeks will be based upon your creative writing. Grades will be determined as follows:

To earn an A:

- Hand in FOUR polished pieces (these pieces must be submitted to me in advance and judged as acceptable).
- Keep copies of all drafts for these and other writing in your writing journal.
- Get written feedback from at least one classmate on each of these four pieces-in-progress.

To earn a B:

- Follow the same procedure as above, producing THREE polished drafts.

To earn a C:

- Follow the same procedure as above in producing TWO polished drafts.

A Focus on Writing

FIGURE 8-2 Writing Menu

> For the past several weeks, we have been studying the Holocaust as we read *The Autobiography of Anne Frank* and excerpts from Miep Gies's *Anne Frank Remembered*. Today, I'd like you to write for about 15 minutes on one of the topics below. You will not have to share your writing with the rest of your group, but I will expect you to talk about some ideas you had as you were writing it and to include this draft in your writing folder.
>
> **Option One:** Imagine you were Miep Gies, and Otto Frank asked if you could assist his family and allow them to hide in the annex. How would you respond to his request? Choose any form: a letter, dialogue, etc.
>
> **Option Two:** Imagine that Anne wrote one diary entry that didn't make it into the published book. Write that entry.
>
> **Option Three:** Could the Holocaust happen today? Are there elements in the world that are similar to those in Hitler's time? Choose any form for your response.
>
> **Option Four:** Think about these two books and write something you're dying to write about in any form.

of marking yourself as an "insider" or "outsider" appear to be quite high. For example, Darius, a seventh-grade boy, reported privately to Margaret that he loved fairy tales. He liked to read and write them and had been doing so for a couple of years until he entered middle school. "It's like not okay to write fairy tales anymore," he whispered to Margaret when she inquired during a writing conference why he wasn't writing. Middle school boys like Darius are beginning to encounter more rigid gender roles that come with what may seem like strict rules in middle school classrooms. Perhaps, what Darius was saying was that in middle school, "Real men don't write about childish things." Middle school students are often extremely vigilant not to mark themselves as childish. Andrea's case, in the Literacy Lesson 8–3, is even more disturbing.

Literacy Lesson 8-3

The F Word: Learning From Andrea

In Andrea's sixth-grade classroom, Mr. Adams set up writing workshop time on every Tuesday and Thursday as time for students to write about self-selected topics. He did not give writing prompts or require certain genres or topics. Students kept their writing notebooks up to date with daily entries that included what they wrote, how much they had written, and which skills they were working to improve. Almost all students wrote fiction. The boys, for the most part, wrote stories about sports and fast-action adventure stories that often included killing and other violent acts. The girls often wrote about friendships and romance.

Andrea found such writing silly. She viewed herself as a writer and dreamed of becoming published. As an avid reader of nonfiction and the newspaper, Andrea liked writing essays addressing the inequalities she observed in the world. To support her writing, Andrea turned to autobiography and historical documents. She became fascinated with the Women's Liberation Movement of the 1960s, reading about Betty Friedan and Gloria Steinem. After she stumbled onto the *Roe vs. Wade* case on the Internet, Andrea became determined to write an editorial for *The Nugget,* the middle school newsletter that went out to all fifth, sixth, and seventh graders in her school. Her essay, titled "The Women's Movement," covered the history of the Women's movement and expressed her views on how women's rights were declining. Her essay stood in sharp contrast to the fiction written by the other students. Boys began calling her "the feminist." This term didn't carry with it any positive connotations with them; whispers began to circulate that called into question Andrea's sexual orientation. Needless to say, Andrea didn't submit another piece for publication.

We're sure you're wondering what to do about the Andreas in your own classrooms, especially when they are often forced into the background and rarely share such embarrassing information with their teachers. As you know, middle school students are often extremely vigilant not to mark themselves as "different" in the eyes of their peers. Free choice is clearly not "free" in the social world of middle school where words and actions may mark students as immature, or worse yet in this developmental period, make their sexual orientation suspect. Choice in the middle school writing curriculum is never as simple as telling students to "write whatever you like." A writing curriculum built entirely around students' free choices will make some students like Darius and Andrea uncomfortable in accepting such invitations. Choices about topic selection, genre, and publication are witnessed by peers, who may assign meanings that mark a student as an outsider in the group. As a result, young men like Darius must keep their interest in fairy tales secret for fear of abandoning their developing masculinity, and young women like Andrea may feel silenced for a lifetime.

It's important to understand that we are not advocating that you limit students' writing choices. We are simply asserting the need to recognize that our well-intentioned choices usually carry consequences for students that are beyond our conscious attention or control. We need to create a classroom that openly challenges the notion that real men don't have feeling or that real women can't be strong or assertive. An antiracist (Hall, 1981; Ny, Staton, & Scane, 1995) or "anti-bias" curriculum where issues like gender, race, culture, and sexual orientation are a conscious part of students' writing, reading, and talk can go a long way in opening up choices for students like Darius and Andrea.

Beyond this responsibility, however, we need to help all students to understand the consequences of "going public" in unfamiliar and potentially hostile environments. It may be a positive, affirming experience for a gay student to "come out" in the comfortable

> **Language Study in Context**
> It's often interesting to ask students to watch popular television shows featuring teenagers and keep a log of the language and behaviors of males and females. Later the class can discuss how television shows give powerful messages about what it means to be "male" and "female" in today's world.

environment of our language arts classroom, but we cannot guarantee that student safe passage in the often cruel social networks that adolescents build in the hallways, the playing fields, or the cafeteria.

For some students, a curriculum built on free choice may make them far too comfortable. Students offered a steady diet of choice may not stretch intellectually, try out new genres, or experiment with rhetorical devices. They may continue writing what they are comfortable writing and not venture beyond those comfort zones. A writing program should seek a balance, creating a place of comfort and safety within which we can nudge students into that uncomfortable place where learning occurs. We must help them to reach the intellectual places that they cannot yet reach independently, what Vygotsky (1978) has called the *zone of proximal development* (ZPD), or the place that learners can only traverse with the help of an adult or a more knowledgeable peer.

Richard Lloyd-Jones, a rhetorician and leading scholar of writing instruction, uses the metaphor of the sand in the oyster to help us think about how to teach writing. He says, "It's the sand in the oyster. You don't want to have so much sand that you kill the oyster, but you want enough to have a pearl every now and then" (quoted in Finders, 1992, p. 507). Your writing instruction should be based upon rigorous but reachable goals for all students. There are many ways to make such standards of writing seem reachable to your middle school students.

Physical Activity and Solitude

For some writers, the need for a quiet, private space is essential. Even the sound of quiet music or the rustle of papers can disturb their writing process. These students need a private area, away from the bustle and noise of the typical middle school classroom. Even a well-placed grouping of pillows on the floor behind a bookcase can provide such a space for these students.

At the same time, the need for physical activity is great in middle school. Movement and hands-on learning activities can make writing and learning in general more meaningful, especially for struggling writers. Middle school teachers will want to allow students to enter writing through drawing and performing. Visual and media literacies (films, videos, cartoons) coupled with physical activities (talk, movement, and performance) can make writing more meaningful and more engaging. In addition, physical activities make writing more real and more relevant to active middle school students whose lives are filled with much more than print literacies.

Physical activities are a way to integrate the language arts and a means to add reality to the writing curriculum. When you think about it, writing in the workforce often includes movement, collaboration, and physical activity. Speech writers collaborate with speakers. Writers of pamphlets and brochures work with others in planning the layout and artwork. Reports and documents often include a public presentation of some kind. Writing that gets work done often includes talk and extensive collaboration with others.

> **Language Study in Context**
>
> You may want your students to research the kinds of writing that their parents or future employers do, investigating what they write as well as the writing, reading, and oral language processes they engage in to accomplish their work. Your students could also explore the ways in which adults often cross disciplinary boundaries in their work. This research could be shared with the whole class through role play, speeches, or dramatic dialogues.

Correctness and Creativity

Teachers must also walk a shaky tightrope between correctness and creativity in the writing classroom. Students may be so concerned with issues of correctness that they doubt their ability to write at all. At the middle school level, issues of grammatical correctness may become more compelling as students prepare for high school placement exams and standardized tests. Likewise, middle school students will need to employ conventions of edited English in order to have their voices heard beyond the classroom. Delpit (1988, 1991, 2002), among others, advocates for explicit instruction so children who are not born into the dominant dialect may gain access to further opportunities that are often denied them due to linguistic stereotyping and prejudice. In the face of this pressing need for access to what has been called "the language of power," early adolescents are still exploring their own interests and identities. A strong focus on correction may constrain and stifle that exploration and creativity.

> **Language Study in Context**
>
> As you discover patterns of errors in students' written work, you might ask them to keep a skills inventory. In a three-column chart they can list (a) a description of the error, written in their own words, (b) two examples of the error in their own writing with corrections, and (c) a gimmick or trick to help them remember how to avoid the error.

As we will argue in Chapter 10, issues of edited English such as grammar, punctuation, and spelling are best taught in the context of students' own language activities. Concentrating on patterns of error rather than editing every error, helping students to keep personal skills inventories of spelling, punctuation, and usage errors, and making "progress, not perfection" your ultimate goal will go a long way in developing your students' knowledge of language conventions without stifling their enthusiasm and creativity.

Personal and Public Writing

Many of our students thrive on the personal understanding gained through private writing in journals or diaries. Just as we may have kept personal writings over the years, our students often bring notebooks or diaries to school in backpacks or keep them hidden in a special place at home. These personal writings serve as a repository of feelings and understanding; at the same time, they mark moments in students' lives and document their personal histories. The trick in classrooms is getting students to believe that some of their writing can be truly private, unedited, not monitored by us.

Schools are incredibly public places. Sponsoring private writing as one part of our curriculum means providing ways for students to fold and staple personal entries in journals or to simply spend some quiet time writing pieces that are not seen by anyone but them. At the same time, we must make it perfectly clear that we are not therapists or guidance counselors. As students enter adolescence, a whole host of personal issues may emerge on the pages of journals: thoughts of suicide, parental abuse, sexual experiences, and other delicate issues with which we as literacy teachers are not prepared to respond. Before assigning journals or logs, we must tell students up-front (and with occasional reminders) that if, as a result of reading their journals, we suspect they may be in danger or may hurt themselves, it is our duty to inform others who can help them. Often, conscious or not, our students' writing may be a call for help, and they will eventually welcome our interventions. But we, and they, must understand that we are in no position to prevent suicide or mediate child abuse without the help of competent professionals.

Just as personal writing is important to middle school students, as their world expands, they will seek out opportunities to gain meaningful relationships beyond their neighborhoods. This is often a time when students see the school's curriculum as less meaningful to their lives. Our job as middle school teachers includes making connections between the school's curriculum and the students' lived experiences. Writing is one means by which the language arts curriculum can become real and relevant, especially if students are given opportunities to make real contributions to their local community and beyond. Sometimes this will demand rigid adherence to particular conventions of edited American English that will allow them to have an impact on others. And sometimes rigid adherence to one set of conventions that do not carry currency in a particular context will prevent their voices from being heard. The ability to move among the multiple ways of writing and make appropriate choices for particular contexts will allow students to write their ways into the larger world.

CREATING A CLASSROOM FOR WRITERS

All of this balancing may seem a daunting juggling act for the middle school writing teacher. Clearly, there is a lot to think about in designing and implementing writing lessons. Even though it may appear almost overwhelming, we need to remember that middle school students are likely to meet writing with eagerness, especially if the teacher approaches the writing opportunities with enthusiasm, a confidence that all students have something important to say, and a belief that all students can learn.

It is now commonly understood that teachers and learners should attend to the processes and products of writing. In many middle school classrooms, you may see wall charts and posters that list steps of "The Writing Process," that move linearly from prewriting to drafting, to revising, to editing, to publishing. A focus on both writing process and product has improved writing instruction, but the linear lockstep approach is problematic. Murray (1994) notes, "I felt no loyalty to a process" (p. 60), arguing that the process of writing should be considered always in the plural. He says that the processes change (a) according to the cognitive style of the writer, (b) according to the writing task, and (c) with experience. Murray goes on to identify the range of writing processes that vary from a three-step process (collect, plan, write), to a five-step process (focus, explore, plan, draft, clarify), and up to a seven-step process (focus, collect, share, order, develop, voice, edit).

The point here is to disrupt the notion that there is one linear progression in the writing process. Leading students through a sequence of writing steps may seem like effective writing instruction, yet this approach is built from the assumption that all writers go through the same steps for all writing. As Murray and many others have demonstrated over the past three decades, writing is recursive rather than linear; effective writers employ only those steps needed for a particular project. As Murray notes, with experience, a writer will internalize some of the planning strategies that are demanded by more familiar tasks and that same writer may need more support with less familiar tasks.

Savvy middle school writers can co-opt any teacher's attempt to force all writers into the same linear process. They may, for example, complete final drafts first and then "mess it all up to make a first draft" to turn into their teachers. Many of us may have been guilty ourselves in writing a final draft for our teachers and then going back and writing out our outlines after the project is completed in order to prove to our well-meaning teachers that we had completed "The Writing Process." That said, teachers will want to give time and instruction to the multiple processes needed for effective writing. Depending on one's purposes and audiences for a particular writing project, some steps will be much more important and some may be omitted altogether.

If a teacher's purpose for a particular writing prompt is for her students to explore their views on an issue, then prewriting strategies such as brainstorming or concept mapping may be the most appropriate means to achieve that goal. Revision and editing may not come into play at all. In contrast, if a student's goal includes publishing in the local newspaper to enlist community members to support a particular position, then revision and editing would clearly be important. That is our hope—that middle school students will begin to see writing has real purposes and the potential for real effects.

Part of creating a welcoming, yet honest climate in your writing classroom involves sharing your own writing processes and struggles. It's a good idea, for example, to write alongside your students. This is a quick way to gauge when a writing activity is confusing or bogus. Sharing your writing with students can also build camaraderie, but you must be careful not to set yourself up as the writing-expert-in-residence or the grammar guru. One way of making your writing process more accessible is to model your own drafting processes aloud for students. You could bring in a blank overhead transparency and ask your students to suggest a few topics. Then proceed to "think aloud" as you move from selecting a topic to creating a rough draft. Before beginning, you might break students into three groups, each with its own task (see Figure 8–3).

After about 15 minutes, stop and ask students to make a list of at least three questions they would like to ask about the composing process. Then ask students to

FIGURE 8-3 Observation Task for Composing Aloud Activity

Instructor to Observers

Group A, take notes on what **behaviors** you see as I write. (for example, I put down my pen, stare into space, scratch my head, etc.)

Group B, take notes on times when I seem to be **struggling** with my writing. What seems to worry me (for example, what others might think about my language choices)?

Group C, take notes on any **decisions** I appear to be making as I write (for example, whether "frightening" or "scary" is a better word).

report on what they have noticed. After this discussion, students are free to ask any further questions about the teacher's writing processes.

Many years ago, Murray spoke at the National Council of Teachers of English fall conference. Although we can't remember his exact words, the gist of his message went something like this: "We have an ethical responsibility to fail more often in front of our students." It's an interesting paradox that, within limits, the more vulnerable we become, the more powerful our teaching becomes. We would all do well to remember that adage as we nurture and develop the multiple writing processes of our middle school students.

We'd now like to focus on an increasingly popular approach that allows teachers to attend to the processes and products of student writing: the writers' workshop.

The Writers' Workshop as a Structure for Learning

A writers' workshop includes time to write, to respond to peers, to confer with the teacher and peers, to share, and to publish. There is no one correct way to set up a writers' workshop in your classroom. Some workshops last an entire semester, some for 3 to 6 weeks. Some teachers sponsor writers' workshops 2 days a week, whereas others hold workshops every day. Some workshop models allow students to be completely in control of what they write; others may be designed around a theme or genre. Atwell (1987) and Rief (1991) provide a wealth of information on how to facilitate a workshop.

In a great many workshops, students enter the classroom and begin to work on their individual writing projects. The teacher may give a mini-lesson (5 to 20 minutes) for the whole class or for those needing to work on a particular strategy or skill. A table may be set up in the corner of the room for conferences. In some, students sign up for a conference with their peers or their teacher on an as-needed basis; in others, teachers hold regular conferences on a rotating schedule. Often the students themselves determine when they are ready to share, but some workshops include regular "sharing circles" each week. Students may share their work in progress or polished pieces. Often classrooms are organized with an area set aside for sharing that includes an author's chair (Graves, 1982). The chair may be a rocking chair, an overstuffed chair, or simply a tall stool placed in a significant location in the room where the author sits to read to peers. Some middle school classrooms have a big couch and a rug for comfortable sharing times. The physical room arrangement may not be critical to a writers' workshop success, but attention to the physical arrangement can help to create opportunities for the kinds of activities that support young writers.

The writers' workshop can be an effective means by which students can learn from, support, and teach their peers. The writers' workshop structure accommodates middle school students' need for social interaction and self-expression, something the National Middle School Association and other middle school specialists advocate. According to the Carnegie Task Force on Education for Young Adolescents (1995), a focus on early adolescents' social needs has overshadowed their needs for academic rigor. Under the skilled and caring guidance of a middle school teacher, a writers' workshop can accommodate both academic rigor and social interactions. The writers' workshop in which students share their writing and their expertise will

FIGURE 8-4 A Writers' Workshop in Progress

create opportunities for students to gain confidence and competence in themselves as writers and as learners. Workshops have proven effective because they balance individual and group work as well as explicit instruction and writing as rehearsal. Workshops often include sharing and publishing to make visible the ways in which writing can have a real impact on self, peers, and the larger community. The photograph in Figure 8–4 shows students writing collaboratively in a classroom setting.

In any writing workshop, the teacher must attend to record keeping. Students often take on many of the responsibilities by keeping a writer's record of their writing, their progress, their skills, and their publications. Such records may be kept in the classroom, or students may be expected to carry their writing folders to class each day. Because many middle school teachers have more than 150 students, it is vitally important to have a system of record keeping. There is no one correct or easy way to manage the paper load. But without an effective and efficient system, the workshop is sure to fail. Harried teachers may simply drop the workshop for some other pedagogical practices that generate less paper management. If you decide to set up a workshop, you must create a comfortable structure within which you and your students can thrive. Depending on the purposes and goals, a writers' workshop can be set in harmony with any approach to literacy teaching, such as text-centered, personal growth, or sociopolitical.

To illustrate more concretely one way in which a workshop might be implemented and monitored, we present Michael's story in Literacy Lesson 8–4. As you read his story, try to tease out the assumptions that appear to guide him in his teaching decisions.

Literacy Lesson 8-4

Facilitating One Writing Classroom

It was late January and Michael had been in his student teaching assignment for just 2 weeks when his mentor teacher suggested that he begin planning for a 3-week writing unit with his sixth graders at Irvin Middle School. Irvin is a rural middle school with a large bussed-in population. As students in a rural township school, all of Michael's students rode the bus at least 30 miles every day. Michael knew very little about his students except that most were farmers, and most were working class or poor. Michael decided to tap the expertise of his students and organize a writing unit around the theme of animals, something many of them had already written about in detail.

After inquiring about a field trip to the zoo 60 miles away, he learned that the school's budget and bus scheduling wouldn't allow for such a trip. As Michael began planning his writing unit, he made decisions about how and when student choice might come into his unit and how too he would infuse some of the department's language arts goals. In an attempt to balance both, Michael developed social and academic goals for his students that included punctuating dialogue correctly, using factual information to support a position, work collaboratively with a small group, and sharing writing in a public forum. After conferring with his mentor teacher about how to make this writing unit real and relevant, he decided that the culminating activity would be to write and perform scripts for a sixth-grade version of *Animal Planet* and invite kindergarteners and first graders to attend.

To support writing, Michael selected clips from the television shows *Dogs with Jobs* and *Animal Planet*. He also selected the short story "Dirk, The Protector" by Paulsen.

From the public library Michael checked out an audiotape of Paulsen discussing his preparation for the Iditarod, the Great Alaskan Dog Sled Race. He planned to ask students to conduct an interview with a pet owner. He also planned to invite Ms. Lawson to come and speak about her seeing-eye dog.

Michael thought this unit would work well to teach his students that language choices are made with a real context in mind. Rather than emphasize issues of correctness severed from context, Michael embedded them in projects to help his students learn that language choices are "correct" when they match the context in which they are used. As a mini-inquiry project, students would collect "bits of language" about pets from two sources: one informal such as family and friends telling stories about their pets, and one more formal such as an encyclopedia, documentary, or guide from a veterinarian. They would then analyze the ways in which the same animal was described in these two different contexts and write about the similarities and differences. He also identified two skills he would address in writing lessons: punctuation marks and the use of paragraphs.

Michael began close to home. On the first day of the unit, he brought in a photograph of his cats, Betty Lou and Big Gray. After sharing a story about how he acquired Betty Lou, he asked students to share orally any stories they had about their own pets. He then conducted a mini-lesson on using quotation marks.

He asked students to pair up and write a brief conversation between his cats and another person or animal. After about 10 minutes of working time, Michael asked if any partnership would like to come to the front of the class to read their dialogues. He

Focus On
Reading and Viewing

Focus On
Language Study

Focus On
Reading and Viewing

Focus On
Talking and Listening

Focus On
Language Study

shared his own short conversation about Betty Lou scolding Big Gray for being so rude to a dog that had come to visit. As pairs read aloud, Michael pointed out when the paragraphs would change to indicate a new speaker and how quotation marks would be used to help readers keep track of who was talking.

Michael concluded that first day with an overview of the coming weeks. There would be workshop time to write stories of real or imaginary animals, small group time to research and plan a script for an animal act for their very own edition of *Animal World*, and partnership time to investigate how realistically animals are portrayed or treated in a movie or television show. He explained that one or two guest speakers would talk about caring for and being cared for by animals. He concluded the day with a short poem about cats by May Swenson.

During the following days, Michael provided much time for students to write individually about their pets and any other animals they found interesting. Their individual writing time was interspersed with whole class discussions and some direct teaching. Each student was expected to complete a writing folder that included stories and poems about animals, one critical analysis of a television or movie with animals in it, and a small group script with costumes and stage directions.

Over the course of 3 weeks, Michael's students worked collaboratively to create scripts and present 5-minute television programs for young children focused on different animals. Students brought in props, drawings, puppets, and even live animals. Michael videotaped these performances, and they were eventually shown to the first-grade and kindergarten classes. His students felt so proud as they saw their work on a television screen, and the eager response of these young people made the experience even more memorable.

Focus On Writing

Focus On Talking and Listening

We can see how Michael works within the parameters of his department and school. While he was very disappointed that a trip to the zoo was not considered possible, he understood the economic concerns for such a trip and was pleased that his enthusiasm had been contagious. As a student teacher Michael's plans and activities were exceptional. He connected to his students' experiences since most were farmers, and many were members of the 4-H clubs. He built in choice and structure. But he struggled with something that challenges many beginning teachers. How does one turn all of this into something to record in a grade book? Michael wanted the video presentations to serve as a celebration for learning rather than as an assessment so he didn't want to assign a letter grade to the videos as products. He didn't want to create any kind of competition among his students to judge the videos or award prizes because he feared that might undermine the collaboration and celebration. As you think about Michael's lessons and read through the NCTE position statement, think about some concrete ways that Michael might build in formative and summative assessments. Think about ways he might assess the multiple language arts and the social competencies as well.

ASSESSMENTS OF WRITTEN LITERACIES

In 1993 the NCTE Committee on Assessment developed an official position statement aimed at securing the best assessment options for students. That statement can be found in its entirety on the Web at: *http://www.ncte.org/positions/writing-assessment.shtml.*

A Focus on Writing

This document notes several important tenets in assessing writing, three that are particularly important for middle school writers:

- Writing is most effective where it accomplishes something the user wants to accomplish for particular listeners or readers. Additionally, assessment must be contextualized in terms of why, where, and for what purpose it is being undertaken; this context must also be clear to the students being assessed.
- Since language by definition is social, assessments that isolate students and forbid discussion and feedback from others conflict with current cognitive and psychological research about language use and the benefits of social interaction during the writing process.
- Writing "ability" is the sum of individual ability and a variety of skills employed in a diversity of contexts. Consequently one piece of writing—even if it is generated under the most desirable conditions—can never serve as an indicator of overall literacy, particularly for high-stakes decisions. Ideally, such literacy must be assessed by more than one piece of writing, in more than one genre, written on different occasions.

In sum, these tenets of assessment from NCTE seem to say that a competent assessment system should encourage middle school students to: write for real purposes and real audiences that they want to address; demonstrate their writing abilities through more than one writing sample; be given time and resources to plan, draft, revise, and edit; and participate in the assessment of their own writing.

MONITORING PROGRESS: FORMATIVE ASSESSMENTS

We begin with the premise that some writing will be abandoned before reaching any final draft stage. For any number of reasons, some middle school students who may have learned a great deal about or through writing will not complete a final writing project. Teaching and evaluations should attend to the processes as well as the products along the way. This sounds simple, but it is often hard to get a handle on exactly what processes to assess and how you might see evidence of them, much less assess them. Here are just a few examples of what you might look for in your students' writing folders and daily behaviors.

Anecdotal Records

Keeping anecdotal records in your journal or plan book is a good way to document student progress and to remind yourself of issues you would like to bring up in writing or evaluation conference. Remember that this list in only a starting place. You'll want to add to it as other ideas occur to you.

- Do students produce multiple drafts for at least some pieces of writing?
- Can they make local (word level) and global (paragraph level or larger) revisions?
- Do you see evidence that they are experimenting with literacy devices, rhetorical strategies, or new vocabulary?
- Can they give substantive oral and/or written feedback on writing to their peers?
- Do they appear to be on task during writing time?

- Can they describe the progress they made and their goals in writing conference with you?
- Can they articulate their writing decisions?
- Can they describe why one piece of their writing is better than another?
- Can they recognize problems in their own writing?
- Do they show progress on the goals you set in evaluation conferences?
- Can they generate writing topics of interest to them?

In addition to assessing processes, you will want to find effective and efficient means to manage the paper load. Students can take on responsibilities for some of the assessments. In the following sections, we present some forms of student-centered assessments.

Writing Logs

Students keep their own records of their writing in progress and their self-evaluations of their development as writers. On a daily basis, students record how they are spending their time and what skills they target. After a writing conference with you, students need to record their weekly progress, including goals and accomplishments. Periodically, you will ask students to create a progress report based on their log entries. Depending on students' experiences, you will want to guide their self-evaluation accordingly. For example, you might ask students to respond to the following prompts before each grading period:

- What are your strengths as a writer?
- What are two goals that you have set for yourself?
- What are two goals that you and I have set for you, and have you met them?

Conferences

In periodic evaluation conferences, you can ask students to look over their writing logs and address how they were accomplishing their goals. Instead of grading or responding to each piece of writing, you can ask students to select one piece of writing that they see as their best and compare it to a draft they wrote earlier in the year in terms of what it shows about their development as a writer. This procedure gives some of the responsibility to students and reduces a teacher's paper load, allowing more attention to the student-selected piece of writing.

Writers' Journals

Similar to learning logs, writers' journals may be places where writers reflect on their writing. In addition, a journal may include generating topics, completing short writing prompts, and reflecting on their development as writers. There's no doubt that, given the class load of the average middle school teacher, we cannot afford to read and respond to every entry in our students' journals. One technique to monitor progress and turn over some of the responsibility to students is to periodically give students two Post-it notes or paper clips and ask them to read through their own journals and select one or two entries to which they would like you to respond. You may or may not want to select one or two more at random. In self-selecting the entries for you to read, the student has greatly reduced the teacher's paper load. More important, they have analyzed and reread their journals with a critical eye.

Peer Group Records and Checkpoints

Asking groups to evaluate their processes is tricky but important. We all know of groups in which one or two students carry the others. But if we value group work, we need to evaluate the processes of the group. Just as with individual projects, some groups learn a great deal that is not readily visible in the final project. You can ask group members to write up a group summary that lists what the group has accomplished to date and specifically addresses the ways in which participants individually contributed to the group's progress.

Creating in-progress checks for understanding may help some groups organize their time and attend to the tasks at hand. Likewise, building in checkpoints will reduce the likelihood that students can simply plagiarize their writing project or procrastinate until the project is compromised. You may provide a progress checklist or create one collaboratively with your students. These checkpoints then can guide group actions and support all learners' involvement in the writing projects, and they will give you feedback to both the group dynamics and production. For example, say a group is planning to write a script and create a radio show to be taped and played for classmates. Their checklist might look something like this:

    ____ Day 3: All group members have selected topics. Topics approved by teacher.
    ____ Day 5: Notes from interviews are shared with group members.
    ____ Day 6: Drafts of new reports are written and shared with group members.
    ____ Day 7: Selected order for reports and practiced. Wrote introductions.
    ____ Day 8: Practiced and all had visuals, costumes, and props at school.
    ____ Day 9: Videotape show.

As noted earlier, middle school students sometimes invest an incredible amount of energy and make tremendous leaps in learning but fail to show these leaps in the finer details of a completed project. Designing checkpoints can assist you in providing structured support along the way for your students and can make visible both processes and products of the learning experiences.

Writing Rubrics

As we noted in Chapter 5, a rubric can make visible your expectations and support learners who may not understand the task at hand. A rubric should be written in language that students understand. It often includes attention to both the processes and products of writing. It may include reflections on students' writing processes and their development as writers. A writing rubric should be intricately tied to writing tasks. Be leery of writing rubrics that are disconnected from the task, audience, or context in which the writing has occurred.

FIGURE 8–5 How We Talk About Our Animals

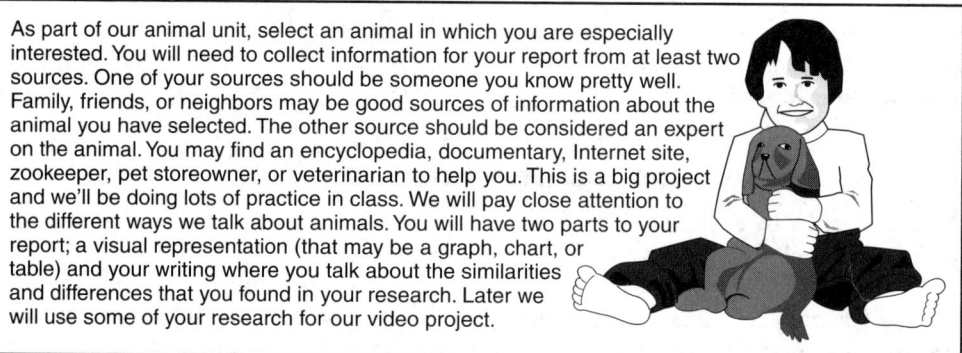

As part of our animal unit, select an animal in which you are especially interested. You will need to collect information for your report from at least two sources. One of your sources should be someone you know pretty well. Family, friends, or neighbors may be good sources of information about the animal you have selected. The other source should be considered an expert on the animal. You may find an encyclopedia, documentary, Internet site, zookeeper, pet storeowner, or veterinarian to help you. This is a big project and we'll be doing lots of practice in class. We will pay close attention to the different ways we talk about animals. You will have two parts to your report; a visual representation (that may be a graph, chart, or table) and your writing where you talk about the similarities and differences that you found in your research. Later we will use some of your research for our video project.

You might have students participate in establishing criteria for the rubric. You could bring in a couple of points that are important to you, such as "Your essay should show a clear cause-effect organizational pattern," and then ask students to help you think of other criteria that should be included in the rubric. As part of his unit on animals, for example, Michael gave out the assignment sheet in Figure 8–5 to his students. Sometime before the project was due, Michael brought in a blank rubric on an overhead transparency and created the grading rubric in Figure 8–6 with his students. Some states have grade-level writing rubrics that will be used to assess students in a standardized testing situation. You will want to familiarize yourself with those rubrics so you can provide meaningful opportunities for your students to learn the content to be tested.

Writing Portfolios

Writing portfolios should include more than copies of students' polished drafts. You may want students to keep drafts-in-progress as well as writing goals and self-assessments. You may ask students to keep process portfolios as well as showcase portfolios. If students do a great deal of writing in your classroom, writing portfolios can become unwieldy. Your room will certainly fill to overflowing. As you think about the portfolio as a tool to document growth over time, consider what central elements will be necessary. Whether your students' writing portfolios are kept in cereal boxes, notebooks, folders, or Web pages, you will want to create something that is manageable. Many teachers discontinue portfolio keeping because they simply cannot physically handle all of the papers or containers. Margaret asked her seventh graders to keep their own writing process portfolios. Periodically she asked them to select one piece to place in their showcase portfolio, which was a single file folder kept in a file cabinet in their classroom.

A Focus on Writing

FIGURE 8-6 Grading Rubric for Animal Project

Research	Excellent	Good	Needs Work
	I have two sources. I give examples from each. I made a good selection for my sources.	I have two sources. I could have included more examples of the different ways that my animal is described.	I didn't have two sources.
Organization	I tell about the similarities and differences. It is easy to see on the graph what I learned. My report is easy to understand.	I jumped around just a little bit, but I did a pretty good job. I could take more time to help my readers follow my ideas.	I didn't help my readers to understand what I learned. My paper is confusing.
Skill Builders	I began a new paragraph when I presented different speakers or ideas. I used quotation marks when I included the exact words that someone said.	I used paragraphs much of the time. I used quotation marks at times, but I didn't always use them in the right places.	I didn't use what we have been learning in class about paragraphs and quotations. I need to put these on my skill-building chart.

Reflective Windows

Along with this single piece of writing to be placed into the portfolio, Margaret asked her students to give her a "window" into their thinking about writing. Some students took the window metaphor literally and drew a window on a piece of paper before writing about their thinking. In these Reflective Windows, students wrote a commentary in which they addressed what they were learning, what they had done particularly well, why they considered this selection a representation of their best work, and how they planned to continue to grow as writers.

Students will need to learn to write differently for different contexts. Think about the different rhetorical decisions you yourself make in writing in different courses, for different jobs, and for different people. Keep these differences in mind as you explore writing in the disciplines in Your Fieldwork Journal 8–3. Think about the ways you might support young writers in making these moves.

Your Fieldwork Journal 8-3

Writing in the Disciplines

Our job as middle school teachers is to guide our students to use writing in more complex ways to reach their goals. Of course, our job is also to help our students make connections with other disciplines in school and beyond. Our students likely will be asked to write in all of their classes. Conduct an interview to find out what kinds of writing are demanded in science, math, social studies, or any other class. If possible, interview a middle school teacher who is teaching many of the same students you are. You may be able to set up an interview at your next team meeting or simply ask to meet individually with one teacher.

During your interview, ask about the kinds of writing that students are expected to do in that class. Also find out about the writing demanded in a profession closely aligned to that subject matter. Be careful not to go in with an agenda to teach or judge your colleagues. Be careful to avoid writing jargon. Write some interview questions to find out about the writing your students must do to perform well in that class. Design additional questions to find out what students must do to write well as scientists, artists, historians, or mathematicians.

You may want to share with others what you have learned about writing in the disciplines. Depending on your teaching circumstances, you may want to design supports for your students based on the writing demands you have identified. You may even be able to collaborate with those on your teaching team to design a writing project to support writing in the disciplines.

USING TECHNOLOGY EFFECTIVELY WITH MIDDLE SCHOOL WRITERS

Jonathan Bush is an assistant professor of English Education who has long been interested in ways of infusing technology into the middle school classroom. In this section, he shares what he has learned in working in middle schools as a teacher, in-service facilitator, and researcher. Jon writes the following to help us learn to think about the ways that technology can enhance our writing classrooms.

Literacy Lesson 8-5

Technology in the Writing Classroom

The middle school literacy classroom is an ideal place for the appropriate integration of new computer technologies. The thematic and interdisciplinary nature of the middle school context, combined with the emphasis on student development and expression,

Technology in Middle School Classrooms

Should
- Work to validate individual students and empower their ability to achieve academic success.
- Enhance traditional print/literature/media materials.
- Amplify students' means of expression and broaden their opportunities to reach meaningful audiences.
- Deepen students' understanding of complex issues and enhance their ability to make global connections.
- Expand the dimensions of literacy.
- Facilitate an open forum for discussion that allows for more free and democratic participation.

Shouldn't
- Replace complex language and development goals with more simplistic "learn the technology" goals.
- Replace traditional print/literature/media materials.
- Disrupt normal classroom community and critically based objectives.
- Stifle students' ability to participate by favoring students with advantaged access to technology.
- Deepen social and economic inequities.
- Replace teacher-student/student-student interaction.

creates many opportunities for effective technology integration. The World Wide Web and other Internet technologies, including class discussion boards, real-time chat, and online document sharing, are effective tools for young writers. Technology also affords various means of publishing, such as Web publishing opportunities, document design, and digital video and audio.

But with these technologies come responsibilities and dilemmas. As teachers of middle school English language arts who use technology, we must consider our goals as teachers and work to ensure that the technologies we integrate into our classrooms do not work to subvert these goals. In particular, we need to consider some potential shoulds and shouldn'ts as we experiment with these technologies in our classrooms.

The list above represents some veteran middle school teachers' concepts of what should and should not occur when technology is integrated into the English language arts classroom. It is important, however, for individual teachers to develop their own guiding concepts of technology based on their unique classroom goals and contexts.

Here are some examples of potentially positive uses of some of these technologies in middle school English language arts.

To expand the dimensions of literacy
- Students explore the genre of the Web site and learn the characteristics of effective WWW-based communication, including means of evaluating online sources and their biases and potential credibility.
- Students can extend their knowledge and perspectives on issues by searching for Internet resources on project elements or classroom issues.

To support teaching

- Class Web sites can be used by teachers to organize information, communicate goals and strategies to parents, and support home-school connections.
- E-mail offers a way for parents to communicate with teachers.
- Free online teaching sites such as blackboard.com offer services that allow teachers to organize classes, archive information and student work, and generally assist in the integration of technologies in class activities.

To support and enhance classroom discussions

- Student-led, small-group, real-time chats and whole class discussion boards can allow for more participation by normally shy or less confident students.
- Follow-up searches of online resources and ancillary materials can be conducted. If a topic/issue interests students during a class discussion, the technology can be used to explore it further.

To create opportunities for expanded publishing/audiences

- Students can create group or individual Web sites as means of sharing research findings with wider audiences.
- Students can interact with others, both locally and internationally, via e-mail, discussion boards, or teacher-led, real-time chats during class time and beyond.
- Students can use visual technologies to create, manage, and design documents, thereby expanding their abilities to express their ideas through new means.

Technology can support our writing goals and those of the young writers in our classrooms. Technologies can help us cross disciplinary boundaries and open our classroom doors to other classrooms, local neighborhoods, and international communities.

The role of the middle school teacher then is to guide students to use writing in a more complex manner, to employ writing as a tool to reach their goals. Too often perhaps in middle school settings, writing is reduced to filling in the blanks. Students are asked to fill in the blanks or respond to a writing prompt that has embedded in it all of the rhetorical decisions that a writer must make to be successful with the task. To gain independence as writers, middle school students need to create their own blanks, to decide what best serves their goals and purposes. But, of course, they will need support to learn to employ the most effective processes to achieve their writing goals. They will need guidance and direct instruction to learn what rhetorical decisions or technological tools to use, what writing steps to take, what conventions to follow. They will need opportunities to practice making choices, practice making mistakes, and practice making connections.

In the next chapter, you'll have an opportunity to explore oral language. We invite you to consider how to create effective speaking and performance activities with middle school students. We turn your attention now to the IRA/NCTE standards.

A Focus on Writing

Standards in Practice

Viewing Your Writing Lessons Through the IRA/NCTE Standards

Locate a copy of the IRA/NCTE *Standards for the English Language Arts* (1996). For an explanation of the standards as well as a table of contents for the volume, an annotated listing of each standard, and chapter excerpts, consult the NCTE Web site at this address: *http://www.ncte.org/standards*.

All of the standards may be relevant to your writing classroom. But, for purposes of this exercise, we suggest you look most closely at Standards 5, 7, and 8. You will notice that within each standard are words or phrases that could be construed as subgoals for your writing classroom. Begin with Standard 5. What subgoals are embedded within this standard? Read this standard closely and attempt to tease apart the multiple goals embedded within it. Highlight the subgoals or list them separately on a piece of paper.

> **Standard 5:** Students employ a wide range of strategies as they write and use different writing process elements appropriate to communicate with different audiences for a variety of purposes.
>
> **Standard 7:** Students conduct research on issues and interests by generating ideas and questions, and by posing problems. They gather, evaluate, and synthesize data from a variety of sources (e.g., print and nonprint texts, artifacts, people) to communicate their discoveries in ways that suit their purpose and audience.
>
> **Standard 8:** Students use a variety of technological and information resources (e.g., libraries, databases, computer networks, and videos) to gather and synthesize information and to create and communicate knowledge.

Now, look at a writing lesson you have created or one you are in the process of writing. If you aren't currently planning lessons of your own, you might want to refer back to Michael's writing lessons about animals, presented in Literacy Lesson 8–4. For each activity in your lesson plan, try to tie it to one or more of the subgoals. As an example, we have paraphrased some of Michael's activities. Beside each activity, we placed the relevant subgoals. For practice, look through Michael's animal workshop against the backdrop of the three standards listed here. Do you note any subgoals that have not been addressed?

Although you can't address all standards in all lessons, on occasion you may want to look closely at the standards to determine how you are addressing them in relevant ways for your particular students in your particular community. There are valid reasons to emphasis some over others. If you find that you do not address some subgoals, you should consider why not. There may be valid reasons for such omissions.

Addressing Standards in Our Practices	
Activities	**Connection to Standards**
• Complete a writing folder that includes stories and poems about animals.	• Employ a wide range of strategies as they write.
• One critical analysis of a television show or movie focused on animals.	• Use a variety of technological resources. • Synthesize data from a variety of sources.
• Videotape script.	• Use a variety of technological resources.
• Show video to kindergartners and first graders.	• Communicate with different audiences.

REFERENCES

Atwell, N. (1987). *In the middle: Writing, reading, and learning with adolescents.* Portsmouth, NH: Boynton/Cook.

Carnegie Task Force on Education for Young Adolescents. (1995). *Great transitions: Preparing adolescents for a new century.* Washington, DC: Author.

Carrington, V., & Luke, A. (in press). Reading, homes and families: From postmodern to modern? In A. van Kleeck, S. A. Stahl, & E. B. Bauer (Eds.), *On reading to children: Parents and teachers.* Mahwah, NJ: Lawrence Erlbaum.

Comber, B., & Simpson, A. (Eds.). (2001). *Negotiating critical literacies in the classroom.* Malwah, NJ: Lawrence Erlbaum.

Delpit, L. (1988). The silenced dialogue: Power and pedagogy in educating other people's children. *Harvard Education Review, 58,* 280–298.

Delpit, L. (1991). A conversation with Lisa Delpit. *Language Arts, 68,* 541–547.

Delpit, L. (2002). What should teachers do?: Ebonics and culturally responsive instruction. In B. Power & R. Hubbard (Eds.), *Language development: A reader for teachers* (2nd ed., pp. 124–128). Upper Saddle River, NJ: Merrill/Prentice Hall.

Edelsky, C. (1996). *With literacy and justice for all: Rethinking the social in language and education (Critical perspectives on literacy and education).* New York: Taylor & Francis.

Elbow, P. (1998). *Writing without teachers.* Oxford, England: Oxford University Press.

Finders, M. (1992). With Jix. *College Composition and Communication, 43,* 497–507.

Graves, D. (1982). *Writing: Teachers and children at work.* Portsmouth, NH: Heinemann.

Hall, S. (1981). Teaching about race. In A. James & R. Jeffcoate (Eds.), *The school in the multicultural society* (pp. 58–69). London: Harper.

Lensmire, T. (1994). *When children write: Critical re-visions of the writing workshop.* New York: Teachers College Press.

Luke, A., & Carrington, V. (2002). Globalisation, literacy, curriculum practice. In R. Fisher, M. Lewis, & G. Brooks (Eds.), *Raising standards in literacy*, pp. 231–250. London: Routledge.

Luke, A., Freebody, P., & Land, R. (2000). *Literate futures: The Queensland state literacy strategy*. Brisbane, Australia: Education Queensland. [http://www.qed.qld.gov.au]

Murray, D. (1994). Knowing and not knowing In L. Tobin & T. Newkirk (Eds.), *Taking stock: The writing process movement in the '90s* (pp. 57–65). Portsmouth, NH: Boynton/Cook (Heinemann).

Ny, R., Staton, P., & Scane, J. (1995). *Anti-racism, feminism, and critical approaches to education*. Westport, CT: Bergin and Garvey.

Rief, L. (1991). *Seeking diversity: Language arts with adolescents*. Portsmouth, NH: Heinemann.

Vygotsky, L. (1978). *Mind in society*. Cambridge, MA: Harvard University Press.

RESOURCES

Print

Allen, J., & Gonzalez, K. (1998). *There's room for me here: Literacy workshops in the middle school*. Portland, ME: Stenhouse.

Alvermann, D. E., Moon, J. S., & Haygood, M. C. (1999). *Popular culture in the classroom: Teaching and researching critical media literacy*. Newark, DE: International Reading Association.

Atwell, N. (1998). *In the middle: New understandings about writing, reading, and learning* (2nd ed.). Portsmouth, NH: Boynton/Cook (Heinemann).

Atwell, N., & Newkirk, T. (1987). *Understanding writing: Ways of observing, learning, and teaching*. Portsmouth, NH: Heinemann.

Berthoff, A. (1981). *The making of meaning: metaphors, models, and maxims for writing teachers*. Upper Montclair, NJ: Boynton/Cook.

Booth, D. (2001). *Reading and writing in the middle years*. Portland, ME: Stenhouse.

Butler, A., & Turbill, J. (1987). *Towards a reading-writing classroom*. Portsmouth, NH: Heinemann.

Christian, S. (1997). *Exchanging lives: Middle school writers online*. Urbana, IL: National Council of Teachers of English.

Dorn, L., & Soffos, C. (2001). *Scaffolding young writers: A writers' workshop approach*. Portland, ME: Stenhouse.

Fletcher, R. (1996). *Breathing in, breathing out: Keeping a writer's notebook*. Portsmouth, NH: Heinemann.

Fletcher, R., & Portalupi, J. (1998). *Craft lessons: Teaching writing K–8*. Portland, ME: Stenhouse.

Fountas, I. C., & Pinnell, G. S. (2001). *Guiding readers and writers (Grades 3–6): Teaching comprehension, genre, and content literacy*. Portsmouth, NH: Heinemann.

Graves, D. (1991). *Build a literate classroom (Reading/writing teacher's companion)*. Portsmouth, NH: Heinemann.

Graves, D. (1994). *A fresh look at writing*. Portsmouth, NH: Heinemann.
Hull, G., & Schultz, K. (2002). *School's out! Bridging out-of-school literacies with classroom practice*. New York: Teachers College Press.
Lensmire, T. (2000). *Powerful writing, responsible teaching*. New York: Teachers College Press.
Mahiri, J. (1998). *Shooting for excellence: African American and youth culture in new century schools*. Urbana. IL: NCTE.
Tobin, L., & Newkirk, T. (1994). *Taking stock: The writing process movement in the '90s*. Portsmouth, NH: Boynton/Cook (Heinemann).
National Council of Teachers of English. (1996). *Motivating writing in middle school. Standards Consensus Series*. Urbana, IL: Author.
Underwood, T. (1999). *The portfolio project: A study of assessment, instruction, and middle school reform*. Urbana, IL: National Council of Teachers of English.
Yagelski, R., & Leonard, S. (2002). *The relevance of English: Teaching that matters in students' lives*. New York: Teachers College Press.
Yancey, K. (1992). *Portfolios in the writing classroom: An introduction*. Urbana, IL: National Council of Teachers of English.

Electronic

Blackboard.Com. Although Blackboard is a commercial software company that creates proprietary software for sale, the company also offers wonderful free resources for teachers on its Web site. This site allows teachers to create their own course site, manage course documents, assist student groups, run course discussion boards and real-time chats, and use numerous other services.

http://www.blackboard.com

Assembly on Computers in English. ACE is sponsored by NCTE and is dedicated to helping English teachers of all levels integrate technology in their classrooms. ACE maintains extensive online and print resources.

http://english.ttu.edu/ACE/

Reading, English, and Communication–Great Web Resources. This site, maintained by Indiana University, provides links to large segments of the ERIC Clearinghouse and other online resources for English language arts teachers.

http://www.indiana.edu/~eric_rec/comatt/websites.html

The National Writing Project. The mission of the NWP is to improve the teaching of writing and improve learning in the nation's schools. Through its professional development model, the National Writing Project recognizes the primary importance of teacher knowledge, expertise, and leadership.

http://www.writingproject.org/index.html

Purdue University's OWL On Line Writing Lab. OWL at Purdue University offers more than 500 pages of handouts, tutorials, and workshops and hundreds of links to other writing resources across the World Wide Web. This Web site provides a wealth of support for writing teachers and includes information on how to set up and use a writing lab. It includes extensive links to other Web resources for writing teachers.

http://www.owl.english.purdue.edu/

NCTE Position on Writing Assessments.

http://www.ncte.org/positions/writing_assessment.shtml

Promising Young Writers. The Promising Young Writers program represents NCTE's commitment to early and continuing work in the development of writing. The program was established to motivate and recognize student writers and to emphasize the importance of writing among eighth-grade students.

http://www.ncte.org/grants/young.shtml

Focus on Critical Literacy. The International Reading Association has created a Web site that offers online resources on critical literacy which includes links to IRA journal articles, book chapters, programs, and position statements.

http://www.reading.org/focus/critical_lit.html

chapter 9

Talking and Listening in the Middle Grades

GUIDING QUESTIONS

1. Why do some teachers feel uncomfortable sponsoring oral language activities in their middle school classrooms?
2. What purposes and forms might talk and listening take in the English language arts classroom?
3. How do issues of race, class, gender, and culture influence middle school students' attitudes toward oral language activities?

A CASE FOR CONSIDERATION
Beyond the "Official Meaning"

Janie, a masters student in her final semester, posted this message to the members of her student teaching listserv:

> *In one of my recent classes, I asked my students why James McBride uses images of water at the end of his book,* The Color of Water. *Some students thought it was totally unintentional, while others began to ask questions that explored possible "deeper meanings" of the text. One student, however, responded in a way that totally shocked me. He said, "What does it matter if the book has a deeper meaning to us? It's whatever the author intended. We will never know what he intended, so there's no use making up stuff about the text."*
>
> *Well, this was by far the most engaged and passionate response I had received that day, so I asked the rest of the class to respond. Everyone began to join in on the conversation, which ranged from students' sharing of personal experiences with the*

book to how we make meaning out of information. I suggested that interpretation and personal response help us explore the author's intent and bring out the multiple perspectives of the people in a classroom. This is what makes literature rich, meaningful, and beautiful. The kids felt that literature was a "mirror" for their lives. . . .

[This experience] made me realize that I need to be aware of my "personal agenda" as a teacher. Maybe my student wasn't just responding to the "pointlessness of interpreting texts," but rather a teacher's way of bringing out one interpretation—her interpretation or the "official meaning." Teachers want their students to use critical thinking and interpretation, but it's not going to do them much good if their interpretations lead them to the teacher's answer or interpretation. Thus, I began to rethink how I've been leading discussion. I want to give my students access to various meanings of the text, but I also want to truly value each perspective and interpretation as adding to the meaning of the text. Any ideas about how this might look in practice???

Janie articulates one of the biggest struggles that English language arts teachers face: How do we balance our agenda—what Janie calls the "official meaning"—with our students' ideas, issues, and concerns in the many forms of talk and listening we sponsor in our classrooms each day? This struggle is particularly compelling in the literature classroom, where we want to invite what Langer (1995) calls a "horizon" of interpretive possibilities in discussion. We must continually be mindful of whose ideas *get the floor* whenever we sponsor a class discussion, group sharing, or public performance. Perhaps most troubling is the question that Janie poses at the end of her reflection: "Any ideas about how this might look in practice?" Let's begin by considering this and some related questions.

FOR DISCUSSION

- How do you prepare for discussion in your middle school classroom (with a list of questions, an activity, or something else)?
- Who tends to "hold the floor" in your classroom and who stays out? How do issues of race, class, gender, and culture enter the picture?
- How do you consciously avoid making your agenda the centerpiece of classroom talk?

THE MANY FACES OF TALKING AND LISTENING

There's no doubt about it. Oral performance is scary stuff, particularly for early adolescents who are so conscious of peer approval. On the other hand, oral performance can enliven and enrich your English language arts classroom immeasurably. This is the dilemma of many of us who were trained to teach the (relatively private) subjects of reading and writing, and have never stepped foot on a theater stage or a public speaking platform. Although, as teachers, we are always "performing" every time we get in front of a class, the idea of teaching theater arts, public speaking, oral interpretation, or other oral activities can feel pretty threatening for those of us without formal preparation.

Luckily, a range of oral language activities is available to us along a continuum from playful and exploratory to more rehearsed, public, and polished. As this chapter will demonstrate, it's not that difficult to give all of our middle school students this broad range of experiences with oral language.

PURPOSES AND FORMS OF ORAL LANGUAGE

Consider all of the possibilities for talking and listening in your middle school classroom. One day your students might role-play a scene from a story they're reading; the next, they might hold a panel discussion or debate; the next, they might create scripts or readers' theater presentations for their classmates or parents. The possibilities range only as far as your (and their) imaginations extend. Far from being a solely performance-oriented art, oral language can involve both *talking to learn* and *learning to talk*. The same is true of listening. Think, for example, of the difference between listening for information to be remembered later on a test and listening for pure pleasure and enjoyment. Figure 9–1 presents just a few of many techniques and forms of talk and listening available to us.

FIGURE 9-1 Techniques and Forms of Oral Language and Listening

group discussions	interviews
debates	mock student congress
dramatic improvisations	memorized speeches
extemporaneous speeches	recitations
dramatic enactments	oral interpretations of literature
panel discussions	dramatic monologues
conversations	choral reading
"pair-shares"	poster sessions
collaborative learning groups	oral demonstrations
jokes	skits
storytelling	problem-solving groups
scripted dialogues	oral reports

FIGURE 9-2 Purposes for Talking and Listening

	Talking and Listening to Explore	Talking and Listening to Learn About Talking and Listening	Talking and Listening to Connect and Transform	Talking and Listening to Showcase
Techniques for Talking and Listening	How might students explore ideas and express themselves through oral language and listening?	How might students become better speakers, collaborators, and listeners?	How might students use talking and listening to connect with others and make an impact on their world?	How might students share or demonstrate what they have learned through talking and listening?

We suggest four purposes for using talking and listening with middle school students: (1) to explore, (2) to learn about talking and listening, (3) to connect with others and transform their worlds, and (4) to *showcase* their learning. These four purposes are summarized in Figure 9–2.

In Your Fieldwork Journal 9–1, we ask you to use this preliminary list as a starting place for considering how these forms and techniques might be used for a variety of purposes.

Your Fieldwork Journal 9-1

Talking and Listening for Multiple Purposes

First, take a look at the list in Figure 9–1. Feel free to add your own forms and techniques for talking and listening to this preliminary list.

Now, create a chart like the one in Figure 9–2. Pick one of the forms or techniques from Figure 9–1 and experiment with the different purposes it might serve in your teaching of writing, reading and viewing, and language study. One example follows. When you've finished this exercise, you might want to share some of your ideas with others.

	Purposes for Talking and Listening			
Forms and Techniques for Talking and Listening	**Talking and Listening to Explore**	**Talking and Listening to Learn about Talking and Listening**	**Talking and Listening to Connect and Transform**	**Talking and Listening to Showcase**
	How might students explore ideas and express themselves through oral language and listening?	How might students become better speakers, collaborators, and listeners?	How might students use talking and listening to connect with others and make an impact on their world?	How might students share or demonstrate what they have learned through talking and listening?
Interviews	• Students interview each other and create commercials, "advertising" the best qualities and talents of their partner. • Students role-play interviews with characters from literature. • Students interview their classmates about early reading and writing experiences and create "literary biographies."	• Students study the language of talk-show hosts for the purpose of creating and videotaping their own talk shows. • Students interview members of their family for the purpose of studying their family's language patterns, pet phrases, and so on. • Students study the dialect in a piece of historical fiction, then stage mock interviews with characters in the dialect of the period.	• Students interview senior citizens about their experiences during the Great Depression as a prelude to reading a novel about this period in history. • Students interview the principal of the nearby high school for the purpose of understanding more about school violence in their area.	• Students conduct schoolwide interviews and create a video segment on attitudes toward teenage drinking in their school. • Students present oral "author studies," based upon televised or print versions of interviews with famous literary figures. • Students present informative speeches, based upon interviews with local experts.

TALKING AND LISTENING WITH MIDDLE SCHOOL STUDENTS

Moffett (1968) said that drama is the matrix from which all other language experiences derive. Think about that concept for a moment. How much of our daily language is devoted to explaining what happened, narrating, or in some way experiencing, enacting, or creating real or imagined events through words? It's this near compulsion to use language as a way of *acting upon each other and the world* that makes talk and listening such a vital part of middle school life. At the same time, we cannot ignore the risks involved, especially for early adolescents who are not situated squarely in the mainstream.

Here are just a few considerations to ponder in creating opportunities for talking and listening with middle school students.

Considerations for Talking and Listening in the Middle School Classroom

- **Middle school students need positive social interactions with peers and adults.**
    - How do we allow opportunities for sharing and performance without putting shy or reluctant learners on the spot?
    - How can we provide opportunities for our students to develop their oral language and listening skills with parents and other interested adults?
    - How can we provide oral language opportunities for students from a variety of cultural and linguistic backgrounds?
- **Middle school students need physical activities to support the development of talk and listening.**
    - How can we get students up and out of their seats more often during the course of reading, writing, and language study?
    - What roles can drawing, viewing, performing, and public presentation play in students' oral language and listening experiences?
    - How can we accommodate our teaching to the vast array of communication styles in our classroom?
- **Middle school students need opportunities for self-definition, creative expression, and a sense of competence and achievement in their experiences with talk and listening.**
    - How do we balance our responsibility to develop students' formal spoken language skills with their need for play, social interaction, and exploration?
    - How can we sponsor activities for talking and listening to learn as well as talking to showcase learning?
    - How can we encourage collaborative and cooperative behaviors among students of various abilities as well as linguistic and cultural backgrounds.
- **Middle school students need oral language opportunities that promote meaningful participation in their families, school, and the larger world.**
    - How might we find authentic and appreciative audiences for students' public performances and demonstrations within and outside our classroom walls?
    - How can our students use talk and listening as a way of exploring the world beyond their schools, communities, and country?
    - How can oral language and listening promote students' involvement in social and political activities of importance to them?

LEVELING THE FIELD: RACE, CLASS, GENDER, CULTURE, AND ORAL LANGUAGE

Many complicating factors are related to oral language for early adolescents. Middle school students are just becoming conscious of peers as they develop their fledgling identities. For some, there are greater penalties for speaking out in class than for others. For example, gender plays a great role in who is likely to contribute and who is likely to stay out of group discussions. At times, discussions of sensitive topics like race or social class hold greater consequences for students from particular backgrounds. Emma, a preservice teacher in her first teaching placement, reflects on this dilemma in a message to the members of her student teaching seminar:

> *I was wondering what sort of experience you're having with your students in regards to their genders? Do you find girls are less or more talkative in discussion than boys? Do you see the same boys ruling the discussion? That's how it is with my [third period class]; however, [the girls in my fourth period class] are vocal and leaders. . . . I went to an all-girl's high school and can see a marked difference between how girls reacted in my high-school classes versus how they react in a coed atmosphere. Just today while working with one of [my host teacher's] classes, I encountered a loud, opinionated boy who reminded me why I choose an all-girls' high school—so I would have a voice that wouldn't be drowned out by one boy's objective to rule the class. However, I'm sure some of you have girls who also attempt to do this, but perhaps in a different manner. Any thoughts on leveling the field?*

> Consider what research says about oral language and listening in the classroom.

As Emma notes, no hard-and-fast rules dictate how gender, race, cultural background, or other factors figure into the likelihood that students will or will not participate in oral language activities. Here are just a few trends that researchers have discovered about the complexities of oral language and listening in your classroom:

- Often, adolescent girls are reluctant to participate in class discussions for fear of looking too smart and therefore jeopardizing their popularity (Sadker & Sadker, 1994).
- Often adolescent males are wary of enjoying traditionally "feminine" activities like keeping journals or reading and writing poetry for fear of losing their status as macho or athletic (Sadker & Sadker, 1994; Salisbury & Jackson, 1996).
- The tenuous status of African American females in school and society is even more profound (Fine, 1995; Fordham, 1996; Grant, 1984; hooks, 1989; McCarthy, 1996; Sadker & Sadker, 1994). According to Fordham (1993), Black teenage girls are more likely to be shunted to the margins of the classroom than any other group. As a result, they typically try to achieve academic success by being "phantoms in the opera." That is, they either remain "voiceless" or impersonate "a male image" (p. 10).

> **Language Study in Context**
> Ask students to study the language of males and females in the literature they are reading, from traditional to more modern day. Discuss how males and females portray gender roles through language and nonverbal behaviors.

Fordham argues that Black girls may unwittingly participate in their own exclusion by engaging in behaviors that alienate their teachers.
- Often, mixed groups of males and females will choose a male as spokesperson, even though females may have done most of the work (Salisbury & Jackson, 1996).
- Teachers often mistake the active communication styles of students from certain racial or ethnic groups as rowdiness or disrespect (Cureton, 1985; Smitherman, 1986).
- By the same token, teachers often correct dialectical miscues, such as "He be going," whereas they tend to ignore nondialectical miscues, such as "Put it over there" instead of "Put it over here" (Cunningham, 1976–1977). This sometimes makes students with nonmainstream dialects reluctant to read aloud in classes.
- Students from some cultural backgrounds have been taught that respect equals silence and that asking questions of teachers means inappropriately questioning authority. Teachers unaware of these cultural differences may interpret their silence as apathy or disinterest.

As teachers, we must be constantly mindful of these social complications, realizing that oral language activities like collaborative learning, sharing circles, group discussion, and public performances are not always equally enjoyable or easy for all students.

> How do issues of diversity complicate your teaching decisions where talk and listening are concerned?

In addition, we must often reach across cultural boundaries to help students whose first language is not English or assist those whose communication styles diverge from what's considered "the norm" because of their family or cultural background. It should not be the burden of students of color or those from countries and cultures outside the United States to "educate" more mainstream students about linguistic stereotyping. It's our responsibility to offer not only oral language and listening experiences, but also opportunities to talk about and explore the many forms of oral language in our diverse society.

> **Language Study in Context**
> Invite students to generate a list of common situations (e.g., making a telephone call, asking to borrow something, inviting someone to their house). Have them role-play these situations and "code-switch," depending upon their conversational partner (e.g., a teacher, parent, employer, best friend).

We should also be aware of different definitions for listening in today's world. Often, statewide or district competency examinations equate listening with taking notes or memorizing details from materials read or presented orally. This limited view unfortunately blinds us to the rich variety of listening purposes beyond the gathering of information, such as listening empathically and responding in a socially appropriate way, listening critically, listening for the subtle nuances in the words of others, listening for pure relaxation and enjoyment, and listening to nonverbal sources such as music.

In the next few pages, we'd like to present some examples of teachers and students using language for the four purposes presented in Figure 9–1: exploring; learning about talking and listening; connecting and transforming; and showcasing.

TALKING AND LISTENING TO EXPLORE

Literacy Lesson 9–1 offers an example of exploring word meanings in class discussions.

Literacy Lesson 9-1

Group Word Webs

During his student teaching placement in a fairly affluent suburban district, Jeff was teaching several vignettes from *The House on Mango Street* by Sandra Cisneros (1991) to his ninth-grade students. One of Jeff's goals was to contrast his students' home lives with that of Cisneros as a young girl. In Jeff's words:

Since many of the vignettes that make up The House on Mango Street *deal with Cisneros's lifelong yearning for a nice home, I had the students create a word web on the board for the word "Home." The students came up to the board and wrote words that reminded them of their homes. I split the class into groups of six or seven students, and one person from each group came up to the board at a time and wrote a word. The students wrote many wonderful things about their homes. They wrote about safety, security, family, food, modern conveniences, athletic equipment, big yards, big rooms, garages, and so on. The webs they created showed their affluence. I then asked the class if Sandra Cisneros had all of these things when she was growing up and they responded, "No.". . . I told the class they were very lucky to have all of the things they have. I urged them to appreciate all that they have and not to take anything for granted. There are many people who do not have all of these beautiful things, who want them badly.*

We then read the vignettes out loud. I asked for volunteers to help me with the reading. After we had read these vignettes and discussed them, I asked the students to think of a metaphor for any one of the characters in the vignettes. This was a difficult assignment, but the students came up with many clever metaphors. One female student wrote: "Esperanza is a butterfly, when she writes she comes out of her cocoon." The students really enjoyed the active participation of creating the word web on the board as well as hearing everyone read their metaphors. [My host teacher] gave me some pointers on not correcting spelling errors in the word web, . . . giving students more time to answer their own questions, and not doing for the students what they can do for themselves. If the students discover things for themselves, they will remember them more than if the teacher gives them the answers. Overall, it was a good day. I enjoyed this lesson, and so did my students.

As Jeff has discovered, talk and listening do not have to involve formal performance. The simple act of walking to the board and writing one word to describe "home" can break up a potentially dreary day and allow students to learn from and with each other. Oral language can be used in many other informal, exploratory ways. Here are just a few examples.

Character Role Plays

Place the desks or chairs in your room in a circle, then choose four or five characters from a story, poem, or novel you are reading. For example, say your students have just finished the novel *The Friends* by Guy (1973). Cluster your students into small groups of four or five, and assign each group a character. You might choose the following characters from Guy's novel: Phylissia (the main character), Edith (her friend), Ruby (Phylissia's sister), Calvin (her father), and Ramona (her mother). To get the ball rolling, hand out a list of open-ended discussion questions for each group (questions like "As the character you are playing, which characters in the book do you like the most or the least?"). Give groups a few moments to discuss the questions *in the voice of their character,* then reconvene in the larger group.

Choose several major events from the book and pose questions about those events to different character groups. For example, you might choose an event like Phylissia's first meeting with Edith. Read an excerpt from the book describing Phylissia's first reaction, then ask the "Phylissias": "When you saw Edith for the first time, did you ever think the two of you would be friends?" Ask the "Ediths" the same question, allowing any and all group members to respond. The more different responses, the better. It's important not to force all group members to respond to each question. Some students will learn more if they are allowed to listen quietly until they feel comfortable joining in. Whether they talk or not, they will learn a great deal through listening to the responses of others.

To Tell the Truth

Consider this variation on the old quiz show *To Tell the Truth*. Ask students to write informally about a series of questions as though they were the narrator of a piece of literature. Choose a text with a fairly unspecified narrator, such as "Stopping by Woods on a Snowy Evening" by Frost (1995). This is a good choice because the speaker in Frost's poem could be male or female, a farmer or a retired investment banker. Questions can range from "What is your name and what were you doing in the woods that evening?" to "What did you mean by 'miles to go' before you sleep?" As soon as students have written for a bit (be sure to ask them to write in the voice of the character), ask for three or four volunteers, each of whom must "swear" to be the narrator in Frost's poem. Students in the audience can ask questions of all narrators, then vote on who they think really stopped by the woods on that snowy evening. At the end of the lesson, ask for volunteers from the audience to read or talk about the different narrators they constructed in their opening writings.

It's often a good idea to engage students in informal oral language experiences outside our classroom walls. In previous chapters, we have discussed the value of inquiry projects that allow students to explore questions of authentic interest and to tap resources beyond traditional print materials found in libraries. Such exploration should be a vital and compelling component of your middle school English language arts program. Before you ask your students to venture into the larger community, however, make sure you lay careful groundwork and help them to understand the interpersonal dynamics of such a move. This is a lesson that Joe Wilson is "still learning" in Literacy Lesson 9–2. He tells the story in his own words.

Literacy Lesson 9-2

Still Learning

I had attended a weeklong institute the summer before to train for a new instructional model. The following school year I had implemented many of the features of the model with some success. That fall I went to a one-day follow-up workshop for the model, and I was eager to try out my latest learning on my students. The learning unit was called "group exploration." Students in small groups were to decide on an area of knowledge in which they had at least some common interest. They then had 5 days to work as a group and individually to garner as much information about the subject as possible. They were restricted to using nontextual sources, and this was pre-Internet, so they were more or less forced to call presumed experts on the phone and interview them to fulfill the requirements.

Focus On
Writing

When the groups had been formed and had found topics, we brainstormed possible resources and ways to get hold of them. We went through basic phone etiquette and formulas of introduction for the purposes of this assignment. I instructed my seventh graders to prepare lists of possible questions before going to the phone, and I remembered to secure permission from the administration for my students to use phones in several areas outside my classroom during my instructional periods. I also got permission for them to make a limited number of long-distance calls; ours is a rural school district with not a wide variety of experts close at hand.

I was exhilarated when my students, some of them nervous, some of them filled with bravado, but all of them excited to try this new form of learning, headed for the four corners of the middle school building to "talk to the experts." I cruised the halls, checking on my young charges, nodding encouragement and flashing the "V" sign when a lit-up face greeted me with the news, "I'm talking to a psychiatrist about dreams!"

My bubble was burst, however, when we returned to the room and began to process the experience. When I asked how things went, Cameron (always the first hand up and, of course, the member of his group to be the official caller) said, "The guy I talked to was really rude. He said he didn't have time to answer my question, and that I should have been better prepared." Cameron's group had selected "astronomy" as their topic. The expert was the head of the department of astronomy at a prestigious state university.

"What did you ask him?" I wondered.

"I just said, 'What do you know about stars?'" Cameron replied.

I suddenly realized I had left out at least one important step in planning. Not only should lists of questions be prepared, they should have been edited. I reflected how an exercise in developing empathy would have been useful. How could I have expected even a bright seventh-grader to understand the knowledge, experience, and attitude of a Ph.D. in astrophysics? The next year I implemented these changes, and we even practiced the interview process with toy phones. I also had a beautiful example of a "no-no" from Cameron's experience to warn future classes of the possible pitfalls of poor preparation!

When you ask them to venture beyond your classroom walls, remember that students like Cameron need to understand the complicated dynamics of talking to others who may not share their experiences and world views. Whether your students are role-playing in the safety of your classroom or journeying out into the world beyond, they must understand the many ways they must tailor their language for various social and interpersonal contexts.

TALKING AND LISTENING TO LEARN ABOUT TALKING AND LISTENING

Interpersonal Communication: Exploring the Language of Self and Others

No chapter on oral language would be complete without a brief discussion of interpersonal communication and its role in students' literacy development. Under the general banner of interpersonal communication lie many important topics: forming impressions of self and others, verbal and nonverbal aspects of communication, active listening, empathy, assertiveness, conflict management, and cross-cultural communication, to name a few. Although your classroom should never resemble an encounter group or a therapy session, students might explore several aspects of interpersonal communication in learning more about how talk and listening function in the social world.

Remember that the activities suggested in the following pages can be somewhat tricky. Students should never feel coerced to reveal personal information or delve too deeply into emotional issues. Especially with early adolescents, it's important to infuse humor and lightheartedness into your teaching, so that students don't feel forced into uncomfortable self-disclosure. Whenever you ask them to write or talk about personal topics, be sure to offer them the opportunity to keep any and all information about their families and personal lives private. If you ask them to write in journals, for example, offer the option of stapling personal pages to let you know not to read them. Here are just a few ideas for exploring the dimensions of interpersonal communication with your middle school students.

> What are the perils and pitfalls of personal sharing in your classroom?

The Power of Names. Ask students to think for a moment about how they would like their friends and family members to view them. As soon as they have thought (and perhaps jotted some notes) about their "ideal selves," ask them to write a one-page "character description" of themselves, something that a novelist might write. Suggest that their description be concrete enough that a stranger could recognize them from this single page and assure them that they may keep this information totally private. Next, tell them to make up a nickname that they would like to have for themselves, something by which they would like to be remembered. This could be a nickname that someone has already given them. Discuss the names they chose and why they chose them.

Now ask them to think about nicknames they have been called in the past. Explain that you don't want them to share the nicknames publicly (some of them may be pretty negative); instead, ask them to consider the power of others in developing our self concepts. What does it mean, for instance, when a child is labeled "the bookworm" or "the comedian" in a family? Next, ask them to read a piece of literature, paying particular attention to how characters are shaped by the way others talk about them.

> **Language Study in Context**
> Have students observe the conversations of peers from a distance in the lunchroom or other location in the school. Stress the fact that they are not expected to eavesdrop on conversations, but to watch from a place far away enough to allow observation only. Ask them to note how others show they are listening through nonverbal behaviors.

Active Listening in Literature and Life. Explain the difference between *hearing* (passively registering the gist or the details of what someone has said) and *listening* (giving nonverbal cues that let a speaker know that he or she has been heard). Stress the fact that *active listening* involves more than just hearing; simple cues like facial expressions, nods, and short words of encouragement like "uh huh" or "how did that make you feel?" can go a long way in promoting successful conversations. Ask them to make a list of situations where they have felt *listened to* and situations where they have been merely *heard*. In groups or pairs, have them make a list of the nonverbal and verbal behaviors of others that encouraged them to feel as they did.

Now, try a bit of modeling. Ask a student to pretend to be asking you for something—say a higher grade in your class. As the student begins talking, demonstrate some of the "hearing" behaviors from the list you just generated: shuffle papers as he or she speaks, look at your watch, yawn, stare into space, mumble an occasional "uh huh" at an inappropriate moment, and make irrelevant or distracting comments. Now role-play the conversation again, this time demonstrating active listening skills: Make eye contact with your student, paraphrase to make sure you've heard what he or she said, ask questions that help you to clarify, and so on.

Once your students have an idea of the difference between hearing and listening, choose a situation of conflict in a piece of literature, preferably one that is alluded to, but not specifically represented in dialogue. An example might be the opening of Myers's story, "The Treasure of Lemon Brown" (1997). As the story opens, 14-year-old Greg is suffering through a lecture by his father about his poor math skills. A week before, Greg asked his father if he could play basketball with the Scorpions, a local team, and was told that it depended upon his next report card. The conversation with Greg and his father is not directly represented in dialogue, but it's clear that a great lack of understanding separates Greg and his father.

Pair each student with a partner and ask them to take turns privately role-playing the scene between Greg and his dad in two different ways: first, using "hearing" techniques, and second, using "active listening" techniques. If you have students who are fairly comfortable with each other, pairs may want to share their improvisations with the whole class. Wrap up the experience by discussing how active listening can go a long way in preventing and mediating interpersonal conflicts.

Nonverbal Criminals. If handled sensitively and with plenty of forewarning about possible consequences, this can be an enjoyable lesson in the "unwritten rules" of nonverbal behavior in social settings. First, ask students to brainstorm a list of literally "unspoken" nonverbal rules that people are supposed to follow in social situations. You might start them off with a few examples such as the following:

- When in an elevator, you are supposed to look at the ceiling or the numbers on the panel above the doors, and not at other people.
- When in a cafeteria, you are not supposed to sit with people you don't know and enter into their conversation as if you were an intimate member of their group.
- When you are in a library, your books and possessions should not invade the space of those at the table with you.

Once you have generated a good list of rules, create a corresponding list of "rules for nonverbal criminals." For example, one rule might be "Enter an elevator and turn toward the people standing behind you. Maintain eye contact with them throughout the entire ride." Although some of your students will probably want to push the boundaries, make sure the list covers petty and not major crimes such as staring at personal body parts or using offensive gestures in public.

For the next several days, have students go out in pairs and break at least two of these nonverbal rules. One student acts as observer and takes inconspicuous notes while the other student violates the rule. At the end of a few days, ask students to make brief reports on how others reacted to them.

As a connection to literature, ask students to read stories or poems, paying particular attention to the nonverbal details that the author chooses to describe characters. A good example might be the character Alphonso in Gary Soto's short story, "First Love." Throughout the course of the story, Alphonso, whose family cannot afford to get him braces, continually pushes on his front teeth in the hopes that he can straighten them himself. Ask students why Soto may have chosen this and other nonverbal behaviors to portray Alphonso's character. Popular television shows with teenaged characters are another good source of information about how characters are portrayed through nonverbal and verbal behaviors. Students can follow up these activities by writing their own stories or character sketches, concentrating on revealing character through nonverbal and verbal behaviors.

Dinner Table Study. This idea is taken from the famous discourse analysis of a family dinner table conducted by Tannen (1981). Although many students might enjoy studying the conversational patterns in their own family gatherings, there are many reasons *not* to make students' own families the centerpiece of an assignment. Issues of privacy and middle-class assumptions about families gathering around dinner tables can get pretty dicey for certain students in your classroom. As an alternative, you might show a segment of a popular television show or movie that depicts a family eating dinner. A good choice might be the dinner table scenes from movies like *Meet the Parents* with Ben Stiller and Robert De Niro, *The Nutty Professor* with Eddie Murphy, or *Father of the Bride* with Steve Martin and Diane Keaton. Ask students to view the scene with an eye toward the nonverbal and verbal behaviors of family members. Assign different conversational features (words, phrases, nonverbal behaviors) to each group, and ask students to take notes on that feature. When they've finished, discuss what roles are revealed by the nonverbal behaviors of different family members. For example, who carves the meat, sits at the head of the table, goes to the kitchen? What is the family's conversational style: Do people take turns talking, have side conversations, argue, or share daily events? When you've finished with this informal discourse analysis, talk about the roles that people learn to play in conversations with peer groups, families, or other close-knit groups.

As you can see by these few examples, the English language arts classroom can be a place where students learn more about the art of effective interpersonal communication at the same time they develop deeper understandings of the social and interpersonal dynamics of their reading, listening, viewing, and writing.

TALKING AND LISTENING TO CONNECT AND TRANSFORM

In the previous chapters, we have presented many ways of inviting students to collaborate through talk, from peer writing conferences to group inquiry projects, literature circles, and teacher-student conferences. Although we believe that the bulk of talk and listening, especially for early adolescents, should involve these informal experiences, there is no denying that whole class instruction remains the mainstay of the middle and secondary classroom. For this reason, we have decided to focus particular attention on making large group discussion a forum for intellectual exploration, personal connection, and social transformation rather than a thinly veiled exercise in teacher control.

Breaking the I-R-E Pattern: Inviting Students' Genuine Responses in Class Discussion

Avoid known-information questions.

Many of us bring heavy baggage from experiences with teachers who relied on a steady diet of what Mehan (1979) has called "known-information" questions, or questions to which they already know the answer. In an article called "What Time Is It Denise? . . ." Mehan presents the following conversation for consideration:

> *What time is it, Denise?*
> *Two o'clock.*
> *Very good, Denise.*

It doesn't take long to recognize that this conversation happened in a classroom. The line "Very good, Denise" is the tip-off. Imagine the response you'd get if you asked a passerby on a city street the time of day and then responded, "Very good." In the real world, a simple "thanks" would suffice. The typical pattern of classroom questioning follows what Mehan and others have called an "I-R-E" or *initiation, reply, evaluation sequence;* that is:

> What time is it? *(initiation)*
> Two o'clock. *(reply)*
> Very good. *(evaluation)*

The evaluative nature of most classroom discourse lets students know that there is one correct answer to their teachers' questions. Lest we give the impression that it's easy to avoid the I-R-E trap, we'd like to make the point that all teachers, ourselves included, struggle with ways to step back from the center and invite our students' authentic responses into the conversation. This is the issue that Susan grapples with in Literacy Lesson 9–3.

Literacy Lesson 9-3

Stepping Out of the Way

For years, I struggled with ways to make my students' responses the center of my curriculum. As a high school and middle school teacher, I was often unaware of how often I took center stage in class discussions. It wasn't as though I knew that much more than my students; in fact, as a new teacher, I often felt less knowledgeable than they. Most of the time, though, I became so excited trying to get my ideas across that I'm sure I would have been mortified if someone had tape recorded my classroom conversations and shown the transcripts to me.

Much later, when I began to study other teachers' classrooms in my research, I saw concretely just how much teacher talk pervades the typical class discussion. In transcript after transcript, I discovered large blocks of teacher talk, followed by truncated or abbreviated students' responses. The I-R-E pattern was alive and well in the classrooms I visited as well as in my own. Even as a university professor who should know better, I still struggled with ways to take myself out of the center of the dialogue, with little success.

This was brought home even more clearly 2 years ago, when I received a sabbatical from my university and was invited by a friend to co-teach in her middle school classroom. I came into that seventh-grade classroom vowing to work more consciously at getting myself out of the center of classroom talk. The first inkling that this might be possible came during a class discussion about racism in America. A few days earlier, my seventh-grade students had been watching a film called *Cornbread, Earl, and Me* (1975). The movie was about a bright and gifted young African American athlete who was gunned down in the street because he was mistaken for a murderer by the police. Our students, many of whom were African American, were understandably shaken by this film. They were disturbed by the trial that followed, where the three officers (one of them African American) were eventually acquitted of his death.

Focus On
Viewing

I knew their strong emotions could be the beginning of a teachable moment, but I wasn't sure how to begin. I wanted to bring the movie (which was set in the 1970s) into the context of more modern-day America. I decided to go back a bit into our history with racism as a country. That night, I got on the Internet and began to download some images of the Rodney King beating, the Los Angeles riots that followed, and the beating of Reginald Denny, the white truck driver who was attacked by a gang of Black youths during the riots. I thought these incidents bore striking similarities to the issues in the film we had just watched.

I started the next day by asking if our students thought that racism was still alive in America. There were points of view all over the map, but the majority of students, Black and White alike, seemed to agree that racism wasn't a daily part of their lives—it was something we had dealt with in the 1960s and was not really an issue in today's world. I knew, though, that these were the students who felt free to talk in the forum of a large class discussion. I wondered about the students who weren't talking, students for whom racism had intimately touched their lives in disturbing and profound ways.

The night before, I had turned some of those Internet photos into color overhead transparencies. That morning, rather than asking a bunch of "known-information questions," I decided to let students take the floor, asking only those questions to which I

Focus On
Viewing and Writing

really wanted to hear the answers. I placed an image of a burning building in the Los Angeles riots on the overhead projector and asked students to write for a few moments about what they saw. I explained that photographs are rather like books, in that each tells its own story. I then asked them to take a few moments, look at the photo, and write about the story that the photograph evoked for them. After students wrote for a few moments, I asked them to share their thoughts. One look at the following transcript shows just how powerful a simple request like "write (or tell) the story that's in your mind" can be in breaking the I-R-E pattern.

Danielle: It looks like it's in [an urban] area. And it looks like it's in the nighttime and maybe a mob might have burned it.

Susan: What gives you a clue that maybe a mob might have burned it?

DeShawn: Because the fire's sort of on the ground and it looks like there are maybe people walking around.

Susan: That's a really good insight. You really looked into this picture.

Brooke: Someone might have blew it up.

Susan: What gives you that idea?

Brooke: Because how, like the building is so high and there's like a little fire going on the street.

Susan: So it kind of looks like a big explosion happened here, huh? . . .

Susan: [pointing to a student] And your name is?

Christie: Christie. Uhm, I thought that maybe it was racism. It looks like there's somebody there.

Susan: It does look like there's somebody there, doesn't it? Now that I look at it, I see somebody there. I'm sorry [this picture is so fuzzy] I had to blow it up. I got it off the Internet. It was a tiny little picture. So you think it might be racism. What gives you the thought it might be racism? Christie?

Christie: (Inaudible)

Selwyn: I think somebody started it on purpose, uhm, somebody might have thought that in life they were losing and they have to let it out on other people.

Susan: Oh that's really quite interesting. I'm not going to tell you what [this photo] is for a few minutes but, remember that [thought] . . .

Pat: I think it was done by an enemy or something. I think they used a firebomb.

Susan: A firebomb. And who do you think the enemy was, you know, an enemy of whom?

Pat: The people who owned the store.

More exploratory discussion followed as, one by one, I placed photographs of the Rodney King beating, the Los Angeles riots, and the beating of Reginald Denny on the overhead and asked students to "tell the story" that the photos suggested. Although my students were only a few years old at the time of these incidents, their comments convinced me that modern-day experiences with violence had informed their perceptions of past events. One student immediately identified the King photo as the result of a "wild police chase." Another suggested that maybe "[S]ome guys . . . want to beat up on the other person because he has a different idea or belief." The photos reminded one student of Jonny Gammage, a man from our city who had been stopped by police on a New York interstate and was shot to death when they supposedly mistook his cellular phone for a gun. Antoine told us that Gammage was his cousin, and things began to hit closer to home.

What followed from that day of exploratory talk was a flurry of interest topics like hate, intolerance, racism, homophobia. Students became interested in hate crimes like the Matthew Shepard murder, the dragging death of James Bird in Texas, the Columbine massacre, the death in our own state of Jonny Gammage and a few weeks later, the death of Amadeau Diallo in a New York City apartment hallway. In the days and weeks that followed, I was constantly reminded of the need to get rid of those known-information questions, allowing my students to explore their own authentic questions about events that touch their lives.

Of course there are a great many reasons why this experience was a success besides the subtle change in the patterns of classroom talk, but I'd like to focus on the talk itself. In terms of sheer numbers of statements, I talk as often as the students do. Yet, there was a marked difference in the quality of the interaction among the students and me. I noticed that most of my questions were truly aimed at gathering information I really wondered about, questions like "What gives you the thought it might be racism?" or "What gives you a clue that maybe a mob might have burned it?" Some of my comments weren't even questions at all, but attempts to paraphrase students' responses so that others in the room could hear them ("It does look like there's somebody there, doesn't it?") or expressions of genuine surprise as students pointed out aspects of the photo I hadn't noticed before ("Now that I look at it, I see somebody there").

Did I know more than my students did about those photographs? Of course! Did I know everything they would teach *me* about their understanding of racism and violence in America? Of course *not!* And that, as Robert Frost would say, has "made all the difference." Despite my attempts to avoid such traps, I noticed when I looked at the transcripts I still fell back on traditional *evaluation* responses like "that's really quite interesting," or "that's a really good insight." However, I remember feeling a genuine spirit of respect and curiosity about students' comments, and their responses continued to amaze me throughout ensuing days.

Transforming the patterns of talk in my classroom is only one aspect of placing students more squarely in the center of their own learning, but it's an important one. Here are some things I've concluded about facilitating class discussion as a result of my recent foray back into the middle school classroom—a list of late-career resolutions, if you will:

- Ask no questions to which I already know (or think I know) the answer; in fact, ask no questions at all, if I can avoid it.
- Allow for "wait time" and rehearsal (in the form of free writing, pair-shares, or just a brief "heads-down" time) before inviting all students into a large group discussion.
- Help students to have something in their hands as well as their heads (a bit of writing, graphic organizer, drawing) before opening a discussion.
- Make abundant use of nonverbal prompts such as movies, songs, and photographs to stimulate discussion.

- Don't get obsessed with the amount of time that I hold the floor (teachers *do* often know more than students, after all), but try to bite my lip whenever a silence seems unbearable or sharing my own personal experience seems more tempting than waiting for students to share theirs.
- Find a way to recognize, but not spotlight, shy or reluctant students.

In Your Fieldwork Journal 9–2, we ask you to try your hand at analyzing the conversational patterns in your own classroom.

Your Fieldwork Journal 9-2

Classroom Inquiry—Discourse Analysis

If you are currently teaching, tape a small segment (roughly 30 minutes) of a discussion you are leading. If you don't have a classroom of your own, observe someone who is teaching and analyze the discussion together. If possible, take the tape home and transcribe the discussion or a part of it. Consider the following questions as you read through the transcript or listen to the tape. Take notes and write about the results of your analysis.

Focus on Your Language
- What kind of roles do you seem to be playing at different points in the discussion (e.g., traffic cop, peacekeeper, and so on)?
- What kind of questions do you seem to be asking at different points in the discussion? Do your questions appear to invite or shut down discussion?

Focus on Your Students' Language
- Do your students typically reply to you or to their classmates? Is their talk different when they direct it to you rather than to each other?
- When do students seem most invested in the discussion? What is their language like when they seem to be invested?
- When do students seem least invested? What is their language like at those times?

Focus on Interrelationships
- What is the proportion of teacher to student talk? Does this balance change at different times in the discussion? Try to mark those places on your transcript. Why do you think these changes are occurring?
- Who has the power at different times in the discussion? What's happening at moments when it seems to switch?

As we think about those teacher questions that shut down exploratory talk or rich interpretation—questions like "What is the name of . . . " or "What happened when . . . "— we would do well to plan some alternatives. Here are just a few ideas for putting those known-information questions on the back burner or getting rid of them altogether.

Question Cue Cards

Ask students to jot down anonymously two or three questions on note cards before, during, or after a lesson. These could be questions pertaining to something you're reading ("Why did he do that?" "What did the author mean when she said . . . ") or to larger issues ("Is it right for people to . . . " "What is the historical period of this story?" "I wonder what his mother is like."). These should be questions that students are actually wondering about at that moment, not questions they think *you* want them to ask. Once the cards are handed in, shuffle the pack and call out the questions. Class discussion from these "wonderings" can last several minutes or a couple of class periods, depending upon student interest. Questions related to longer or more provocative texts can serve as a seedbed for future research projects.

KWL Activity

This is another simple approach to use with both fiction and nonfiction texts. For example, you may be teaching a unit on Japanese internment camps, the bombing of Pearl Harbor, the Holocaust, or the Women's Liberation Movement. To begin this activity, you can ask students to write any facts they know about the issue you are about to explore on one side of an index card labeled *K* for "What do I *know?*" On the other side, ask them to write questions they have under the label *W* for "What do I *want* to know?" After the cards are passed in, you can make three columns on an overhead transparency or piece of poster board, filling in the first two columns with students' responses (see Figure 9–3). Periodically during the unit you can return to this chart, filling in any new information and adding new questions as they arise. Eventually, after you have engaged in some discussion, reading, or research, you can work with students in filling out the last column: *L* ("What did I *learn?*").

Handing over more of the authority to our students isn't easy, but it is perhaps most fully accomplished as we help students to see how their talk and listening can make an impact on the larger world. This is a lesson that Harry Webb learned in his first teaching job. Harry tells the story in his own words in Literacy Lesson 9–4.

FIGURE 9–3 KWL Chart

What do we Know?	What do we Want to know?	What have we Learned?

Literacy Lesson 9-4

"A Foot in the Door": Service Learning in an Alternative Classroom

"Your main task will be to get these kids interested, just to get them to come to school."

Those were the instructions I received from my principal during the interview for my first teaching job; I would be teaching "at-risk" eighth graders in an alternative classroom. Originally I thought of the job as my foot in the door of an "excelled" school district. The students had grown up in an educated, upper-middle class city whose citizens placed great importance on a quality school system. The writing skills of my students were not lacking, but their motivation was. Despite the achievements of my district, or any district for that matter, there will always be those students who slip through the cracks, and these were the kids I faced for the very first time 4 years ago in my classroom. I now know that I got my foot in the door of an exciting classroom with some amazing kids. But in the beginning I wasn't sure what to do.

Where did I go from there? How was I supposed to motivate 20 students to write? To read? To engage in school literacy? Students who all had juvenile officers and none with both biological parents at home? For one quarter I tried the methods that my college had taught me: journals, literary response letters, essays, reports, newspaper articles, etc. The students were doing little writing, some did nothing, and all did not care that they were failing. I quickly found that college had given me many great ideas on teaching motivated kids, but I held no strategies for the unmotivated ones. That's when I discovered service learning.

By working on service projects that moved them out of the classroom and into the community, my students had a greater desire to attend school and complete the educational tasks. They worked in the community to achieve tangible goals, and when they returned to the classroom, they had a shared concrete experience that inspired their writing. I used the same writing assignments as before but this time drew from their personal experiences during service learning.

In one of our projects, students wanted to improve their school grounds as a way of giving our school and community a better reputation. Students chose an element that needed improvement, gathered supplies, made a scale model, wrote letters, and made phone calls. The actual project involved buying supplies and learning new skills such as using power tools, pouring concrete, building, and landscaping (see the accompanying figure).

Focus On
Talking and Listening

In addition to improving their written expression, students also increased their proficiency with oral language. Students needed to make phone calls. It was in that "need" that their oral skills came into play. They wanted projects to be successful, and they couldn't do it alone. They needed to communicate with each other, and they needed to go beyond the classroom for help. Much of their oral language development came in the process of getting the project off the ground. But they also needed to advertise their success beyond our classroom. I designed assignments to help them promote their projects and, more important, themselves. One such assignment was a reflection on the entire school year and all the service learning projects we had completed. The class put together a film documenting the many contributions to the community and the skills they used and learned as a result of their work. The film required a written script and voice narration. Once again, with a shared concrete experience and results in which

Focus On
Talking, Writing, and Viewing

Talking and Listening in the Middle Grades

Service Learning Project—Improving School Grounds

ROPES COURSE

Spring 2001-Spring 2002

Step One: Identify Community Need

- We wanted to make our school grounds better.
- Give students a physical and mental challenge.
- Gave our school and community a better reputation.

Step Two: Plan and Prepare

- Choose an element
- Supplies
- Made scale model
- Wrote letters and made phone calls
- Measure area
- Plan for future development

Step Three: Go to Community and Perform Service

- Bought supplies
- Constructed elements
- Used construction skills (power tools, carpentry, concrete, landscaping)
- Teamwork skills
- Communication skills

Step Four: Reflection and Celebration

- Used the ropes course
- Community service awards
- Made a film and presented our work at a conference

they had pride, the students were able to complete the assignment in the classroom with much success.

Another successful example of "at-risk" students using oral proficiency by means of service learning was their elementary school presentations. The eighth-grade class took numerous trips to local elementary schools in the district to read stories, teach the youngsters about dangerous household chemicals, the dangers of strangers, and ways to avoid troublesome situations in their neighborhoods.

It was amazing to see kids who normally had a hard time talking in front of a group shine as they spoke about something they knew about in front of an audience of as

Focus On
Focus on Talking

many as 50 five- to seven-year-old children. As a great celebration for this particular assignment, the class was designated as the "Volunteers of the Month" by the city in which they live and were granted the award in a ceremony by the mayor.

Last fall, my students decided that needy children might like to have bicycles for the holidays. Realizing that many community members would probably be willing to donate bikes that could be repaired with a little effort, they set about collecting and repairing bicycles for these children. They sent out flyers and made phone calls, asking for donations. In addition to gathering tools and creating a work area, they learned about bicycle repair and eventually created some special holiday gifts for children in our community (see the accompanying figure).

Service Learning Project—Bicycle Repair

BICYCLE SHOP

Fall/Winter 2001

Step One: Identification of a Community Need

- Needy children might like to have bicycles for the holidays.
- A lot of old bikes are just sitting around and could be used with a little repair.

Step Two: Plan and Prepare

- Collect bicycles with flyers and phone calls
- Get tools and a work area
- Get parts and accessories
- Learn about bike repair

Step Three: Go to the Community

- Do the bicycle work
- Donate to a worthy cause
- Contact the media

Step Four: Reflection and Celebration

- There are many different types of reflection activities we are working on, from written projects to artwork.
- Celebration – we are going to celebrate by giving the children bikes and seeing smiles on their faces.

These "at-risk" students have routinely written reflections of their service work using journals, newspaper articles, reports, essays, scripts, skits, creative stories, poetry, and letter formats. In addition, some of the actual work for the projects required writing as part of the preparation, proposals for grant money, letters of permission, flyers, storybooks for children, and public service announcements. Where do I go from here?

Literacy is only one piece in the complex puzzle of helping the "at-risk" child, though it is a large one. I'm continuing to study and practice ways of increasing motivation by incorporating service learning while improving literacy. The job that started four years ago as my "foot in the door" continues to be the biggest and most rewarding challenge of my life.

Focus On Writing

TALKING AND LISTENING TO SHOWCASE AND PERFORM

Opportunities for performance can range from informal activities like reading or role playing to more elaborate performances such as public speeches, readers' theaters, skits, or plays. It is clearly beyond the scope of this book to describe all of these performance activities in depth. In the next few pages, we'll offer a few general suggestions for how you can enliven your English language arts classroom with performance opportunities suitable for early adolescents.

Speeches, Demonstrations, and Presentations

Often the formal nature of much public speaking intimidates students and teachers alike. Especially at the middle school level, we suggest that public speeches and presentations should be extemporaneous rather than heavily scripted and memorized. On occasion, you might want students to memorize a famous public address, skit, or dramatic monologue. Usually, however, you'll want your students to be adept at speaking from note cards or cue sheets rather than formal manuscripts.

It takes a great many years of practice to make a scripted presentation sound fresh, engaging, and spontaneous. This kind of practiced informality is beyond the scope of most middle school students, or their teachers, for that matter. Furthermore, we believe that presentations and speeches for this age group should range from a minute to no more than 4 or 5 minutes. Here are just a few suggestions for brief performance opportunities.

Soapbox Speeches. One way of introducing students slowly to the concept of impromptu or extemporaneous speaking is to set up an area of the room and ask students to talk informally for no less than 1 and no more than 2 minutes on an item of current interest to them. Set up a small wooden box or platform in the front of your classroom. Explain how, in earlier days, speakers used to pull up a makeshift platform (often a wooden soap box) and make informal, impromptu speeches to anyone who would listen.

Tell your students you will devote the first 5 minutes of each class period to these "soapbox" speeches. Give students a couple minutes after they settle in to make a few notes or think about what they might say. Then invite them to stand on the soap box and talk for a minute or so about topics ranging from opinions on current events to announcements about school plays, meetings, and dances. Invite them to tell funny stories or share interesting experiences. The idea is not to produce polished presentations, but to get students comfortable with the idea of getting up and talking in front of peers about something that engages them. Give students a check mark in your grade book each time they speak, making sure to give those who haven't spoken the first chance to do so each day. At the end of a marking period, you can refer to these marks in assigning class participation grades or deciding whether to move students who are between grades up to a higher grade.

Grab Bag Speeches. Collect small objects and keep them in a paper bag in your classroom. Whenever you have a few moments left at the end of a class period, invite students to pull out an object. Give each student 1 minute to jot down ideas for an introduction, three major points, and a conclusion. They might create an advertisement for the object, describe its useful features, tell a story about "a day in the life" of that object, or draw some completely unexpected connections to it. It's not necessary to grade these speeches. Simple marks in your grade book will document how many times students have spoken. Give students a few "passes" during the grading period, so they don't feel forced to perform every time. Write a "P" in your book each time a student chooses to pass. Once all passes are used up, students must speak every time you call on them.

"Process" Speeches and Informative Reports. Periodically, or as a culmination to inquiry projects, students might present information about topics related to their expertise or experience. Consider asking them to create visuals such as charts, graphs, or electronic slide shows to assist them in making their presentations. Students might explain a process like "jump starting an engine," a historical event like "the destruction of the World Trade Towers," or a skill like "planning a yard sale."

Mock Legislatures. Particularly if you are teaming with a social studies teacher, you could sponsor an informal classroom congress. The National Forensics League Home Page, listed in the Resources section of this chapter, gives rather lengthy rules for student congress; however, you needn't be this elaborate.

If you don't want to get caught up in the particulars of *Robert's Rules of Order* (Robert, 2000) or other complicated topics like how a bill becomes a law, consider asking students to work in teams of about four or five students, researching issues that involve some kind of change in our current laws or public policy (for example, homelessness or the death penalty). Ask each group to create at least two "bills" that could be debated in a student congress. (The National Forensic League Student Congress manual at *http://debate.uvm.edu/NFL/congressmanual.html* provides the format for a sample bill.)

Once each group has drafted at least two bills, set aside a class period for group representatives to make short presentations of the bills and submit them to the entire class for a vote. Depending on your time limits, you can narrow your choice to one bill or allow two or three bills for debate. Give students a few days to work in teams, gathering information to support or argue against the chosen bills. Eventually, each student should prepare an informal 2- or 3-minute persuasive speech for or against a bill, including evidence from reliable sources.

During the session (which can last one class period or several days), pull the desks together, so that affirmative ("pro") speakers are on one side of the room and negative ("con") speakers are on the other side, with a podium in the middle. All students should have an equal chance to speak throughout the time period. Each student should speak no more than 3 minutes, with a 1-minute follow-up time for questions from the opposing side. Evaluate speeches on a 1 to 3 point scale and use these points to determine final grades.

Beyond Round-Robin Reading: Oral Interpretation, Choral Reading, and Readers' Theater

One of the most tried (or trite) and true approaches to reading dramatic literature in the secondary or middle school classroom is what has been called *round-robin reading*. Although a good many students enjoy reading aloud in class, others find it dreadfully dull, and for good reason. How many of us can remember holding our collective breath as some poor classmate struggled to produce a cold reading of Shaw or Shakespeare?

If you are going to ask students to read aloud, consider assigning parts or characters a day beforehand and asking students to rehearse before coming to class. Better yet, avoid round-robin reading altogether and substitute a bit of choral reading, oral interpretation, or readers' theater. If you're at a loss about where to begin, there are lots of excellent books, articles, and Web sites listed in the Resources section of this chapter. You might want to begin with Aaron Shepard's Web Page at *http://www.aaronshep.com*. Aaron sells his books and scripts, so this is a commercial site, but he also offers plenty of "resources and treats for teachers, librarians, storytellers, children's writers, parents, and young people" at no cost.

If you spend an hour surfing some of the Web sites at the conclusion of this chapter, you should return to your classroom armed with some good ideas and even a few scripts to begin your first foray into the world of oral interpretation. First, a few explanations. As opposed to *presentational theater,* where props, costumes, and settings are often realistic, *oral interpretation* is more like a theater of the mind, which allows the audience to imagine many aspects that would be presented to them in a stage play or movie. Since oral interpretation, and its close relatives readers' theater and choral reading, rely on minimal or no props, costumes, and settings, the audience is expected to participate imaginatively, as they would in reading a book, as opposed to seeing a movie. Much of the interpretation is accomplished through the performers' expression, intonation, and limited movement and gestures rather than props, settings, or other trappings of traditional theater.

At its simplest level, oral interpretation involves the dramatic verbal and vocal representation of a piece of literature in a way that conveys a particular tone, mood, feeling, or other aspect of the interpreter's understanding. To illustrate the differences to your middle school students, you might want to engage them in a few activities like those in Literacy Lesson 9–5.

Literacy Lesson 9-5

A New Twist on an Old Tale

Begin by explaining that you're going to take a popular story or poem and experiment with a bit of performance. Your choice of text can range from folktales to poems with strong imagery, rhyme, or verse. For our example, we've chosen the popular children's verse, "Mary Had a Little Lamb," though most middle school students would probably find it far too juvenile. Quite frankly, we're using it here because it's short and it doesn't violate copyright restrictions. You be the judge of whether your particular students can get over the "little kid" nature of the piece and have fun with it.

Once you've chosen a text, make some copies and pass one out to every student. If you're using "Mary," you might not even need to make the copies. Next, ask for volunteers to read (or say) the words aloud, using different vocal inflections and nonverbal behaviors to convey emotions such as anger, disgust, worry, or surprise.

From this starting place, move to a bit of choral reading. *Choral reading* involves the oral reading of literature by more than one reader, using combinations of vocal qualities, rhythm, and intonation patterns to create a strong impression. First, divide your class into three groups. Assign each to the "high," "medium," or "low" group, depending on their vocal quality. Then hand out another script like the following.

High Voices:	Mary had a little lamb,
All:	little lamb, little lamb,
Medium Voices:	Mary had a little lamb,
Low Voices:	Its fleece was white as snow.
High Voices:	And everywhere that Mary went,
All:	Mary went, Mary went.
Medium Voices:	Everywhere that Mary went,
Low Voices:	The lamb was sure to go. (and so on)

Have students sit in a circle at their desks or on the floor and practice reading lines together in groups of high, medium, and low voices. Next, work on vocal intonation and feeling. Ask students to consider who the high voices might represent (Mary herself?), the medium voices (a narrator? Mary's teacher?), and the low voices (the lamb?). Questions might include "How does the teacher feel when she says the line 'which was against the rules'? What gestures might we use to convey her feelings (e.g., hands on hips, waving a warning finger?)?"

After a bit of choral reading, you're ready to try your hand at *readers' theater.* Ask students to take their original text and lead them through a bit of script cutting. Begin by asking, "How many different speakers or voices can you hear in this piece?" Responses may include Mary, her classmates, the lamb, the teacher, a narrator, and even people who aren't directly mentioned in the script like Mary's mother or father. Place students into small task groups of four or five. Hand out highlighting pens or ask them to underline lines or segments of lines, assigning them to different speakers. As an example,

> He followed her to school one day, ^{Narrator}
> School one day, ^{Lamb}
> School one day, ^{Lamb}
> He followed her ^{Narrator} to school one day, ^{Lamb}
> Which was against the rules. ^{Teacher}

After groups of students have cut their script and practiced for a bit, invite them to perform their different readers' theater renditions for the class.

From this point, you are limited only by your collective imaginations and the time you have available for performance activities. Here are just a few considerations you might keep in mind in creating readers' theater presentations.

- *To stage or not to stage?* Interpreters can stand on platforms or risers, sit on stools, read from scripts, or use simplified props, blocking, and pantomime. The idea is to be representational rather than real. Characters can pantomime actions like drinking from a glass or opening a door. Sometimes a few stage props (a plant, framed photograph on the wall, a chair) can "say more" about a story's setting than a more elaborate set. Slides and music can enhance elements of tone, characters' emotional states, or other aspects of the script.
- *To memorize or not to memorize?* Because it eliminates the need for scripts, memorization allows interpreters more freedom in moving around a stage, gesturing, and pantomiming. If students do memorize their parts, consider using what is called "offstage focus" (having interpreters look out at the audience as they are saying lines, rather than other characters on stage). This gives audience members a feeling of intimacy and allows them to see subtle facial expressions and other nonverbal nuances of the interpreters.
- *To costume or not to costume?* If you decide to use costumes, keep them to a minimum. One item of clothing (a scarf, pipe, or cane) can represent a character. As a way of minimizing expense, decide in advance which items of clothing students already have (e.g., black tee shirts and jeans) and use these rather than purchasing or making costumes.
- *Published versus student-created scripts?* Although a growing number of published readers' theater scripts are available (many of which are based upon traditional materials with no copyright restrictions), we see more instructional value in having students cut scripts and assign parts themselves or with your help. Collaborative and critical skills are developed as students explore questions about the various possibilities for which speakers or voices to identify in a piece of literature when a line shifts perspective, or which poems seem to go together in the context of a larger script.

The book *Something Is Going to Happen: Poetry Performance for the Classroom* by Wolf (1990) is a great source for approaching poetry interpretation with middle school students. It includes commonsense descriptions of issues like blocking and script cutting and a nice variety of short sample scripts with suggested stage directions.

Although the possibilities for readers' theater and oral interpretation in your English language arts classroom are nearly endless, here are just a few ideas for your consideration.

- *Performance Anthology.* Decide on a unifying theme (*"Life Cycles"*) and commission student writings on various aspects of the theme (e.g., growing up, childhood, teenage years, and parenting). Rather than creating a print anthology of student writing, create a *performance anthology* or a collection of oral renditions of student writings, arranged according to themes. Students can perform their own pieces or ask class members to do so. Consider using popular or original music, slides, and other artistic touches. Invite friends and family members to attend the final performance.
- *Collaborative Script Writing.* Engage your students in writing and performing a script for a soap opera or simple melodrama—the cornier the better. Decide on a clever title (e.g., "As the Eyeball Turns"), a cast of characters, and a basic plot line. Together with your students, map an outline of the plot onto a piece of chart paper and break it into three or four short scenes. Assign each scene to a scripting group. Once the script is created, you can duplicate copies, assign parts, and read or perform it aloud.
- *Thematic Montage.* Tie together several short pieces under some unifying theme with several subthemes. For example, excerpts of "The People, Yes" by Sandburg (1990) can be interwoven with other poetry about America and slides of American life. If you have access to a stage, consider using lighting and music to add yet another dimension to the performance. Share your students' work in an assembly or on parents' night.

EVALUATING ORAL LANGUAGE AND LISTENING

Oral language and listening are perhaps the hardest language acts to grade and evaluate. Any kind of performance, whether a formal public speech or a class comment, is loaded with emotion and personal investment, especially for early adolescents. The question is how to encourage students to develop their oral language abilities without squelching their often tentative attempts at expression and fluency.

In Chapter 5, we argued for the importance of negotiating the criteria upon which students will be graded or evaluated. This is perhaps most crucial in the areas of oral language and listening. Students need to know what is expected of them, and you must be adept at guessing what is appropriate to grade and what is best left ungraded.

> Provide many ungraded opportunities for oral language and listening.

Just as in the writing classroom, you should sponsor a large number of ungraded, exploratory oral activities before assigning a grade. Above all, don't use the forum of a public discussion or performance as an opportunity to correct students' grammar or usage. Awareness of usage issues is probably best approached in private, as you talk with students about their writing. Simply rephrasing a grammatically incorrect statement in what has been called "the language of wider communication" as you respond orally to students will most likely let them know in a subtle way that they've made a mistake.

Once students become comfortable talking and listening in informal situations, you may want to assign more formal tasks like presentations or speeches. As an introduction to formal public speaking, consider making a humorous example of yourself. If you are a bit of a ham, walk into the classroom with your shirt untucked or hair mussed, and place a sheaf of notes on a podium. Make sure to drop the notes and rearrange them several times before beginning to speak. Announce your topic: "Ten Tips for Delivering a Public Speech." As you speak from a list of 10 pointers, illustrate each one by doing the exact opposite of what it says. For example, as you say "avoid distracting behaviors," rock the podium back and forth, pace from one end of the room to the other, or fiddle with your jewelry. As you say "be sure to make eye contact with each member of your audience," look at the floor or above the heads of the audience. Be sure to lower your voice so that even people in the front row can't hear you, and clear your throat often. Your students will get the idea pretty quickly. Use this as a springboard for discussing a few general criteria on which you might judge their first public performance. Turn these criteria into a simple rubric and grade students on a 3- or 5-point scale for each criterion.

If students are creating readers' theater presentations, you might want to grade aspects of the *process* (e.g., creating a script, contributing published or student writing, rehearsing), but leave the performance itself ungraded. Consider creating a contract in which students can lose points for failing to show up for rehearsals or using group time unproductively, but which leaves other, more risky, aspects of the performance ungraded. The contract could allow students to earn extra points for things like bringing in props, creating slides for a show, writing an original song, or creating a tape or CD of background music. These extra points could serve as a reward for shy students or those who have a limited knowledge of English and would rather not perform.

If you are serious about integrating the language arts in your classroom, there will be plenty of opportunities to grade or evaluate more formal and polished aspects of student work. Just as you wouldn't grade individual entries in a personal journal or learning log, you'll want to avoid assigning grades to students' tentative, exploratory attempts at talking and listening. Formal public speeches and debates lend themselves more readily to grading, but even these should be handled with care. Finally, we believe it's always important to give lots of *formative evaluation* (in the form of informal feedback at every stage of preparation) before arriving at a final grade.

> Give credit for both preparation and performance.

The best advice we can offer applies not only to oral language and listening but to all language arts: Look closely, beneath the surface of a student's classroom behavior. Most students are like icebergs. A great deal of their interest, their skill, their preferences and proclivities, the key to what moves them to passion or bores them to death, is hidden beneath the surface of their classroom performances. Some are what Jim, a preservice teacher in his final placement, likes to call "slacker savants." Literacy Lesson 9–6 offers Jim's final reflection for the members of his student teaching seminar.

Literacy Lesson 9-6

The Slacker Savant

What's Going On

There is one student like this in every class. A student that is too withdrawn from everyone and everything to give a damn about school. This student might be the one that shouts out things that are irrelevant to class; it also may be the student sitting in the back corner asleep. Usually, this student might tend to turn in very little work, if any. Yet we, as educators, are enamored by this kind of mentality. "I came up with the most interesting community builder about yadda yadda, and all STUDENT X could do was sleep!" is our battle cry. Plagued with constant absences, trips to the office, detention, and expulsion, we are left to ask, where does it end?

Maybe we are asking the wrong questions. I think we should ask, where does it start?

Yesterday

There was a student in my 8/9 period class. For privacy reasons, let's call him Dan. Dan was the student that always stumbled into class late, orange juice in hand, Discman hidden under his hooded sweatshirt, five o'clock shadow on his face. He would pick his seat in the corner, slump into it, and nod off to sleep. He rarely turned in work and didn't contribute to class in a positive manner.

All in all, I had no reservations about who I believed Dan was. I pictured him a slacker, a student with no ambition and drive. I saw his multiple absences as cuts; not times he was sick, but days he just didn't feel like going to school. When pushed, I figured he would do as little as he could to survive and waste the rest of his, and my, time.

All this changed when Dan handed in his first writing assignment, 2 weeks late. It was a very polished, deep, dark poem on drug use. I was expecting something a lot more elementary, and I was floored. I read his poem over and over again, wondering how he could waste so much time during class and turn in a piece of work that was phenomenal. I then deemed Dan the Slacker Savant.

In keeping with Dan's love for music, I have decided to use popular song quotes for the headings of this reflection. This is important because, although it does have something to do with Dan's love for music, it also works to show where we have moved to and from as a teacher and a student, and a student and a teacher.

Right Now

Now that I had my beliefs about Dan disproved, I was ecstatic. I felt that it would be a whole new world for the two of us, as I would be able to ask things of him, and he would do them. In all actuality, things went back to the same way they were before, where he would come in, sit down, and "veg" out. This was troubling to me, as I wondered how I could bridge the gap between the two of us, find out what exactly made him act this way, and how I could get him to produce better, and more frequent, work.

I began by observing the way he acted in my class. I had him toward the end of the day in a class that was fairly small, so it was easy for me to keep an eye on him while I taught the class. At first, I noticed he liked to talk to some of the nearby students, but many kids in the class did this, so it didn't strike me as odd. I also noticed that when he was supposed to be reading his free-read book, which we provided time for in class, he had his head down and he was napping. I looked back roughly 5 minutes later to see him with his book open, reading.

On the next day, which was a writing day, again I followed his movements as I went about my daily routine. I didn't want him to know I was observing him, as I figured it would change what he was doing. During the mini-lesson, he had his head down, napping. When the class moved on to peer editing their writing pieces, he again took a few minutes more than everyone else, but he managed to begin editing his writing with another student.

Throughout the semester, I noticed he would never turn things in when we asked him to, but the quality of the work was always right there. I began to question what Dan's beliefs were about school and the school environment. In my own school days, I tended to produce the same habits as Dan because I was not a fan of the structure of school. I was a more independent learner and tended to do things on my own schedule. This was my hypothesis for the way Dan worked.

I thought it would be a great idea to talk with Dan about his final project, and I could then use the conversation as a gateway to a somewhat informal interview of Dan on his opinions toward his work, his study habits, and school in general. I believed that a normal interview wouldn't be a good idea because it would prove to be too regimented for Dan, and he would favor a conversation that went normally, as opposed to a conversation where I took down his words or taped them.

Dan and I talked about his final project, which would be on building soapbox racers. We then began talking about his inability to hand things in on time and often enough. When I asked Dan if he thought he was a good student, he said, "I dunno." When pressed, he said his work was average and he didn't like doing small assignments like the ones we had him doing because he felt they "wasted [his] time." When we moved on to talking about school, Dan said exactly what I believed he was going to say: "School sucks." He began detailing the fact that he didn't like school because he wasn't an early person and didn't like the fact that everything was so scheduled and organized. He said he liked doing things at his own pace and liked to take more time on things that he enjoyed because they meant more to him.

As my student teaching semester came to a close, I began to ask Dan's opinions on some of the lessons we had done in class. I was always happy that he would give me an honest response, which would really tell me how things went. The class we had fed off its own energy and we became a tighter knit class and got more work done as a result of it.

When I sat down to analyze Dan's literacy, I came to a resounding conclusion. Dan can do the work. It isn't a question of whether or not he can do it, because he can. The challenge is getting him to do the work. The thing I found out about Dan, and about *slacker savants* in general, is that in many cases they aren't lazy or slow. They just aren't into it. These students don't want to waste their time on busywork, because they believe their time is worth more than that. In many ways, I agree with them.

Don't Stop Thinking About Tomorrow

Since we know what we know about Dan, we can use what we have learned about him to better the learning environment of our classes. What we must first realize is that we aren't going to get a classroom of 30 students just like Dan. Many students, if you ask them to recopy the dictionary, will get their pens ready. These are the students who not only want to succeed, but also might believe that every assignment we give them is going to be required for graduation. Now, I don't want to put any kind of student above another, but I favor a student who is resistant to learning. When you have a student who does everything you ask of him or her, there isn't much of a challenge. I had a challenge in Dan in that he challenged me to come up with lessons he would enjoy, lessons he would do, and lessons from which the entire class would benefit.

I agree with Dan that he should be assigned work that is worth his time. I think we might want to work toward giving students like these more independent roles inside and outside of the classroom. When I asked Dan about his final project, he was adamant about working on it. I believe he was enthralled with it because it involved something he enjoyed, and it wasn't tied down into the classroom. . . . If we give students who are more independent the opportunity to use their own time for their own reasons, we might see a better work output from them.

All in all, I think a slacker savant isn't a bad thing. I think students who push us, as educators, to adapt our needs to more than one kind of student are positive because they broaden who we are as educators. The trick is to accept that all students are not bright balls of sunshine who are happy to be with us and doing what we are doing for every waking moment of the school day. When educators begin to use this kind of mentality, our classes will be the better for it.

From teaching our students to become better communicators and listeners to becoming more careful observers of their verbal and nonverbal behaviors in our classroom, much can be gained by making talk and listening a significant part of our English language arts curriculum. It may seem scary at first to think about performance activities like readers' theater, public speaking, debate, or drama, but the benefits far outweigh the costs. As Miss Frizzle says in the popular children's television show, *The Magic School Bus*, it's important to "take chances, make mistakes, get messy!" As James observes, our teaching, our students, and our classes are bound to be "the better for it."

Standards in Practice

Viewing Your Oral Language Lessons Through the IRA/NCTE Standards

Locate a copy of the IRA/NCTE *Standards for the English Language Arts* (1996). For an explanation of the standards, a table of contents for the volume, an annotated listing of each standard, and chapter excerpts, consult the NCTE Web site at this address: *http://www.ncte.org/standards*.

For purposes of this chapter, we suggest you look most closely at Standards 11 and 12. Read each standard closely and attempt to tease out the multiple goals embedded in each one. We have highlighted words and phrases in these standards that you might use in critically analyzing your own lessons.

> **Standard 11:** Students participate as knowledgeable, reflective, creative, and critical members of a variety of literacy communities.
>
> **Standard 12:** Students use spoken, written, and visual language to accomplish their own purposes (e.g., for learning, enjoyment, persuasion, and the exchange of information).

Now, look at a lesson you have created or one you are in the process of creating that involves talk and listening. If you aren't currently planning lessons of your own, you might want to refer back to Literacy Lesson 9–4 on Harry Webb's service learning projects presented earlier in this chapter. For each activity in your lesson plan, try to tie it to one or more of these subgoals. As an example, we've paraphrased some of the activities in Harry Webb's service learning project. Beside each activity, we placed the relevant subgoals of Standard 11:

Activities	Connections to Standards
Landscaping Project	
• Choosing an element that needed improvement	• Students participate as knowledgeable, *reflective, creative,* and *critical members* of their classroom community.
• Making phone calls • Writing letters	• Students use spoken and written language to *accomplish their own purposes* (e.g., for *learning, persuasion,* and the *exchange of information*).
• Learning new skills	• Students use spoken language to *accomplish their own purposes* (e.g., for *learning* and the *exchange of information*).
• Writing reflections on the entire year	• Students use written language to *accomplish their own purposes* (e.g., for *learning*).

Critically examine one of your lessons (or Harry's) against the backdrop of the two standards listed at the beginning of this section. Do you note any subgoals that have not been addressed? Although you can't address all standards in all lessons, on occasion you may want to look closely at the standards to determine how you are addressing them in relevant ways for your students in your particular community. There are valid reasons to emphasize some over others. You may find that you do not address some subgoals. If so, consider why that is the case.

REFERENCES

Cisneros, S. (1991). *The house on Mango Street.* Madison, WI: Turtleback Books.

Cunningham, P. M. (1976–1977). Teachers' correction responses to black-dialect miscues which are non-meaning changing. *Reading Research Quarterly, 12*(4), 637–653.

Cureton, G. O. (1985). Using a black learning style. In C. K. Brooks, L. C. Scott, M. Chaplin, D. Lipscomb, W. Cook, & V. Davis (Eds.), *Tapping potential: English and language arts for the black learner* (pp. 102–108). Urbana, IL: National Council of Teachers of English.

Fine, M. (1995). Silencing and literacy. In V. Gadsden & D. Wagner (Eds.), *Literacy among African-American youth: Issues in learning, teaching, and schooling* (pp. 201–222). Cresskill, NJ: Hampton Press.

Fordham, S. (1993). Those loud black girls: (Black) women, silence, and gender "passing" in the academy. *Anthropology and Education Quarterly, 24*(1), 3–32.

Fordham, S. (1996). *Blacked out: Dilemmas of race, identity, and success at Capital High.* Chicago: University of Chicago Press.

Frost, R. (1995). Stopping by woods on a snowy evening. In R. Frost, *Collected Poems, prose, and plays*. New York: The Library of America.

Grant, L. (1984). Black females' "place" in desegregated classrooms. *Sociology of Education, 57*(2), 98–111.

Guy, R. (1973). *The friends*. New York: Holt Rinehart & Winston.

hooks, b. (1989). *Talking back: Thinking feminist, thinking black*. Boston: South End Press.

Langer, J. (1995). *Envisioning literature: Literary understanding and literature instruction*. New York: Teachers College Press.

Manduke, J. (Producer/Director) (1975). *Cornbread, Earl, and me*. United States: Orion Home Video.

McCarthy, C. (1996). Multicultural policy discourses on racial inequality in American education. In R. Ng, P. Staton, & J. Scane (Eds.), *Anti-racism, feminism, and critical approaches to education* (pp. 21–44). Westport, CT: Bergin and Garvey.

Mehan, H. (1979). What time is it Denise? Asking known-information questions in classroom discourse. *Theory into Practice, 18*(4), 285–294.

Moffett, J. (1968). *Teaching the universe of discourse*. Boston: Houghton.

Myers, W. D. (1997). The treasure of Lemon Brown. *The language of literature, 7th grade* (pp. 18–26). Evanston, IL: McDougal Littell.

Robert, H. M. (2000). *Robert's rules of order*. New York: HarperCollins.

Soto, G. (1992). First love. In J. C. Thomas (Ed.), *A gathering of flowers: Stories about being young in America* (pp. 135–151). New York: HarperCollins Children's Book Group.

Sadker, M., & Sadker, D. (1994). *Failing at fairness: How our schools cheat girls*. New York: Simon and Schuster.

Salisbury, J., & Jackson, D. (1996). *Challenging macho values: Practical ways of working with adolescent boys*. London: Falmer Press.

Sandburg, C. (1990). *The people, yes*. San Diego: Harcourt Trade Publishers.

Smitherman, G. (1986). *Talkin and testifyin: The language of black America*. Detroit, MI: Wayne State University Press.

Tannen, D. (1981). New York Jewish conversational style. *International Journal of the Sociology of Language 30,* 133–149.

Wolf, A. (1990). *Something is going to happen: Poetry performance for the classroom—A teacher's companion book*. Asheville, NC: Iambic Publications.

RESOURCES

Print

Drama

Barnes, D. (1968). *Drama in the English classroom*. Urbana, IL: National Council of Teachers of English.

Johnson, L., & O'Neil, C. (Eds.). (1984). *Dorothy Heathcote: Collected writings on education and drama*. London: Hutchinson.

O'Neil, C., & Lambert, A. (1982). *Drama structures: A handbook for teachers*. London: Hutchinson.

Wagner, B. J. L. (1998). *Educational drama and language arts: What research shows*. Portsmouth, NH: Heinemann.

Teacher Questioning

Bloome, D. (1986). Building literacy and the classroom community. *Theory into Practice, 25,* 71–76.

Dillon, J. T. (1990). *The practice of questioning.* New York: Routledge.

Hynds, S. (1991). Questions of difficulty in literary reading. In A. Purves (Ed.), *The idea of difficulty in literature* (pp. 117–139). Albany, NY: SUNY Press.

Hynds, S. (1992). Challenging questions in the teaching of literature. In J. A. Langer (Ed.), *Literature instruction: A focus on student response* (pp. 78–100). Urbana, IL: National Council of Teachers of English.

Raphael, T. (1986). Teaching question-answer relationships, revisited. *The Reading Teacher, 39*(6), 516–522.

Talk in the Classroom

Barnes, D. (1976). *From communication to curriculum.* Harmondsworth, England: Penguin.

Barnes, D., Britton, J., & Torbe, M. (1987). *Language, the learner and the school* (3rd ed.). Harmondsworth, England: Penguin.

Brice Heath, S. (1983). *Ways with words: Language, life, and work in communities and classrooms.* Cambridge, England: Cambridge University Press.

Cazden, C. (1988). *Classroom discourse: The language of teaching and learning.* Portsmouth, NH: Heinemann.

Gere, A. R. (1990). Talking in writing groups. In S. Hynds & D. L. Rubin (Eds.), *Perspectives on talk and learning* (pp. 115–128). Urbana, IL: National Council of Teachers of English.

Hynds, S., & Rubin, D. L. (Eds.). (1990). *Perspectives on talk and learning.* Urbana, IL: National Council of Teachers of English.

Lundsteen, S. W. (1979). *Listening.* Urbana, IL: National Council of Teachers of English.

Marshall, J. D., Smagorinsky, P., & Smith, M. W. (1995). *The language of interpretation: Patterns of discourse in discussions of literature.* NCTE Research Report No. 27. Urbana, IL: National Council of Teachers of English.

Mehan, H. (1979). What time is it Denise? Asking known-information questions in classroom discourse. *Theory into Practice 28*(4), 285–294.

Moffett, J., & Wagner, B. J. (1992). *Student-centered language arts, K–12* (4th ed.). Portsmouth, NH: Boynton/Cook, Heinemann.

O'Keefe, V. (1995). *Speaking to think/thinking to speak: The importance of talk in the learning process.* Portsmouth, NH: Boynton/Cook, Heinemann.

Sorenson, M. (1993). Teaching each other: Connecting talking and writing. *English Journal, 82*(1), 42–47.

Sowder, W. H. (1993). Fostering discussion in the language arts classroom. *English Journal, 82*(6), 39–42.

Torbe, M., & Medway, P. (1981). *The climate for learning: Contexts for language.* Montclair, NJ: Boynton/Cook.

Weinberg, S. K. (1996). Unforgettable memories: Oral history in the middle school classroom. *Voices from the Middle, 3*(3), 18–25.

Wells, G. (1985). *The meaning makers: Children learning language and using language to learn.* Upper Montclair, NJ: Heinemann.

Electronic

International Listening Association Home Page. This site is a treasure trove of inspiration that includes thought-provoking, fun quotes about listening. A favorite of ours is from Pooh's Little Instruction Book: "If the person you are talking to doesn't appear to be listening, be patient. It may simply be that he has a small piece of fluff in his ear."

http://listen.org

The Internet Theatre Bookshop. This is a great site to browse for play scripts. You can search by genre, nation, author's name, or keyword. Includes a brief synopsis and casting requirements for each play.

http://www.stageplays.com/index.html

Gallery of Poets. Focused primarily on classic poets such as Poe and Frost, this is a good site for finding CDs, films, reviews, and other resources helpful for the oral performance of poetry.

http://www.galleryofpoets.com

Virtual Presentation Assistant. This site provides an online tutorial to help students develop public speaking skills such as determining purpose, topic selection, and so on. The site is intended for students at the college level, but the language is accessible to younger folks as well. Links to other sites focused on public speaking are also available.

http://www.ukans.edu/cwis/units/coms2/vpa/vpa.htm

Shakespeare Bookshelf. Sponsored by a group called the "Internet Public Library," this is a great source if you want to find full-text electronic versions of all the Shakespearean plays.

http://www.ipl.org/reading/shakespeare/shakespeare.html

Art of Speaking in Public. This nonprofit site includes several quick tips for beginning public speakers.

http://www.artofspeaking.com/main.htm

National Forensic League Home Page. If you sponsor or wish to work with a speech and debate program, several features on the National Forensic League (NFL) Web site might interest you, including a detailed description of the rules and regulations of "student congress," an explanation of different debate formats, and the current national topic for high school students.

http://debate.uvm.edu/nfl.html

National Junior Forensic League (NJFL). This is an arm of the NFL designed for middle school students. Teacher sponsors can assign points to students for participation in various speech events. Membership information can be accessed at

http://debate.uvm.edu/NFL/AnnouncingNJFL.html

Middle School.Net Debate Sites. Advertised as a resource "for teachers by teachers," this site contains many valuable links for teachers interested in starting a debate program or using debate techniques in their classrooms.

http://www.middleschool.net/activities/debate.htm

Storytelling, Drama, Creative Dramatics, Puppetry & Readers Theater for Children & Young Adults. As its title implies, this is a great site for links to storytelling speaking, oral interpretation, and drama resources. If it's not on their list, chances are, it doesn't exist.

http://falcon.jmu.edu/~ramseyil/drama.htm

Aaron Shepard's Storytelling Page. As with his popular readers' theater page, Aaron Shephard again provides valuable resources for the middle school teacher—everything from articles on storytelling to sample scripts.

http://www.aaronshep.com/storytelling/index.html

The Drama Teacher's Resource Room. Beginning teachers are often "chosen" to sponsor the drama club, even though they may have no clue as to how to hold tryouts, plan a rehearsal schedule, or build a set. This site is a good place to start and includes everything from creative dramatics icebreakers to a sample rehearsal schedule.

http://www3.sk.sympatico.ca/erachi/

Aaron Shepard's RT Page. Billed as a place to go for "scripts and tips" for readers' theater, this site provides just that. Aaron sells books and other materials, but you don't need to purchase a book to use the many informative materials and free scripts provided on this Web page. His tips on cutting your own scripts are particularly informative.

http://www.aaronshep.com/rt/

Poetry Alive. This organization brings oral interpretation techniques to teachers and schools through its workshop opportunities and assembly performances. Tapes, CDs, and books are available from this Web site. Of most interest to teachers are the free texts of poetry for various grade levels and the many links to author information and biography. Ideal for texts suitable for readers' theater scripts.

http://www.poetryalive.com

Dramatic Storytelling in the English Classroom Prepared by Dianne Pizarro and Ruth Buchanan. This site provides a commonsense explanation of the characteristics of readers' theater, along with sample texts and scripting techniques.

http://www.aspa.asn.au/Projects/english/rtheatre.htm

The Dramatic Exchange. If you're looking for a playscript involving 11 males and 1 female or a mystery, musical, or screenplay, this would be a good place to start. Includes brief synopses of hundreds of plays.

http://www.dramex.org/plays.html

Learn Improv. This site is a good source for quick creative dramatics exercises. You can also contribute an idea for other teachers to access if you're so inclined.

http://www.learnimprov.com/

Improv Games Collection. This is an excellent source for improvisational games.

http://www.humanpingpongball.com/gm.html

Classroom Lesson Plans for Creative Dramatics. This Web site is created by a teacher for teachers. Great ideas for simple exercises you can use in your classroom.

http://www.geocities.com/Broadway/Alley/3765/lessons.html

Gender Equity in Middle School Education—An Ask ERIC InfoGuide. This site lists an array of articles related to gender issues in early adolescence.

http://www.askeric.org/Old_Askeric/InfoGuides/alpha_list/gender_98.html

Tolerance.Org. This is a good site for students interested in becoming active in social justice, service learning, or community service projects. Sponsored by the Southern Poverty Law Center, this site is dedicated to promoting tolerance and fighting hate. Students can access a feature called "Tolerance Watch" to be alerted to instances of hate and injustice, one called "Do Something" if they are interested in ways to become involved, or one called "Dig Deeper" if they want to examine their own prejudices and attitudes.

http://tolerance.org

chapter 10

A Focus on Language Study

GUIDING QUESTIONS

1. What does language study include?
2. How can we help students understand how language varies and changes in different regions, across different cultural groups, and across time periods?
3. How does a middle school teacher foster and monitor language development?

A CASE FOR CONSIDERATION

"I Never Thought About Words Before"

Mr. Williams had his back turned to the empty class as he quickly attempted to erase from the blackboard all traces of the words that his third-period class had been discussing. Suddenly Anna came tumbling into his seventh-grade classroom with her best friend Sarah. She could barely contain her enthusiasm or the scraps of paper that seemed to be exploding out of her writer's notebook.

"Mr. W., you won't believe what I found! You won't believe it! Did you know that there are really word detectives? Did you know that there are people who go around listening? That's their job. I'm not kidding. Someone has the job to go out and just listen. And did you know," she interrupted herself in her excitement, "you won't believe what Aunt Mary said about dictionaries. She knows, and she heard on the radio, that a dictionary has a life span. And if it is too old it is dead, because the words may be too old."

Mr. Williams tried to quiet her. "Anna, can you wait until the bell rings? I'd like you to tell everybody what you discovered in your detective work." Like Anna, Mr. Williams could barely contain his pleasure in learning that a student was really excited about language. In his experience in 10 years of teaching seventh-grade language arts, he had struggled to find ways to make language study not only fun but more important, to make it meaningful for his students. This project seemed to interest at least one student. He hoped there would be more in the days to come.

A week before, he had filled the room with old book of Victorian and Elizabethan poetry, 19th-century novels, even a few textbooks that were written around the turn of the century. Some he had gotten from the school librarian who brought them to his room on a cart, and some he had been collecting over the years from thrift shops, used bookstores, and garage sales. He told his students up front that some of the words in these books would seem foreign to them. They might have dropped out of current usage altogether. Others might be words that have changed meaning since they were used in an earlier time period—words like "gay" or "radical" or "awesome."

His students discussed current slang terms that probably had different meanings in earlier times. For example, Morgan suggested that the word "ridiculous" (pronounced REEEEdiculous) could be used to describe something that a person really loved or really hated. Rolf explained, "If my dad asked me how I liked a concert, I'd say, 'REEEEdiculous!' If it was good or bad depended on how I said the word."

After a bit of fun discussing popular slang terms, Mr. Williams asked his students to read as many pieces as they could and keep a word notebook, listing all of the words or phrases they found interesting or those that had changed meaning since the time they were written. "For the next few weeks, you're going to become 'word detectives,' " Mr. Williams challenged. After creating their word lists, he explained, students would choose three words and do some detective work, finding out not only the multiple meanings of the words, but the way they have changed over time. As a start, they could use one of the dictionaries on his bookshelves, but they should try to move beyond these sources, eventually searching Web sites or even going to the public library to consult the *Oxford English Dictionary*. As a culminating activity, students would create visuals displaying their three words, their current definitions, and a brief explanation of their different meanings over time. On a selected day, he planned to have a poster session in which students could walk around the room, visiting each other's word detective displays.

Anna's class had been working on the project for the past 5 days. As other students began filing into their seats, there was the usual commotion as they dropped their notebooks and backpacks on the tables and began to settle in. The room was still abuzz, but Anna's voice could be heard above the others as she began opening her notebook, "You know, I never thought about words before!"

FOR DISCUSSION

- What might you assume about Mr. Williams's goals for the word detective's notebook?
- What might Mr. Williams have students do next with their detective work?
- What are some other means by which a middle school teacher might help students to "think about words"?

WHAT COUNTS AS LANGUAGE STUDY

In considering teaching in a middle school, preservice teachers often have a long list of questions and concerns about language study:

> "I don't know all of the rules. I don't remember what an adverbial clause is. How can I ever teach in middle school?"
>
> "Is there a handbook I can buy?"
>
> "Don't middle school students hate language arts because of all of the grammar stuff?"

Many of us had (and still have) similar worries about language study. We tend to equate this term with *grammar* and feel ill prepared to teach the tiny particulars about parts of speech and punctuation that we once knew but have long since forgotten. Worrisome questions flood our minds: What's a dangling participle, a gerund, a predicate nominative? What's the difference between a predicate and a verb? These questions plague us every time we consider teaching about language. We probably learned to read, write, and speak with some semblance of grace, or we wouldn't be teaching English language arts. But is that enough? Do we need to know all the parts of speech in order to write? What technical terms do we need to teach our students so they'll become competent writers, readers, and language users? When the students in her preservice teaching classes ask questions like these, Susan always asks, "Do you need to know all the parts of a sewing machine to make a dress?" Of course not! But still, those worries nag us. We're afraid we'll be at a party with a bunch of English teachers and won't know the difference between a dangling modifier and a dangling participle.

Let's begin by recognizing that the study of formal language and grammar is only one small (however important) part of the study of language. What "counts" as language study, you might ask? The answer to that question is "many things." First, it's an understanding of the social and political aspects of language use: the multiple language communities within which we and our students live, the rules of communicative competence within those different communities, and the political implications of being a language "outsider." Next, it involves the history of language. Much as Mr. Williams's students were discovering in the opening Case for Consideration, our students should see language as fluid, flexible, changing. Language study also includes discovering how words function across the curriculum—discovering how scientists, mathematicians, and historians write and speak. We need to help our students with questions like "How do I write a report for my earth science class?" or "How do I understand the language of story problems in mathematics?"

Your classroom should be a place where students openly discuss issues of language diversity, including the study of dialect issues and what counts as "correctness" in different social contexts. They need to value the language of home and neighborhood at the same time they master the conventions needed to succeed in a wider sphere. Of course the study of grammar and usage should be integrated into every aspect of your English language arts curriculum, from reading and viewing to writing, oral language, and listening. We know from research and from our own common sense as teachers that teaching isolated rules from grammar textbooks or making copious editorial marks on student papers rarely results in better or more "correct" language. Issues of grammar and usage should emerge naturally at the point of use, when students are most ready to learn about them and incorporate them into their daily language activities. Finally, and most importantly, your middle school students will embrace language study most willingly if you set aside some time in your teaching for language play. Language games and activities go a long way in teaching students how to exploit the fun as well as the power of language in their daily lives.

Language study is much more than imparting rules of correctness. English is a living language. Words change. Rules change. Yes, it is the study of correctness, but it is the study of correctness in context. You might say it is the study of appropriateness. It's also the study of language play. It is the study of the history of language. It is the study of language in use. It encompasses the critical study of the language of power and the social and political consequences of language use. In other words, language study is the study of words and how they circulate, live, change, and die. In this chapter we want to shift the lens of language study from the texts (whether they be oral or written) to learners and contexts.

Throughout this chapter, think about the lens of reading and viewing, the lens of writing, and the lens of oral language. Consider how language study can be contextualized and integrated into meaningful literacy lessons. We begin by reflecting on what is unique about approaching the study of language with early adolescents. Think about these questions as you consider how you might incorporate language study into your own classroom.

Considerations for Teaching Language Study with Middle School Students

- **Middle school students need positive social interactions with peers and adults.**
  - How might we tap the expertise of community members to foster an appreciation of diverse language use in our students?
  - How do we support students moving among multiple contexts and communities?
- **Middle school students need physical activities to expand their language use.**
  - In what ways are art, movement, games, and sports connected to language use?
  - How might performance support language study?
- **Middle school students need opportunities for self-definition, creative expression, and a sense of competence and achievement in their language experiences.**
  - How can we create opportunities to practice new competencies without the threat of correction?
  - How might we tap the creative expression and language competence that middle school students bring to the classroom?
- **Middle school students need language opportunities that promote meaningful participation in families, school, and the larger world.**
  - How can language study promote students' effective involvement in social and political activities in their communities?

DISCOURSE COMMUNITIES AND COMMUNICATIVE COMPETENCE

> An integrated approach to language study focuses on the contexts and communicative competence demanded by them. The goal of language study is to help students move adeptly among multiple communities of readers, writers, speakers, viewers, and listeners.

Sociolinguist James Paul Gee (1990) argues that to appreciate language in its social context, we need to focus not on language but rather on what he calls *discourses*. He writes, "A Discourse is a sort of 'identity kit,' which comes complete with the appropriate costume, and instructions of how to act, talk, and often write, so as to take on a particular social role that others will recognize" (p. 142). He notes that another way to think about discourses is to approach them as "clubs with (tacit) rules about who is a member and who is not and (tacit) rules about how members ought to behave (if they want to continue being accepted as members)" (p. 143).

Students learn how to interact in multiple discourse communities. Different groups have different ways of talking, thinking, acting, and even dressing. A child who grows up in a "soccer family," for example, learns the rules of the game in terms far beyond the playing field. She learns how to talk, think, act, and dress soccer, and she learns what linguists call "code switching" when she prepares for other memberships. She knows how to talk, think, act, and dress soccer and can easily shift to talk, think, act, and dress church choir. Because social practices valued in one discourse community may not be valued in another, students learn to switch codes across different contexts. A student who is a member of Honors Choir is expected to dress, talk, and even walk across the stage in a particular manner. That same student may need to change "costumes" and "scripts" when he prepares for a poetry slam or performs in his basement band. Most middle school students know how to talk, think, act, and dress school. It is easy to identify those students who, for any number of reasons, do not. Our job as literacy teacher is to help students move effectively into different contexts.

In much the same way, students in different disciplines need to learn the rules of multiple communities, discovering how scientists talk about experiments or how artists critique a painting, for instance. Learning to participate in each of these communities requires that students learn certain social practices valued in these different communities. In looking through the lens of language study, you might ask yourself, "What are the multiple contexts or 'discourse communities' in which members of my middle school classroom and their families live and work?"

Anthropologist Dell Hymes (1972) defines *communicative competence* as "what it is a member of society knows in knowing how to participate" (p. 66). Hymes (1996)

> In looking through the lens of language study, you might ask, "What do students need to do and know in order to participate fully in a particular context?"

notes that the term *competence* "should not be a synonym for ideal grammatical knowledge" (p. 58) but should be understood in terms of actual communities and the consequences for persons in that community. Our judgments of middle school students' competence with language in use must be expanded beyond issues of grammar. Both oral and written communicative competence should include attention to intentions and expectations within a context.

Examine your own discourse communities in Your Fieldwork Journal 10–1.

A Focus on Language Study

Your Fieldwork Journal 10-1

A Little Detective Work Into Your Discourse Communities

For this activity, we ask you to explore a couple of your own discourse communities. First, select two settings: (1) an informal setting where you are with a group of close friends or family, and (2) one in which you are in a formal learning setting such as a university classroom or a professional organization. If possible, bring in a tape recorder and tape the talk in each setting. If not, make some quick notes about the language you used in each setting. Try to capture both verbal and nonverbal practices in which each community engages. Now for the detective work: What is it that a member of this group must know in order to participate?

If you were able to tape record the talk, listen to the first tape and try to make explicit at least three "rules" that someone must follow in order to indicate that he or she is a fully functioning member of this "club." Your rules can include verbal and nonverbal actions. You might list such things as

"Address members by humorous nicknames."
"Raise your hand and wait to be called on before speaking."
"End your conversational turn taking by calling on the next speaker by name."

Now do the same thing with the second tape. When you're finished, try to create at least three language rules that are exactly the same for both contexts. Record these rules in a Venn diagram like the one that follows.

Language Rules in Context

Context:
Informal Context Rules
1.
2.
3.

Context:
Formal Context Rules
1.
2.
3.

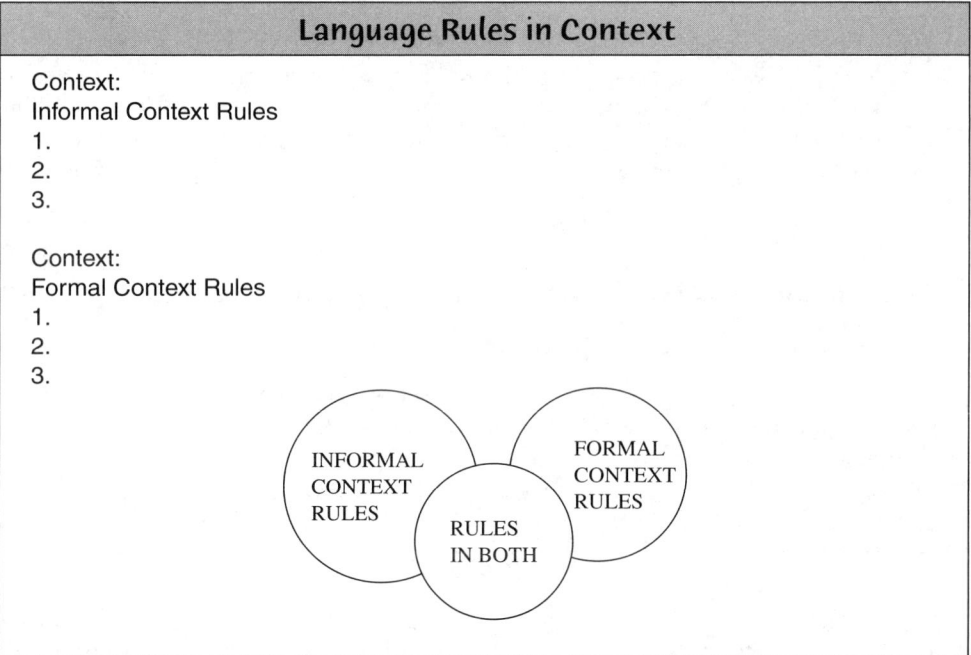

Now, listen to the tape or consult your notes again and think about any language infractions that mark someone as an outsider to this "club." What infractions might mark someone as less than a fully functioning member of this group? If someone were to break the rules, what might the members do to "school" this individual in more appropriate ways with words? Write these infractions in the area surrounding each side of the Venn diagram.

Keep in mind what you learned from this exercise as you think through the ways in which you can create a language-rich classroom for your students. Ask yourself, "What are the multiple contexts or discourse communities in which members of my middle school classroom and their families live and work? What do students need to do/know in order to participate in a particular context, and how can I help them in my classroom to do this?"

HELPING STUDENTS UNDERSTAND THEIR DISCOURSE COMMUNITIES

Heath (1983) notes that children learn language through the process of socialization in their neighborhoods, communities, and schools. The idea that there is one "correct" English denies our own practices as we talk on the telephone to our best friends, our professors, our families, or telemarketers. In both fostering and monitoring language study in your middle school classroom, you might begin by asking your students to help you to examine the demands and expectations of particular contexts in which they live, learn, and play. A simple way to help students to understand the role of language as a social practice is to ask them to list the different language groups to which they belong. This is also a good way to get to know your students. In Literacy Lesson 10–1, Mrs. Harmon asks her students to explore their multiple communities. When Mrs. Harmon asked her students to do this at the beginning of their sixth-grade year, she wasn't surprised to find that many of her students were fluent speakers of many languages.

Literacy Lesson 10-1

French Cooking and Multiple Memberships

I begin with an official language; that's easy. And they are usually amazed at the many languages spoken by their peers. And then I want to lead them to a more complex understanding of the ways we talk. I start with myself. I brainstorm with them to deepen their understanding of language in use. I tease them with the ways in which I can talk like an English teacher, but that is not the only way I know how to talk. I talk differently to my family and friends, to telemarketers, and to Mr. Wilkens, the principal.

I like to bring in a phone and talk into it and ask students to tell me who they think I am talking to and what evidence they have to support their views. They can quickly see that it is word choice, body language (even over the phone), tone, and inflections that give clues as to who I am talking to and what my relationship is with that person. For example, I pretend to talk to my grandbaby. Then we talk about the "rules" for motherese. Students will often ask to try out a particular way of talking to challenge their classmates. They are actually quite savvy and quite aware of particular sets of language rules.

Next, on the blackboard, I begin with my own personal list of memberships in language groups. I write something like: *school English, Spanish, French cooking, the language of bridge playing.* When I wrote "French cooking," one of my students interrupted, "Mrs. Harmon, I didn't know you spoke French."

"Well, I don't speak French," I replied, "I speak French cooking. I understand and use the language of French cookbooks." I then gave her some examples: "*Chiffonnade* means vegetables cut into ribbons or shreds, *aromates* means herbs and spices, and *à la Broche* means to cook on a skewer over a flame. I need to know how to use these words so I can cook and follow recipes." I told her that she probably spoke a little French cooking too. I asked, "Do you know what *à la mode* means?"

She said, "Yeah, it means you want ice cream on top."

"See, you do speak French cooking."

This is how I start the class thinking about the different rules we use when we talk or write. I begin where they are experts. I ask them to list their memberships and list three words they must know to be a member. Because I start by talking about my grandbaby and my hobbies, I think they can see and hear that it isn't only official clubs that influence the ways people talk. This too eases any sense that I think talking like an English teacher is the only right way to talk.

Language study in the middle school classroom should consist of fostering students' language purposefully, critically, and creatively. Just as Anna exclaimed, "I never thought about words before!" middle school students need opportunities to think about words and structures of the language they use in written and oral texts. They need to make intentional decisions and employ strategies to engage, persuade, and interact with others. They also need chances to critically examine texts and the social contexts in which they were produced. Equally important, they need to understand the social nature of texts, examining the rules in terms of who uses them and for what purposes. Middle school students need opportunities to play with language, to engage creatively with the rhythms, repetitions, cadences, humor, and beauty in language.

One question you may want to hold on to as you progress through this chapter is "How does language study support reading, viewing, oral language, and writing?" By itself, language study can be interesting, motivating, and engaging. Most students will probably enjoy researching how and for what purposes words come into being. For example, they might study the arrival of the computer and how it transformed our language—that is, how "computerese" has slipped into our everyday language. Similarly, dialect journals, designed to capture language in use in multiple contexts, may be a fun way for middle school students to keep track of how context shapes meaning.

Middle school teachers can help students understand the differences demanded in formal and informal contexts by asking them to create dramatic scripts or role plays in which they act out how their language changes in different settings or with

Focus On
Oral Language

different people. One teacher asked her fifth graders to work in groups and create a short skit in which they were to explain something to three different individuals. She gave them several open-ended prompts from which to choose such as, "You borrowed your sibling's jacket without permission and tore it while performing a spectacular acrobatic feat on your bike. Now, confess this to your sibling, your best friend, and your parent." When designing oral language activities, give students a free reign to take the lead in creating situations that best match their experiences and needs.

> Note the ways in which the study of language can integrate the multiple language arts. Here we see how looking through the lens of language study can expand students' understanding of oral and written texts.

It's also important to share with students the ways in which oral and written texts shape meanings differently. They might, for example, compare the language of essays with those of extemporaneous and formal public speeches on the same or similar topics. Or, closer to home, they might compare how you talk to a friend, e-mail that same friend, and write a schoolwide invitation that all students and parents will receive.

STANDARDIZATION AND "POWERFUL" LANGUAGE

Just as we can explore the social dimensions of language with students, we should also look at its political dimensions. Such a study may seem pretty risky at first glance. After all, we're English language arts teachers, not politicians. Clearly, though, a study of language is a study of politics, and it's important not to deny it. As Edelsky (1992) so eloquently argues,

> Many people, especially in the United States, think of politics only as dirty and "backroom stuff." As a result, we regard it as not polite to engage in controversial arguments or politics; we don't want to politicize.... The schools, because they are public schools, supposedly do not advocate any particular position. But we ignore the fact that embedded in every textbook, every basal reader, and every classroom discussion is a political perspective. (p. 325)

Studying language is a political act. Christensen (2002) notes,

> Asking students to memorize the rules without asking who makes the rules, who enforces the rules, who benefits from the rules, who loses from the rules, who uses the rules to keep some in and others out, legitimates a social system that devalues my students' knowledge and language. (p. 176)

A wide variety of activities can help middle school students learn about how language varies and changes in different regions, across different cultural groups, and across different time periods. Equally important, students can teach you and their peers about the multiple ways they adapt their language for work and play.

Middle school teachers may find themselves torn between honoring the language of the home and helping students to acquire "standard" English or what we call "edited English" in this book. Delpit (2002), a leading scholar on teaching and learning language in settings of cultural diversity, addresses this dilemma and notes that teachers must understand that language

> ... is intimately connected with loved ones, community and personal identity. To suggest that this form is "wrong" or, even worse, ignorant is to suggest that something is

wrong with the student and his or her family. To denigrate your language is, then, in African-American terms, to "talk about your mama." Anyone who knows anything about African-American culture knows the consequences of that speech act! (p. 125)

On the other hand, Delpit goes on to say that to deny students access to a politically powerful dialect denies these students access to succeed economically. So the answer to a middle school teacher's question about which approach to take with language is quite simple: Do both. But how?

Before we go further, we need to address briefly what "standard" we are talking about. The very label *standard* indicates that some students in our classrooms are below standard. Those students who do not come with the social and cultural background that gives them access to one particular way with writing or talking are often viewed as deficient in classrooms. For that reason, many scholars refuse to call one particular code "standard." Instead, they choose terms like "edited American English," "cash code," or "power code." Beyond our own classrooms, we know our students will be judged according to some version of "standard" language use, and our language study can address the politics of such definitions.

To understand how social context affects language, middle school students can monitor their own language use. Explicit attention to language variations of all kinds can help middle school students learn to make appropriate language choices for a wide array of settings, including home, school, and workplaces. Middle school students are not too young to understand the politics of language choices. In fact, they are keenly aware of the power of language to mark them as insiders or outsiders, of who controls and enforces the rules, and who benefits from them.

Gee's (1990) notion of discourse communities is not beyond the abilities of middle school students. During middle school, friendship networks often flourish around literacy activities that come with a need to create new language variations. For example, when Margaret was visiting a middle school, one group of sixth-grade boys spent their leisure-time activities creating monster magazines and using electronic publishing on the Web to showcase their new creations. For whatever reasons, new vocabulary sprang up around these activities. A "Mo-Mo," for instance, was someone within the group who had created his own monster. And a "MO-Te" was a writer who used other writers' monsters in his writing. Likewise, many students in this middle school classroom begin to create words around their interests—music, fashion, and technology—to name a few. When adults or other outsiders attempt to co-opt their language, early adolescents usually poke fun at these feeble attempts to enter their discourse community. This is because, in the life of the average middle school student, there are many "languages of power." It's useful for us to keep our perspective as we teach about "standard language." Remember that talking like an English teacher would make many of our students seem "deficient" in their elaborate social networks of peers.

Guiding Practice With Varieties of English

Middle school students can learn the rules of standard English when they understand the multiple rule systems in operation. But what exactly might this look like?

Margaret guided one of her student teachers, Rhonda, in a study to examine the ways in which adolescent boys and girls were characterized in popular teen magazines.

Rhonda began by asking her seventh-grade students to look at copies of popular magazines targeted for boys *(Sports Illustrated)* and girls *(Seventeen)*. They examined the cover art, table of contents, advertisements, and articles. Students began collecting snippets of language that seemed to characterize the ways in which the magazine publishers constructed what it meant to be a boy or a girl through their language use. It wasn't hard for the seventh graders to begin to identify some concerns. Why weren't girls encouraged to be strong and powerful? Why were there so many boys in the girls' magazines but not any girls in the boys' magazines? Why did the boys have highly technical language about playing a game, but the language for the girls was all about romance and beauty? How would such articles sound if they didn't follow these perceived rules? Rhonda's students enjoyed making magazine pages for boys and girls that seemed to "break the rules." This activity made two things about language visible to her students: (1) how rule systems work, and (2) how social practices enable and constrain the ways we think people should be.

Focus On Oral Language

Similarly, Mr. Williams wanted his students to investigate language use. Rather than rely only on textual worlds, he designed an inquiry into the lived worlds of his students. Mr. Williams found that his students often were quite savvy about the ways in which they needed to move among multiple discourse communities. But he also found that they did so without explicit attention to these necessary moves. He often found them ridiculing a friend for what they perceived to be acting, talking, or dressing in inappropriate ways. He didn't like it when he'd overhear his students making fun of the way someone talked, and he was even more upset when he heard the word "poser" often used among friends to describe peers who appeared to sell themselves out and make moves that were not "true" to their character.

Focus On Oral Language

To attempt to disrupt the notion that there is only one "correct" or "true" way to talk and be in the world, Mr. Williams asked his students to select an individual from the sporting or entertainment world and to collect the ways that they talked in different settings. As an example, he brought in video clips of one of his favorite singers performing on *Sesame Street* and *Saturday Night Live* and at a concert. He also brought video clips of a professional football player talking about winning a big game and then on a public service announcement asking parents to read with their children. He directed students in a whole class inquiry in which they watched the news as it was delivered on different stations. Together they teased out the rules for appropriate language use that include words, actions, and dress. He also asked students to articulate the ways in which teenagers should talk among their friends. They then designed skits to teach alien adolescents how to get it right in different group-selected settings such as in the classroom, in the cafeteria, on the playing field, and even with probation officers or in the courtroom. In an attempt to help students understand the necessary shifts that all effective language users make and to make the politics of language choices central to his middle school curriculum, Mr. Williams designed many language study activities, such as the "word detectives" exercise described in the opening case study, as a way of helping his students examine their own language use. Here are some suggestions for activities and projects to help students to (a) understand how and why the English language varies and changes, (b) learn English appropriate for many settings, and (c) analyze how social context affects language use.

> Language study can help students understand the social and political nature of language in use. Teachers are often more comfortable creating activities with a focus on language variations in oral texts than in written texts. Can you think of reasons this might be so?

Language Histories. In addition to studying language in textual and real worlds, middle school students can investigate the ways in which language changes over time. This can be done in a variety of ways. One way Ms. Evans found was to ask her sixth graders to interview family members who were at least 20 years older than they. Their task was to investigate the ways in which "teenage talk" has shifted over time. Students interviewed grandparents, aunts, uncles, and parents. They asked questions about how they talked about friends, about music, about parents. The students then prepared an oral presentation in which some dressed in their parents' clothes, some played music, and all were amused with the silly ways their elders spoke. As a reflection on the experience, Ms. Evans asked them to collaborate on a time capsule about the language of the teenager today and to predict what might amuse their grandchildren. As a means to integrate language study with reading and viewing, students can investigate the ways in which characters in books, films, and other media speak, teasing out the implicit rules and examining the historical settings.

Word Detective Inquiries. Word detective inquiries can be drawn from old television programs or books. Students can look for the ways that words, phrases, and even sentence patterns shift over time, geographic region, or cultural groups. Students can create and mail out surveys to investigate the study of language in use across regions. Middle school students might create translation dictionaries based on technical language, generational language, or peer group language. These dictionaries can be created individually or in small groups. They can be the result of interviews, Internet searches, or text-based research.

Language Locks. Students can create codebooks to record secret friendship codes. They can select a hobby or profession and look at highly specialized language that is accessible only to those few who have the technical expertise, social competence, and/or language "keys" to unlock the codes. The Internet is a helpful source for students to investigate language locks, as are instant messaging, e-mails, and their own experiences to use language to "lock" some out.

Biased Communication Investigations. Even at the middle school level, students can look for bias in language. A comfortable place to begin is with sports reporting. They can look at newspapers or listen to television news and record the ways in which some teams are given priority treatment over others. But don't underestimate your students. They can study bias in language in other arenas as well. For example, they can examine how their neighborhoods are characterized in the media. When Margaret worked at an alternative middle school, she asked the students to examine the ways in which adolescents appeared in the local newspaper. Fifteen-year-old Angel noted that her peer group was written about differently than the athletes. "They make it look like we are all in trouble or on welfare or something like that. They try to make it look like we are all wards of the court. That's BS." Understanding the language bias in the local newspaper, Angel set out to right the characterizations of students like her. She wrote an editorial to the newspaper that began, "We the students of TLC would like to speak out on our own behalf and rights. We are not all troubled kids or wards of the welfare system."

PLAYING WITH LANGUAGE

Be sure to make space for language play in your classroom. Poetry, word games, rhymes, puns, and riddles can make language visible to students in creative and fun ways. Such activities work like finger exercises on a piano, helping students to gain control over their language. Working with homonyms, for example, students can play with understandings and twist meanings for the pleasure of their peers. Mrs. Vingant's fifth-grade students each selected a set of homonyms and created very short "poems" such as "I'll visit you on the Isle of Capri if you walk down the aisle with me." They also began to understand how poetry could work on multiple levels by looking for and then creating "hidden meanings" in poems. One girl came up to Mrs. Vingant excited with this secret message in the poem she had just composed:

> Craig is some boy
> He stole her heart
> And then your hand
> Kept in golden pens

She asked, "Do you get it? Can you see my secret meaning?"

To which Mrs. V. replied after studying the short poem, "Is it that golden means more than just the color?"

"No. No. Read it across." After a few attempts, she read diagonally, beginning with "Craig," and the secret revealed itself: "Craig stole your pens." She then asked Craig to return the missing pen set.

Getting the Knack, by Stafford and Dunning, has many accessible poetry exercises that allow students to play with language. Another rich source is *The Weighty Word Book* (Levitt, Guralnick, & Stevens, 1999), which offers one-page stories that playfully illustrate difficult vocabulary words. One, for example, tells the story of two sisters who always go everywhere together until one of the sisters, Kate, decides she will take a trip without her sister so friends will have to say a separate bye for Kate, illustrating the word, "bifurcate." Margaret's seventh-grade students always groaned when she read one of these stories aloud, but they used this book in two ways. They turned the stories into short scripts to perform, and they also created their own "weighty word" stories, illustrating the meaning of a challenging word through drawing and writing.

Middle school students may connect with language through visual, dramatic, or kinesthetic ways of playing with words. They might illustrate adjectives making them look, feel, or even smell like what they are. They might create short scripts. They could illustrate the literal meanings of euphemisms or colloquialisms. One teacher even brought in large cookies and had students write on them with frosting tubes so they could "eat their words." The Internet offers great sources for playing with words. Students can examine and/or create Web sites in which playful language is employed for multiple use: to amuse and entertain, to include and exclude, or to attend to particular groups, for example.

LANGUAGE STUDY ACROSS THE CURRICULUM

History, mathematics, and science all have a language. The specialized languages of subject matter and professions are a rich source for inquiry. Especially as they move into the upper grades, middle school students need explicit attention to content-specific languages. Specialized vocabularies and language uses can be taught across disciplinary boundaries with the other middle school teachers on the team. It might be a rich opportunity for the guidance counselor, parents, and community members to share their specialized language competencies. Students may interview or invite guest speakers from professions that they are considering for their future. Such activities can be informal and ongoing or culminate in activities like career fairs. In Ms. Robinson's sixth-grade class, for example, students created storyboards and career dictionaries about their chosen professions. They each wrote a short script and enlisted one or two classmates to help them demonstrate the ways in which dentists, mathematicians, electricians, and other professionals might talk. Below is a snippet of Sally's. Can you guess her chosen profession?

> The study of language is the study of language in context. Can you think of additional activities that allow students to attend to the communicative intentions and expectations in contexts that are important for them?

Sally: The galleys are late.
C'Koh: Well, have you seen the copy?
Sally: I have to have them proofed within 48 hours. We need the galley proofs right away.

Language Diversity and Grammar Instruction

Teaching grammar should still be a central part of any literacy program. But as we have said throughout this chapter, grammar should not be reduced to isolated drills. How might this approach to grammar instruction work? Clearly, standard written English is not identical to standard oral English. Grammar may be paired with writing, reading, or oral language. Differences in oral and written standard should not be ignored in the teaching of grammar. Likewise, rather than a rigid adherence to traditional drills, teachers can design mini-lessons according to the needs of the students they are teaching. Mini-lessons can include data sets in which students work to tease out the rules beneath the patterns. Mini-lessons might focus on a published story in which students look at the ways in which the author selected language to situate a story in a particular region or period of history.

    The study of language through literature or film can expose students to language in use in a particular context, helping them to acquire words, phrases, and language structures. Delpit (2002) suggests that role play and drama to practice standard English are viable alternatives because they remove the threat and embarrassment of correction. Videotape or audiotape conversations allow students the opportunities to listen to language in use. This is a useful means to help students learn to monitor their own language use. Read-alouds by the teacher are another viable means to support language learning. Reading to your middle school students is especially beneficial to second language learners who may benefit from hearing language in use.

TABLE 10-1 Teaching Grammar in Context

Less Attention	More Attention
• The use of terminology • Memorization of definitions • Analysis of sentences • Usage exercises	• Inquiry • Effective grammatical structures in reading • Production of effective sentences • Discussion and investigation of questions of usage • Exploration of the power of dialects through literature and film • Consideration of different effects that differing dialects have in different circumstances

Source: Adapted from *Teaching Grammar in Context* by C. Weaver, 1996, New Jersey: Boynton/Cook.

Teaching Grammar and Usage in the Middle School

Much of a middle school language arts curriculum may be devoted to the teaching of grammar. As noted previously, a focus on grammar is not a focus on a singular rule system. Weaver (1996) documents an overwhelming body of research demonstrating that the teaching of grammar in isolation does little to improve reading, writing, or even standardized test scores. In *Teaching Grammar in Context,* Weaver provides a wealth of resources, examples, and strategies to help teachers use grammar to support the language arts. In teaching grammar, Weaver recommends that teachers shift the focus of their instruction from labeling to the function of the language. Table 10–1 may be useful as we think about designing language study for our middle school students.

Second Language Learners

It's likely that your middle school classroom will include a diverse student population. There will be students whose home language is not English. Unfortunately, many middle schools do not have an ESL teacher to help you design and guide language development for your students. It's important to understand theory and research of second language acquisition so you don't base your program on myths that commonly circulate about students. Likewise, it's important to understand that learning standard English varies from individual learner to individual learner within and across cultural groups. Samway and McKeon (2002) list some features of second language acquisition, which might help you think about the ways you can support your middle school students.

- Language learning involves hypothesis testing. Errors are integral to language learning.
- Understanding language usually precedes language production. A "silent period" is normal.
- Mastering academic language may take second language learners up to 7 years.
- Second language acquisition and academic success are influenced by (a) personality, (b) cultural affiliation, (c) prior schooling, and (d) teacher expectations. (p. 63)

A language-rich classroom will be a key to success. Even if a second language learner doesn't appear to be participating, remember that silence is part of the normal developmental sequence. The teacher and peers are often a great source of English for second language learners. Setting up meaningful interactions is a key means to support language development for all students, especially for second language learners. Just remember that participation doesn't mean the student must speak. Through listening, the student can begin to formulate hypotheses about language patterns. Small-group interactions with peers may provide a more comfortable setting for students. While selecting materials that are accessible, keep in mind that materials should seem age appropriate for your students. Invite students to share their experiences and teach their peers so they feel that they are a part of your classroom. Making lists and using art, charts, drawings, and other graphic organizers are ways to help students build vocabulary and learn the language system.

> As you think about setting up small-group interactions, attempt to design the tasks so that each student can be a valued contributor. Think about nonlinguistic means by which you may tap the expertise of your second language learners.

Weddel and Van Duzer (1997) suggest that beginning-level students can write in both English and their native language if need be. As students become more competent in English, the teacher can enlist them to assess their language needs by asking them questions such as "Where do you use English?", "For what purpose do you want to use English?", and "What language skills are you interested in developing?" Most important, understand that language learning doesn't take place in isolation. Language learning is social. To support all language learners in your classroom, find out as much as you can about your second language learners. That means reading research, talking with support personnel such as ESL teachers, and, most important, talking with your students and their families. Tap the resources that students bring to your classroom. Create a language-rich classroom. Provide nonlinguistic support such as artwork, drama, and role play, and focus on meaningful interactions with important others.

MONITORING LANGUAGE DEVELOPMENT

It's important for middle school teachers to understand that sometimes an "error" in a student's work is actually a developmental leap or experimentation with something that is just beyond the student's reach, something over which the student does not yet have control. When Margaret taught a group of seventh graders how to use apostrophes to show ownership, for instance, she noticed that apostrophes began appearing after almost any *s* that ended a word. Similarly, second language learners often gain an understanding of correct patterns and then apply it to words that are exceptions to the rules. If they have not heard particular words in use, they may apply a language principle incorrectly. For example, they may correctly apply rules of how to form past tense by adding *-ed* to a word such as "go" which becomes "goed" rather than "went." According to Samway and McKeon (2002), these errors for second language learners "are an integral part of the second language learning process, helping learners to refine and revise their understanding of how the second language works" (p. 63). But for all your middle school students, they may be making great leaps in language use that may look to you like errors. Errors can be signs of growth.

> Teachers need to be sensitive about correcting students' errors in oral and written texts. Correcting students in front of their peers may send the message that something is wrong with these students and with their families. What are some ways to show genuine respect for the rich language variations that students bring to your classroom while expanding their abilities to move among multiple discourse communities?

> Errors might indicate carelessness or leaps in learning. They might indicate you are not a member of the community for which the student is writing or speaking. How might you find out the reasons for the error?

Shaughnessy (1979) suggests that in addition to noting the errors a student makes, teachers need to understand the reason for the error. Middle school teachers often notice particular usage errors that appear throughout an individual student's work or with an entire group of students. This becomes an opportunity to teach those particular skills. Middle school teachers can teach a mini-lesson to the entire class or to those students identified as needing support with this particular skill. Focusing on the students' text is a good starting place as long as students are not put in embarrassing situations in front of their peers.

Skills to Remember

Students can keep track of their individual skills work in a skills-building section of their Writer's Notebook. The purpose is to help middle school students understand their own errors and take responsibility for them. After you have taught a mini-lesson on a particular skill or set of skills, ask those students involved to record comments in their "skills to remember" section of their notebooks. You may also circle error patterns you notice in a student's work and hold a conference with that individual to discuss the error. As students become more familiar with grammar and usage rules, they may be able to identify error patterns with partners. You may mark student-written work by placing a checkmark in the line where an error has occurred and ask them to find and correct the error. Figure 10–1 is an example of one teacher's guidelines to her students, designed to help them learn to monitor their language use and development.

If you note in reading a draft that a particular error appears again and again, you might circle the error. You can create a shorthand such as checkmarks and circles that let students know they need to correct errors and gain knowledge of the

FIGURE 10-1 Goals and Growth Record

A Special Section of Your Writer's Notebook—"Skills to Remember"

It's important for you to understand the common spelling mistakes, punctuation conventions, and usage errors that you make. I would like you to take charge of your language learning this semester. In your Writer's Notebook, create a section called **"Skills to Remember."** Each time you hand in written work, I will make an *X* in the margin next to any errors I find. If I notice that you are making the same mistake over and over again, I will circle the *X*. It is your job to (a) discover what this error might be, and (b) find a trick or gimmick to help you remember the correct form. Sometimes we will be working on these together with all of your classmates. Sometimes I can meet with you individually. You can also ask someone in your writing group to help you if you can't find the error. And you can always look in your English book or in some of our classroom resources, specifically a few grammar and usage handbooks in our writing corner. This section of your notebook should be continually expanded as you progress through the semester and beyond.

rules behind the errors. A circle on their paper, for example, can be an indication to students that they need to go to their "Skills to Remember" section and record the skills they are addressing.

Literacy Lesson 10–2 offers an example of a "Grammar Derby" implemented by a new teacher to engage her students.

Literacy Lesson 10-2

Grammar Derby

As a first-year teacher, Janet Hart inherited an eighth-grade curriculum that caused her great discomfort. All of her students had been required to purchase three disposable workbooks, one each for grammar, vocabulary, and spelling. The second 9-week curriculum guide addressed grammar and usage. She didn't want to assign worksheets every day, but there was an expectation that students should use their workbooks. Writing was to come in the fourth 9 weeks. She wanted to teach grammar and usage in context. She wanted to engage the students, and she guessed from her own middle school experience that the isolated skills-driven approach would not pique their interest. She also felt that as a beginning teacher, she didn't want to stray too far from the curriculum. So she decided to weave in some things that she thought would be of interest to middle school students: television, music, and the world around them. She designed a game that she called Grammar Derby. She asked her students to find rule violations in their daily interactions. Her purposes were to help them integrate them into their speech and writing and to understand that context and expectations made a difference as to how rule violations were received. The game sheet looked like this:

Grammar Derby

(Points: Adults, 5 points; children under 12, 1 point; characters on TV, 3; song lyrics, 3; in print, 5)

Usage Rule	Violation	Who Said It	Where Said	Points	Total Points
Subject-verb agreement	You don't love me.	Singer	Radio	3	3
Double negatives	You don't love me no more.	Singer	Radio	3	6

As you might guess, students were highly motivated. Some came with two or three sheets filled in a night. It was working just great, she thought. She was planning some discussion prompts to help her students understand the complexities of language in use one morning at 7:30 when Mr. Bilke stormed into her classroom. Mr. Bilke was the eighth-grade math teacher on her team. Without a greeting, he interrupted, "What's this grammar derby stuff you got the kids doing?"

Janet was caught off guard and began, "I asked my students to listen for errors and then . . ."

"Well it's interfering with my class. I said something about something and about half the class took out some sheet of paper and they all started writing something down. They said I said something like, 'can't not.' And they were smirking and laughing. I'm sure I didn't say it. But it was disrespectful. And I want it stopped."

Janet apologized and tried to explain that she wanted her students to understand that everybody doesn't follow the rules all the time. She was still trying to explain when Mr. Bilke turned away and walked out of her room. "I want it stopped," he repeated.

In striving to make connections to real-world applications, Janet hadn't thought through how her activity might actually put students, parents, or teachers in disrespectful or embarrassing situations. She learned an important lesson about language. She knew that she would need to explain to her students how language use is connected to issues of power and status. And she knew she wouldn't use Mr. Bilke as an example. She also knew she would change the game and ask students to seek examples only in print, audio, and video forms. She knew she had embarrassed her teaching colleague and that she still had a lot of learning to do.

Your Fieldwork Journal 10–2 offers an exercise to explore your philosophy of teaching language study.

Your Fieldwork Journal 10-2

A Letter Home

As a middle school teacher, you will need to communicate to parents, colleagues, students, or community members your views about language study, specifically in terms of language variations. Some parents may express concern if their son's or daughter's paper comes home without errors corrected. Some parents bring a set of assumptions about what and how you should teach language study and may believe that language study is only the grammar and usage worksheets they experienced in their junior high English classroom. If parents do not know why you are doing what you are doing, some parents may feel that your activities are designed to disrespect their home.

Your task is to write a letter to parents to explain your philosophy. Before you can do that, you will want to articulate for yourself what will count as language study in your classroom. Working with a partner or small group, think about the ways in which you might design learning experiences for your middle school students to address some or all of the goals listed on the following chart:

A Focus on Language Study

Designing Language Experiences			
To analyze how social context affects language use	To learn English appropriate for many settings, including workplaces	To monitor their own language use	To understand how and why the English language varies and changes

Using some of the goals and concrete strategies from the completed chart, write a brief letter home, explaining some of the things their middle school students will be doing this year in your classroom and reasons for such activities.

When you have completed your letter, discuss some other ways to reach parents and community members to explain your approach to language study. Also share your ideas about how you might tap the expertise of families and community members to enhance and support the kind of language-rich classroom you might envision.

Goals and Growth Records

Monitoring students' language development is no easy task. One way is to ask students to set goals and assess their own progress. This will take some modeling and practice, but it will help students learn to monitor their own development and take further responsibility for their own learning. Periodically ask students to set two or three language goals. Then regularly ask them to record their progress. Below is an example of a student's progress report from Mr. Martin's sixth-grade classroom.

> Hey Mr. M,
>
> I had three goals. 1 bring my pencil to class. 2 write sentences 3 write its and it's right. how I am doing so far. I usully brang my pencil. thats good. I write sentences. I use a period and a question mark. I am good. I don't use its so no problem. next time you told me to make some more goals so I am.
>
> Your favorte student
>
> William S. Walters

Mr. Martin met with William, who brought his progress letter and growth record to his language conference. During their meeting together, Mr. Martin helped William to create appropriate and reachable language goals. When he met individually with students during their language conference, Mr. Martin wanted students to begin taking the responsibility of keeping their own written records of the goals they negotiated.

> Students can learn to write language goals that integrate with reading, writing, viewing, and speaking. They can learn to address social and political aspects of language as they examine and experiment with their own language choices. But to do so, they will need guidance and support to move beyond the kind of goals that William sets for himself at the beginning of the year.

FIGURE 10-2 Goals and Growth Record

Student's Name _____
Grading Period _____

Date	Goals Set	Conference Date Scheduled	Progress and Plans	Teacher and Student Agreed
Sept. 4	• Bring writing materials • Use end marks • Use *its* and *it's* correctly	Oct. 4 set	• Good job with pens • Periods and question marks are coming • Not so important	MJM + WSW 10/04
Oct. 5	• Use end marks • Use capital letters to start a sentence • Share in small group			

Although Mr. Martin has more than 150 students, he also keeps a record so he can guide student development and monitor progress. He keeps six 3-inch black notebooks behind his desk, one notebook for each of six class periods. When he meets with William or other sixth graders, he too records the goals and progress during the conference. All of this record keeping is done at the time of the 3- to 5-minute conference. Although he would like to take more time, as a veteran teacher, Mr. Martin knows that managing the paper load is vital to his success, so he has created a shorthand way of keeping track and has turned over some of the responsibility to his sixth graders. Figure 10–2 offers an example of the goals and growth records that he and his students keep together.

Portfolios

As noted in Chapter 5, portfolios are another effective means to monitor growth over time. Students can include writing samples, audiotapes, self-assessments, and conference notes in their portfolio. These student records and reflections on their language use can be useful to help the teacher monitor their progress.

Error Analysis

Another activity that can help students to discover and monitor their usage patterns and problems in context is through explicit error analysis. Since we all make mistakes, this can be done without embarrassment if handled well and if designed with

A Focus on Language Study

FIGURE 10-3 Discovering Your Usage Patterns and Problems

Error Analysis
The point of this exercise is not to achieve perfection, but to become more acutely aware of your own personal set of usage errors. Each time you have someone proofread a piece of writing, make note of your problems in a double-entry journal. If you aren't sure what the problem is, consult a friend, a handbook, or me. List each problem under these categories along the left side of a double-entry journal.

"Clever Reminders"
Now, on the right side of your double-entry journal, beside each error, create a "clever reminder" (acronym, catchy saying, or other bit of verbal gymnastics) to jog your memory whenever you encounter each of your problems in the future.

Example of Double-Entry Journal

Problem	Reminder
Write an explanation of a problem you have been having	Create a gimmick, trick, or rule to help you remember the correct way.
(Example of student record keeping) I get mixed up with *they're, there,* and *their*.	*They're* means "they are" and it has the word "they" in it. *There* has the word "here" in it. So I can think of here and there. *Their* has "heir" in it. The heir is the one who gets to keep it.

---

the understanding that mistakes are mistakes in context, not an indication that someone is deficit. The point of this exercise is not to achieve perfection, but to become more acutely aware of a personal set of usage errors. The teacher may want to model her own usage problems. Margaret, for example, always had to stop and think about *its* and *it's*. Only through her computer software program was she able to use *which* and *that* correctly with commas or without. She might start with a text on the overhead with her own sets of errors embedded in them and think aloud to demonstrate how she is trying to learn to monitor and correct her problem areas.

Figure 10–3 is a handout used to help students begin to address their own sets of language errors.

What does language study include? In this chapter we hope we have helped you to "think about words" with some of the same enthusiasm that Anna expressed in the opening Case for Consideration. Understanding how language varies and changes in different regions, across different discourse communities, and across time can support middle school students expand their repertoire of effective language practices. Provide opportunities to help your students examine the social and political aspects of language in use. Give students opportunities for examining and experimenting with their own language choices. Allow students to set their own purposes in contexts that are important to them. Expand the range of contexts in which your students can comfortably move. Allow students time to play with words. Language study can be effectively integrated with reading, writing, viewing, and speaking activities. Tapping students' expertise with language can make your classroom a rich and productive discourse community.

Throughout this book, we have introduced you to professional organizations and other professional opportunities to help you continue your development as a middle school teacher. In the final chapter, we review some of these and provide some concrete tips on how to best prepare for the job and the job interview at the middle school level. Before we do, we turn your attention back to language study.

Standards in Practice

Language Study Standards

In this chapter we have focused the lens of language study on learners and on contexts. We have written the following standards. They express what we think middle school students should know and be able to do with language study.

- Middle school students can analyze how social context affects language in use.
- Middle school students know how to make appropriate language choices for many contexts.
- Middle school students can monitor their own language use and development.
- Middle school students show respect for language variations.
- Middle school students understand how and why the English language varies and changes across cultures, ethnic groups, geographic regions, and historic periods.

For this exploration, we'd like you to locate a copy of your state English language arts standards. Find the standards that specifically address language study. Try to unpack the assumptions of what language study should include. Attempt to tease out how your state addresses issues of correctness and standardization.

1. Now answer the following two questions regarding your state's approach to language study.
    What counts as language study?
    What evidence do you find that the standards support or undercut an integrated approach to language study?
2. Working with a partner or in a small group, articulate your views of what counts as language study. What points of agreement can you find with your state's standards, your views, and our list? Where do your views depart? Consider in your group how easy or difficult it might be to prepare your middle school students for standardized tests based on your state's standards.

REFERENCES

Christensen, L. (2002). Whose standard? Teaching standard English. In B. Power & R. Hubbard (Eds.), *Language development: A reader for teachers* (2nd ed., pp. 173–177). Upper Saddle River, NJ: Merrill/Prentice Hall.

Delpit, L. (2002). What should teachers do? Ebonics and culturally responsive instruction. In B. Power & R. Hubbard (Eds.), *Language development: A reader for teachers* (2nd ed, pp. 124–128). Upper Saddle River, NJ: Merrill/Prentice Hall.

Edelsky, C. (1992). A talk with Carole Edelsky. *Language Arts, 69,* 324–329.

Gee, J. (1990). *Social linguistics and literacies: Ideology in discourse.* New York: Falmer Press.

Hall, S. (1981). Teaching about race. In A. James & R. Jeffcoate (Eds.), *The school in the multicultural society* (pp. 58–69). London: Harper.

Heath, S. B. (1983). *Ways with words: Language, life, and work in communities and classrooms.* New York: Cambridge University Press.

Hymes, D. (1972). Models of the interaction of language and social life. In J. Gumperz & D. Hymes (Eds.), *Directions in sociolinguistics: The ethnography of communication* (pp. 35–71). New York: Holt, Rinehart and Winston.

Hymes, D. (1996). *Ethnography, linguistics, and narrative inequality: Toward an understanding of voice.* London: Taylor & Francis.

Levitt, P., Guralnick, E. S., & Stevens, J. (1999). *The weighty word book* (2nd ed.) Boulder, CO: Court Wayne Press.

Samway, K., & McKeon, D. (2002). Myths about acquiring a second language. In B. Power & R. Hubbard (Eds.), *Language development: A reader for teachers* (2nd ed., pp. 62–68). Upper Saddle River, NJ: Merrill/Prentice Hall.

Shaughnessy, M. (1979). *Errors and expectations: A guide for the teacher of basic writing.* New York: Oxford University Press.

Stafford, W., & Dunning, S. (1992). *Getting the knack: 20 poetry exercises.* Urbana, IL: National Council of Teachers of English.

Weaver, C. (1996). *Teaching grammar in context.* Montclair, NJ: Boynton/Cook.

Weddel, K. S., & Van Duzer, C. (1997). *Needs assessment for adult ESL learners* (ERIC Digest). Washington, DC: National Clearinghouse for ESL Literacy Education. (ERIC Document Reproductive Services No. ED 407882).

RESOURCES

Print

Boran, S., & Comber, B. (2001). *Critiquing whole language and classroom inquiry.* Urbana, IL: National Council of Teachers of English.

Cazden, C. (1988). *Classroom discourse: The language of teaching and learning.* Portsmouth, NH: Heinemann.

Dudley-Marling, C., & Edelsky, C. (2001). *The fate of progressive language policies and practices.* Urbana, IL: National Council of Teachers of English.

Edelsky, C. (1996). *With literacy and justice for all: Rethinking the social in language and education (Critical perspectives on literacy and education).* New York: Taylor & Francis.

González, R. D., & Melis, I. (2000). *Language ideologies: Critical perspectives on the official English movement. Volume 1: Education and the social implications of official language.* Urbana, IL: National Council of Teachers of English.

González, R. D., & Melis, I. (2001). *Language ideologies: Critical perspectives on the official English movement. Volume 2: History, theory, and policy.* Urbana, IL: National Council of Teachers of English.

McWhorter, J. (2000). *Spreading the word: Language and dialect in America.* Portsmouth, NH: Heinemann.

Ng, R., Staton, P., & Scane, J. (1995). *Anti-racism, feminism, and critical approaches to education.* Westport, CT: Bergin and Garvey.

Power, B., & Hubbard, R. (2002). *Language development: A reader for teachers* (2nd ed.). Upper Saddle River, NJ: Merrill/Prentice Hall.

Wallace, R., & Hunter, S. (1995). *The place of grammar in writing instruction: Past, present, future.* Montclair, NJ: Boynton/Cook.

Weaver, C. (1998). *Lessons to share on teaching grammar in context.* Montclair, NJ: Boynton/Cook.

Weaver, C., Gillmeiser-Krause, L., & Vento-Zogby, G. (1996). *Creating support for effective literacy education.* Portsmouth, NH: Heinemann.

Electronic

Center for Multilingual Multicultural Research. CMMR is an organized research unit at the University of Southern California. The center focuses on multilingual education, English as a second language, foreign language instruction, multicultural education, and related areas. The center's comprehensive Web site addresses language policies and rights and includes Asian-Pacific Island resources, Latino/Latina and Hispanic resources, Native American/American Indian, and African American resources. This site also includes a collection of articles on the Ebonics debate.

http://www.usc.edu/dept/education/CMMR/

For a collection of articles on the Ebonics debate:

http://www-rcf.usc.edu/~cmmr/African_American.html#ebonics

International Reading Association. The IRA has three Web sites that address critical issues of language study and adolescent literacy: Focus on Critical Literacy, Focus on Language and Cultural Diversity, and Focus on Adolescent Literacy.

- **Focus on Critical Literacy:** This Web site was organized to help teachers and their students to understand, develop, and adopt a critical perspective on literacy. It offers online resources on critical literacy, including links to IRA journal articles, book chapters, programs, position statements, and more.

    http://www.reading.org/focus/critical_lit.html

- **Focus on Language and Cultural Diversity:** This Web site addresses issues related to teaching students whose first language is not the primary language of instruction and whose culture and values may differ from those in mainstream schools and of the larger community.

    http://www.reading.org/focus/langdir.html

- **Focus on Adolescent Literacy:** This Web site focuses on the literacy demands that adolescents encounter. The International Reading Association believes that the ongoing literacy development of adolescents is just as important, and requires just as much attention, as that of beginning readers. The site includes their position statement on adolescent literacy.

http://www.reading.org/focus/adolescent.html

On Line Writing Lab. OWL at Purdue University provides a wealth of support for teaching second language learners as well as teaching grammar, punctuation, and spelling. This site includes an extensive list of links to other Web resources for ESL teachers and learners.

http://owl.english.purdue.edu/

chapter 11

Entering the Profession: Lessons for Literacy and Life

GUIDING QUESTIONS
1. Where do effective middle school language arts teachers turn to seek out opportunities to learn from and contribute to the learning of their students, colleagues, communities, and profession?
2. How do effective middle school language arts teachers prepare for a job interview?

A CASE FOR CONSIDERATION
Teaching in Troubling Times

Early adolescence is often characterized as a troubling time. Everywhere in the media, we read about adolescents at risk. We are told that adolescents are becoming all the more dangerous to others and to themselves. Amid a growing concern with acts of school violence, rising illegal drug use, and ever younger teen pregnancies, we invite you to become middle school teachers. Why would anyone accept such an invitation? Noting the difficulties that teachers face, Kohl (1984) writes,

> Why teach, then? Are there reasons that override these negatives and can make teaching a wonderful way to spend a life? The answer for some people—and I'm one of them—is finally yes, because there still are children. The prime reason to teach is wanting to be with young people and help them grow. (p. 162)

He concludes his personal account on becoming a teacher by saying that all of the reasons not to teach are actually the most compelling reasons to become a teacher, "because there still are children."

You can hear a commitment to young people come through vividly in the following e-mail correspondences from three student teachers to their student teaching peers, all nearing completion of their student teaching experience.

Hi,

I am sooo happy to hear that you have been having a very rewarding student teaching experience. I too have been blessed with a remarkable host teacher and mentor. I have been student teaching at Larkwood Middle School, eighth grade ELA. I had so many worries and concerns when I started. I worried about developing lesson plans, how I was going to get the students to focus, etc., etc. . . . However, since I began teaching there, I have realized the bond I have developed with these students. I just had to get into their heads and their hearts. I had to learn their likes and dislikes. I had to learn their different moods, and what might trigger them. THEN, I could do anything to help them learn. One by one I began to develop a relationship with these kids.

They are a special bunch! Just today, I realized how much I'm really going to miss them. I too hope they know that I have learned from them! As much as I hope they have learned from me.

Trisha

* * *

Hi all,

My students have also become phenomenal teachers. I hope they walk away from my placement with half of the knowledge they have taught me. They have taught me very valuable lessons such as always be prepared to explain and back up the material that I present, always be prepared to support those who need support while still challenging advanced students, and always have an upbeat and supportive attitude because that reflects onto others. My students have also taught me many light-hearted lessons, such as how to appreciate being called "YO MISS." This is a very important thing! My students have truly made me realize why I want to teach. Even though there are endless nights of work and preparation, I always know that in the morning I have something wonderful to look forward to.

I have never done so much work, been so exhausted, been so frustrated, or so mind boggled. At the same time, I have never been so sure of something in my entire life—I love teaching and I love knowing that I will be doing something that will always have new twists and turns. We are officially preparing ourselves to be lifelong learners, underpaid and over-loved.

Rayann

* * *

Why is everyone getting so sentimental? I can't take it! I am sitting here reading Trisha's words to Rayann and I AM getting all misty-eyed. Now it's time for a little Craig thought. . . . Jerry Springer flavor.

Everyday I come into class ready to learn. Never before have I had this kind of anticipation for a day full of ups and downs, and that is what makes it exciting. One period could be the worst in your life, and your host teacher (if she is anything like mine) does her best to convince you that "these things happen" or "you did great!" I wonder what would really happen if my host teacher wasn't there? Who would pick up the pieces? You guys? No. You do that too much already. Let me tell you who has been there for me so far this semester. It's the kids. You glow from head to toe when they come in with a smile on their face and call you their, oh so charming, nickname that they have given you. And you, with your best teacher face and best-friend heart, say, "Nick, I don't mind if you call me that, but please don't do it in school. It is not appropriate, OK?"

"OK, Mr. Newcomer. Sorry."

To be able to call a classroom our own. To have that parent phone call that says you are doing a great job. To get the little pats on the back after a rough period. To get a high-five in the hallway. The smile from the student who has the crush on you. The grimace from the student who doesn't. The grin, from ear to ear, that your students get when they did well on an assignment. OK, OK, now I'm getting sentimental. See you tomorrow.

Craig

FOR DISCUSSION

- Trisha mentions the "worries and concerns when I started." The ways we imagine our middle school students have everything to do with how we will teach them. What were your expectations in working in a middle school language arts classroom? Looking back through your work this semester, in what ways have your views been confirmed, reinforced, or challenged?
- How might teachers sustain over time the kind of enthusiasm and commitment to the students that beginning teachers like Trisha, Craig, and Rayann express?

PROFESSIONAL SUPPORT: WHERE DO YOU GO FROM HERE?

Note that Craig mentions that he depends on his teacher and his student teaching peers for support. If we expect middle school teaching to be exhausting, frustrating, and mind-boggling as Rayann suggests, where can we turn for support? A professional learning community is vital to ensure your success. So how does one go about joining a professional learning community? In this chapter, we will focus on the resources that are readily available to you locally, nationally, and internationally.

Professional Memberships

Throughout this book, we have introduced you to professional organizations. Many offer conferences, books, journals, and other professional opportunities to help you continue your development as a middle school teacher. Those that might be most beneficial to you as a literacy teacher are the International Reading Association, the National Council of Teachers of English, and the National Middle School Association.

The International Reading Association headquarters is located at 800 Barksdale Road., P.O. Box 8139, Newark, DE 19714-8139, and IRA can be found online at *http://www.ira.org/*. IRA provides members with access to a broad range of professional meetings, publications, and other resources. Two of their journals may be of particular interest to middle school teachers.

- *The Journal of Adolescent & Adult Literacy* is intended for those involved in the literacy and language arts education of adolescents and older learners. This journal includes practical ways of teaching and studying literacy and also addresses the challenges teachers face in rapidly changing cultural, economic, and social contexts.
- *The Reading Teacher* is intended for those involved with literacy education of children to the age of 12. This journal focuses on practices, research, and trends in literacy education and related fields.

The National Council of Teachers of English addresses the teaching and learning of English and the language arts at all levels of education. Headquarters is located at 1111 Kenyon Road, Urbana, IL 61801-10996, and NCTE can be found online at *http://www.ncte.org/*. NCTE publishes several professional journals and books. Three of its journals may be of particular interest to those teaching at the middle school level.

- *English Journal* is intended for middle and secondary English language arts teachers. Issues include articles written by and for teachers on the teaching of writing and reading, literature, and language. Each issue includes reviews of current materials, including books and electronic media.
- *Language Arts* is intended for literacy and language arts teachers of children prekindergarten through the eighth grade. Like other NCTE publications, research-based and practical classroom articles and up-to-date relevant reviews of professional materials are included.
- *Voices from the Middle* is devoted to literacy and learning at the middle school level. Each issue includes articles written by middle school teachers. Reviews of adolescent literature, a technology column, and professional resources for teachers are also included.

The National Middle School Association offers resources and services for middle school curriculum coordinators, teachers, and administrators. NMSA Headquarters is located at 4151 Executive Parkway, Suite 300, Westerville, OH 43081, and the association can be contacted online at *www.nmsa.org*. NMSA publishes the *Middle School Journal*, a journal focused on all aspects of middle level education, specifically focusing on the educational and developmental needs of young adolescents.

Local, state, and regional affiliates of these organizations or other professional organizations likely provide support in the form of local chapter meetings, conferences, and publications a little closer to home. You may locate these through the national Web sites or through professional colleagues in your building.

Don't underestimate the tremendous expertise that is just down the hall from you. Seek out experienced teachers and other professionals. They will view your requests for advice as a compliment and a mark of your professionalism, not a sign of weakness.

Help Down the Hall

Media Specialists. Get to know the media specialist in your building as soon as you arrive. Media specialists can provide great resources for you. They know books, Internet resources, available media, and local community resources. They likely know the culture of the school and the official rules for operating there.

If you have a project in mind, go to your media specialists early, and they can help you locate additional resources. Mrs. Peters, a media specialist with more than 20 years of experience says, "Just have them come to me early. I can order materials through interlibrary loan. I can purchase materials. I can get audio and videotapes to support most any project that teachers are developing. But I can't do it with a couple of days' notice." She goes on to suggest that the media specialist might be a great person to make friends with early in one's career. Here is a list of questions that she offers for beginning teachers to find out about during their first weeks at their new school.

1. What is the school's Internet use policy?
2. How do I reserve space in the library for my classes?
3. How do I order videos, books, and other materials?
4. How do I sign up for computer use?
5. What are the school policies on censorship?
6. What counts as fair use in terms of copying?
7. What's here in the library? What seems to be popular with my students?

Guidance Counselors. A school guidance counselor's job is configured differently from district to district. You will want to find out how your particular school defines the job of the guidance counselor. In most schools, the counselor works closely with teachers, parents, students, and community support personnel. Counselors may be in charge of programs for students who are facing social, academic, or legal problems. Some schools sponsor peer support activities through the guidance office. In other schools, the guidance office may handle only course and standardized test schedules. Most counselors know a great deal about the local community and can help you learn what local resource agencies are available to you and your students. Your guidance counselor will likely know a great deal about the standardized tests that are administered in your school. He or she most likely works directly with special needs faculty and family support personnel. The counselor can help you get to know your students, their families, and the community.

Social Workers. Some schools have full-time social workers. Others do not. If your school has a social worker, you will want to get acquainted and learn what support systems are available to your students and their families. If there are special support groups for middle school students, you will want to know what they are. If you have concerns about a particular student, the social worker or guidance counselor can help you identify warning signs and locate support or interventions when needed. As a language arts teacher, you may learn through your students' writing information that is far beyond your expertise. Don't try to take on the responsibilities of a social worker or guidance counselor. Work closely with these professionals who can guide you when further action may be in the best interest of any particular student. They might suggest referrals, additional testing, or other interventions. The main thing to realize is that they are support personnel who are highly trained to help students and to help you.

School Nurses. You will want to know the school policies and practices regarding health and accidents before you need to know them. Ask your nurse about any concerns you may have regarding the health and well-being of your students. Also, find out the specific ways to handle blood and bodily fluids so you will be prepared in case an accident should occur in your room. You may have students who have special medical needs. Alert the nurse if you have concerns. At this developmental stage, many students are growing and changing quite rapidly. Medications that have been effective in the past may no longer serve early adolescents in the same ways. Girls often begin their menstrual cycles and may be unprepared. Work closely and confidentially with your school nurse so that students' medical needs are handled as discreetly and promptly as possible to ensure the well-being of your students and to avoid classroom disruption and student embarrassment.

Special Education Teachers. As you know, the special education teacher can help you design and modify lessons for students with special needs in your classroom. To determine appropriate levels of support or modification that may be necessary for a student with a disability, special education teachers can assist you. They may also lead you to some curricular materials that may support all learners in your classroom. The special education teacher can also offer guidance in working with students and their families. If you are unsure if a student needs additional help, a special education teacher can help you to request appropriate additional testing and to make referrals. If you need advice on how to hold a conference with parents and other professionals, the special education teacher can help to arrange appropriate meetings, make referrals, or facilitate other supportive interactions among parents, social service providers, and school personnel.

ESL Teachers. It's likely that your middle school classroom will include students whose home language is not English. An English as a second language (ESL) teacher will be a vital resource to help you to design and guide language development for these students. The ESL program may have additional funding to provide you with alternative texts and materials for your second language users. Even if no additional funding is available, ESL teachers can help you to adapt your instructional materials. They will be able to guide you in understanding some aspects of second language acquisition and help you think about the ways you might support all middle school students in your classroom.

Teachers and Administrators. Seek out a teacher who can help you get acquainted with the school and community. If you do not have a teaching mentor assigned to you, ask your principal to assign one. Teaching colleagues will help get you through the hard days and help you celebrate small victories. They can help you understand the school routines. At the middle school level, many nonteaching duties can be streamlined if you know they are coming. Ask your colleagues about taking attendance, sending sick or disciplined students to the office, collecting tickets at games, distributing books, and creating a record book. Find a colleague who can provide support and who is willing to go out after school for a cup of coffee. This person can in a very real sense serve as your advocate and your lifeline.

Parents. Contrary to popular folk wisdom, middle school parents and middle school students are often closely connected, and most like it that way. Although many parents may have jobs that prevent them from participating during regular school hours, most will be happy to assist in any way they can. Some parents may be unfamiliar with the ways they might contribute to their children's education, and your invitations may not be accepted because of families' diverse home and school experiences. Finders and Lewis (1994) suggest that instead of assuming that absence means not caring, teachers must understand and break through the barriers that hinder some parents from participating in their children's education more fully. They note that parents' own school experiences, diverse economic and time constraints, and diverse linguistic and cultural practices at times make parents feel uncomfortable and unwelcome in school settings. You'll want to create opportunities to get to know parents and invite them into your classrooms in ways that make them feel confident and comfortable. As you think about your literacy lessons, consider the ways you can tap the expertise of your students' families. Parents can offer great insight into and assistance for their children. They can be significant collaborators in designing effective literacy lessons and offer a direct link to the local community.

Community Organizations. Find out what resources are available in your community that might provide guest speakers, enrich your curricular materials, or help you to design appropriate community projects. Community connections are a hallmark of an effective middle school program. Community connections can make literacy learning real and relevant in your middle school classroom. Each community has rich and unique resources that should be tapped. Begin with your students to find out who and what is available in your community. Ask parents and other community members to help you make connections that will link your classroom with the local community and beyond.

SECURING A JOB

Before you can begin to make these professional connections, you will need to secure a job. Now is a good time to be in the job market because there are jobs. It is estimated that by the year 2005, there will be a 50% turnover in current teaching positions. The teaching profession across the nation is growing older; much of the current teaching force is nearing retirement age. Teachers are retiring earlier. That means simply that there are and will continue to be many job opportunities for you. But how might you prepare for those at the middle school level?

Gaining Experiences

Margaret conducted telephone interviews with 50 middle school principals and asked them specifically, "What in particular makes one candidate's materials rise to the top of the application files?" This section explores the main reasons that principals gave for deciding who they would interview. The list is rank-ordered by importance from the perspective of the middle school principals interviewed.

Explicit Interest in Teaching at the Middle School Level. Enthusiasm for this age group was by far the number one consideration that principals expressed in their reasons for inviting a candidate for an interview and for hiring. One noted that even though she receives applications from those who are certified in elementary school as well as those in secondary schools, "I am not so concerned with the certification. I want to know that they are looking for a teaching position at the middle school level, not just looking for any teaching position. I read their letters and look for specifics about their interest in middle school students." Of course, in some states, certification at the middle level is a requirement. For some states, however, middle schools can and do attract applications across certification programs. Scan your letter and resume and look for implicit and explicit messages about your interest in teaching at the middle school level.

Classroom Experiences and Evidence of Success at the Middle School Level. According to several principals, letters of reference from middle school teachers and principals who have observed the candidate at this level are important selection criteria. Principals reported that they scrutinize resumes for evidence of contact time and successful experience with middle school students. "I want to know that they can be successful and happy working in my building," one said.

Some mentioned that they were especially interested in finding candidates who had demonstrated leadership with this age group, which included such things as organizing outings, attending field trips, and overseeing major projects. One noted that even if the candidate does not have teaching experiences at this level, he looks for individuals who have experiences with young people of middle school age through community clubs, recreational sports organizations, and religious and other programs. Well before it's time to think about applying for a teaching position, seek out opportunities to work with middle school students. While you are working in a middle school setting, invite department chairs, principals, or other professionals in to your middle school classroom so they can speak to your competencies in working with this age group.

Abilities to Work on Teams. Quite often teaching is characterized as an individual activity. Some teachers tend to close their doors and work privately. Not so in the middle school. An effective middle school teacher must be a team member. Since middle school teachers often work across disciplinary boundaries, principals want to know how well an individual can work with others. Seek out opportunities to gain experience in working on a team. Then consider ways to demonstrate your emerging competence in teamwork. An interdisciplinary unit or letters from colleagues in other content areas are two ways you might showcase your competencies.

Credentials in More Than One Content Area and/or Additional Teaching Endorsements. A middle school teacher who has certification in more than one content area is highly desirable. A candidate who can teach math, science, or social studies in addition to language arts will certainly be regarded as employable. Since class sizes may shift from year to year, principals often find they need additional sections of one subject for a short period of time. They may need 1.5 teachers in one subject and .5 in another. Middle school teachers who can teach multiple subjects make it easier for principals to accommodate such needs.

That said, do not add endorsements just to secure a job. Do so because you have an interest in another subject. Although for a number of reasons it may not be possible for you to complete a second endorsement at the same time as you complete your literacy certification program, you may find time in your schedule to complete some of the requirements. If so, make it clear to principals and other hiring personnel that you are working toward a second endorsement. You may be hired with the understanding that you can complete the requirements during your first few years of employment.

Abilities to Work With Students Beyond the Academics. Many middle schools offer social and academic programs beyond the traditional classroom experiences. In addition to your preparation in English language arts, consider what areas of expertise you bring to the middle school. You will want to gain experience with middle school students during your course work at the university, and you'll want to showcase those experiences when you apply for a position. Think about ways you might volunteer or gain experience through paid positions. Also think about the types of outings, explorations, and performances you might contribute to a middle school program. Think about how you might showcase the hobbies, social issues, local concerns, and expertise that you could share with interested middle school students.

Specific Course Work in Middle School. "Does this applicant know anything about the middle school philosophy?" That's what several principals asked. Whereas all beginning teachers will need support and guidance, principals hope to hire those who bring a working understanding of middle school with them. They want to build on that existing knowledge without the feeling, as one put it, "We often have to start from scratch because the new teachers don't know much about middle schools and how they work." In your letter, résumé, and/or portfolio, you will want to make it clear that you understand the central components of effective middle school programs and can put them into practice.

Understanding the Needs of At-Risk Students and Those With Special Needs. One principal noted, "All students enter the middle school, but this is where we really begin to lose them. I want my teachers to find ways to support all learners. We need to keep them in school. It's in my building where we can lose them for good." As classrooms become more inclusive, middle school teachers work with a wide range of students. We do want all middle school students to complete middle school successfully and go on to high school. We don't want to "lose them for good." Gain as much experience as you can with programs and practices that are having a positive impact with students who have not been successful in traditional classroom settings.

Need for Seamless Integration of Technology. Principals reported that they like to hire individuals who are technologically proficient. Many middle schools do not have a technology teacher, and technological support in a building may be minimal. So middle school teachers must be able to integrate technology into their curriculum. In some states, you may be able to work toward a technology endorsement. But for many principals, demonstrated competence is enough. Successful completion of a single course or workshop can make your application shine. You may want to showcase your technological skills through course Web pages or an electronic portfolio.

Knowledge of Local, State, and National Standards and Standardized Tests. With increasing accountability demands, principals want to hire those with extensive skills in assessment strategies and those who bring a deep understanding of the ways in which state and national standards can be integrated into the local curriculum. You may want to draw from some of the exercises in this book to showcase your understanding of national standards and appropriate assessment strategies.

Competence in Subject Matter. Clearly, all teachers must have a deep and broad understanding of their subject matter. To design, implement, and adapt teaching strategies, teachers must make appropriate connections between the structure of the discipline and the experiences that students bring to the classroom. In addition to teaching the content effectively, middle school teachers must have a strong content knowledge in order to work across disciplinary boundaries, specifically to anticipate and make curricular connections through interdisciplinary work.

This list might serve you in multiple ways. It might guide you early on as you select courses and gain professional experiences in school and community settings. It can also help you later as you prepare for teaching applications and interviews. It might be useful to refer back to this list as you create a professional portfolio.

Preparing a Professional Portfolio

A professional portfolio is more than a collection of documents that represents your views of teaching and learning. You may want to consider it a process-folio because it is a way for you to document not only what you and your students do, but also how you think and make decisions as a teacher. The purposes of a professional portfolio are (a) to reflect on your practice and (b) to make visible to potential employers what you can do in the classroom and what you know about the subject area, your students, and teaching. The following questions may serve to facilitate discussions among your teaching colleagues and give some direction for you as you plan for and design your professional portfolio.

Considerations for Your Middle School Portfolio

- How do I design for and put into practice positive social interactions with peers and adults?
- How do I incorporate physical activities into meaningful literacy experiences?
- How do I build on the competence and experiences that middle school students bring to my classroom?
- How do I promote meaningful participation with families, school, and the larger world?
- How do I work collaboratively with other teachers and support personnel to promote the social and academic development of middle school students?
- Given all this, how can I make these emerging competencies visible through the selection of appropriate artifacts?

For much of your professional development, you will want to examine the way in which you can improve your teaching. But when it comes time for interviews, you will want to turn your process-folio into a showcase portfolio. It will be shorter and much more polished. You will want your showcase portfolio to show off your competencies in the best possible light.

Considering the Showcase Portfolio. The showcase portfolio, as its name implies, should be designed to showcase your strengths as a beginning teacher. Much of the value of your showcase portfolio will come from the thought and time you put in during its construction. Reflecting about your beliefs and practices will help you to articulate them during the interview. Many beginning teachers are dismayed with the little time and attention that an interviewing principal or department head seems to give to the portfolio. But the preparation of the portfolio should help you interact professionally during the interview regardless of how much attention the interviewers give to the portfolio during the interview. You may want to make multiple copies of certain pieces so you can leave them after the interview.

Here are some quick hints.

- Be professional, not cute.
- Be concise. Don't include everything you have ever done. Select representative examples.
- Use tabs or labeled dividers so you can turn quickly to a section.
- Make one-page overviews of key documents (e.g., middle school philosophy, interdisciplinary unit, assessment practices, classroom management plan, and résumé). Make these summaries concise and professional, and make multiple copies so you can leave them if requested to do so.

There is much to do in the coming weeks as you prepare for and seek out a middle school teaching position. But as one of Margaret's student teacher reports, "mistakes are the best learning experiences." Becca Harkavy not only survived her student teaching experience in a seventh-grade classroom, but she thrived. She went on to create the pamphlet in Figure 11–1 for her future teaching colleagues.

We leave you with Literacy Lesson 11–1, which might help you to answer the question, "Why teach at the middle school level?"

STUDENT TEACHING SURVIVAL GUIDE

(Illustration: frazzled teacher labeled with:)
- pen you can't find
- bald spot
- up until 2 AM planning lessons
- caffeine!
- clothing: hip conservative
- Black tights to hide the tattoo that seemed like such a good idea at the time
- false smile
- feigned pose of confidence

Weeks 3–5

TIPS AND ENCOURAGEMENT FROM THE SURVIVORS

Mistakes are the best learning experiences.
Don't be afraid to say "No."
Beg, borrow and steal: Copy everything and keep a copy.
Ask questions.
Practice, practice, practice.
Relax when you have your evaluations; you are not expected to be perfect.
Take pictures.
Let yourself laugh.
No matter how hard it gets, try to maintain your enthusiasm.
OVERPLAN: plan 2 days into 1.

ORGANIZATION TIPS

- Have 2 folders for each class, one labeled: "Grade," the other labeled: "Return."
- Somewhere in the room keep the week's assignments posted.
- For each class write down ahead of time what you will be covering for the day. That way they know. Plus you'll always have that one kid who reminds you, "Don't we have a quiz today?" You think you wouldn't forget that now, but just wait. You'll love that child.
- Establish as much of a routine as possible. This doesn't mean boring. It means that you remember to do things like taking attendance and reading announcements.

"I love lists. I think they are what keeps me sane."

ODDS AND ENDS

<u>Rubrics:</u> These are very important. I did not realize just how important until I student taught. Be sure that you know how you are going to evaluate something before you assign it. This will save you a great deal of time in the long run, and, more importantly, it will allow you to be much more objective in your grading. Tell your students what the rubric is (i.e., how much is each part of this worth) when you give the assignment. This way there are few surprises.

<u>Policies, procedures and rules:</u> Establish these ahead of time. You may want to use the same structure as your supervising teacher. Regardless of that, go over your expectations with your students. Perhaps you would want to give them a handout. In this you should cover such things as: rules, homework policies, sleeping in class, make-up work, emergency procedures and late work.

<u>Make-up work:</u> When you are creating assignments or planning activities for class, try to remember to consider what you will do if a student is absent. I tell students it is their responsibility to come to me to get their make-up work.

THINGS TO LOOK FORWARD TO

- When your students say something hilarious and appropriate.
- When they write and write and write.
- When a parent, student, or another teacher compliments you.
- When a student looks at you and says, "Oh, I get it now."
- When they really enjoy one of the activities you plan.
- When a quiet student participates.
- When you have a meaningful discussion that developed from a tangent.
- When you overhear them saying how strict you are.
- When you overhear them saying that they like your class.

(Illustration: composed teacher labeled with:)
- hair growing back
- bright-eyed
- clothes: still no teacher sweater!
- calm, relaxed demeanor
- genuine smile
- caffeine free? Dream On.

Weeks 9 & 10

Literacy Lesson 11-1

The Last Day of School

Mrs. Everett set up her writers' workshop on a 3-week rotating basis. By that, we mean that she had her students engaged in writing workshop for 3 weeks and then shifted to literature instruction, direct writing instruction, public speeches, and other lessons. She retained a workshop element in each of her instructional units, which included time to write and share. During writers' workshop, she allowed students opportunities to self-select topics and write about what interested them most. During the 3 weeks of the unit, students came into the classroom, picked up their folder from the wire baskets at the front of the room, and started to work. Mrs. Everett circulated around the room to help reluctant writers get started. At the end of each day, she took an oral roll call, asking students to announce what they had accomplished that day. She concluded the 3 weeks with a celebration that included a whole class book and a public reading for their peers.

It was the last day of school; Mrs. Everett's seventh graders had been finishing their writing so they could take their turn in the author's chair for one last time. They had been in and out of the computer lab. They had been peer editing and proofreading each other's work so that their end-of-the-year class book would be perfect. For the entire last week, students had come to school early, and others stayed late to help with typing, drawing, and arranging the layout to be just the way they wanted it.

Finally all their work was done, and the last day arrived. The students were excited to see their writing in this thick book, almost 50 pages! Sean had designed the cover. He was a big, gangly boy who had been in more than his share of trouble in and out of Mrs. Everett's room. Sean loved to write science fiction adventure stories, and Mrs. Everett on more than one occasion had asked him to remove some writing that included violent acts against his classmates. Sean was an exceptional writer, an amazing artist, and a class clown. He didn't like authority and rarely made it to class on time, if at all. He was quite proud of his final work for this class, a five-page story. He asked to read first and lumbered to the front of the room. He sprawled out in the oak rocker, stretching his legs out onto the braided rug in the front of the room. The other seventh graders scooted back to allow room for Sean's long legs. Sean read, students clapped loudly, and he slid out of the chair dramatically onto the rug, rolling over those closest, bumping against his classmates before squeezing into a group of girls, grinning all the while. Mrs. Everett quietly asked him to get seated and called for the next reader.

Shawna raised her hand. Sean jumped up to help her navigate her wheelchair through the others to get to the front. He helped her move from her chair to the author's chair and stepped quietly behind her to give her the stage. Shawna's hands shook as she began, "The Day I Won the Race: A True Story by Shawna Rice." She stumbled over her words as she told about her event in the Special Olympics; her hands began to shake so fiercely that she couldn't read. The class was dead silent. Shawna started to cry. Sean quietly slipped the class book from her hands and continued for her. In a dramatic voice he concluded, "My chair was moving fast. I was fast. When I crossed the finish line, they all hugged me. I WAS a champion." The class broke into applause for Shawna. She lifted both her arms over her head, waving them as she had done at the end of her race. As the clapping died down, Sean lifted Shawna into her chair and wheeled her to the side of the rug. Caesar asked to read next.

Standards in Practice

Standards, Standards, Standards

As you have seen throughout this book, a variety of organizations can provide support for what you do in your middle school classroom. Throughout this book, we have asked you to think about your philosophy and practice against the backdrop of a particular set of standards. We do so with a sense of unease. You may note that some of the standards work against others. Some hold multiple and conflicting views of language and literacy—just as we all do. As you enter your middle school classroom, you will be faced with standardized tests that tell your students who they can and can't be, where they can and cannot go. You will encounter local and national standards that hold small or great consequences for you and your students. We leave you with a set of critical considerations about how standards might shape your daily interactions with middle school students.

Select one set of standards that you have used in this text or a set that has a strong influence on a local school district. Find out as much as possible about the history and origin of the standards, the time period when these standards were developed, and the people involved in their construction. Ask yourself these questions:

- Under what social and historic circumstances did the standards originate?
- What inferences can I draw from this set of standards about what is to be highly valued and what is to be ignored?
- Whose perspective does this set of standards ask me to assume?
- How might this set of standards impact my students' lives?
- Who loses in this equation?
- How can I support all of my students while working with these standards?

These questions guide you to speculate on how a set of standards might impact you and your students. As you complete this task, it might be valuable to share with others who have looked at a different set of standards. Often schools are expected to work from multiple and, at times, conflicting standards. As you talk with your teaching peers, discuss the ways in which sets of standards might create both obstacles and opportunities in your middle school classroom.

REFERENCES

Finders, M., & Lewis, C. (1994). Why some parents don't come to school. *Educational Leadership, 51*(9), 50–54.

Kohl, H. (1984). *Growing minds: On becoming a teacher.* New York: Harper and Row.

RESOURCES

Print

Alvermann, D., Hinchman, K., & Moore, D. (2000). *Reconceptualizing the literacies of adolescents' lives.* Mahwah, NJ: Lawrence Erlbaum.

Burke, J., & Claggett, M. F. (1999). *The English teacher's companion: A complete guide to classroom, curriculum, and the profession.* Montclair, NJ: Boynton/Cook.

Hubbard, R. S., & Power, B. M. (1993). *The art of classroom inquiry: A handbook for teacher-researchers.* Portsmouth, NH: Heinemann.

Moje, E. B. (2002). *All the stories that we have: Adolescents' insights about literacy and learning in secondary schools.* Newark, DE: International Reading Association.

Moore, D., & Alvermann, D. (2000). *Struggling adolescent readers: A collection of teaching strategies.* Newark, DE: International Reading Association.

Moore, D., Bean, T., Birdyshaw, D., & Rycik, J. (1999). *Adolescent literacy: A position statement for the Commission on Adolescent Literacy of the International Reading Association.* Newark, DE: International Reading Association.

Muth, K. D., & Alvermann, D. (1999). *Teaching and learning in the middle grades.* Needham Heights, MA: Allyn & Bacon.

Tchudi, S., & Tchudi, S. (1999). *The English language arts handbook: Classroom strategies for teachers.* Montclair, NJ: Boynton/Cook.

Vinz, R. (1996). *Composing a teaching life.* Montclair, NJ: Boynton/Cook.

Wilhelm, J. (1996). *Standards in practice, 6–8.* Urbana, IL: National Council of Teachers of English.

Electronic

Assembly on Literature for Adolescents. ALAN is a special-interest group of NCTE. ALAN's membership includes teachers, authors, librarians, publishers, teacher educators, and others who are particularly interested in the area of young adult literature.

http://www.alan-ya.org/

Center for Multilingual Multicultural Research. The CMMR has established an extensive list of resources for beginning teachers.

http://www-rcf.usc.edu/~cmmr/BofA_induction.html#BTSA

Center on School, Family and Community Partnerships. The Center supports research and projects aimed at increasing an understanding of practices of partnership that help all children succeed in elementary, middle, and high schools in rural, suburban, and urban areas. The focus is on how members of communities can work together to improve schools, strengthen families, and enhance student learning and development.

http://www.csos.jhu.edu/p2000/center.htm

Education Association. This organization provides a Parent Involvement Home Page that includes suggestions for how parents can support their children with reading and other content areas. It also lists publications, grant opportunities, and other resources for parents.

http://www.nea.org/parents/

National Council of Teachers of English. The NCTE offers resources and support for beginning teachers at:

http://www.ncte.org/newteach/

Rethinking Schools. This online publication emphasizes problems and promises facing urban schools, particularly issues of race. It addresses a broad range of educational issues such as vouchers and marketplace-oriented reforms, funding equity, and school-to-work. Articles are written by and for teachers, parents, and students.

http://www.rethinkingschools.org/

Index

Active listening skills, 250–251
Activity modifications, 95
Administrators, support of school, 308
ADOL. *See* Adolescence Directory On Line
Adolescence, 7
Adolescence Directory On Line, 20
Advisory programs, 13
Aesthetic dimensions of language learning, 35
Aesthetic reading, 174
Affective dimensions of language learning, 35
ALAN. *See* Assembly on Literature for Adolescents
ALAN Review, The, 36, 199
Alberto, P.A., 107
Allen, H.A., 19
Alternative assessments, 118–128
Alvermann, D., 20, 87
Anecdotal records, use of, 225–226
Applebee, A.N., 34, 43, 45, 144, 178, 196, 199
Appleman, D., 178, 179, 196
Armstrong, W.H., 86
Assembly on Computers in English, 236
Assembly on Literature for Adolescents, 36, 46
Assessment of early adolescent learners
    alternative assessments, 118–128
    authentic assessment, 115
    conferences and interviews, 120–121
    cultural influences, 141–142
    defining, 112
    fishbowl discussion, using a, 122
    grading criteria, 128–130, 135–136
    graphic representations, use of, 119–120
    inquiries and investigations, 123–124
    integrating assessment, 113–114
    large groups, evaluating, 122–123
    learning logs, use of, 118–119
    linear model of assessment, 115–116
    performance assessment, 115, 118, 122
    portfolio assessment, 128
    purposes and audiences, identifying, 112–113
    recursive model of assessment, 116–117
    self-assessment, 120
    small-group work, evaluating, 121–122
    standardized testing, role of and preparation for, 136–137
Assumptions concerning early adolescents, 4–5, 5–6, 8, 57–58
At-risk students and special needs, experience with, 310–311
Atwell, N., 35, 43, 87, 183, 188, 197, 234
Authentic assessment, 115
Authentic voice, encouraging the development of the, 35

Barbieri, M., 39, 43, 86
Barnes, D., 34, 43
Barry, H., 8, 19
Bay Area Writing Project, 36
Beach, R., 33, 43, 45, 124, 143
Bean, T., 20
Beane, J.A., 19
Behavioral objectives, influence of, 31
Bender, W., 108
Berberich, C., 108
Biased communication investigations, 287–288
Bilingual considerations, 151–152
Biological changes in adolescents, influence of, 6, 8
Birdyshaw, D., 20
Bishop, K.D., 108
Bondi, J., 20
Books and the Teenage Reader, 36
Braddock, R., 33, 43
Britton, J., 34, 43, 165
Brooks, C., 31, 43
Brooks-Gunn, J., 7, 18
Brown, R., 114, 118, 143, 144
Brozovic, S.A., 107
Brumberg, J.J., 7, 18
Bruner, J., 33, 43
Bucher, K.T., 20
Burgess, T., 43

Calkins, L.M., 35, 43
"Call-response" communication pattern, 180
Capper, J., 144
Carlsen, G.R., 36, 43
Carnegie Council on Adolescent Development, 9, 10
Carr, J., 59, 86
Carrington, V., 206, 207, 234, 235
Caught in the Middle: Educational Reform for Young Adolescents in California Public Schools, 9
Censorship and text selection, 181–182
Center for Adolescent Studies, 20
Cheville, J., 144

319

Child labor laws and compulsory schooling laws, influence of, 8
Chomsky, N., 33, 43
Choral reading, 263
Christensen, L., 299
Class, race, gender, and individual life circumstances, influence of, 8
Co-teaching, 98
Cognitive dimensions of language learning, 35
Cohen, J., 144
Coleman, J.S., 19
Collaborative approaches, 14, 37, 64–65, 211–214
Collaborative learning chart, 186
Collaborative teaching, 98
Collaborative writing groups, 54
Colleagues, support of, 308
Comber, B., 207, 234
Commercialization of the educational process, 27
Communicative competence, 280
Community-based activities, integration of learning projects with, 14
Community context influences, 56
Community organizations, support of, 308
Competition, de-emphasis on, 14
Complexity of developing literacy skills, 50–51
Comprehension strategies, 176–177
Compulsory schooling laws, influence of, 8
Conferences and interviews, assessment of, 120–121, 226
Connect and transform, talking and listening to, 252–261
Connecting stance, 175, 176
Constructivism movement, 37
Consultative support, 97–98
Control, determination of boundaries of student and teacher, 59
Cooperation, role of, 14
Coots, J.J., 108

Correctness and creativity, balancing, 218
Council for Exceptional Children, 107, 108
Crane, R., 108
Creative expression, importance of, 17
Credentials, 310
Critical Encounters in High School English: Teaching Literacy Theory to Adolescents, 178
Critical theory, strategies of, 178–179
Culminating activity, designing a, 14, 74
Cultural boundaries, influence of, 39, 141–142, 180, 244–245
Cunningham, P.M., 245, 271
Cureton, G.O., 245, 271
Curriculum guide, review of your school's, 58
Curriculum views, changing, 10

Daily lesson plans, 68, 70, 71
Dana, T., 144
Dartmouth Conference, 32, 33
"Decoding" perspective, 31
Delpit, L., 218, 234, 284, 299
Demonstrated leadership, proof of, 309
Developing Educational Standards, 42, 46
Developmental needs of early adolescent learners, 17–18
Dickinson, T., 17, 19, 20
Dinner table studies, 251–252
Dionisio, M., 87
Disabilities, learners with
  activity modifications, 95
  assumptions, 90
  Council for Exceptional Children, 107
  environmental modifications, 96
  evaluation of student performance, 104–106
  inclusion, philosophy of, 91
  incorporation into classroom, 88–90
  Individual Education Program, 90–91, 93–94
  Individuals with Disabilities Education Act, 90
  instructional modifications, 95–96
  least restrictive environment, 90, 91
  materials modifications, 96
  peers, interaction with, 99–100
  support team, development and implementation of, 91–92, 94–95, 97–98, 101
Discourse communities, interaction in multiple, 50–51, 280, 282, 285
Diversity of the middle school classroom, 50–51, 54–55, 149–150, 289
Dixon, J., 32, 43
Dowdy, C., 108
Drama in the English classroom, important role of, 34
Dunn, P., 108
Dunning, S., 288, 299

Eagleton, T., 45
Eccles, J., 19
Economic and structural influences on adolescent programs, 16
Edelsky, C., 38, 43, 207, 234, 299
Efferent reading, 35, 174–175
Elaborated calenders, 66
Elbow, P., 45, 150, 166, 234
Elliott, G., 19
Emig, J., 33, 43
Endorsements, teaching, 310
English Journal, 305
Environmental modifications, 96
Erb, T., 17, 19, 20
Error analysis, 296–297
ESL teachers, 307–308
Evaluation and grading methods, determining, 74–75, 104–106, 193–194, 266–267
Everhart, R., 8, 19
Evolution of schooling, historical, 8
Expectations of working with middle school students, 3–4
Experiencing stance, 175, 176

Exploratory programs, 14
Explore, talking and listening to, 245–249
Expressive nature of language, 33, 34
Extending stance, 175, 176
Extracurricular opportunities, professional, 310

Fader, D., 32, 36, 43
Falvey, M.A., 108
Family participation, importance of, 17
Farrell, E.J., 45
Feldlaufer, H., 19
Feldman, S., 19
Feminist criticism, 179
Feminist movement, role of the, 39
Financial constraints on exemplary middle schools, impact of, 16
Finders, M., 8, 19, 39, 43, 114, 143, 198, 217, 234, 315
Fine, M., 244, 271
First impressions chart, use of, 184
Fishbowl discussion, using a, 122
Five, C.L., 87
Flexible scheduling, potential for, 14
Flower, L., 33, 43
Focus on Critical Literacy, 237
Fordham, S., 244, 271
Formal instructional plans, 70
Fostering students' language skills, 283–284
Framework methods, choosing, 73–74
Free-choice independent reading time, 54
Freebody, P., 207, 235
Friend, M., 108
Frye, N., 33, 43

Gardner, H., 36, 43, 62, 65, 86, 114, 143, 195, 197
Gateways, 137
Gee, J.P., 50, 86, 170, 197, 280, 285, 299
Gender, influence of, 6–8

Gerrick, W.G., 20
Gill, K., 144
Goodman, K., 36, 43, 44
Goodman, Y., 36, 43, 44
Grab bag speeches, 262
Grading criteria, 128–130, 135–136, 194–195
Graham, P., 114, 143
Grammar instruction, 290
Grant, L., 244, 272
Graphic representations, use of, 119–120
Graves, D.H., 35, 44, 144, 221, 234
Grenot-Scheyer, M., 108
Growth model, 33
Guidance counselors, support of, 306
Guided imagery, use of, 185
Guided practice skills, 285–288
Guralnick, E.S., 299

Hall, G. Stanley, 7, 216, 234, 299
Hands-on activities, incorporating, 13–14
Harris, J., 32, 44
Hayes, J.R., 33, 43
Heath, S.B., 38, 44, 282, 299
Heathcote, D., 34, 44
Hiebert, E.H., 37, 44
Hinchman, K., 87
Hinton, S.E., 35, 44
Historical criticism, 179
Histories, use of language, 287
Holland, N.N., 33, 44
Hood, W., 36, 44
Hook, J.N., 45
Hooked on Books, 32, 36
hooks, b., 244, 272
Hormonal role in adolescent behavior, 7
Hughes, M.A., 107
Hunt, I., 31, 33, 44, 197
Hunt, K.W., 44
Hymes, D., 280, 299
Hynds, S., 19, 150, 166

I-R-E patterning, 252–256
IDEA. *See* Individuals with Disabilities Education Act
In the Middle, 35

Inclusion practices, 91, 179–180
Independent reading system, development of, 187
Individual Education Program, 90–91, 93–94
Individual life circumstances, influence of, 8
Individual support, 98
Individuals with Disabilities Education Act, 90
Inferior form of language, myth of speech as an, 150–151
Informative reports, 262
Inhelder, B., 33, 44
Inquiries and investigations, evaluating, 123–124
Instructional modifications, 96
INTASC. *See* Interstate New Teacher Assessment and Support Consortium
Integrated language arts, 149–150
Interdisciplinary planning, 71–72
Interdisciplinary teams, 13
Interest inventories, use of, 60–61
International Reading Association, 46, 305
Interpersonal communication, 65, 249–250
Interstate New Teacher Assessment and Support Consortium standards, 84–85, 142–143
Intrapersonal communication, 65
Iver, D.M., 19

Jackson, D., 244, 245, 272
Jackson, R., 108
Job market, entering the
  at-risk students and special needs, experience with, 310–311
  classroom experiences, 309
  credentials, 310
  demonstrated leadership, proof of, 309
  endorsements, teaching, 310
  extracurricular opportunities, 310
  interest in teaching, expression of, 309

portfolio, developing your professional, 311–313
standards, knowledge of local, state, and national, 311, 315
subject matter competency, 311
team player, evidence of being a, 309–310
technology, familiarity with contemporary, 311
Jones, T., 197
Journal of Adolescent & Adult Literacy, 305
Journals, use of writers', 226–227

Kellough, N.G., 19
Kellough, R.D., 19
Kernel sentences, 33
Kinesthetic activities, 65
Klein, H., 7, 19
Kohl, H., 302, 315
Krogness, M.M., 183, 197
KWL activity, using, 257

Labov, W., 38, 44, 197
LaMorte, K., 87
Land, R., 207, 235
Lang, G., 108
Langer, J., 44, 174, 197, 272
Language arts
 application of, 149
 bilingual considerations, 151–152
 diversity within student body, role of, 149–150
 inferior form of language, myth of speech as an, 150–151
 integrated language arts, 149–150
 lenses, concept of language, 149, 152–158
 myths, common, 150–152
 standards, 165
Language Arts, 305
Language study
 application, 278–279, 294
 biased communication investigations, 287–288
 communicative competence, 280
 definition of, 278
 discourse communities, interaction in multiple, 280, 282, 285
 diversity, language, 289
 error analysis, 296–297
 evaluation of, 291–293
 fostering students' language skills, 283–284
 goals and growth records, 295–296
 grammar instruction, 290
 guided practice skills, 285–288
 histories, use of language, 287
 lens of, 155–156, 157
 locks, use of language, 287
 opportunities, providing study, 297–298
 playing with language, 288
 political dimensions of language, 284–285
 portfolios, use of, 296
 second language acquisition, 290–291
 social context, role of, 285
 specialized languages of subject matter, 289–291
 "standard" language, 284–285
 word detective inquiries, use of, 287
Large groups, evaluating, 122–123
Learn, talking and listening to, 249–252
Learner-centered focus, 26, 37
Learning logs, use of, 118–119
Least restrictive environment, 90, 91
Lee, C., 108
Lenses, concept of language, 149, 152–158
Lensmire, T., 234
Lesson plans
 daily lesson plans, 68, 70, 71
 elaborated calendars, 66
 formal instructional plans, 70
 organization of, 66–71
 purpose and audience, defining your, 66
 weekly calendar, 66–68, 69

Levitt, P., 288, 299
Lewin, L., 144
Lewis, C., 315
Lewis, S., 87
Life stage, growing recognition of adolescence as a separate, 8
Linear model of assessment, 115–116
Linguistic activities, 64
Literacy
 cognitive process, as a, 28, 32–35, 41
 personal growth, as, 28, 35–37, 41
 sociocultural process, as a, 28, 37–38, 41
 sociopolitical practice, as a, 38–40
 sociopolitical process, as a, 28, 41
 text, as, 28, 30–32, 41
"Literacy club," encouragement of the, 180
Literal questions, using, 176
Literary and nonliterary reading, comparison of, 174
Literature as Exploration, 33, 174
Lloyd-Jones, R., 217
Locks, use of language, 287
Logical-mathematical activities, 64
Logs, use of writing, 226
Long-range planning
 culminating activity, designing a, 74
 evaluation and grading methods, determining, 74–75
 formalizing your plan, 76–77
 framework methods, choosing, 73–74
 goals, determining your overall, 72–73
 materials and resources, identifying, 74
 relevance and usefulness, identifying, 73
 techniques, strategies, and procedures, describing ongoing, 75–76

Lord, S., 19
Lowly, L., 86
LRE. *See* least restrictive environment
Luke, A., 38, 44, 86, 107, 170, 197, 206, 234, 235
Lustig, K., 144

Macrorie, K., 32, 44
Manning, M.L., 19, 20
Marxist criticism, 179
Materials and resources, identification and assessment of, 61–62, 74, 96
McCarthy, C., 244, 272
McEwin, C., 17, 19, 20
McKeon, D., 290, 291, 299
McLeod, A., 43
Media, presentation of adolescents in the, 4
Media specialists, use of, 306
Mehan, H., 176, 197, 252, 272
Middle School Journal, 305
Midgley, C., 19
"Mini" high schools, 8–9
Mitchell, D., 87
Mock legislatures, 262–263
Moffett, J., 34, 44, 243, 272
Moore, D., 20, 87
Moore, T., 166
Multiculturalism, role of, 38
"Multiliteracies," 206
Multiple intelligences, theory of, 36, 62–64
Multiple literacies, theory of, 50
Murphy, S., 108
Murray, D.M., 35, 44, 219, 235
Musical activities, 65
Muth, K.D., 20
Myers, J., 124, 143
Myers, W.D., 272

National Board for Professional Teaching Standards, 20, 84
National Center for the Study of Writing and Literacy, 46
National Coalition of Education Activists, 145
National Council of Teachers of English, 21, 36, 47, 87, 305
National Information Center for Handicapped Children and Youth, 108
National Middle School Association, 10, 21, 305
National Research Center on English Learning and Achievement, 46
National Writing Project, 36, 47, 236
Naturalistic activities, 65
NCTE/IRA Standards for the English Language Arts, 165, 167
Negativity associated with teaching middle schoolers, 3
"New Criticism," 31, 32, 34, 178, 179
"New literacies," 206
Newkirk, T., 45
Nonliterary reading, comparison of literary and, 174
Nonverbal rules, 250–251
"Normal behavior," assumptions regarding, 5
North, S.M., 45
Nurses, support of school, 307
Ny, R., 216, 235

Oral language activities
  active listening skills, 250–251
  "call-response" communication pattern, 180
  choral reading, 263
  cultural boundaries and, 244–245
  dinner table study, 251–252
  evaluation criteria, 266–267
  explore, talking and listening to, 245–249
  factors of participation, complicating, 244–245
  forms, 240–241
  grab bag speeches, 262
  I-R-E patterning, 252–256
  importance of, 34
  informative reports, 262
  interpersonal communication, 249–250
  KWL activity, using, 257
  learn, talking and listening to, 249–252
  mock legislatures, 262–263
  nonverbal rules, 250–251
  opportunities for talking and listening, creating, 243
  oral interpretation, 262
  peer approval, role of, 239
  performance, talking and listening for, 261–266
  "process" speeches, 262
  purposes, 241, 242
  question cue cards, use of, 257
  readers' theater, 263, 265–266
  role playing, 246–247
  soapbox speeches, use of, 261–262
  social complications and, 244–245
  speeches, 261–263
  techniques, 240–241
  To Tell the Truth, 247–248
  vital role of, 243
Orientations, school, 9, 16
Outsiders, The, 35

Palladino, G., 7, 19
Parents, support of, 308
Participation, complicating factors of student, 244–245
Patton, J., 108
Peer dynamics, influence of, 99–100, 211–213, 214–216, 239
Peer group records, 227
Peer support, 98–99
Performance, talking and listening for, 261–266
Performance assessment, 115, 118, 122
Perl, S., 33, 44
Perrone, V., 144
Personal experiences of students, influence of, 33

Personal growth and development, concern for students', 28
Personal sharing technique, 37
Personal writing, role of, 218–219
Phelps, S., 87
Physical activity, importance of, 13–14, 17, 34, 217
Piaget, J., 33, 44
Pierangelo, R., 108
Plan, developing your teaching and classroom. *See also* Lesson Plans; Long-range planning
 change and revision, planning for, 83–84
 control, determination of boundaries of student and teacher, 59
 curriculum guide, review of your school's, 58
 goals, establishment of, 58–59
 interdisciplinary planning, 71–72
 long-range planning, 72–77
 multiple intelligences, planning for, 62–64
 organization of, 66–71
 "rule of three," 59
Playing with language, 288
Political dimensions of language, 284–285
Polloway, R., 108
Popular culture in literacy learning, role of, 39
Portfolio, developing and assessing your, 128, 228, 296, 311–313
Postman, N., 32, 44
Postmodernism movement, role of the, 39
Process-centered approach
 approaches and materials, teaching, 29
 cognitive process, literacy as a, 32–35
 curriculum focus, 28
 personal growth, literacy as, 35–37
 teacher responsibilities, 29
"Process" speeches, 262
Product-centered approach
 approaches and materials, teaching, 29
 curriculum focus, 28
 teacher responsibilities, 29
 text, literacy as, 30–32
Products of student learning, preoccupation with, 26, 28
Professional memberships, 305—306
Progressivist rhetoric of the early 1970s, 32
Project Zero, 62–63, 87
Psychological changes of adolescents, influence of, 6
Public writing, role of, 218–219
Purpose and audience, defining your, 66, 112–113, 207–209, 241, 242
Purves, A., 33, 44, 45

Question cue cards, use of, 257

Race, influence of, 8
Ransom, J.C., 31, 44
Readability test, conducting, 61
Reader-focused approach, 178
Reader-Response Criticism, 178, 179
Reader response perspective, teaching from a, 33–34, 35
Reading and viewing
 aesthetic reading, 174
 assessment methods, 191–195
 censorship and text selection, 181–182
 collaborative learning chart, 186
 comprehension strategies, 176–177
 connecting stance, 175, 176
 critical theory, strategies of, 178–179
 cultural differences, influence of, 180
 definition of, contemporary, 170
 efferent reading, 174–175
 evaluation methods, 193–194
 experiencing stance, 175, 176
 extending stance, 175, 176
 first impressions chart, use of, 184
 grading methods, 194–195
 guided imagery, use of, 185
 hierarchies, 175
 inclusion practices, 179–180
 independent reading system, development of, 187
 lens of, 153–154
 "literacy club," encouragement of the, 180
 literal questions, using, 176
 literary and nonliterary reading, comparison of, 174
 "New Criticism" *See* "New Criticism"
 organization methods, 182–183
 responding experiences, 191–193
 small-group reading methods, 187–188
 stances, intellectual, 175
 standards, 195–196
 text selection, 181–183
 texts and techniques, 170–171, 172–173
 viewing sheet, use of, 185
 "wait time," importance of, 180
 whole-class instruction methods, 183–187
 workshop teaching methods, 188–191
Reading Teacher, The, 305
Recursive model of assessment, 116–117
Reflective windows, use of, 229
Reif, L., 87, 144, 183, 188, 197, 235
Reiter, E.O., 7, 18
Research in the Teaching of English, 87
Responding experiences, 191–193
Responsive middle school, principles of the, 10
Reuman, D., 19
Ripperre, V., 33, 44
Risk factors of early adolescents, 9
Robert, H.M., 262, 272

Index

Rogers, C.R., 35, 44
Role playing, 246–247
Rosen, H., 43
Rosenblatt, L.M., 33, 35, 44, 174, 197
Rubin, D.L., 150, 166
Rubric, grading, 128–130, 135–136, 227–228, 229
"Rule of three," 59
Rycik, J., 20

Sadker, D., 244, 272
Sadker, M., 244, 272
Sailor, W., 108
Salisbury, J., 244, 245, 272
Samway, K., 290, 291, 299
Santrock, J.W., 7, 19
Scales, P., 17, 19, 20
Scane, J., 216, 235
Schlegel, A., 8, 19
Schmidt, H., 197
Schurr, S., 87, 144
Second language acquisition, 290–291
Self-assessment, 120
Self-definition, opportunities for, 17
Shaughnessy, M., 292, 299
Shewey, K., 87
Shoemaker, B.J., 144
Showcase, writing to, 209
Simpson, A., 207, 234
Skinner, B.F., 31, 44
Small-group reading methods, 187–188
Small-group work, evaluating, 121–122
Smith, F., 166, 180, 197
Smith, T., 108, 151
Smitherman, G., 38, 44, 245, 272
Soapbox speeches, use of, 261–262
Social and economic influences on adolescence, 7, 9, 244–245
Social/contextual approach, 28, 29, 37–40
Social expectations, shifting, 7
Social interaction with adults and peers, importance of, 17, 34

Social workers, support of, 307
Sommers, N., 33, 44
Soto, G., 166, 180, 197, 272
Special education teachers, support of, 307
Specialized languages of subject matter, 289–291
Speeches, 261–263
Splittgerber, F., 19
Squire, J., 45
Stafford, W., 288, 299
Stances, intellectual, 175
"Standard" language, 284–285
Standardized testing, influence of, 28, 60, 136–137
Staton, P., 216, 235
Stevens, J., 299
Stevenson, C., 59, 86, 288
Stiggins, R.J., 144
Stover, L., 87
Student-centered approach, 36
Student retention, perceived need for, 8
Subject matter competency, 311
Sunstein, B., 144
Support team, development and implementation of, 60–62, 91–92, 94–95, 97–98, 101, 306–308

Taber, T.A., 107
Takanishi, R., 20
Talking and listening. *See* Oral language activities
Tannen, D., 251, 272
Tchudi, S., 87, 144
Teacher accountability, preoccupation with, 28
Teacher-centeredness, requirement of, 39
Teaching as a Subversive Activity, 32
Teaching materials and resources, assessment of, 61–62
Team player, evidence of being a, 309–310
"Technoliteracies," 206
Technological advancements, role of, 39, 206, 230–232, 311

Teen mothers, changing perspectives and, 2–3
Text, definition of, 50
Text-centered approach, 27
Text-focused approach, 178
Text selection, 181–183
The Reader, The Text, The Poem, 35
Theater, readers', 263, 265–266
Tippins, D., 144
Title IX prohibition of sex discrimination in education, 9
To Tell the Truth, 247–248
Tobin, L., 45
Transition programs, 14, 16
Trumbull, V., 108
Turning Points: Preparing Youth for the Twenty-first Century, 9

Unit planning
  culminating activity, designing a, 74
  evaluation and grading methods, determining, 74–75
  formalizing your plan, 76–77
  framework methods, choosing, 73–74
  goals, determining your overall, 72–73
  materials and resources, identifying, 74
  relevance and usefulness, identifying, 73
  techniques, strategies, and procedures, describing ongoing, 75–76
Uphan, D., 108

Vacca, J.L., 61, 86
Vacca, R.T., 61, 86
Van Duzer, C., 291, 299
Varied instruction, importance of, 13–14
Vars, G., 87
Viewing sheet, use of, 185
Visitation days, value of, 14
Visual/spatial activities, 64

Voices from the Middle, 305
Vygotsky, L., 33, 37, 44, 217, 235

Wagner, B.J., 34, 44
"Wait time," importance of, 180
Walley, C.W., 20
Watson, C.R., 20
Weaver, C., 290, 299
Weddel, K.S., 291, 299
Weekly calendar, 66–68, 69
Weingartner, C., 32, 44
Weiser, I., 144
Whole-class instruction methods, 54, 183–187
"Whole language" movement, 36
Wiener, R., 144
Wiggins, G., 114, 117, 143, 144
Wiles, J., 20
Wilhelm, J.D., 20, 197, 198
Willinsky, J., 38, 44, 45
Winograd, G., 144
Wolf, A., 266, 272
Word detective inquiries, use of, 287
Workshop teaching methods, 35, 37, 188–191
Writing
  anecdotal records, use of, 225–226
  application of, 203
  approaches to classroom programs, 206–207
  assessment techniques, 224–229
  assumptions, 204, 206
  choices, creating project, 214–217
  collaboration and privacy strategies, 211–214
  comfortable writing environment, developing a, 211
  conferences, evaluation, 226
  connect and transform, writing to, 209
  correctness and creativity, balancing, 218
  design and implementation strategies, 219–221
  explore, writing to, 209
  external influences, 206
  goals, writing program, 206
  journals, use of writers', 226–227
  lens of, 154–155
  logs, use of writing, 226
  "multiliteracies," 206
  "new literacies," 206
  opportunities, creating writing, 211, 213
  peer dynamics, influence of, 211–213, 214–216
  peer group records, 227
  personal writing, role of, 218–219
  physical activity, importance of, 217
  portfolio techniques, 228
  public writing, role of, 218–219
  purposes of, multiple, 207–209
  reflective windows, use of, 229
  rubrics, development of writing, 227–228, 229
  showcase, writing to, 209
  solitude, creating, 217
  "technoliteracies," 206
  technological influences, 206, 230–232
  technology, application of, 230–232
  writers' workshop, development and use of a, 221–224
  zone of proximal development, 217
Writing Across the Curriculum movement, 33, 47

Yancie, K., 144
Young Adult Library Services Organization Web Site, 199
Your Reading, 36

Zone of proximal development (ZPD), 37, 217